Longitudinal Field Research Methods

Organization Science

Series Editor: Arie Y. Lewin

Books from Sage Publications, *Organization Science*, and the Institute for Operations Research and the Management Sciences

The Sage Publications **Organization Science** book series reprints expanded Special Issues of *Organization Science*. Each individual volume is based on the original Special Issue that appeared in *Organization Science*. It includes all-new introductions by the editors as well as several chapters which did not appear in the original Special Issue. These new chapters may include reprints of papers which appeared in other issues of *Organization Science*, relevant papers which appeared in other journals, and also new original articles.

The book series is published by Sage Publications in partnership with INFORMS (the Institute for Operations Research and Management Sciences) the publisher of *Organization Science*. The Series Editor is Arie Y. Lewin, the Editor in Chief of *Organization Science*.

Organization Science was founded in 1989 as an international journal with the aim of advancing the field of organization studies by attracting the publishing innovative research from across the social sciences. The term "Science" in the journal's title is interpreted in the broadest possible sense to include diverse methods and theoretical approaches. The editors of *Organization Science* believe that creative insight often occurs outside traditional approaches and topic areas, and that the role of *Organization Science* is to be broadly inclusive of the field by helping to integrate the diverse stands of organizational research. Authors are expected to describe theoretical concepts that give meaning to data, and to show how these concepts are relevant to organizations. Manuscripts that speculate beyond current thinking are more desirable than papers that use tried and true methods to study routine problems.

Initial books in this series:

Longitudinal Field Research Methods: Studying Processes of Organizational Change
   Edited by George P. Huber and Andrew H. Van de Ven

Organizational Learning
   Edited by Michael D. Cohen and Lee S. Sproull

For information on subscriptions or submission guidelines for *Organization Science*, please contact INFORMS at: INFORMS, P.O. Box 64794, Baltimore, MD 21264-4794, 1-800-446-3676.

Longitudinal Field Research Methods

Studying Processes of Organizational Change

George P. Huber
Andrew H. Van de Ven
Editors

Organization Science

SAGE Publications
International Educational and Professional Publisher
Thousand Oaks   London   New Delhi

For information address:

 SAGE Publications, Inc.
2455 Teller Road
Thousand Oaks, California 91320
E-mail: order@sagepub.com

SAGE Publications Ltd.
6 Bonhill Street
London EC2A 4PU
United Kingdom

SAGE Publications India Pvt. Ltd.
M-32 Market
Greater Kailash I
New Delhi 110 048 India

Printed in the United States of America

Library of Congress Cataloging-in-Publication Data

Main entry under title:

Longitudinal field research methods: studying processes of
    organizational change / edited by George P. Huber, Andrew H. Van de Ven
        p.   cm.—(Organization science)
    Includes bibliographical references and index.
    ISBN 0-8039-7090-0 (alk. paper).—ISBN 0-8039-7091-9
(pbk.: alk. paper)
        1. Organizational change—Longitudinal method.   I. Huber, George P.
II. Van de Ven, Andrew H.   III. Series.
HD58.8.L663   1995
658.4′063—dc20   95-16852

This book is printed on acid-free paper.

95   96   97   98   99   10   9   8   7   6   5   4   3   2   1

Sage Production Editor: Astrid Virding
Sage Typesetter: Andrea D. Swanson

Contents

Introduction

ANDREW H. VAN DE VEN
GEORGE P. HUBER

The study of organizational change tends to focus on two kinds of questions:

1. What are the antecedents or consequences of changes in organizational forms or administrative practices?
2. How does an organizational change emerge, develop, grow, or terminate over time?

The vast majority of research to date has focused on the first of these questions. Recently, however, there has been a growing interest in studying the second question, which is concerned with the temporal sequence of events that unfold as organizational change occurs. Process studies are fundamental to our understanding of the dynamics of organizational life and to the development and testing of theories of organizational adaptation, change, innovation, and redesign. This book focuses on longitudinal field research methods for studying processes of organizational change.

Answering the first of the above questions usually calls for a variance theory explanation of the input factors (independent variables) that statistically explain variations in some outcome criteria (dependent variables). Answering the second question requires a process theory explanation of the temporal order in which a discrete set of events occurred, based on a story or historical narrative. In terms of causality, to answer the first question one must find evidence of covariation, temporal precedence, and absence of spurious associations between the independent and dependent variables. To answer the second question, one must explain an observed sequence of events in terms of underlying generative mechanisms or laws that cause events to happen and the particular circumstances or contingencies that exist when these mechanisms operate.

An example will clarify these and other important distinctions between the two questions and how researchers often address them. A typical formulation of the first question might be, Do yearly increases in R&D funding (an input) increase organizational innovativeness (an outcome)? To answer this question, a researcher would operationalize R&D funding and innovativeness as independent and dependent variables, respectively, and measure them on numerical scales at different points in time. Changes in states of these variables can be calculated as the differences between scores obtained at various points in time on each variable. As Monge notes in Chapter 10 of this volume, these change scores on a variable can be examined in terms of their continuity, magnitude, rate of change, trend, periodicity, and duration. The researcher can then use modeling techniques to examine how changes in R&D investment precede similar changes in a lagged innovativeness variable.

Monge goes on to distinguish this class of so-called process theories, about changes in variables over time, from another class of process theories that focus on sequences of events that explain these changes. For example, with respect to the second question above we might ask, Do product innovations develop through a characteristic sequence of events or stages, such as invention, prototype development, testing, commercialization, and so on? To address this question, the researcher would gather data on the chronological sequence of activities that occurred within the period when the innovative product was developed. The researcher could code the observed activities as indicators of a discrete set of events associated with product development states. The researcher could then identify the sequence of these events for each innovation and compare the event sequences of different product innovations. As Abbott discusses in Chapter 8, the researcher could make these comparisons using a variety of pattern-matching methods to examine various characteristics of event sequences, such as event duration, order, and recurrence. Further comparisons could involve subsequences or reoccurring strings of events within the overall product innovation event sequences.

In this example, we could decompose the product development process into a series of input-output analyses by viewing each event as a change in a variable (i.e., as the difference between nonexistence at the beginning state and existence at the ending state of each event), and then by examining whether changes of state are explained by some other variables (such as R&D investment). From this perspective, events represent changes in variables, and these changes are the building blocks of process in an input-process-output model. Importantly, because our process question is not whether but *how* a change occurred, we also need a story that narrates the sequence of events that unfolded as the product innovation emerged. Once we find a sequence or pattern of events in a developmental process, we can turn to questions about the causes or consequences of the events within the process pattern. Abbott suggests that to understand how an organizational change occurs, researchers should alter their typical methods of analysis. Rather than first generalizing in terms of variables, he notes, researchers should first generalize in terms of a narrative history or a story. Only in this way will they preserve the key properties of order and sequence of events in making theoretical generalizations about processes of organizational change. Of course, alternative processes can lead to the same change outcomes—an application of the principle of equifinality.

Although clearly different in substance and method, our two introductory questions are highly related, and both are important for the understanding of organizational change. To answer the first question, one typically assumes or hypothesizes an answer to the second question. Whether implicit or explicit, the logic underlying an answer to the first question inevitably consists of a process story about how a sequence of events unfolds to cause an independent (input) variable to exert its influence on a dependent (outcome) variable. For example, to say that R&D investment causes organizational innovativeness is to make important assumptions about the order and sequence in which R&D investment and innovation events unfold in an organization. Thus one way to improve significantly the robustness of answers to the first question is to examine explicitly the process theory that is assumed to explain why an independent (input) variable influences a dependent (output) variable. Doing so requires that the researcher open the proverbial black box between inputs and outcomes, taking process seriously by examining temporal sequences of events.

Continuing with the relatedness of the introductory questions, we note that process studies that provide answers to the second question tend to be uninteresting or irrelevant without an answer to the first question. Indeed, as Pettigrew argues in Chapter 4, theoretically sound and practically useful research on change should explore the context, content, and process of change, together with the interconnections of these contingencies through time. Just as change is perceptible only relative to a state of constancy, an appreciation of a temporal sequence of events requires an understanding of the starting (input) conditions and ending (outcome) results. In short, answers to both questions are needed concerning the inputs, processes, and outcomes of organizational change.

A basic problem, however, is that although methods for examining the first question are well known and codified in standard research methodology texts, relatively little attention has been given to the development of methods for conducting research on the second question. Few guidelines are available to researchers who are interested in studying processes of change in organizations. As a consequence, researchers undertaking process studies have been developing their own methods through trial and error. With the current growing interest in organizational processes, it is timely to articulate the results of their experience, to assess their scientific standards carefully, and to make them available to others who are undertaking longitudinal field studies of organizational change processes.

The chapters in this book are of two types: those focused on the design and conduct of longitudinal research in the field and those dealing with methods for analyzing and interpreting process patterns in longitudinal data collected in the field. Chapters 1 and 2 describe studies undertaken by individual researchers engaged in tracking processes of technology adoption (Barley) and transfer (Leonard-Barton). In Chapter 3, Eisenhardt describes how theories can be constructed from the data obtained from these and similar case studies. The subsequent three chapters describe large research programs involving multiple teams of researchers studying processes of strategic corporate change (Pettigrew), organizational redesign (Glick, Huber, Miller, Doty, and Sutcliffe), and innovation (Van de Ven and Poole) in many different sites. In Chapter 7, McPhee describes alternative approaches for integrating the results of studies of this nature.

In Chapter 8, Abbott describes methods for systematically treating sequences of data, and in Chapter 9, Subherwal and Robey describe a longitudinal study in which one of these methods was used to find and examine alternative sequences in organizations that introduced computer-based information systems. Monge uses Chapter 10 to provide a thoughtful examination of what is entailed in a rigorous longitudinal study directed at improving organizational performance. Finally, in Chapter 11, Meyer, Goes, and Brooks describe the challenges researchers face when studying organizations under hyperturbulent conditions, where change is discontinuous and beyond the adaptive capability of the organizations being studied.

Although there is some inevitable overlap, the seven empirical studies presented here emphasize different sets of methodological issues involved in conducting longitudinal field research on organizational processes. They include ethnographic methods (Barley), longitudinal and comparative case studies (Leonard-Barton and Pettigrew), event-history analysis (Glick et al., Meyer et al., and Sabherwal and Robey), and real-time tracking of events as they occur over time (Van de Ven and Poole). The studies also address various methods and analytic procedures that can be used to tabulate, code, and interpret both quantitative and qualitative longitudinal data collected in the field. Taken together, they provide rich insights into the practical problems and methods researchers experience in conducting longitudinal field observations and in analyzing data to examine empirically the processes of organizational change. In this regard, we encouraged the authors to reveal and evaluate their methodologies, and to make their work open for scrutiny so that readers could profit from what the authors have learned.

DESIGN AND CONDUCT OF
LONGITUDINAL RESEARCH IN THE FIELD

The seven chapters describing individual longitudinal field studies can be arrayed on a continuum, from the Barley chapter, which describes how a researcher serves as the observer and interpreter of the process, to the Meyer et al. chapter, which describes how researchers use participants as key informants to construct event histories of organizational change. In either case, the researcher faces the problem of the observer's perceptual and cognitive limitations, as well as the problem of the observer's not being aware of some events. Each of these problems occurs, of course, whether the observer is the researcher or a participant in a change process. In addition, each of these two methodological approaches has unique problems. The researcher-as-observer faces the problems of influencing the system being observed and of correctly interpreting what is observed. As Barley makes explicit, if you are sensed by a social system, then you are part of it. If you are part of it, you affect it. If you affect it, you cannot observe the system in its natural state and can report only the processes of a disturbed system. This is the social science equivalent of the Heisenberg principle, a "fact" universally accepted in the physical sciences as having no exceptions. It is, of course, much more of a problem in social sciences, where the observer's presence is so apparent. Barley and Leonard-Barton candidly discuss these matters in the context of their studies. In contrast, the use of participants as key informants raises the problems of identifying the best informants, ensuring that they correctly understand the investigator's queries and provide veridical answers, and maintaining informant participation through the duration of the study. Glick et al. candidly discuss these matters in the context of their study.

A host of additional important issues need to be addressed concerning the conduct of longitudinal field research. Which sites or cases should be selected for observation? In what temporal intervals and for how many intervals should data be collected? What are the research outputs? Who are the users of the research? How should researchers present their findings to different audiences? How do researchers handle the problems of complexity and simplicity associated with longitudinal comparative studies on change? As these questions suggest, the mobilization of ongoing support and participation in a longitudinal field study requires researchers to develop an extensive set of craft skills. Based on his experiences in carrying out longitudinal field studies for a score or more years, Pettigrew discusses his evolving theory of method, which articulates the craft skills that researchers require to study organizational change while in the field.

The sheer labor intensity required to observe an organizational change process over time limits an observer/investigator to studying no more than a few cases at a time. As a result, serious questions are often raised about the generalizability of in-depth case studies. Further, given the fact that qualitative event data are slippery and ambiguous symbols, problems of researcher bias and replicability loom quite large. Leonard-Barton takes a somewhat unusual approach and describes a "case replication" methodology to test the generality of particular findings from a single longitudinal case study by examining whether or not these findings are present in other cases studied retrospectively. Such an approach attempts to minimize the limitations and maximize the benefits of longitudinal and retrospective case studies, when conducted separately. This methodology makes it possible for a single researcher to generalize key findings and economize on fieldwork, but, as Leonard-Barton notes, there are two thorny problems associated with it: (1) the difficulty of selecting other cases on spatial and temporal criteria that permit meaningful comparisons with the findings from the longitudinal case, and (2) the difficulty of comparing process findings obtained from real-time observations with retrospective observations.

An alternative approach is to maximize the generalizability of a longitudinal field study by obtaining retrospective event histories on hundreds of organizational changes and, in the process, sacrificing in-depth knowledge of how individual changes unfolded. This approach was adopted by Glick et al. in their longitudinal study of a wide variety of changes in a diverse set of organizations and industries. As the authors report, this large-scale nomothetic research strategy was chosen to address our first introductory question, namely, What are the antecedent conditions and consequences of changes across a variety of organizational forms, contexts, and leaders? Retrospective event histories were obtained through periodic interviews with participants in the change processes to capture the major events in each change process, and their antecedents and consequences were examined with longitudinal data on organization forms, contexts, and leaders.

As we noted earlier, change processes are themselves composed of events with antecedents and consequences, and when these are understood and connected in the form of a story or historical narrative, an understanding of the process is often the result. Meyer and his associates provide an example of this method. Drawing on the approach adopted by Glick et al., but limiting their study to a single industry (so that they could compare series of events from different organizations) and adding more open-ended questions to their interviews, Meyer et al. were able to answer both of the questions posed at the opening of this introduction. Their chapter is also noteworthy for calling to our attention the fact that many research practices are so ingrained in the normal science research paradigm that deviating from them is akin to heresy, but that certain of these practices must be discarded in the study of organizational change under hyperturbulent conditions.

UNDERSTANDING TEMPORAL PROCESSES
IN LONGITUDINAL FIELD DATA

Whatever sampling strategies and data-collection methods are used to observe change processes in the field, all of the contributors to this volume report that over time, data mount astronomically and overload the information-processing capacity of even a trained mind. Rigorously drawing inferential links between data and theory requires methods that go beyond subjective "eyeballing" of raw qualitative data to identify process patterns. Unfortunately, data analysis methods are rarely reported in detail in published case studies or ethnographic reports. One cannot ordinarily follow how a researcher got from hundreds of pages of field observations to his or her final conclusions, even though the research may be sprinkled with vivid—yet idiosyncratic—quotes from organizational participants. Given the sheer volume of data amassed in a typical longitudinal study of an organizational change process, most research reports violate a basic canon of scientific reporting, which demands presentation of the data as distinct from analyses and inferences drawn from those data.

The chapters by Van de Ven and Poole, McPhee, Eisenhardt, Monge, and Abbott address methods and standards for analyzing longitudinal data. Based on their experiences in the Minnesota Innovation Research Program, Van de Ven and Poole focus on methods for transforming raw data obtained from longitudinal field studies into a form useful for examining process theories of innovation development. They propose seven specific steps for tabulating and coding qualitative data into a chronological event sequence and for transforming these qualitative data into a quantitative form that permits the application of linear and nonlinear methods of time-series analyses to examine systematically time-dependent patterns of relationships among event sequences and stages.

Whereas these steps provide a systematic way to examine the order and sequence of events over time *within* a given case, Eisenhardt and McPhee both address the problem of how to draw comparisons *between* different cases of organizational innovation or change. Comparing different cases may be moderately challenging when the cases simply represent different data points, but McPhee addresses the even more complex and interesting situations that arise when the cases were studied by different research teams who had different explanations or conceptual images in mind when designing and conducting their studies. These latter situations are particularly relevant where multisite, multimethod, and multiteam programmatic research are undertaken, such as at Pettigrew's Centre for Corporate Strategy and Change, Huber and Glick's program of research on change in organizational design and effectiveness, and Van de Ven's Minnesota Innovation Research Program. McPhee proposes three different approaches for comparing and integrating cases as well as a useful set of diagnostic methods for determining the possibilities and limitations of each approach.

Finally, the chapters by Abbott and Monge provide two useful and complementary primers of the analytic concepts and techniques available for examining various models of changes in variance and process theories about sequences of events or stages. In addition to the contributions we have already summarized, Monge makes the important observation that one reason organization science has made little progress in developing dynamic process theories is that its tool kit has largely been limited to verbal or linguistic analysis and correlational research at a single point in time. He focuses on the time-dependent processes of how individual variables may change over time, and then explores dynamic relationships between process-related variables across time: their history, the time lag, rate of change, magnitude of change, and the permanence of change. He also discusses the important issue of feedback in process theories, and concludes with a typology of alternative methods for analyzing process data.

Abbott provides a useful primer for introducing organization scientists to the basic logic and methods entailed in studying processes of organizational change. He alerts us to an important deficiency in most analyses of organizational change and change processes: the recognition that the history of how an initial state came to be is often of critical importance when one attempts to use this state to predict a change in a later state. This fact is not accounted for in the Markovian thinking that underlies most of the analytic techniques currently used by organization scientists in their studies of change processes. To diminish this obstacle to the development of process theories, Abbott notes, we need to think in terms of processes (sequences of events); he provides guidance in the conceptualization, measurement, and analyses of sequences.

Taken as a whole, the chapters in this book provide a repertoire of methods for undertaking longitudinal field research studies of organizational change. They surface a number of philosophy of science issues that underlie the research problems and methods introduced above.

1

Images of Imaging

Notes on Doing Longitudinal Fieldwork

STEPHEN R. BARLEY

This chapter discusses the problems and processes involved in conducting longitudinal ethnographic research. The author's field study of technological change in radiology provides the context for the discussion. Specific attention is paid to how researchers can design a qualitative study and then collect data in a systematic and explicit manner. Consequently, the chapter seeks to dispel the notion that participant observation and quantitative data analysis are inimical. Finally, the social and human problems of gaining entry into a research site, constructing a research role, and managing relationships with informants are illustrated.

Whether longitudinal, cross-sectional, observational, archival, or experimental, all research stems from and remains caught in a tangled web of practical, personal, and theoretical agendas. Accordingly, this chapter offers for scrutiny what Van Maanen (1988) calls a "confessional tale" of my field research on computerized imaging technologies (Barley 1984, 1986a, 1986b, 1988a, 1988b, 1990). The telling weaves together the rational and the irrational, the planned and the unplanned, the personal and the impersonal to approach a sense of realism often lacking in the methods sections of most

This chapter appeared originally in *Organization Science,* vol. 1, no. 3, August 1990, pp. 220-247.

journal articles. The narrative's details trace two general, and somewhat conflicting, themes. First, the doing of longitudinal field research is far more deliberate, disciplined, and mindful than most critics grant or most new converts sense. Good ethnography is not simply the taking of copious, journalistic notes on one's chumming with the natives. Yet, regardless of calculated attempts at discipline, fieldwork inevitably intensifies the tensions, the relationships, and the serendipitous events that influence all research. It is in the precarious balance between the controlled and the uncontrolled, the cognitive and the affective, the designed and the unexpected that fieldwork finds its distinctive vitality and analytic power.

CONTEXT AND BACKGROUND

The Project's Genesis

Contextual Influences

The story of any research program rightfully begins with the decision to investigate a specific topic. Although some social research is undoubtedly formulated, as textbooks advise, to answer nomothetic questions or to expand on previous research, my work on radiology began as an attempt to fill what I thought was an interesting empirical void. To be sure, theoretical concerns played a background role insofar as they provided a frame of reference and a set of sensitizing concepts. The study was, in fact, guided by two tenets integral to a symbolic interactionist's notion of social structure: (1) that social structures emerge gradually out of an ongoing process of negotiation and interaction and (2) that technology should occasion structural change by altering roles and relationships. However, like most ethnographers, I embarked on the project with little more than a handful of general questions and no strongly articulated hypotheses. Far more important for determining the study's focus were my personal interests and the circumstances of my location in time and space.

Few students at MIT in the late 1970s could avoid the perception that computers and other advanced technologies would slowly but surely transform the infrastructure of society, and that this transformation would stem from changes in the workplace. Even in the Institute's School of Management, conversations frequently turned to talk about computer-aided design and manufacturing, computer networks, fiber optics, genetic engineering, artificial intelligence, parallel processing, decision support systems, and a host of other technologies far too esoteric to mention. Most of these machines and techniques were designed for use by professionals and semiprofessionals, the so-called knowledge workers of Daniel Bell's (1973) postindustrial society. Yet, then as now, most social research on technical change concerned either mid-level managers or blue-collar and lower-white-collar workers.

Most previous research had also failed to examine closely the dynamics by which technologies might occasion social change. Although many studies of technology were wittingly or unwittingly premised on Marx's notion that shifts in the technical infrastructure transform societies by altering modes and relations of production, few researchers had actually traced organizational and occupational changes to shifts in the nature of work or the manner in which work is performed. Instead, most had settled for auguring such broad trends as decentralization, deskilling, and reskilling, without many data and with little firsthand knowledge of how machines are actually used. This state of affairs was particularly true for the managerial and organizational literature on new technology, where it seemed that only the early sociotechnical theorists (Trist and Bamforth 1951, Rice 1958, Herbst 1962, Fensham and Hooper 1964) and a handful of others (Mann and Williams 1961, Meissner 1969) had ever bothered to observe the actual turning of a machine's cam.

Largely because I had a keen interest in occupational dynamics and because I had been steeped in Everett C. Hughes's (1958, 1972) brand of occupational sociology, the time seemed ripe for closely studying the process by which computerized technologies were altering the work of professionals and semiprofessionals. Such a study would chronicle the actions, interactions, and interpretations occasioned by specific machines to explain how technically induced changes in an interaction order (Goffman 1983) might lead to organizational and occupational change. Given this rather broad mandate, the specific decision to examine radiological technologies was largely opportunistic.

Discovering Radiology

Since a large number of researchers were already examining how managers used computers, and since, whatever else it might be, management hardly fit any sociologist's notion of a profession, I resolved to stay away from corporate offices and boardrooms. Medicine seemed a more desirable setting on several counts. Compared with other professions, the institutional structure and daily activities of medical work had been well investigated by sociologists of occupations (e.g., Becker et al. 1961, Strauss et al. 1964, Mechanic 1968, Freidson 1970, Freidson and Lorber 1972, Larkin 1978, 1983). This literature provided a sufficiently solid backdrop for assessing whether a technology reinforced or challenged the social contours of medical practice. Moreover, with the possible exception of engineering and science, no professional setting had experienced more technical change during the 1970s than had medicine. From digital thermometers and monitoring devices to expert programs that simulated a physician's judgment, computational technologies were rapidly infiltrating and transforming the way doctors diagnosed and treated disease.

Medicine also seemed appropriate for personal reasons. As a teenager, I had been deeply interested in the life sciences and was certain that I would pursue a medical career. Not only had I studied molecular biology and human physiology as an undergraduate, but during high school I had worked in a hospital's pathology lab. Consequently, the physician's task was less foreign to me than the work of an engineer or lawyer, and since I was interested in understanding how technologies alter the details of professional practice, it seemed pragmatic to look for a setting where I had some understanding of the science on which the practice was based. In retrospect, these affective and personal motives proved to be extremely critical, for without an intrinsic interest in medicine, I would have probably jettisoned the project in face of the frustrations and difficulties I encountered while negotiating entry.

In the early fall of 1981, I began shopping for a suitable medical technology. I initially investigated several expert programs and a number of computerized devices used in surgery or intensive care. However, all proved to be either uninteresting or else sophisticated prototypes located in medical centers where physicians were themselves primarily researchers. I eventually stumbled across radiology and the medical imaging revolution quite by accident during a conversation with Dr. Octo Barnett, a member of the staff at Massachusetts General Hospital and an expert in the use of computers in medicine. After explaining that I wanted to study a technology that was already affecting medical practice, but that was still in the early phases of its diffusion curve, Dr. Barnett counseled, "You ought to study radiology. If there's any area in medicine where computers are transforming medical practice, radiology is it."

After spending several weeks reading the radiological literature, I concluded that radiology indeed offered an opportune setting. Since the late 1960s radiology had been jolted out of its technical calm by a series of innovations, most of which involved computers and each of which represented a new way of looking inside the human body. Three of these technologies—special procedures, ultrasound, and computerized tomography (CT) scanning—had become prevalent in community hospitals. Common wisdom was that the new technologies had occasioned a revolution in medical diagnosis (Banta and McNeil 1978, OTA 1978, 1981, Stocking and Morrison 1978, Wiener 1979). Hoping that the influx of sophisticated technologies had also occasioned social change, I began to design a study for determining whether and how new imaging devices had altered the social organization of radiological work.

Research Design

Three broad and interrelated, but distinct, questions guided the research design. Did the social organization of special procedures, ultrasound, and CT scanning differ from the social order surrounding radiology's traditional technologies, radiography and fluoroscopy? If so, why did such differences exist? Finally, were the differences peculiar to specific hospitals or were they to be found in any radiology department that had adopted the technologies? To answer each question, data were collected from three distinct vantage points, which might be called, respectively, the synchronic, the diachronic, and the parallel.

Synchronic Analysis

Any social setting can be read as a historical document of itself shelved momentarily between past and present. Whatever the current social order, we know it became so from what it was in the past. To wherever the social order evolves, we know it will arrive there by some transformation of what it is now. But although all social settings so summarize their pasts and sire their futures, some register their histories more visibly than others. Most social orders leave behind few relics of their reigns. The traces that do survive as artifacts or rituals are often but mere shadows of some long forgotten substance. What existed and why it existed can be culled only from the memories of people who lived during the period or from records that survived their time. In other situations, rare by comparison, a prior social order continues to exist side by side with what has come since and with what is likely to come in the near future. When living traces of a former order reside alongside vestiges of a new, it is possible to compare the two simultaneously.

The sociology of technology and work is perhaps blessed for this reason. In periods of technical change, workplaces often become mixtures of old and new technologies operated concurrently. Associated with each technology is the social order that grew up around its use. Because the mixture occurs in the same setting, one can essentially hold constant variations brought about by the organization's cultural, historical, environmental, and social idiosyncrasies in order to see more clearly the ramifications of the technologies themselves.

Radiology departments were (and remain) living, Januslike documents of their social and technical evolution. In most hospitals, radiographic and fluoroscopic equipment stands juxtaposed to the newer devices and techniques of ultrasound, CT, and special procedures. This temporal and spatial concurrence is especially propitious for analyzing old and new imaging technologies synchronically. Because of the average department's technical mix, one can treat each technology's context as if it were fixed in time. Although clearly fictional, the assumption of stasis enabled me to compare simultaneously the various technologies' operation with an eye to determining whether the new devices' social contexts were similar to each other and yet different from the social organization of radiography and fluoroscopy. In particular, I anticipated that a synchronic analysis would highlight differences and similarities in the tasks, roles, and role relationships of the radiologists and technologists who worked with each device.[1] If the new technologies had indeed engendered social change, then the data should show that the roles of radiologists and technologists in new areas were different from the roles of those who worked with older technologies.

Diachronic Analysis

Should the synchronic analysis show that the new technologies had occasioned social orders that were similarly different from the social organization of radiography and fluoroscopy, then one might reasonably claim that the new devices had pointed the practice of radiology in a more or less consistent direction. However, from synchronic data alone one could not determine how or why a new social order had evolved. Understanding how the new technologies had breached radiology's structural and cultural traditions required charting changes as they occurred. In other words, a diachronic perspective was also necessary. Whereas a synchronic analysis would freeze time and look across a radiology department as a whole, a diachronic analysis would seize time and examine the developmental path of a specific technology's use. Said differently, a synchronic analysis would compare technologies with each other, whereas a diachronic analysis would contrast earlier and later periods of a single technology's use.

Diachronic analysis was also most compatible with a symbolic interactionist's notion of a negotiated order: the idea that social structures sediment out of a stream of ongoing actions, interactions, and interpretations that gradually define the contours of tasks, roles, and relationships as well as a technology's identity as a social object (Strauss et al. 1963, 1964, Berger and Luckmann 1967, Strauss 1978, Giddens 1984, Barley 1988c). Since the events of day-to-day life fade quickly into the flow of experience, participants in a work setting may not notice their cumulative import. To be sure, participants may realize retrospectively that changes have occurred, but they are unlikely to remember how or why the changes arose. Thus, if researchers are to understand how a technology becomes embedded in a particular social order, they need to observe the actions and interactions that actually generate the order. The most accurate way to collect such data is to follow the use of a new technology from the moment it goes on-line.

Parallel Analysis

Although the combination of synchronic and diachronic data seemed necessary for showing that new technologies had altered the social organization of radiological work and for explaining how such change occurred, even in combination, the two seemed insufficient for lodging credible claims. The idiosyncratic culture and history of a radiology department could easily shape the use of any technology it acquired. Thus distinguishing between setting-specific effects and global processes occasioned by a technology's physical attributes required that the synchronic and diachronic analyses be bolstered by a third axis of comparison: the parallel.

By conducting parallel studies in several hospitals, one could more readily identify each organization's cultural and structural idiosyncrasies as well as pinpoint their commonalities. From the vantage point of a parallel analysis, cultural elements would cut across the use of all technologies at a given site and yet appear site specific when compared with practices in other hospitals. Because a parallel analysis would also highlight generalizable differences between technologies, it could also point to what might be credibly construed as the social ramifications of the technologies themselves.

At first glance, *synchronic, diachronic,* and *parallel* may appear to be little more than pretentious synonyms for terms such as *cross-sectional, longitudinal,* and *comparative.*[2] If linguistic prowess were all that was at stake, more common terms would indeed be preferable. However, the unfamiliar terms highlight distinctions glossed by traditional vocabularies. For instance, synchronic and parallel analysis could both be properly described as *cross-sectional.* However, to use the latter term would be to obscure the fact that synchronic analysis and parallel analysis address different units of observation. Synchronic analysis involves a comparison of intraorganizational phenomena, in this case different technologies, while parallel analysis entails interorganizational comparisons. Similarly, *longitudinal* and *diachronic* both refer to chronologically arrayed data. However, the former term does not carry the latter's evolutionary connotation. An evolutionary perspective is especially important if one wishes to analyze transformations of action rather than merely identify and examine historical trends. Finally, even though diachronic, synchronic, and parallel analyses all entail a comparative stance, each implies a distinct focus of comparison.

By clearly distinguishing among the three comparative foci, researchers may better substantiate their claims. A synchronic analysis is particularly useful for making statements that generalize across members of a class of events, objects, persons, or activities. For instance, the claim that computerized technologies are associated with certain outcomes is more credible when it can be shown (1) that similar outcomes are occasioned by numerous computational devices and (2) that these outcomes are not associated with devices that lack computational capacities. In contrast, diachronic analysis is crucial for explaining the etiology of the differences. Computerized devices could conceivably be associated with different outcomes for reasons independent of their computational core. Only diachronic data that capture unfolding events can clarify such ambiguities. Finally, parallel studies allow one to generalize synchronic and diachronic findings across similar social settings. Only by parallel analysis can a researcher conclude that an organization's idiosyncrasies do not account for the outcomes associated with a set of computerized devices.

More important, conclusions become problematic when research questions are paired with an inappropriate comparative stance. For example, synchronic data may seem to suggest that similar outcomes are rooted in similar processes. However, similar outcomes may arise from different processes and different outcomes may arise from similar dynamics (Barley 1986a). Only diachronic data can disentangle such possibilities. By itself, a parallel study of a class of events, objects, or activities may also lead to wrongful conclusions. Suppose, for instance, that one were to investigate the effects of new technologies by studying CT scanning in a number of hospitals. Even if one found that all CT scanners occasion similar phenomena, one could not be sure whether the findings would apply to all computationally based imaging devices or only to CT scanners. A synchronic analysis of several technologies conducted in tandem could resolve this issue. In other words, the synchronic, the diachronic, and the parallel represent three distinct axes of comparison that, when used in combination, allow researchers to examine explicitly the spatial and temporal boundaries of their claims.

For these reasons, I chose to pursue the triple comparative focus summarized in Figure 1.1. The triple focus, in turn, strongly constrained the universe of potential research sites. Since synchronic differences can be assessed through the mere comparison of the daily uses of different technologies, any of a large number of radiology departments could have served as sites for the study's synchronic thrust. However, the diachronic agenda severely restricted freedom of selection. At the time of the study, only whole-body CT scanners were being widely adopted by community hospitals in Massachusetts. Most radiology departments had already implemented special procedures and ultrasound, and only the largest medical centers were using magnetic resonance imaging. The goal of conducting a diachronic comparison, therefore, left little choice but to target hospitals that were about to receive their first body scanners. The diachronic agenda also required that I begin the research before the scanners went on-line. Finally, the performance of a parallel comparison required that I study at least two sites, each of which satisfied the diachronic criteria.

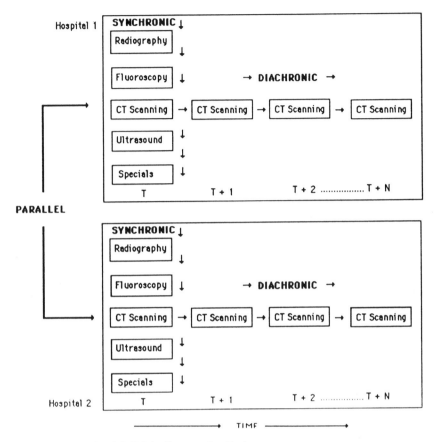

Figure 1.1. The Study's Triple Comparative Design

EXECUTION

Entry

Like most states, Massachusetts limits the number of hospitals allowed to purchase costly medical devices through a "determination of need" process (OTA 1978, Banta and Behney 1980). Because CT scanners cost between $500,000 and $1.5 million, only four Massachusetts hospitals were permitted to purchase body scanners during 1982, the year the study was slated to begin. In January 1982, I obtained the four hospitals' identities from the Massachusetts Public Health Council. Of the four, one was too distant to afford frequent access. In February, I contacted the three remaining hospitals in hopes of persuading at least two to participate in the study.

I presented the study as basic social science aimed at better understanding of the social implications of computerization. Although I played on the widespread perception that radiology was in a period of transformation, I purposely distanced myself from economists and other critics who were at the time writing articles on radiology's contribution to the high cost of medical care. Instead, I emphasized my affiliation with MIT, a well-known haven for technophiles, and, as would therefore be expected, expressed great interest in the technologies themselves. I also marketed myself as an anthropologist. An anthropological rhetoric not only allowed me to justify more easily why I wanted to spend a year as a participant observer, it enabled me to skirt any prejudice associated with my being a sociologist.[3] While I readily suggested that the study might provide information useful for understanding the changing nature of radiological work, I studiously avoided creating the impression that I would serve as an organizational consultant. In fact, I candidly explained that, as an ethnographer, I could not ethically use my knowledge to intervene in the "culture" I was investigating.

Negotiations for entry proceeded fitfully for five months, driven by dynamics of which, at the time, I was only dimly aware. Knowing no one who could arrange formal introductions, I began to negotiate access by placing telephone calls directly to the chief of radiology at each hospital. The chief radiologist at the first hospital referred me to the department's administrator. I arranged by phone to meet with the administrator and acknowledged our conversation with a brief letter and research proposal. Within the first five minutes of our meeting, the administrator firmly informed me that the radiologists had discussed the proposal and concluded they had no desire to participate. Although officially rejected because of the project's potential disruption to the department, I later learned from a prominent and well-connected radiologist that the hospital had been reprimanded a year earlier for attempting to skirt the determination of need procedure. My research proposal had apparently aroused the radiologists' suspicions of investigative surveillance, an interpretation whose viability seems less fanciful given events at the second hospital.

There, I began by negotiating directly with the radiologists as well as with the department's administrator. The proposal was relatively well received within the department, in part because one of the more influential radiologists had once worked with a team of anthropologists in New Guinea and was therefore kindly disposed toward ethnographers. However, the proposal encountered snags at higher levels of the hospital's administration.

Unbeknown to me, during the previous year a journalist had entered the hospital posing as a researcher. He later published an article critical of the cost of medical care, in which he cited physicians' names and annual salaries. The incident left the hospital's administration hesitant to open doors to other persons claiming to be social scientists. Moreover, two former members of the radiology department's staff had recently been indicted for selling silver recovered from X-ray film on the black market. The hospital's higher-ups apparently suspected the purity of my investigative motives for this reason as well.

At the third radiology department, I was referred to the hospital's second in command. Although the hospital's higher administrators proved enthusiastic about the research, their enthusiasm did not filter down to the radiology department. I was eventually able to present my case to the department's chief administrator, but I was unable to meet with the radiologists. In fact, over the next four months I called the third hospital on a biweekly basis, hoping to arrange a meeting with the chief radiologist or to learn from the chief administrator whether the department had made a decision regarding the study. The receptionists always told me that neither person was in his office, and although the receptionists promised to forward my messages, neither the administrator nor the chief radiologist returned my calls. I had greater success contacting the administrator at the second hospital. However, on each call I was politely informed that the hospital had not yet acted on my proposal.

As the weeks dragged on without word from either hospital, I began to fear that I might never gain access. By May, my fear of wasting a year of preparation became so acute that I decided to observe scanner operations at a local medical school as a fallback position. The radiologist in charge of CT operations at the medical school eventually spoke on my behalf with the chief radiologist at the third hospital.[4] Within three days of the radiologist's intervention, I was granted access to the third hospital. Later that same week, the second hospital cleared the study. I do not know whether the second hospital's timing was coincidental or whether the administration there had also been contacted by my newfound champion. At any rate, only after successfully, but blindly, working my way into the radiologists' professional network did "Urban" and "Suburban" finally grant access. Aside from a promise that I would not reveal the identify of either hospital, no strings were placed on my participation. In particular, I was not obligated to provide feedback at the end of the study. The experience underscored a crucial lesson about gaining entry that I have since relearned on several occasions: Despite an academic's proclivity to think otherwise, who you know is often far more important than what you know.

Methods

Sustained Observation

Negotiated order theorists assert that social order consists largely of patterned activities and shared interpretations that smooth the vagaries of daily life by establishing the bedrock of consistency and coherence necessary for sustained action. Without such patterns, persons would often not know how to behave or what to think. As a result, organized activity would crumble against the wake of ongoing experience and be washed aside by complexity and novelty. From this perspective, it follows that if new technologies are to change a social order, they must do so by altering old patterns and creating new ones.

If social orders are patterns and if technical change alters those patterns, then investigations of a technology's implications for the organization of work would seem to require sustained observation, for unless one observes, one is unlikely to uncover the behaviors and interpretations that compose the patterns. Moreover, unless one's observation is sustained, one can document neither recurrence nor consistency. Sustained observation is also crucial for tracing the evolution of social institutions. Institutions do not arise fully formed. Instead, habits and definitions of reality accrue over time as problematic incidents demand interpretation and action (Berger and Luckmann 1967). Once an interpretation is posed, an act executed, and the result deemed sufficient, all three fade into the past to become taken-for-granted aspects of the present (Schein 1985). Studies of technical change based solely on interviews or archival materials are, therefore, quite likely to depict the dynamics of social change inaccurately. It was to avoid the difficulties associated with retrospective interpretation that I chose sustained observation as my primary methodology.

In the second week of June 1982, nearly a year after the project's inception, I began a year-long stint as a participant observer in the radiology departments at Urban and Suburban. With the exception of a seven-week hiatus from the field in the middle of the year, I spent an average of 4 days a week in observation. By alternating sites on a daily basis, I logged 84 days of observation at Urban and 87 at Suburban. My typical routine was to arrive on site between 8 a.m. and 9 a.m., spend six to seven hours accompanying technologists or radiologists as they went about their day's work, and then leave by 3:30 p.m., when the day shift ended. In the evening after each day's observation, I expanded my field notes at a typewriter. On average, 20 pages of single-spaced typed field notes were compiled each day, yielding a total corpus of slightly more than 2,500 pages for the entire project.

Systematization

Like most participant observers, I cite the volume of my field notes as evidence of sustained observation and as a not-so-subtle indicator that real work was done. But while sustained observation and copious notes are necessary for adequate fieldwork, in my opinion, they are not sufficient. In addition, observation needs to be both systematic and explicit. Tactics for making observations systematic and explicit are notoriously difficult to specify before fieldwork begins. Not only do the structures of social settings vary, but in most cases researchers are initially ignorant of how the setting is organized. Nevertheless, as one gains familiarity with a setting, its routines suggest avenues for structuring inquiry.

Because the synchronic thrust of the research was to discover how the social organization of work varied across different technologies, I required an observational strategy that would allow a systematic charting of the tasks, roles, and role relations associated with each modality. Preferably the strategy would also be relatively unobtrusive and attuned to the rhythm of the each department's work. Shortly after entering the field, I discovered that radiologists and technologists parsed their work into what were variously called "procedures," "studies," and "examinations." A procedure entailed using a particular device in a certain way to produce pictures of a specific anatomical region. The flow of work through each technology, therefore, consisted of a stream of examinations, each with a discrete beginning and end. The work of technologists and radiologists revolved around an unfolding series of such studies, and since most interactions between radiologists and technologists occurred during examinations, procedures were the stage on which role relations were enacted. For these reasons, procedures seemed to be an ecologically natural unit of observation for studying the social organization of each imaging device. During the third week of the study, I began to use the occurrence of procedures to structure daily observations.[5]

To systematize the data collection, I created the observational matrix displayed in Figure 1.2 by cross-classifying roles and role relations by procedures. My strategy was to observe multiple instances of the most frequent exams conducted with each technology in order to fill the cells of the matrix with redundant descriptive data. Once the matrix was complete, I could compare any procedure synchronically with another. More important, by combining all procedures subsumed under each technology, I could compare the use of different technologies. Because a scanner's later use could be contrasted with its earlier use by examining how the particulars of the data in CT columns evolved with time, the matrix also proved useful for collecting diachronic information.

Since technologists and radiologists were usually assigned to one (or at most two) technologies each day, I habitually attached myself to a radiologist or technologist in the morning and then followed that person over the course of the day. Which person I observed on any given day depended on two considerations: (1) which of the matrix's cells required more data and (2) whether by choosing an informant I could observe a procedure being performed by someone whom I had not repeatedly observed in that context. As

Procedures by Technology

	Radiography		Fluoroscopy		Special Procedures		Ultrasound		CT Scanning	
	Routines	I.V.P.'s	Barium Enemas	Upper G.I.'s	Angio-graphy	Nephros-tomy	GYN's	Cardiacs	Heads	Chests
Work Roles										
Radiologists' Work										
Technologists' Work										
Role-Relations										
Radiologist-Radiologist										
Technologist-Technologist										
Radiologist-Technologist										
Radiologist-Patient										
Technologist-Patient										

Figure 1.2. Observational Matrix

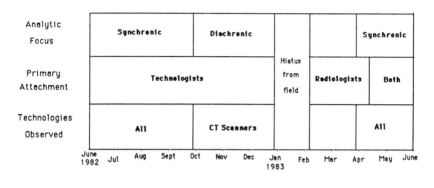

Figure 1.3. Phases of Observation

the second criterion implies, I attempted to observe all radiologists and technologists who operated each technology in order to distinguish more easily their social regularities from their individual habits and idiosyncrasies.

Guided by the observational matrix and the study's triple comparative design, the substantive focus of the investigation changed over the course of the year so that discrete phases of observation emerged. The phases reflected the CT scanners' arrival, decisions to alternate between collecting synchronic and diachronic data, and variation in attention to the work of technologists and radiologists. Figure 1.3 arrays the phases schematically along a timeline representing the study's duration. From mid-June to late September, I collected data for a synchronic comparison of technologies. During that time, observation shifted on a daily basis among radiography, fluoroscopy, ultrasound, and special procedures. I attached myself exclusively to technologists and observed the department from their perspective.

By late September the scanners had been assembled, and by the first of October both departments had brought their scanners on-line. From the end of September to the end of December, I observed, almost exclusively, the body scanner operations and their day-to-day development. During this period the analytic focus shifted from synchronic to diachronic. The physical layout of the two CT departments and the nature of the radiologists' duties when assigned to CT allowed me to observe the flow of radiologists' and technologists' work more or less simultaneously. However, during this period I continued to attach myself primarily to the technologists.

From Christmas to Valentine's Day I withdrew from the field to spend time with the data I had collected. During that period, I spent a day at each site at two-week intervals to maintain connections, to provide assurances that I would return, and to keep abreast of major developments. In mid-February, daily observation of the scanners resumed, but now primarily from the point of view of the radiologists. By the end of March, I shifted from exclusively observing CT work to observing the radiologists in other areas of the department.

From the first of April to the end of May, I once again adopted a synchronic orientation and observed the entire range of procedures per-formed in the departments. However, rather than attach myself primarily to either technologists or radiologists, I alternated back and forth between their company. Most of my time was spent outside the CT areas, but I logged at least two hours a day with the scanners' personnel so that I could continue to chart developments. In general, this rather complicated schedule of obser-vations enabled me to collect data for a synchronic analysis of all technolo-gies, as well as a diachronic analysis of the two CT operations, while capturing the perspectives of both radiologists and technologists. It is critical to note that the observational schedule was devised during the course of the study in light of issues of timing as well as imbalances in the data, both of which would have been difficult to anticipate in advance.

Explicitness

Social scientists often draw rigid distinctions between qualitative and quantitative studies. Methods texts ritualistically extol the former for their richness while advocating the latter for their explicitness and presumed replicability. Although explicitness is perhaps easier to attain in survey or experimental research, there is no reason to conclude, a priori, that explicit-ness is inimical to qualitative research. The value of sustained observation is not simply its suitability for revealing patterned complexities. Sustained observation also increases the odds that researchers will uncover meaningful indicators of those patterns. After all, if participant observers succeed in identifying patterned activities and interpretations, they must do so by attending to repetitive cues.

Although it is impossible to document all facets of a setting that lead to ethnographic insight, some can be isolated more or less precisely. In fact, one value of longitudinal fieldwork is that it increases the likelihood of the researcher's identifying setting-specific cues. The reason is simple: Repeated observation of repetitious actions or events becomes boring. Not only is boredom a sure sign that repetition is taking place, but the events that occasion boredom may represent useful setting-specific indicators. The power of a setting-specific indicator is its capacity to make more explicit the grounds on which one has drawn one's conclusions. By carefully documenting the frequency of setting-specific indicators, researchers not only can describe what happened, they can prove that it did, in fact, occur.

The value of interplay between description and documentation in qualitative research is often discussed, but rarely demonstrated.[6] To be sure, researchers cannot usually know ahead of time what will count as indicators of the patterns they discover while in the field. Nevertheless, they can devise indicators as their studies develop, presuming, of course, that they stay in the field long enough to assemble the indicators once they discover them.[7] Two general tactics for augmenting an ethnographic account with explicit, even quantitative, indicators proved particularly useful in the course of my work: the keeping of behavioral records and the use of nonobservational data.

Radiological work is fortuitously composed of visible physical and verbal behaviors. The execution of procedures involves human action as well as the mechanical or electronic responses of machines. Even the interpretation of films by radiologists usually entails conversations among radiologists or between radiologists and referring physicians. Given this wealth of observable behavior, after several weeks in the field I settled on a general stance toward note taking: to capture the chronological stream of events, actions, and interactions that occurred over the course of an exam. Metaphorically, I resolved, to the best of my ability, to become a human camera.[8]

From the beginning of the study I made no secret of the fact that I would be constantly taking notes on what was going on around me. However, to reduce intrusion, I worked with small spiral notepads that fit easily in the palm of my hand. During the course of a procedure, I jotted down a running record of as many actions and bits of conversation as I could record. As part of the regimen, I noted the times at which the procedure began and ended, as well as the times at which actors entered and left the scene. Since all procedures took place in examination rooms, entrances and exits were easily distinguished. When the timing of beginnings, ends, entrances, and exits became habitual, my timekeeping expanded to the duration of each procedure's major phases. Once a procedure's repetitive aspects began to appear routine, I devised a shorthand to document more parsimoniously the actions and idioms that recurred across all instances of a particular exam.

Because my notes took the form of behavioral records, they provided a sufficiently detailed database for supporting a number of explicit analyses. For example, it was possible to calculate from field notes the proportion of a procedure's duration during which radiologists and technologists were in face-to-face contact. This particular measure of interaction was used to substantiate an ethnographic account of role relations among radiologists and technologists operating different technologies (Barley 1990). Similarly, because the notes recorded who had made what decisions during the course of each CT scan, it was possible to plot when, and at what rate, decisions shifted from the domain of radiologist's work to the domain of technologist's work (Barley 1986a). As a final example, because interactions were chronicled in considerable detail, it was possible to identify the scripts that guided interactions and to analyze the distribution of those scripts not only across technologies but, in the case of the CT scanners, over time (Barley 1984, 1986a, 1990). One value of such setting-specific indicators is that they can be analyzed using standard statistical techniques. However, unlike most measures, which are formulated prior to the study, indicators captured in a chronology of field notes enhance a study's ecological validity because they remain close to the phenomenon under investigation.

In addition to recording countable behaviors, I also sought greater explicitness by augmenting observational data with a number of observationally independent sources of information. For example, even though I became adept at recording snippets of conversation, it was physically impossible to capture on paper the complexity of longer exchanges. To address this problem, I secured permission to tape-record exams during the last three months of the study. The taping was done with a small microcassette recorder kept in the pocket of my lab coat or held beneath my memo pad. The tapes were later transcribed and the transcripts were used to document verbal parameters of role relations among radiologists and technologists.

After three months of observation, I compiled a set of sociometric questionnaires based on topics of technical and social conversation common among radiologists and technologists. The questionnaires were distributed to all members of the departments in August, and again in May. The sociometric data served two purposes. First, they were useful for verifying qualitative observations regarding role relations among radiologists and technologists. Specifically, the sociograms confirmed that role relations in CT had, in fact, come to resemble those of ultrasound and special procedures. Second, the sociometric questionnaires allowed a graphic representation of the larger social network for each department and, hence, an examination of the global structure that emerged from the various role dyads (Barley 1990).

Finally, both departments granted free access to the records they routinely compiled. Whenever a particular set of records seemed as if it might shed light on some pattern, I arranged to raid the department's archives. For example, duty assignment sheets were particularly helpful for verifying how the new technologies had affected the demographic distribution of radiologists' work (Barley 1990). Daily CT schedules, with their cancellations and "add-ons," offered measures of work flow and workload. Other records allowed me to test hunches regarding the scanner's ability to substitute for older radiographic procedures, such as the myelogram. As a final example, data recorded by the scanner's computer on hard copies of images represented an unobtrusive measure of the rigidity or flexibility of standard operating procedures. Since the CT technologists set a number of these parameters, their variance across time provided a small indication of the technologists' increasing control over the particulars of their work.

As with the content of the sociometric questions, the relevance of these and other unobtrusive indicators became clear only as I gained familiarity with the social order of the radiology departments. Just as the most celebrated network analyst could not determine ahead of time what interactional content would meaningfully tap the social structure of a radiology department, so an expert in unobtrusive observation could not predict the sociological relevance of specific records in the departments' archives. Ironically, then, researchers may actually need to wait until they have observed for some period of time before they can begin to be explicit about their observations, for only with time and familiarity can they recognize which indicators are sociologically relevant in a given setting.

Data Analysis

Although participant observation and other forms of qualitative research pose a variety of challenges foreign to most quantitative studies, perhaps the most daunting occurs after leaving the field: ordering and analyzing what many would consider to be an overwhelming corpus of descriptive data. Unlike survey researchers or experimentalists whose data come precategorized, ethnographers face the task of developing analytic categories a posteriori. While participant observers may find, in retrospect, that they have insufficient data for making strong claims about some of the phenomena captured by their field notes, my own experience suggests that the analytic task is far less troublesome than critics claim.

Contrary to popular opinion, the analysis of field data actually begins during a study's observational phase. By utilizing a comparative research design and by actively attempting to systematize sustained observations, researchers increase their odds of accumulating a body of field notes amenable to orderly analysis. Moreover, as Glaser and Strauss (1967) suggest, by stopping to analyze one's field notes from time to time during data collection, one can develop tentative theoretical notions and hypotheses that direct one toward even more systematic and telling data. For this reason, I routinely reviewed my field notes on weekends and on the basis of these reviews wrote "analytic memos" that recorded the results of my tentative analyses. Similarly, halfway through the project I withdrew from the field for seven weeks to analyze the body of data I had collected since June. The interlude allowed the formulation of tentative hypotheses and the identification potential indicators that gave greater direction to later observations. For example, during an analysis of early field notes I sensed that radiologists seemed less authoritarian when making requests of technologists who operated newer technologies (Barley 1984). The difference seemed to be lodged in the syntactic structure of the radiologists' utterances. The idea drove me to tape-record examinations and to analyze speech acts.

From an ontological point of view there is little reason to believe that analytic categories developed after the collection of the data are any more or less valid than those developed before or during data collection. In each case, the researcher risks imposing an overly simplistic and inaccurate framework on social reality. In fact, to the degree that field data contain a representative sample of actions and interpretations, one can argue that a posteriori categories are less likely to be biased by the researcher's own fantasies, since the categories tend to emerge from, and remain closer to, the data (Glaser and Strauss 1967, Geertz 1973, Van Maanen 1979). More pragmatically, however, there exist numerous strategies for making the analysis of field data more systematic, explicit, and hence, valid, replicable, and convincing.[9] To gain some of the flavor of how field notes can be systematically analyzed, consider how the scripts that characterized daily life in the two radiology departments were identified and analyzed.[10] The analytic activity progressed through four phases: (1) developing categories, (2) grouping data, (3) identifying patterns or scripts, and (4) comparing and contrasting scripts both synchronically and diachronically.

Developing Categories

Because of their richness, any set of field notes can be analyzed from a variety of perspectives. In general, however, the first step is to develop categories for sorting the data. Although one's actual categories ultimately depend on the particulars of the study, several general categorization schemes described by Lofland (1976) proved useful as a starting point for identifying the scripted properties of radiological work. One scheme entailed constructing a *typology of episodes*. All social life tends to have an episodic flavor. Social episodes tend to be repetitive and to have discrete temporal and spatial boundaries as well as explicit names. As noted earlier, the episodic nature of radiological work is grounded in a stream of procedures or examinations. Hence *types of procedures* not only guided the data collection, they also provided categories for organizing much of the analysis.

Types of interaction offered a second categorization scheme. Whereas episodic categories usually demarcate recurrent forms of situated activity, types of interactions involve role-based encounters. Although it is possible to develop interactional categories based on the content or tenor of an encounter, I chose categories formed on role dyads. Specifically, the central roles of a radiology department were cross-classified to create a listing of common interactional pairs: (1) radiologists interacting with radiologists, (2) technologists with technologists, (3) radiologists with technologists, (4) radiologists with patients, and (5) technologists with patients.

A third scheme was based on the notion that role incumbents have *typical days*. That is, a role incumbent's round of activity often inscribes a routine. Thus the flow of events, actions, and interactions experienced by a class of actors can be taken as a focus of analytic attention. I used the notion of typical days to analyze the temporal properties of the work of radiologists and technologists assigned to different technologies (Barley 1988b). Even finer category systems were developed by cross-classifying two or more categorization schemes: for instance, "interactions among radiologists and technologists during a barium enema," "a typical day of a technologist assigned to intravenous pyleograms," and so forth.

Grouping Data

With a single category system in mind, I read and reread the entire corpus of field notes, placing appropriate codes in the margins near passages relevant to particular categories. The notes could then be sorted by category. For instance, all field notes that described barium enemas were isolated and grouped together in a file according to their order of occurrence. Similar files were compiled for other procedures as well as for types of interactions and typical days. Because grouping involved sorting the field notes into separate files, and because I worked without the aid of a computer, I used a separate set of photocopied field notes for each typology. The duplicates allowed me to cut and rearrange relevant sections of a day's notes as the analysis required.

Identifying Scripts

After sorting the field notes by procedure, interaction type, or typical days, and after arranging incidents within each category in chronological order, my next task was to examine the data for the presence of patterns or scripts. Scripts may be thought of as outlines or plots of recurrent behaviors that define, in observable terms, the essence of the roles and actions that characterize a particular interaction order (Goffman 1959, 1967, 1983). For instance, like most recurrent episodes, each procedure consisted of a set of behaviors and activities that unfolded in a series of more or less invariant stages. These stages encoded the procedure's plot: the recurrent structure of unfolding that defined a procedure's unique character.

Turn-taking structures and the distribution of speech acts (requests, demands, questions, and so on) among role incumbents were examined to identify scripts that undergirded interactions. For example, one script characteristic of encounters between radiologists and technologists was dubbed "direction seeking." Although instances of direction seeking varied widely in content, each was characterized by the same interactional structure: (1) A technologist inquired about an appropriate course of action, (2) a radiologist provided the technologist with an answer, and (3) the technologist acted in accordance with the radiologist's answer. Scripts underlying typical days were defined in terms of the duration of events and cycles or sequences of activity. Once a script was identified, a code indicating its presence was written in the margin of the field notes.

It is critical to recognize that not all instances of a general category, such as "interactions between radiologists and technologists in CT," will evince the same script. In fact, instances within any given category are likely to exhibit several possible patterns. Analysts should not be disturbed if they find a multiplicity of patterns, since the goal is to specify the structural order of all activities and interactions observed. In other words, the objective is to develop a more refined set of categories based on the scripted properties of ongoing action. By the end of the analysis, one aims to be working with categories (such as "direction seeking") more refined than those with which one began (e.g., "interactions between technologists and radiologists").

Once one has identified a set of recurrent scripts, one can then compare scripts to uncover commonalities or shared global properties. The guiding notion is that certain scripts encode overarching or general structural principles. For example, regardless of duty assignment, the scripts of a radiologist's typical day evidenced what Hall (1969, p. 173) has called a polychronic order (Barley 1988b). This was quite different from the monochronic ordering of a technologist's day. Similarly, certain interactional scripts seemed to encode radiology's traditional status structure and its associated distribution of knowledge, while other scripts encoded the converse (Barley 1986a). Theoretically, such commonalities represent the institutionalized core of an interaction order.

Comparing Scripts Synchronically and Diachronically

Once the scripts evident in the field notes from each hospital were identified, the final step in the analysis was to analyze the scripts synchronically and diachronically, both of which were relatively straightforward procedures. At this point, the analysis acquired a quantitative edge. For the synchronic analysis, I simply tallied each script's occurrences across different technologies. Scripts that occurred in radiography and fluoroscopy but not in the newer technologies (or vice versa) offered evidence for a technologically occasioned shift in the social order of radiological work.

HOSPITAL PHASE		SUBURBAN						URBAN					
		Phase 1			Phase 2			Phase 1			Phase 2			Phase 4
		UV	AQ	PS	CT	RR	BT	DG	CM	UC	DS	UCrit	AcQ	TC	ME
Suburban	1	6	9	0	0	0	0	10	0	0	5	0	0	0	0
	2	2	3	2	13	14	7	11	0	0	5	0	1	9	7
Urban	1	0	0	10	0	0	1	47	12	12	21	0	2	0	0
	2	0	0	1	0	0	2	14	1	7	13	11	6	0	0
	3	0	0	1	1	0	0	50	4	9	33	4	7	0	0
	4	0	0	0	0	1	0	13	0	3	11	1	0	11	10

Legend   UV = unsought validation   CM   = countermand
         AQ = anticipatory question   UC   = usurping the controls
         PS = preference stating   DS   = direction seeking
         CT = clandestine teaching   UCrit = unexpected criticism
         RR = role reversal   AcQ = accusatory question
         BT = blaming the technologist   TC   = technical consultation
         DG = direction giving   ME   = mutual execution

Figure 1.4. Distribution of Scripts in Urban's and Suburban's CT Operation During Specific Phases of Each Scanner's Evolution

The diachronic analysis was executed by tallying each script's frequency during specific phases of each CT scanner's evolution. Phases were identified by noting the dates on which significant changes occurred in personnel assignments or in the scanners' general operating procedures. Figure 1.4 (which is discussed more fully in Barley 1986a) provides an illustration of how diachronic distributions were tallied and analyzed. Across the top of the figure are arrayed the scripts characteristic of each hospital's interaction order. Suburban's scripts are to the left of the solid vertical line drawn through the body of the figure; Urban's scripts are to the right. Each hospital's scripts are further grouped by the phase of structuring where they appeared to be most heavily concentrated in the field notes. The rows within the figure are ordered by hospital and, within hospital, by the phases of structuring hypothesized for that hospital. A solid horizontal line separates Suburban's and Urban's phases. Accordingly, each cell of the figure reports the number of times a specific script occurred in the field notes from a particular phase of structuring at a particular hospital.

Consider the two-by-two division of Figure 1.4 formed by the solid vertical and solid horizontal lines. Cells in the upper-left-hand and lower-right-hand quadrants (i.e., the main diagonal) report the occurrence of scripts in the hospital where they were thought to be most characteristic. Cells contained in the off-diagonal quadrants represent the occurrence of one hospital's scripts in the field notes from the other. Examination of this figure shows that Suburban and Urban were characterized by different scripts, given that Suburban's scripts are more frequent in the upper-left-hand quadrant and Urban's scripts are most frequent in the lower-right-hand quadrant. Moreover, it is also clear that within each hospital, different sets of scripts did indeed characterize different phases of structuring. For example, unsought validation (UV), anticipatory questions (AQ), and preference stating (PS) were more common at Suburban during Phase 1 than during Phase 2. Similarly, clandestine teaching (CT), role reversals (RR), and blaming the technologists (BT) did not appear at Suburban until Phase 2. By comparing the structural commonalities of the various scripts at each hospital, it was then possible to indicate in what general direction and at what rate the social order of the two CT scanners had evolved (see Barley 1986a).

BECOMING A RESEARCH TOOL

Critics often claim that the pitfalls of participant observation are primarily epistemological. The foregoing sections have shown that epistemic difficulties can be managed. In sharp contrast to the rhetoric of most methods texts, I submit that participant observation is far more likely to be tainted by emotional, social, and moral difficulties. To be sure, such problems accompany all forms of research, but they acquire special poignancy whenever researchers decide to use themselves as research tools. Longitudinal observation serves only to intensity the complications, for the longer one is in the field, the more the research task takes on the interpersonal trappings of daily life.

Periods of intense pleasure and elation certainly punctuated my year in the hospitals. However, I recall most vividly the darker emotions and the interpersonal complexities that haunted my daily routine. I was acutely aware, from the very outset, that the project's continuation rested largely on my being tolerated, accepted, and even liked by others. Each day, therefore, carried with it the nagging threat that I could always be expelled from one or both sites for committing a faux pas. As a result, I became more concerned with how others perceived me than I had been at any other time in my life since junior high school. Such self-consciousness consumed considerable energy. Like an actor in Goffman's essays or a freshman at a college mixer, I schemed, plotted, and worried constantly about how to present myself. Did that comment sound insufferably academic? Would asking this question go beyond the bounds of propriety? What effect would my being friendly with this person have on my relations with others? Should I laugh at racist or sexist jokes?

I resolved to manage such difficulties by taking cues from others and by engaging in behaviors commonly valued in other walks of life. For instance, I attempted to be congenial at all times. I avoided discussions of emotionally charged topics and belittled my education lest I be perceived as self-important. When possible, I went out of my way to do favors. I bought doughnuts, made coffee, and refrained from speaking ill of anyone, including those who were widely disliked. Even though I could not bring myself to laugh at racist or sexist jokes, I also did not confront their tellers.

As I gained familiarity with the people at each site, and as I learned more about the technologies, I gradually began to take a more active part in the departments' day-to-day routines. Although I was legally constrained from running the machines and although I was wary of harming patients while trying to be helpful, I nevertheless devised small measures of usefulness by assisting technologists with their "grunt work." I routinely helped lift patients off gurneys and onto tables, held urinals for feeble males, carried messages back and forth between technologists and radiologists, and lugged countless film cassettes for those who needed them. After several months of observing the CT scanners, I also found that I had learned a great deal about the software. When technologists and radiologists discovered that they could use me as "walking-talking" documentation, they did not hesitate to do so. My ability to be of assistance reflected the fact that I had worked with computers, whereas most of the technologists and radiologists had not. Moreover, I had observed problems encountered at both sites. In contrast, most technologists and radiologists knew how to cope only with those glitches that had plagued their own scanners.

The Emergence of Trust

Fieldworkers often wax poetic on the necessity of gaining the trust of informants. Many suggest that, as in everyday life, trust and acceptance are based largely on what the researcher is able to do honestly for others. While give-and-take is undoubtedly important, in my experience trust cannot be easily managed and is only partially contingent on familiarity and congeniality. In retrospect, any acceptance I gained appears to have been largely determined by events and perceptions over which I had little control.

For instance, building trust and friendship at Urban was exceptionally difficult because of a long history of conflict within the department. Urban's X-ray technologists, at least initially, regarded me with intense suspicion, and some hypothesized that the administration had sent me to spy on them, a perception never voiced, even indirectly, at Suburban. In fact, Urban's administrator had made overtures about my consulting with him on managerial issues. During the first several months, therefore, I had considerable difficulty engaging technologists in conversation unless I asked them direct questions, to which I usually received curt, and not always polite, replies.

Although I cannot pinpoint exactly when relations began to unfreeze, I suspect the X-ray technologists gradually lowered their guard for four reasons. First, I studiously avoided the department's administrator and made certain that we spoke only on public turf, so that witnesses could overhear our conversations. Second, in the first days of the study I developed good relations with the technologists who ran Urban's head scanner.[11] Because of a staff shortage in early July, the CT technologists were forced to work briefly in the X-ray department. Their demonstrations of acceptance during this period may have worked to my advantage. Third, I had several opportunities to express verbal solidarity with technologists after witnessing particularly nasty encounters involving technologists and radiologists. However, the most important factor was undoubtedly my relationship with Urban's sonographer, who was tied to the dominant clique of X-ray technologists and who went out of his way to vouch for me to his friends. Once the members of the dominant clique became more open, most of the other X-ray technologists followed suit.

Gaining the support of key insiders also proved critical at Suburban. Although far more hospitable than their counterparts at Urban, Suburban's technologists also remained aloof for several months. My relations with the technologists were transformed almost overnight by a completely serendipitous event. A patient from a neighboring hospital was to have a nephrostomy at Suburban. The procedure had been performed twice before, but each time the catheter had become dislodged. The third nephrostomy would require a catheter of unusually large diameter to prevent slippage. Suburban had only one such catheter on hand. A specials tech, who was also the most central person in the department's network, had prepared the catheter the night before the procedure was scheduled. However, an hour before the nephrostomy was to begin, he discovered that a janitor had thrown the catheter in the trash. After a number of phone calls, the technologist located a replacement at a hospital in Boston, but because he was unfamiliar with the city, he feared he would not be able to get to the hospital and back within an hour. Because I knew where the hospital was located and because I also owned a relatively fast car, I offered to drive him. We succeeded in making the round trip in 45 minutes, without encountering the highway patrol and without the radiologists ever learning that the catheter had been missing. Thereafter, I had no difficulty getting any of Suburban's technologists to cooperate.

Anxieties and Shortcomings

With time, then, most technologists and radiologists seemed to accept my presence. Some even showed friendship. Ironically, however, achieving interpersonal acceptance proved to be a double-edged sword. As in any social group, there were persons with whom I felt uncomfortable and some whom I actually disliked. Yet I could neither avoid their presence nor confront them about any of their behaviors that bothered me. The problem was particularly pointed at Urban, where the authoritarian culture led many technologists to be distrustful, distant, cynical, and, at times, openly hostile. In fact, the atmosphere at Urban was so distasteful that I eventually had to bolster my resolve to return on a daily basis. On many a morning I found myself driving aimlessly around the streets of Boston for as much as an hour before I succeeded in talking myself into the hospital's parking lot.

The longitudinal component of the study brought with it another set of unanticipated anxieties and predicaments. I was constantly plagued by the fear that I may be overlooking important social dynamics. The desperate and irrational thought that I might complete the study empty-handed led me to spend far too many hours questioning the "real" meaning of what I had seen or heard. Halfway through the project, boredom reared its head. I began to think that I had seen all there was to see. From time to time, I even found myself nodding off as I watched exams or listened to conversations. On the heals of boredom, however, came guilt, which renewed my anxiety about overlooking important details. Thus a spiral of complacency and doubt arose. The discipline of writing analytic memos proved crucial for managing these difficulties, as did periodic rump sessions with my colleagues and fellow ethnographers: Edgar Schein, John Van Maanen, and Gideon Kunda.

A final difficulty, partially associated with the experience of boredom, was a phenomenon that anthropologists term *going native*. The primary intellectual risk of long-term participant observation is that one may eventually come to view the setting entirely from an insider's perspective. As a result, situated behaviors and interpretations begin to appear normal, unsurprising, and commonsensical. When going native, the ethnographer forgets that he or she must remain, above all else, a "professional stranger" (Agar 1981).

By the end of the year I had certainly gone native on several fronts. Like the radiologists and technologists, I had long become numb to patients and their emotional outbursts. I not only regarded patients almost entirely as biological organisms, but I even began to appreciate how such emotional armor could allow one to execute tasks that might otherwise be too disturbing to perform. For instance, like my informants, I ceased to question how I could watch a barium enema performed on an elderly, groaning patient, while talking nonchalantly about what I had eaten for lunch. The upshot of my conversion was that I now have little of sociological importance to say about the patients I observed.

Finding a Niche

Thus the underbelly of long-term participant observation partially consists of the effects of the research act on the researcher. The remainder involves the researcher's influence on the setting. With the possible exception of archival research, all studies probably affect the people who are studied to some extent, even though researchers often pretend otherwise. Nevertheless, the probability seems particularly acute during ethnographic research. By becoming a participant observer, one creates for the ecology of an organization a role that did not exist before: namely, the role of the ever-present and ever-curious observer. Aside from allowing one's research to be used by management as part of an organizational intervention, it is difficult to imagine how a research act could be more intrusive for a longer period of time.

During the last week of the study, I brought a camera to both departments, intent on capturing mementos of the previous year. Taking pictures instantly became a farewell rite between myself and my informants. A number of technologists and radiologists even offered to take my picture after I took theirs. I accepted on the condition that they pose me in a stance typical of my observing. As my informants directed me on where to stand and how to hold my body, I found their attention to detail alarming. For instance, several of the technologists refused to take my picture until I had taken the cap off the top of my pen and placed it in my mouth. They realized, as I did not, that when observing I had often used my teeth to pull the cap off my felt-tip and that I habitually held the cap in my mouth. All of these photographs show me standing in a corner of an examination room (or directly behind technologists seated at a CT scanner), holding a pen in my right hand and a notepad in my left. For every picture, I was instructed to write. What, then, can be said about a role that appears, as I look at these photographs, so incongruent with its surroundings?

Although I made no secret of my intentions, my note taking was certainly more than a little suspicious, especially at first. Early on, a few of the bolder radiologists and technologists ventured to ask what I was writing. Not wishing to appear secretive, I decided to offer my notebook to whoever expressed interest in seeing what I had written. Since most of my notes pertained to the flow of action, those who accepted my offer expressed surprise that I had recorded the obvious and that I could find such pedestrian matters interesting. Nevertheless, most technologists and radiologists were initially quite self-conscious whenever something even slightly embarrassing occurred in my presence. On these occasions, they made jokes ("Steve, did you get all that down?") accompanied by nervous laughter, of which the most nervous was probably my own. I resolved early to take no notes when events turned to the untoward or when I sensed that a compromising situation was about to unfold. Although I might later jot down a summary of these events while secluded in a bathroom stall, in doing so I remained acutely aware that I should not be seen as someone after the department's "dirt."[12]

I prefer to think that with time, most of the technologists and radiologists made peace with my notebook, even if they did not completely forget its presence. On more than one occasion, a technologist took the pad from my hand and wrote down events that I had not myself noted. In all cases, this behavior followed a stream of events that I had been studiously attempting to ignore. Similarly, after several months, radiologists routinely informed me of events that I had not witnessed, but that they thought I would find interesting. It therefore seems reasonable to conclude that over the course of a year my presence as observer became more or less routine for the technologists and radiologists with whom I interacted on a daily basis. In fact, contrary to popular opinion, one reason for pursuing fieldwork longitudinally is that it actually enables researchers to get beyond presentational rhetoric and behavioral shows. People simply find it difficult to monitor their behavior or to dissemble for an entire year. Consequently, there is little reason to believe that my presence had a deleterious effect on my informants' lives or that my observations skewed their behaviors. But what of the patients, whom I rarely encountered twice? How did they understand my presence?

Both radiology departments accepted student technologists from local training programs. Interns were common at Urban and, from the perspective of a patient, interns would not have been out of place at Suburban. Without planning it to be so, my implicit cover became that of "student," although neither I nor anyone else mentioned what kind of student I might be. In other words, without solicitation, technologists and radiologists gave me a situational identity so that I could blend into the setting as a plausible anomaly. At Suburban, I was given a white lab coat identical to those worn by doctors and male technologists. The technologists always introduced me to patients in a manner that suggested my right to be in the situation. If patients directly questioned my identity, technologists would usually respond before I had the chance: "He's trying to learn what we do," "That's just Steve, he's learning the scanner with us," and so on. In point of fact, however, patients rarely questioned my identity (or, for that matter, anything else). Since the technologists and radiologists treated me as if I belonged, so did most of the patients. Being a pragmatist, I was more than willing to take advantage of any definition of my role that might felicitously arise.

In general, then, I do not believe that my presence skewed the social dynamics of the departments or that the act of observation led to filtered information. At the same time, one should not conclude that my presence had no implications or that my role was merely that of a fly on the wall. Instead, the social ramifications of long-term participant observation may simply be more subtle than most critics suggest. In fact, it seems that the most significant effects of my presence were fashioned less by the research act than by where I became situated in each department's social ecology. As with all other roles, the role of participant observer is fashioned by how the researcher's presence meshes with an ongoing stream of interaction to create a niche more or less unique to the context in which the observer is embedded.

Political Alignments

The phased nature of my observational strategy highlighted the nature of my role as well as what may be the most significant hazard associated with all forms of field research. Because I had initially approached the study from the technologist's vantage point, I found switching to the radiologist's perspective difficult. However, the difficulty was not simply a matter of my inability to change frames. Instead, it resulted largely from how my presence had been defined by others. When settings contain multiple groups with potentially conflicting interests, one is inevitably perceived as being more aligned with one group than another. At the time of the switch, I had not only yet to establish the type of rapport I had developed with the technologists, but, more important, I had not yet overcome the radiologists' perception that I was primarily interested in and aligned with the technologists.

A similar transition occurred when I returned to the synchronic strategy at the end of the year. The X-ray technologists were suspicious of the fact that I had spent so much time with the CT technologists and the radiologists, who they perceived as having interests different from their own. Fortunately, by this time I knew the technologists well enough to confront the situation head-on and to explain my position both as a researcher and as a person. The stance appeared to work, in that during the last two months I easily moved from one group to another without apparent ill feelings. However, had I not been engaged in longitudinal research, and had I not consciously chosen to view the department from the perspective of different groups, I would probably not have become cognizant of the political nature of the research act.

Given the salience of political analysis in recent organizational theory, it is surprising that most methods courses completely overlook the political implications of doing research. My experience suggests that in stratified organizations informants are quick to ascertain with which group the researcher appears to side. Moreover, it is extremely difficult for the researcher to alter the definition of his or her role once an alignment has been drawn. Such definitions undoubtedly influence the nature of the cooperation and information that researchers receive. The unfortunate fact is that most organizational researchers align themselves with one faction or another unwittingly and fail to appreciate how the alignment may affect their data.[13] One of the most important advantages of longitudinal fieldwork may be that extensive immersion in an organization enables a researcher to appreciate more fully, and perhaps to counteract, political definitions of his or her role.

From the very beginning, I sensed that technologists and radiologists were watching to see if I would pass potentially sensitive information to other persons in the department. Whether or not my perception was accurate, I cannot say for sure. Nevertheless, I was careful never to repeat what technologists or radiologists told me unless I was specifically asked to carry a message or unless the information was obviously meant to be public (i.e., "Don't use Room 2 because the film changer is jammed"). I can remember only one occasion on which I broke my self-imposed vow of confidentiality.

In late spring, the cardiologists at Suburban attempted to usurp cardiac ultrasound. I had been informed of the cardiologists' intentions by sonographers and radiologists alike. However, several radiologists did not know that I knew about the turf battle, even though I thought that my knowing was common knowledge. Under this assumption, I asked two radiologists a rather pointed question regarding the progress of the conflict. One immediately demanded to know how I knew about the situation. Taken aback, I named another radiologist as the person who had informed me. At first I thought I had betrayed my informant. However, as it turned out, the radiologist was glad to hear that it had not been a cardiologist who had told me. Afterward, the radiologist became more open with me than he had been up to that point in time. His openness led to the discovery that he had known my father-in-law while he was a resident. My faux pas thus ironically led our relationship onto firmer ground.

With time, I believe I came to be seen as a harmless, but perhaps eccentric, individual without factional loyalties. In fact, judging by the actions of the technologists and radiologists themselves, I would venture that my situated identity became that of a trusted neutral. For instance, after Christmas several of Suburban's technologists came to speak to me about difficulties they were having with one of their colleagues. They claimed that they had decided to talk with me because they were certain I "wouldn't talk."

A far more dramatic incident occurred at Urban.

Near the end of the study, I witnessed an instance of extreme hostility between a technologist and a radiologist that resulted in the radiologist's calling the technologist a number of unflattering names. The technologist, who felt that she had quietly borne a long history of affront, was quick to recognize that my presence meant she could successfully lodge a formal grievance, if I would be willing to testify on her behalf. The technologist lost no time in asking for my aid. After a moment of agony, I decided that I could not risk compromising my position as researcher. I therefore lamely told the technologist that I could not assist her because I could not attribute blame or malicious intent when I had no access to the radiologist's thought processes. The technologist became justifiably indignant, and I feared that my refusal would prove costly.

To my surprise and great relief, on returning to the department four days later, I was told that in my absence the technologists had discussed the issue of how I should have responded. While one or two felt I should have sided with the technologist, the consensus had been that I had all along been a neutral party and that I should not be expected to sacrifice that status now. My informant told me that to do so, the technologists had decided, would jeopardize my work. God bless them!

CONCLUDING COMMENTS

Although longitudinal field research seems particularly well suited for studies of the social ramifications of new technologies and perhaps even most organizational change, like all research methods, mine suffer from biases and limitations that should be made explicit. First and foremost, my approach to ethnographic field research is decidedly structuralist in orientation and realist in tone (for an elaboration of these genres, see Van Maanen 1988). Nowhere have I sought to offer an ethnographic account of the "native's point of view." Instead, my methods and tales are weighted toward what an anthropologist would call an *etic* or formal analysis. Had I been interested in writing a description of native viewpoints, I would have focused on other types of data and would have chosen other analytic and descriptive techniques.[14] It would, therefore, be a mistake for readers to treat my work as paradigmatic of all ethnographic research. Ethnography has many faces; I have described but one.

My approach to fieldwork is also rather costly, at least in terms of time. From beginning to end, the project took two and a half years to complete. I am still analyzing some of the data that I collected in 1982. Long-term observational fieldwork is not something that can be done on an occasional afternoon. It requires a considerable commitment of energy, a high tolerance for ambiguity, and, in some cases, a strong stomach. Moreover, the ethnographic stance is, in general, incompatible with the intent to prescribe or intervene, a stance that frequently characterizes research in organizational behavior. As on the voyages of the starship *Enterprise,* the watchword of careful ethnographic research is the "Prime Directive."

At the same time, however, organizational studies might profit both theoretically and empirically if more researchers were to embark on observational travels framed by an ethnographic sensitivity. For this to occur, we will surely need to change the way we reward our students and ourselves. The study that I have described was conducted as work toward a doctoral dissertation. As a graduate student, I had few organizational constraints on my time and I experienced no pressure to crank out articles to earn tenure (or, for that matter, to complete my degree by an arbitrary date). At first glance, conducting longitudinal ethnographic research would seem to be more difficult for academics carrying full-time teaching loads in institutions where the sheer number of annual publications is used as a blunt measure of reward. Nevertheless, researchers can overcome such obstacles by juggling their schedules creatively to allow solid blocks of time for research. Far more limiting are geographic constraints. Suburban and Urban were located within half an hour's drive of my residence. Had I been located in a less urban area, the study would have been far less tractable.

Finally, if I had it to do over again, I would probably do the study differently. For example, I can imagine (1) employing coders to help analyze data, (2) using Abbott's techniques for analyzing sequences to study temporal structures (see Chapter 8, this volume), or (3) taking on a partner and doing a team ethnography. I would have also begun my tape-recording much earlier. If I were undertaking the study today, I would also undoubtedly use a microcomputer and a word-processing program instead of a typewriter to compile my field notes. There now exist numerous software packages that enable field researchers to code portions of a text file and then reassemble those coded sections in a separate database. Several of these packages are commercially available (e.g., Note Bene, Go Ask Sam). Others have been explicitly written for and by ethnographers (Shelly 1988). The ability to sort, search, merge, and scan text files electronically seems far more efficient than the manual methods on which I relied. In fact, such programs should enable a researcher to compile counts and distributions rapidly and then subject these numeric data directly to statistical analysis.

Note, however, that all of these "improvements" aim at making the observation and analysis even more explicit, systematic, and credible. As such, they bow to empiricist, though not necessarily positivist, canons. While I am personally most comfortable with an empiricist's stance, there are insights to be gained from approaches more interpretive, and more lyrical, than my own. In fact, measured against such standards, my own work is little more than hackwork. Caveat emptor.

Acknowledgments

The research discussed in this chapter was supported, in part, by a doctoral dissertation grant from the National Center for Health Services Research (HS 05004). Collegial readings by Gideon Kunda, Pam Tolbert, Andrew Van de Ven, and several anonymous reviewers were valuable in checking my excesses.

Notes

1. The occupational groups most central to the work of a radiology department are radiologists and technologists. Radiologists are physicians who specialize in the interpretation of medical images. Technologists are individuals with associate's degrees in radiological technology. Technologists produce the films that radiologists interpret.

2. The terms *diachronic* and *synchronic* are adopted from linguistics. *Parallel* is, to the best of my knowledge, my own creation.

3. In my experience, the general population has greater esteem for anthropology than for sociology. Anthropology probably has a better name for a variety of reasons. Most people not only know less about anthropology than sociology, but because of the popularity of Indiana Jones, National Geographic television specials, and some PBS programming, anthropology has acquired a certain mystique. In contrast, since the 1960s sociologists have gained high visibility in the media as society's professional muckrakers. Because of difficulties encountered in my earlier research on funeral directing, I learned that ethnographers run less risk of premature rejection when they present themselves as anthropologists rather than sociologists.

4. However, he did so only after learning that Edgar Schein was a member of my committee. Several years earlier, the chief radiologist had been a Sloan Fellow at MIT and had done a thesis with Schein. Although I make no pretense of understanding the radiologist's motives and interpretations, for whatever reason he apparently felt that my ties to Schein were a sufficient reason for him to champion my cause.

5. Note that choosing procedures as a unit of analysis focused my attention in one direction rather than in the others that were possible. The choice seemed reasonable given my concern with behavior and interactions. However, had I been primarily interested in mapping insiders' interpretations, I would have probably chosen another tactic for collecting data. For instance, I might have relied more heavily on ethnosemantic interviews to construct linguistic taxonomies and semantic contrast sets.

6. A number of researchers talk about *triangulation,* the use of several methods to make findings more believable (Webb et al. 1966, Jick 1979). However, fewer researchers actively attempt to triangulate. Meyer's (1982) study of hospitals facing an anesthesiologists' strike and Faulkner's (1983) work on the careers of Hollywood composers are masterful examples. On tactics for making qualitative and ethnographic observations explicit, I have found the work of Michael Agar (1980, 1981), Miles and Huberman (1984), and Roger Barker (1963, 1978) to be extremely useful. Barker's studies of the "stream of behavior" and his methods for documenting it are classics of qualitative empiricism too often overlooked by modern fieldworkers.

7. At this point it seems appropriate to make clear one of my pet peeves. The reason so much of the so-called qualitative research in organizational behavior is thin and of questionable worth has little to do with the fact that the research is qualitative in nature. Rather, the difficulty arises from the fact that researchers have shied away from sustained observation. Three weeks' worth of unstructured interviews with a handful of respondents (usually top management) does not make for ethnographic understanding—much less allow for the possibility of collecting data on setting-specific indicators. From my perspective, when an ethnography does not involve extended periods of fieldwork, it does not deserve the name.

8. Although my behavioral focus differs from that of most ethnographers who have been primarily concerned with insiders' interpretations, I certainly did not ignore interpretations. Not

only did I record interpretive comments as part of my note taking, but if participants did not verbalize their interpretations of events spontaneously, I elicited them between procedures or when action was otherwise in a lull.

9. I have found the following to be particularly useful guides for conceptualizing the task of analyzing field data: Glaser and Strauss (1967), Schatzman and Strauss (1973), Lofland (1971, 1976), Agar (1980), Spradley (1980), Burgess (1982), Miles and Huberman (1984).

10. As noted in the text, a script is fundamentally a structuralist notion. The reader should, therefore, note that the analytic techniques reflect a decidedly formalist orientation to ethnographic research.

11. Although neither Urban nor Suburban had previously used a body scanner, Urban had been operating a head scanner since 1977.

12. I was also conscious that my field notes could be subpoenaed should a patient decide to sue a radiologist for malpractice. For this reason, I avoided recording any information on the interpretive mistakes that radiologists made. I also took no notes on procedures performed on lawyers, an occupation of whose members physicians appear to be justifiably wary. In fact, the radiologists were themselves especially careful whenever they encountered patients who were known to be lawyers or lawyers' wives.

13. Because of my experience, I now have serious reservations about the accuracy of any piece of research conducted by researchers who even remotely engage in what might be construed as a consulting role or who align themselves with the management of an organization. Perhaps it is time organizational researchers gave as much attention to the biases of their alignments as they do to the biases of their methods. I fear that we may actually find the former to be more epistemologically damaging than the latter.

14. Those interested in learning more about emic ethnographies may want to consult the work of Dalton (1951), Geertz (1973, 1983), Douglas (1966, 1975), Spradley (1980), Gregory (1983), and Kunda (1991).

References

Agar, Michael (1980), "Getting Better Quality Stuff: Methodological Competition in an Interdisciplinary Niche," *Urban Life,* 9, 34-50.

Agar, Michael (1981), *The Professional Stranger,* New York: Academic Press.

Banta, David, and Clyde J. Behney (1980), "Medical Technology Policies and Problems," *Health Care Management Review,* 5, 45-52.

Banta, David, and Barbara J. McNeil (1978), "Evaluation of the CAT Scanner and Other Diagnostic Technologies," *Health Care Management Review,* 3, 7-19.

Barker, Roger G. (1963), *The Stream of Behavior,* New York: Appleton-Century-Crofts.

Barker, Roger G. (1978), *Habitats, Environments, and Human Behavior,* San Francisco: Jossey-Bass.

Barley, Stephen R. (1984), "The Professional, the Semi-Professional and the Machines: The Social Ramifications of Computer Based Imaging in Radiology," doctoral dissertation, Sloan School of Management, MIT.

Barley, Stephen R. (1986a), "Technology as an Occasion for Structuring: Observations on CT Scanners and the Social Order of Radiology Departments," *Administrative Science Quarterly,* 31, 78-108.

Barley, Stephen R. (1986b), "Changing Roles in Radiology," *Administrative Radiology,* 5, 32-41.

Barley, Stephen R. (1988a), "The Social Construction of a Machine: Ritual, Superstition, Magical Thinking and Other Pragmatic Responses to Running a CT Scanner," in M. Lock and

D. Gordon (Eds.), *Biomedicine Examined* (pp. 497-539), Dordrecht, Netherlands: Kluwer Academic.

Barley, Stephen R. (1988b), "On Technology, Time, and Social Order: Technically Induced Change in the Temporal Organization of Radiological Work," in F. A. Dubinskas (Ed.), *Making Time: Ethnographies of High Technology Organizations* (pp. 123-169), Philadelphia: Temple University Press.

Barley, Stephen R. (1988c), "Technology, Power, and the Social Organization of Work: Towards a Pragmatic Theory of Deskilling," in N. DiTomaso and S. Bacharach (Eds.), *Research in the Sociology of Organizations* (Vol. 6, pp. 33-80), Greenwich, CT: JAI.

Barley, Stephen R. (1990), "The Alignment of Technology and Structure Through Roles and Networks," *Administrative Science Quarterly*, 35, 61-103.

Becker, Howard S., Blanche Geer, Everett C. Hughes, and Anselm L. Strauss (1961), *Boys in White: Student Culture in Medical School*, Chicago: University of Chicago Press.

Bell, Daniel (1973), *The Coming of the Post-Industrial Society*, New York: Basic Books.

Berger, Peter L., and Thomas Luckmann (1967), *The Social Construction of Reality: A Treatise in the Sociology of Knowledge*, Garden City, NY: Doubleday.

Burgess, Robert G. (Ed.) (1982), *Field Research: A Sourcebook and Field Manual*, London: George Allen & Unwin.

Dalton, Melville (1951), "Informal Factors in Career Achievement," *American Journal of Sociology*, 61, 407-415.

Douglas, Mary (1966), *Purity and Danger: An Analysis of the Concepts of Pollution and Taboo*, London: Routledge & Kegan Paul.

Douglas, Mary (1975), *Implicit Meanings: Essays in Anthropology*, London: Routledge & Kegan Paul.

Faulkner, Robert R. (1983), *Music on Demand: Composers and Careers in the Hollywood Film Industry*, New Brunswick, NJ: Transaction.

Fensham, Peter J., and Douglas Hooper (1964), *The Dynamics of a Changing Technology*, London: Tavistock.

Freidson, Eliot (1970), *Professional Dominance: The Social Structure of Medical Care*, New York: Atherton.

Freidson, Eliot, and Judith Lorber (1972), *Medical Men and Their Work*, Chicago: Aldine.

Geertz, Clifford (1973), *The Interpretation of Cultures: Selected Essays*, New York: Basic Books.

Geertz, Clifford (1983), *Local Knowledge: Further Essays in Interpretive Anthropology*, New York: Basic Books.

Giddens, Anthony (1984), *The Constitution of Society*, Berkeley: University of California Press.

Glaser, Barney G., and Anselm L. Strauss (1967), *The Discovery of Grounded Theory: Strategies for Qualitative Research*, Chicago: Aldine.

Goffman, Erving (1959), *The Presentation of Self in Everyday Life*, Garden City, NY: Anchor.

Goffman, Erving (1967), *Interaction Ritual: Essays on Face-to-Face Behavior*, Garden City, NY: Anchor.

Goffman, Erving (1983), "The Interaction Order," *American Sociological Review*, 48, 1-17.

Gregory, Kathleen L. (1983), "Native-View Paradigms: Multiple Cultures and Culture Conflicts in Organizations," *Administrative Science Quarterly*, 28, 259-377.

Hall, Edward T. (1969), *The Hidden Dimension*, Garden City, NY: Anchor.

Herbst, P. G. (1962), *Autonomous Group Functioning*, London: Tavistock.

Hughes, Everett C. (1958), *Men and Their Work*, Glencoe, IL: Free Press.

Hughes, Everett C. (1972), *The Sociological Eye*, Chicago: Aldine.

Jick, Todd D. (1979), "Mixing Qualitative and Quantitative Methods: Triangulation in Action," *Administrative Science Quarterly*, 24, 602-611.

Kunda, Gideon (1991), *Engineering Culture: Control and Commitment in a High Tech Corporation,* Philadelphia: Temple University Press.

Larkin, Gerald (1978), "Medical Dominance and Control: Radiographers in the Division of Labor," *Sociological Review,* 26, 843-858.

Larkin, Gerald (1983), *Occupational Monopoly and Modern Medicine,* London: Tavistock.

Lofland, John (1971), *Analyzing Social Settings: A Guide to Qualitative Observation and Analysis,* Belmont, CA: Wadsworth.

Lofland, John (1976), *Doing Social Life: The Qualitative Study of Human Interaction in Natural Settings,* New York: Wiley.

Mann, Floyd C., and Lawrence K. Williams (1961), "Observations on the Dynamics of a Change to Electronic Data-Processing Equipment," *Administrative Science Quarterly,* 5, 217-256.

Mechanic, David (1968), *Medical Sociology: A Selective View,* New York: Free Press.

Meissner, Martin (1969), *Technology and the Worker,* San Francisco: Chandler.

Meyer, Alan (1982), "Adapting to Environmental Jolts," *Administrative Science Quarterly,* 27, 515-532.

Miles, Matthew B., and A. Michael Huberman (1984), *Qualitative Data Analysis: A Sourcebook of New Methods,* Beverly Hills, CA: Sage.

Office of Technology Assessment (1978), *Policy Implications of the Computed Tomography (CT) Scanner,* Washington, DC: Congress of the United States.

Office of Technology Assessment (1981), *Policy Implications of the Computed Tomography Scanner: An Update,* Washington, DC: Congress of the United States.

Rice, A. K. (1958), *Productivity and Social Organization: The Ahmebabad Experiment,* London: Tavistock.

Schein, Edgar H. (1985), *Organizational Culture and Leadership,* San Francisco: Jossey-Bass.

Schatzman, Leonard, and Anselm L. Strauss (1973), *Field Research: Strategies for a Natural Sociology,* Englewood Cliffs, NJ: Prentice Hall.

Shelly, Anne L. (1988), "Analytic Strategies and Computer Assistance as Tools of Qualitative Researchers," unpublished paper, School of Computer and Information Science, Syracuse University.

Spradley, James P. (1980), *Participant Observation,* New York: Holt, Rinehart & Winston.

Stocking, Barbara, and Stuart L. Morrison (1978), *The Image and the Reality,* London: Oxford University Press.

Strauss, Anselm L. (1978), *Negotiations,* San Francisco: Jossey-Bass.

Strauss, Anselm L., Rue Bucher, Danuta Ehrlich, Melvin Sabshin, and Leonard Schatzman (1963), "The Hospital and Its Negotiated Order," in Eliot Freidson (Ed.), *The Hospital in Modern Society* (pp. 147-169), New York: Free Press.

Strauss, Anselm L., Leonard Schatzman, Rue Bucher, Danuta Ehrlich, and Melvin Sabshin (1964), *Psychiatric Ideologies and Institutions,* Glencoe, IL: Free Press.

Trist, E. L., and K. W. Bamforth (1951), "Some Social Psychological Consequences of the Longwall Method of Coal Getting," *Human Relations,* 4, 3-38.

Van Maanen, John (1979), "The Fact of Fiction in Organizational Ethnography," *Administrative Science Quarterly,* 24, 539-550.

Van Maanen, John (1988), *Tales of the Field: On Writing Ethnography,* Chicago: University of Chicago Press.

Webb, Eugene J., Donald T. Campbell, Richard D. Schwartz, and Lee Sechrest (1966), *Unobtrusive Measures: Nonreactive Research in the Social Sciences,* Chicago: Rand McNally.

Wiener, H. (1979), *Findings in CT: A Clinical and Economic Analysis of Computed Tomography,* New York: Pfizer.

2

A Dual Methodology for Case Studies

Synergistic Use of a Longitudinal
Single Site With Replicated Multiple Sites

DOROTHY LEONARD-BARTON

This chapter describes a case study methodology that combines a real-time longitudinal (three-year) study with nine retrospective case studies about the same phenomenon. These two kinds of case studies offer opportunities for complementary and synergistic data gathering and analysis. That is, specific strengths in each method compensate for some particular weakness in the other. For instance, the retrospective studies offer the opportunity to identify patterns indicative of dynamic processes and the longitudinal study provides a close-up view of those patterns as they evolve over time. The combination of the two types of case studies also enhances three kinds of validity: construct, internal, and external. The author also discusses problems with and shortcomings of this dual methodology and suggests the circumstances for which the methodology is especially appropriate.

This chapter reports on a case study methodology used to investigate the process of transferring new technologies from their developers into the hands of their users. The methodology, a combination of a longitudinal case study

This chapter appeared originally in *Organization Science,* vol. 1, no. 3, August 1990, pp. 248-266.

of a single site and a retrospective analysis of case studies, has significant advantages, including some that are synergistic, over either component methodology.

The research methodology is the focus here, rather than the research topic (technology transfer). Therefore, I present the substantive issues motivating the study in which the methodology was used only very briefly before moving to a description of the field methods used and of both the expected and serendipitous synergies obtained through the particular blend of methods. The third section of the chapter presents some principal weaknesses and failings in the methodology, and I conclude with suggestions about issues and research contexts best suited to this methodology. The methodology draws on or is related to the work of numerous other researchers, who have discussed both the hazards and the richness of qualitative data-gathering methods (e.g., Miles and Huberman 1984, Van Maanen 1988); who have developed systematic, rigorous approaches to developing theory through comparative case study (Yin 1984, Eisenhardt 1989); or who have demonstrated the value of similar approaches by their own field-based case research (e.g., Bower 1970, Pettigrew 1979, Bourgeois and Eisenhardt 1988).

The particular phenomenon studied here is the internal development and deployment of equipment, processes, and software tools intended to increase the productivity of employees as they produce goods or services for their corporate employers. The research topic of new technology implementation is conceptually linked to a large body of literature about organizational innovativeness. However, much of this literature has focused on those characteristics of the organization as a whole that covary with innovative behavior—for example, the degree of decentralization, complexity, or formalization (Kimberly and Evanisko 1981, Moch and Morse 1977, Burns and Stalker 1961). In contrast, one objective of the research described here was to evolve theory about the nature of the innovation process itself, reflecting the complex interaction of individual and group motivation and behavior with technical problem solving. Empirical work supporting the development of theory about the process of innovation is relatively scarce outside of the engineering literature (a similar observation has been made by Van de Ven 1986). A secondary objective was to produce some managerial insights into those factors aiding and impeding the transfer of the new technology from its inventors/developers to its users within an organization. These two objectives—one theoretical and one oriented toward practice—necessitated a methodology capable of capturing dynamic processes. Moreover, the process description had to be at a level of detail that could provide understanding of individual, work group, and organizational behavior over time.

METHODOLOGY

Major Methodological Choices

Three major methodological choices were made to accomplish the two objectives described above: (1) to use process-focused case studies; (2) to include enough such studies (nine) that the potential generalizability of the emerging theory would be beyond that offered by a single implementation situation, as suggested by Yin (1984); and (3) to complement the retrospective cases with the simultaneous conduct of one longitudinal (three-year), real-time field case study. The novelty and benefits of the methodology described below lie in the synergistic interaction of these last two decisions, and therefore the discussion focuses mostly on them.

Case Study Methodology

The phenomenon being researched always dictates to some extent the terms of its own dissection and exploration. Because this study focused on a "how" and "why" question about a contemporary set of events (Yin 1984, p. 13) and, as noted above, addressed a process not yet thoroughly researched, a case study was the logical methodology. A case study is a history of a past or current phenomenon, drawn from multiple sources of evidence. It can include data from direct observation and systematic interviewing as well as from public and private archives. In fact, any fact relevant to the stream of events describing the phenomenon is a potential datum in a case study, because context is important (Franz and Robey 1984, Stone 1978).

Rather than seeking degrees of freedom from a large standardized data set, the case study tests "theory with degrees of freedom coming from the multiple implications of [the] theory. The process is a kind of pattern-matching" (Campbell 1975, p. 182). In the research on technology development and implementation discussed here, no single perspective, however numerous the observations from that one vantage point, would reveal the entire pattern. In order to understand all the interacting factors (for example, the criticality of the technology to the business, alteration of the technology during implementation, or the actions of champions on behalf of the new technology), it was necessary that the research methodology slice vertically through the organization, obtaining data from multiple levels and perspectives. Therefore a case study approach was appropriate and was used. However, the methodology of the study was not limited to a single case.

Multiple Cases

A single case study is subject to limits in generalizability and several potential biases, such as the misjudgment of the representativeness of a single event (Tversky and Kahneman 1986), exaggeration of the salience of a datum because of its ready availability, or biasing of estimates because of unconscious anchoring (see Jaikumar and Bohn 1986). Multiple cases augment external validity and help guard against observer biases. Yin (1984) argues that the logic underlying a multiple case study approach is similar to that guiding multiple experiments, and that each case should be selected so that it "either (a) predicts similar results (a literal replication), or (b) produces contrary results but for predictable reasons (a theoretical replication)" (pp. 48-49). Because the objective of the research was to produce theory relevant to numerous different managerial situations and capable of explaining success or failure, a methodology including both literal and theoretical replication was required. As described below in some detail, nine retrospective case studies of internal technology transfer were conducted to fulfill this requirement.

Longitudinal Study

The most significant limitation of wholly retrospective research is the difficulty of determining cause and effect from reconstructed events. Moreover, although studies have shown that the participants in organizational processes do not forget key events in these processes as readily as one might suppose (Huber 1985), the participant informant in a wholly retrospective study may not have recognized an event as important when it occurred and thus may not recall it afterward. Therefore, whereas multiple retrospective studies increase the external validity of a research design, a longitudinal, real-time study can increase internal validity by enabling the researcher to track cause and effect. For this reason, simultaneously with the nine retrospective studies, I conducted one in-depth, three-year study of the development and deployment of a technology. Table 2.1 presents a timeline and description of the data sources used in the 10 cases.

Study Context and Structure

Retrospective Cases: Context and Structure

As Table 2.1 shows, the first retrospective case study (Structured System Analysis, or SSA) included extensive data-gathering efforts in 1983-1984. First, a highly structured interview guide was developed in a pilot study of

TABLE 2.1 Description of Methods Used: Timeline and Data Sources

				Primary Data Sources		
				Interviews		
Date	Method	Technology	Population	Structured	Unstructured	Secondary Data Sources
1983-1984	First of multiple, retrospective cases	SSA (used by programmers)	Programmers (pilot)	$N = 25$		Archival
			Programmers (three site, full-scale)	$N = 145$		
			SSA developers	$N = 2$	$N = 5$	
			Upper-level managers		$N = 3$	
1984-1986	Eight more multiple retrospective cases	Copper	Users of technology	$N = 2$ to 4	$N = 2$ to 22	Archival
		CAD	Developers of technology	$N = 2$	$N = 2$ to 8	
		Smartwave				
		Solagen	Upper-level managers		$N = 1$ to 4	
		XCON				
		Polymer Process				
		Circulator				
		Diagnostic				
1984	Single-site, in-depth, longitudinal	XSEL (used by sales force)	Sales representatives (pilot)	$N = 20$		Archival
			Sales representatives (national sample, *first survey*)	$N = 98$		Personal observation
						Attendance at meetings

Year	Site	Group	N (sample)	N (interviews)	Method
		User Design Group members	N = 16		Informal conversations
		System managers	N = 7	N = 8	
		Developers		N = 5 to 8	
		Other managers		N = 5 to 10	
1985	XSEL	Sales representatives (national sample, *second survey*)	N = 95		Archival Personal observation
		Trainees before and after training	N = 23		Attendance at meetings
		Developers		N = 5 to 8	Informal conversations
		Other managers		N = 5 to 10	
1986	XSEL	Sales representatives (national sample, *third survey*)	N = 96		Archival Personal observation
		Developers	N = 2	N = 5 to 8	Attendance at meetings
		Sales unit managers	N = 46		
		Other managers		N = 3 to 6	Informal conversations

43

25 computer programmers, and then that guide was applied in 145 personal interviews with the computer programmers who constituted the population targeted as users of the SSA software and techniques. The data from these interviews at three different organizational sites provided a comprehensive view of users' opinions about SSA (e.g., strengths and weaknesses of the technology, influences on users' adoption decisions) at one point in time. However, the 145 interviews added only bulk, not depth, to the research database. That is, the information gathered in the full-scale study was largely redundant with the insights I had already obtained in the 25 pilot interviews. True, I gathered enough additional degrees of freedom from the large-scale survey of 145 interviews to test those initial insights with statistical modeling techniques (Leonard-Barton 1987a). However, all the data (both pilot and full-scale survey) emanated from one perspective: the users'. I had to return to the organization for mostly unstructured interviews with the SSA developers and with other managers in order to understand the whole story from multiple perspectives. Therefore, in the next eight retrospective studies, conducted 1984-1986, I interviewed fewer respondents but drew them from populations representing multiple perspectives. These unstructured interviews were supplemented with a short (two-page) questionnaire filled out by two technology developers and at least two representative users at each of the eight study sites.

The eight retrospective case situations were selected so as to vary deliberately the context of the technology transfer and the nature of the technology, for greater generalizability. Including the SSA site, the nine cases were drawn from six different corporations, and the technologies studied ranged from chemical processes to new materials (see Table 2.2). However, "literal replication" in multiple sites requires that the phenomenon being studied be defined by some characteristics common to all the research situations (Yin 1984). In each corporation, a representative from the technology development organization drew up a preliminary list of technologies that had been transferred into operations, with varying degrees of success. The eight technologies that I finally selected, after consultation with the company representative, matched the initial SSA site in meeting the following requirements: They were developed internally, for internal use, within the past five years. These three selection criteria enabled me to limit numerous potential influences originating outside the firm (such as the effects of external vendors, of external market competition and demand, or of historically different industry conditions), as possible sources of variance in project outcomes.

In addition, all nine cases were matched on three dimensions that controlled for irrelevant sources of variance originating within the firm. First, the technologies selected had all passed some baseline tests of technical feasi-

TABLE 2.2 Description of 10 Cases of Technology Transfer of an Innovation

Technology	Degree of Success
1. Polymer Process: A chemical reaction producing a new polymer that is used in the production of toner for copier machines. Developed in corporate research laboratories of "Alpha" Corporation on the East Coast and transferred into manufacturing operations in the Midwest.	High success. In full use in plant as scheduled.
2. XCON (eXpert CONfigurer): An expert system that checks the configuration of complex computer systems before they are ordered from manufacturing to ensure that all needed components are included in the design and that they are compatible, i.e., that the system can be manufactured. Originated at Carnegie Mellon University, transferred into AI systems group within manufacturing at Digital Equipment Corp. and then into manufacturing operations to be used by 14-17 technical editors.	High success. In use by all 16 technical editors for 98% of orders.
3. Rolling Mill Diagnostic: A mathematical computer program designed to detect the source of irregularities occurring in the rolling of aluminum sheeting. Originated in Alcan Research Laboratories and transferred into rolling mills at Oswego, New York.	High success. In regular use by plant engineers.
4. Computer-Aided Design: A computer-aided design tool intended for use by engineers who are designing circuit packs. CAD generates a schematic (drawing) representation of the circuitry that then goes to drafting for fine-tuning and on to the manufacturing site to guide the production of prototype circuit boards. Designed in Corporation Information Systems group of "Shield Electronics" and diffused nationwide.	Moderately high success. Used in 70% of intended cases after 18 months in field. (Use is strongly mandated.)
5. XSEL: An expert system designed for use by sales representatives in a computer company that sells complex customized systems. XSEL checks the sales reps' configurations for accuracy and completeness before the order is submitted. Designed in AI systems group (located in manufacturing) and transferred to more than 2,000 sales representatives nationwide.	Moderate success. Use by 50% of intended users 18 months after full-scale introduction to field. (Use not mandated, with some exceptions.)
6. Structured Systems Analysis: A structured methodology for constructing software, used by systems analysts in their first attempts to "scope out" the business their system is to serve. Accompanied by computerized aids that help generate the diagrams and standardized notations used to communicate the analysis (thus akin to word processing). Developed in Corporate Information Systems group of "Cairn" Corporation, transferred throughout the corporation worldwide to hundreds of design groups and thousands of systems analysts.	Moderate success. Adoption by an average of 60% of the intended users 36 months after full-scale introduction to field. (Use is weakly mandated.)

(continued)

TABLE 2.2 Continued

Technology	Degree of Success
7. Copper Process: The substitution of copper for silver in the production of hybrid circuit boards. Originated in northern research laboratories; transferred to southern manufacturing site.	Failure at first. Eventual forced implementation after months of difficulty. Full potential never reached.
8. Smartwave: An expert system (a type of artificial intelligence that mimics human judgment and can represent heuristics) designed to diagnose defects occurring during the process of passing circuit boards over a molten wave of solder to connect lead wires on the backs of boards. Developed in manufacturing AI systems group, transferred to one manufacturing site.	Failure in original form. Revived in different form after the study ended.
9. Solagen: A chemical reaction designed to speed up and better control the deterioration of animal bones and hides into gelatin. The original process took six weeks and involved decomposition in a lime pit. Solagen takes 48 hours. Implemented on a pilot plant basis at Kodak Park in Rochester, New York.	Total failure. After pilot plant, withdrawn from active status.
10. Jumping Ring Circulator: An electromechanical pump designed to stir recycled aluminum scrap into a molten metal bath. Designed in corporate Research Laboratories, manufactured outside, implemented on an experimental basis in rolling mills.	Total failure. Withdrawn from operations after months of experimentation.

bility. This provision eliminated from study any cases in which the failure to transfer to users occurred simply because the technology was technically infeasible. Second, all the technologies selected altered the work environment in some obvious (albeit not necessarily important) way. This selection criterion eliminated cases in which transfer success could potentially be imputed to users' lack of awareness of any innovation—that is, that anything had been changed. For instance, a software compiler project was rejected because the technology transformed the internal workings of a computer, but without any noticeable alteration to the interface visible to users. Third, the transfer stages included in the study were consistently defined across projects. All projects focused on the time from the first establishment of technical feasibility until the user organization used the technology in full production mode, or, in two cases of failure, until the project was canceled. This definition set bounds on the transfer situation, confining it to a series of transactions between developers and the earliest users, thus providing additional control over undesired variation among cases.

Whereas the majority of the cases were literal replications of the first SSA study circumstances, several were selected for the purposes of "theoretical

TABLE 2.3 Comparison of the Two Methodologies

| | Methodology | |
Research Activities	Single-Site In-Depth, Longitudinal	Multiple-Site Retrospective
1. Data Gathering		
a. Efficiency	Low; danger of data overload; many unusable data	Relatively high; focused data gathering
b. Objectivity	Danger of too deep involvement, developing unconscious biases	Danger of unconsciously accepting respondent bias
c. Pattern recognition	Microscopic examination of details of process	Recognition of overall patterns in process
2. Establishing Validity		
a. External validity	Low generalizability	Relatively high generalizability; variety of situations
b. Internal validity	Relatively high; good opportunity to establish cause and effect	Lower; potential confusion about cause and effect
c. Construct validity	Opportunity to test sensitivity of construct measures to passage of time	Opportunity to validate stability of construct across situations

replication," that is, so as to explore conditions under which technology transfer failed. In selecting the total 10 cases, the original intent was to match 5 complete failures with 5 highly successful cases, and informants from the corporations were asked to make these judgments during the initial selection process. However, making such absolute distinctions between success and failure proved to be highly problematic for most of the cases. Of the 10, 2 were complete failures, 2 were initial failures (eventually revived), 3 were moderately successful, and 3 were highly successful. (Measures of success included informants' opinions during the unstructured interviews, their responses to scaled questions on the questionnaire, and archival data.)

As I had discovered in my first case study (SSA, conducted in 1983-1984), retrospective studies often leave one hungry for the details that enrich understanding of process. Informants were occasionally quite vague about the timing of events and therefore, when archival data were not available, it was difficult to be certain of the direction of influence—that is, which was cause and which effect. Moreover, sometimes informants were reluctant to talk about "political" issues, believing it unwise to dredge up old problems.

Yet understanding the resolution of those issues was often critical to the theory-building process. Recognizing these disadvantages to reconstructing events after the fact led me to conduct the longitudinal, real-time, in-depth study simultaneously with the final eight retrospective studies.

Longitudinal Study: Context and Structure

The purest form of a longitudinal field study—namely, daily participant observation—was not feasible. I could visit the research site only once or twice a week. Therefore, most of the data were obtained through retrospective reports gathered shortly after events occurred. However, a longitudinal study involving a series of multiple interviews about recent events offered the obvious benefit of proximity in time to current events, and thereby increased the likelihood that I could determine the sequence and nature of events accurately. Moreover, there were many opportunities to collect data through personal observation at meetings and training sessions.

The context of the longitudinal research was the development and deployment of XSEL, an "expert system" (a type of artificial intelligence software) intended to help sales representatives at Digital Equipment Corporation configure (select components for and design) the very large semicustomized computer systems sold by Digital. Accuracy in this complex task is very important, for small omissions (e.g., omitting a connector cable) or incorrect assumptions about the compatibility of parts (e.g., communication hardware used to link computers) can render a computer system impossible to manufacture in the form ordered by the sales representative (for a detailed account, see Leonard-Barton 1987b). Therefore, XSEL could potentially save Digital much time, effort, and money by helping sales representatives configure systems correctly at the time they placed customers' orders.

During the three-year period in which I followed the XSEL development and implementation (1984-1986), I gathered data using both highly structured and unstructured methods. The formal, highly structured efforts included (1) three annual surveys (two telephone, one mail) of a representative national sample of about 100 sales representatives, with almost all of the questions replicated from year to year; (2) questionnaires filled out by members of the "User Design Group" (sales representatives who met every few months with software developers to review and guide the progress of the software); (3) a telephone survey of 46 sales unit managers (the immediate supervisors of the representatives who were to use XSEL); (4) archival data; and (5) structured interview sessions with the developers to analyze the number and kinds of technical changes or additions being made to the software (see Table 2.1).

Unstructured data collection included notes taken during User Design Group meetings and meetings of the XSEL program office with various other groups important to implementation. For example, I traveled to a national meeting of the "systems managers," seven computer operators, each of whom was in charge of the machine dedicated in each sales region to the running of XSEL. Data were also obtained in unstructured interviews with very early XSEL users across the country and with people around the company whose work would be affected by the advent of XSEL. These informants included people in the information systems office traditionally responsible for supporting software and three of the seven regional sales managers whose opinions influenced use or rejection of XSEL by the sales representatives reporting to them. In addition, I held many informal meetings with the XSEL program office personnel and with their (sole) counterpart in the sales organization. Altogether these sources produced a plethora of data, which were paradoxically both the strength and the weakness of the in-depth longitudinal study. As discussed later in greater detail, the method promoted a rich, full understanding of the context and the process from the perspective of someone who has lived through events. However, it was clear even at the beginning of the study that such abundant data could also smother me, obscuring the very process patterns I wished to discern.

The Synergy of Combined Methods

Two sets of advantages are obtained from combining the longitudinal real-time study with the replicated historical cases: (1) specific strengths in the data-gathering process for each method that compensated for some particular lack or weakness in the other, and (2) complementary approaches in each method that, because of the synergy obtained by combining the two, enhanced external, construct, and internal validity.

Because "all research methods are seriously flawed—though each is flawed differently" (McGrath, Martin, and Kulka 1982, p. 15), the challenge to the researcher is to "choose—and often to devise—a set of measures . . . that together, transcend one another's methodological vulnerabilities" (McGrath 1982, p. 99). In data gathering, the real-time study and the replicated retrospective cases methodologies have compensatory strengths in (1) efficiency and (2) objectivity.

Data Gathering

Efficiency. The more the in-depth, real-time longitudinal study approximates a true ethnographic, participant observation methodology, the more the researcher sacrifices efficiency for richness of data. In such studies, delegating data gathering leads to unacceptable losses in the investigator's grasp of important details. Further, in order to observe critical events, one must often spend an inordinate amount of time on noncritical ones and in building relationships with the people involved (see also Van Maanen 1988 on this point). Therefore, the ethnographic study is deep rather than quick.

The three-year study described here did not achieve the depth of ethnographic immersion described by Van Maanen (1988) or undertaken by Barley (1986). However, the study did involve spending whole days and evenings at the site, because the phenomenon of interest—namely, the development and implementation of new technology—could not be tracked totally through any particular set of meetings or known events. For instance, although the XSEL program office held meetings with a User Design Group of representatives from the sales force, these irregularly held meetings could not provide insight into all the dynamics of interest. Not only were many other types of meetings and sessions important, but many critical events occurred outside of formal situations.

Many useful data emerged from informal conversations at lunch, in hallways, and during breaks in formal meetings. For example, such conversations with a senior sales representative and (on a separate occasion) with a system manager, both of whom had extensive computer science training, revealed the depth of the shift in development methodology and architecture that the artificial intelligence approach to computer software represented for people trained traditionally. To a programmer accustomed to the precise, sequentially ordered logic of COBOL or FORTRAN, the rule-based system created in XSEL appeared undisciplined, chaotic in short, like poorly written software code rather than differently constructed code. Understanding this viewpoint led me to include questions in the three annual national surveys identifying a subpopulation of sales representatives hostile to XSEL because of what I termed their "signature skill," that is, their close emotional and cognitive ties to traditional programming approaches. The two or three individuals who had initially alerted me to that reaction to expert systems became over the period of the study advocates of XSEL, thereby demonstrating that their original aversion was not necessarily permanent. Their attitudinal shift, which I followed informally, was mirrored over the three years in the annual national surveys. (That is, the subpopulation of sales representatives identified in the 1984 national sample as having programming as a signature skill changed from hostile to at least neutral attitudes toward XSEL by the 1986 survey.) Although following this kind of research thread in the longitudinal research was very important to the overall study, it was extremely time-consuming to attend so many meetings, go out to lunch with the program office managers many days, or arrange to be available late on

Friday afternoons when the managers were able to take the time to sit back and reflect on the week's problems and progress.

In contrast, the replicated, multiple-site cases were relatively efficient. Most of the data for the retrospective studies were gathered in two almost simultaneous phases. First, I held unstructured interviews with developers of the technology and with the internal corporate users of the innovations, and tapped archival sources. This process generally took two very concentrated days on site plus some follow-up telephone calls. Interviews at the first several retrospective studies were much less efficiently conducted than those at the last, for (as noted below) findings and observations from the longitudinal study often suggested issues that had been inadequately covered in the initial interviews in the retrospective studies. Consequently, some of the follow-up telephone interviews were quite substantial. All of these interviews were tape-recorded, unless the informants objected to that practice. They were promised anonymity, in that nothing they said was attributed to them personally (verbally or in writing) to anyone else within or outside their organization, until and unless they gave me permission to quote them. No one had access to the tapes besides one research assistant and me.

In the second phase of the research, I mailed out the two-page questionnaire, responses to which provided standard outcome measures for all 10 cases. When I received these back, I compared the opinions of the technology developers with those of the technology users and telephoned for further discussion and clarification those few informants whose evaluations of outcomes in a particular project were widely discrepant from others'. Next I mailed back to one previously designated representative at each field site the draft narrative of the project events as we had reconstructed them, for review. This historical document usually underwent several iterations, with informants providing additional details for the document, correcting inaccuracies in it, and sometimes (unfortunately) altering their earlier statements even though all the quotations had already been individually released for inclusion in the document. This process of obtaining agreement that the story had been accurately (and completely) presented was the most time-consuming part of the studies.

Objectivity. In a real-time longitudinal study, the researcher is in danger of losing objectivity—of becoming too involved with the organization, the people, and the process. Students of innovation are notoriously prone to a "pro-innovation bias" (Rogers 1983), and that likelihood is increased by proximity to the managerial struggle to launch the innovation. One may be perceived as, and may in fact become, an advocate rather than an observer. In retrospective studies, it is easier to maintain both in appearance and in fact an appropriately open mind about the desirability of the innovation.

The retrospective studies could not counter any specific pro-XSEL biases I had developed over the years of association with the expert system. However, the retrospective cases at least alerted me to the possibility of a general pro-innovative bias, because in several of the replicated studies, opposition to the innovation was very well founded and articulately presented. I could not possibly dismiss it as merely a simplistic "not-invented-here" reaction. In assessing the anti-innovation stances in the multiple cases, I was continually prompted to reexamine my own attitudes toward XSEL. In short, the retrospective cases helped "keep me honest."

On the other hand, in the retrospective studies, the danger is not so much that one may surrender to one's own biases as that one may unconsciously accept those of the informant. The innovation is seen through the lenses of the informants chosen, and the researcher may take the story as told, without questioning interpretations. In such research, the interviewer does not have as much access to corroborating or refuting details as does a researcher in an in-depth longitudinal study. Thus the researcher using retrospective reports to investigate historical events has to work harder to be a critical audience, aware of everyone's vulnerability to subjective perceptions (Sears and Freedman 1974).

The XSEL study provided some striking examples of political expediency that came to my attention only because of my deep involvement with the project, and that alerted me to the potential for similar events in the retrospective studies. For instance, I attended a dinner meeting one evening at which a manager spoke to the XSEL User Design Group. I took copious notes, writing down verbatim some quotations about actions this individual said he had taken in support of the innovation. These public statements turned out to differ greatly both from the reports of others and from written memos he had previously issued.

Experience with such self-serving revisionism led me to be cautious in the retrospective studies about accepting self-report as the only source of evidence about any incident or personal stance vis-à-vis the new technology. This caution was especially necessary in investigating mutual adaptation (i.e., the degree to which the technology was adapted to the organization during the development and implementation process and the degree to which the organization was adapted to fit the requirements of the technology; see Leonard-Barton 1988a). Participants differed in their perceptions of both the extent of adaptation and in their attribution of responsibility for those changes. Forewarned by my experiences with XSEL, I focused as much as possible on certifiable technical and organizational changes, such as the mid-project capital investment in a new dryer for a polymer process, indicating an initial oversight in equipment needs, or additions to a job performance checklist used to evaluate a buyer in the Purchasing Department. Such lists of documented changes helped guard against revisionist history.

Pattern Recognition. The replicated studies and the in-depth tracking of XSEL focused on the same issues. However, the difference in perspective was akin to that on a computer when one first views the pattern from some distance and then zooms in, enlarging some segment or line until the individual pixels are visible. This variance in depth of vision allowed me to identify some pattern or process of interest from the macro perspective of the retrospective studies and then, in effect, examine it in the XSEL study with a microscope, either to dissect it further into component parts or to understand the forces that drove it.

For instance, somewhat related experimental findings in marketing (Anderson 1973, Oliver 1977), combined with empirical observations from the replicated cases, suggested that inflated expectations about an innovation led, soon after initial trials, to discouragement and dislike of the new technology when the person trying it for the first time discovers how far short of his or her expectations it falls. The XSEL study allowed the opportunity to examine that drop at some depth, to identify those subgroups in the sales force most vulnerable to such initial disillusionment, and to understand through structured interviews why the drop occurred and how and why an innovation could recover. As noted earlier, members of one subgroup in the sales representative population, skilled software programmers, were initially critical and then changed their minds about XSEL; another group, skilled configurers, became increasingly critical over time. This detailed understanding of the user reactions enhanced the insights that I had obtained from the research in the replicated cases. However, keeping the macro perspective in mind was also valuable for the XSEL study. Recognition of the common patterns in innovation implementation led me to anticipate a bottoming out of the negative reactions when the XSEL project was going through that initial drop in acceptance levels, because evidence from the other cases suggested that the downward trend could be reversed among at least some users, and indeed that is what occurred. User evaluations surveyed in 1986 were higher than they had been in 1985.

Similarly, although informants in the replicated cases often identified innovation "assassins," it was not clear from those retrospective accounts exactly how such individuals had destroyed or delayed an innovation by strategic inaction as well as by deliberate anti-innovation action. A close-up view of an innovation assassin at work in the XSEL case provided real insight into some of the ways an individual can block progress in the innovation simply by delaying action while still professing support for it. Understanding those dynamics in turn inspired me to question informants in the replicated cases about critical individuals' lack of action as well as about their overt actions.

Establishing Validity

External Validity. Multiple case studies on a given topic clearly have more external validity—that is, generalizability—than does a single case. For instance, the mutual adaptation of technology and organization that occurred within the XSEL project could have been driven by the nontraditional software development processes employed in constructing expert systems or by the unusual management decision to employ a User Design Group very early in the development project. If so, then many of my observations about XSEL would have little applicability to other technology development and implementation situations. By expanding the sample of cases to include hardware, chemical processes, and other software projects conducted in several different companies, I was able to offset somewhat the XSEL study's lack of external validity.

Construct Validity. Because a construct is an abstraction, its definition consists in part of "sets of propositions about [its] relationship to other variables—other constructs or directly observable behavior" (Selltiz, Wrightsman, and Cook 1976, p. 173). Therefore, one validates a construct by observing whether predictions made on the basis of those propositions about its relationship to other variables are confirmed when tested. Multiple sources of evidence, if they yield similar results, are evidence of a construct's convergent validity. If the construct as measured can be differentiated from other constructs, it also possesses discriminant validity (Campbell and Fiske 1959). The dual research methodology described here provides better opportunity for construct validation than either design would alone, as the following example illustrates.

One construct that was of some importance to the theory under development in this study was the "communicability" of a technology, defined as "the degree to which a technology's operating principles (know-how) and underlying scientific principles (know-why) can be communicated to people other than its developers" (Leonard-Barton 1988b, p. 7). Multiple measures of this construct were possible, ranging from what are often considered "objective" measures (e.g., level of user documentation and availability of training) to more "subjective" measures (e.g., the ease of use, relative to the perceived skill level of the users). Informant responses to numerically scaled questions about communicability in the XSEL annual surveys and to less structured questions in the retrospective studies were consistent in their relationship to such other variables as evaluation of the technology by users, and the relationships proved to be in the expected direction. Moreover, the construct was defined to be conceptually quite distinct from the related concept of preparedness: "the extent to which technology has shown proof of technical feasibility in a laboratory or in an operational setting" (Leonard-

Barton 1988b, p. 7). However, as again indicated by responses in both the annual XSEL surveys and the retrospective case studies, both communicability and preparedness contributed to the users' perceptions of how ready the technology was for transfer. The two studies thus provided corroborating evidence of both convergent and divergent validity for the construct.

However, the special value of doing both kinds of studies was the opportunity to recognize how sensitive were measures of the construct to the point in time at which they were administered. Communicability varied across time and relative to different groups of users. In fact, the construct had validity only if its measurement was associated with a given, consistently specified point in the transfer process—and for a particular group of technology receivers. The XSEL study illuminated these points, because it was possible to measure communicability at a number of different points during the implementation process. This opportunity for measurement at multiple stages in turn led to the need to select one defined point that could be identified in all cases and thus compared consistently across them. The point selected (the very first use of the technology in a routine production task) could be identified with a satisfactory degree of precision and marked the implementation stage of greatest theoretical interest. Thus the longitudinal study aided in precise definition, and the retrospective studies demonstrated the consistency of the predicted patterns of relationship between the construct and other variables.

Internal Validity: Cause and Effect. One of the greatest advantages of the dual methodologies derived from the ability to move back and forth between the two, formulating theory in one setting and then immediately placing the embryonic ideas in the context of the other kind of study for potential disconfirmation. This cutting and pasting of ideas was particularly useful in establishing internal validity, for the combination of the two types of case studies provided better evidence for hypotheses about causal relationships between variables than either could have alone.

For example, in the first several retrospective studies, a direct casual link was made verbally by respondents between the innovation's level of transferability (preparedness and communicability) and the transfer effort's problems or outright failure. That is, informants in the organizations that were to use the new technologies told me that the technologies failed because they were released by the developers too soon, before they were proved technically (although one of the case selection criteria had been some proof of technical feasibility in the laboratory) and before adequate documentation and training were available. This cause-and-effect relationship seemed reasonable and in keeping with marketing and diffusion literature.

However, in the XSEL case study, I saw that although the technology measured quite low on transferability, changes were being made on both the software system and in the sales organization where it was to be used, and these changes were moving the project out of the doldrums and, in some sites, toward success. Was this an anomaly? Or was there in fact an intervening variable between the independent variable of transferability and the dependent variable of success or failure? Judging from the XSEL case, initial lack of transferability was not a direct determinant of success or failure. Rather, the degree of adaptability in the technology and/or in the receiving organization intervened, and the relationship was best described by a mediated model (see Venkatraman 1989 and Leonard-Barton 1988a, 1988b). In short, the observed effect of success or failure was directly caused by the degree of mutual technical and organizational adaptation undertaken during the project in reaction to the initial conditions of the technology.

Once I had made this hypothesis, I then returned to the multiple sites in which I was conducting interviews and probed more deeply into the superficial cause-and-effect relationships that had been suggested to me. I found that in the more troubled projects, the developers had refused to adapt their innovation to the user environment and/or the users had refused to adapt their organization in any way. In contrast, the success stories included technologies that were initially of very low transferability, but mutual adaptation of technology and organization had occurred.

This causal relationship is unlikely to have been so apparent to me from retrospective studies alone, because in the minds of some of the respondents, the direction of causality was confused. After a project became very difficult, respondents tended to reflect that the technology had never been "ready to transfer." Similarly, after a project was acknowledged to be a success, respondents apparently underestimated or even totally forgot the accommodations that had been made in order for the transfer to succeed. Yet when I ferreted out the changes in technology and/or organization that had been made (or, in the less successful cases, evidence of inability or unwillingness to change) and fed the story of sequential events back to the respondents, they confirmed the causal relationship—sometimes acknowledging that their initial explanations to me had been "oversimplified." Of considerable interest was the tendency to take the changes for granted when they were made and to have never considered such adaptations when they were not. Without the longitudinal study, I might never have seen the intervening variable. Without the retrospective studies, I could not have confirmed the pattern.

PROBLEMS WITH THE METHODOLOGY

No methodology is perfect. Some of the shortcomings of the one promulgated here are inherent in the methodology, and others are attributable to inadequate operationalization. I turn now to discussion of a few of the most important problems encountered.

Problems Inherent in the Design

The inherent limitations of qualitative case studies—such as the vulnerability of the data to subjective interpretation and the difficulties of compiling in one's head evidence about relationships among variables—are well known and need not be elaborated here. Miles and Huberman (1984) provide a useful guide to overcoming some of these problems. The time-consuming nature of ethnographic studies and hence the labor intensity of the longitudinal portion of the dual design is self-evident. Finally, because a number of the potential biases inherent in both the longitudinal and the retrospective cases have been explored above, I need not explore them further here. Rather, I will discuss two problems more particularly associated with the dual methodology: the difficulty of coordinating the different data-collection approaches and the difficulty of dealing with the volume of data generated by the combined approaches.

Coordinating Data Collection

Among limitations inherent in the dual methodology described here, perhaps the most important is the difficulty of managing the data collection. Because many of the opportunities for synergy between the retrospective and the in-depth studies arise from the recognition of patterns or different perspectives on the same phenomenon, the research has to be very tightly coordinated. Case facts are open to interpretation. Therefore, it is best to have at least two researchers, who can challenge each other's observations. Moreover, conducting an adequate number of multiple cases at geographically dispersed sites to complement the simultaneous in-depth study is physically demanding, if not impossible, for one person.

However, confining all the mental analyses to one mind would be a more efficient way to obtain the needed synergy between studies. During the three years of these studies, I had the continuous assistance of one researcher, albeit that position was held successively by two different people. I found it difficult to transfer completely to that research assistant the emerging intuitions I was gaining from my greater involvement in the XSEL study. Such intuitions were important guides in identifying issues to be probed in the much more superficial and brief interviewing situations in the multiple cases. At each of the multiple case sites, although I conducted at least the first day of interviewing, the assistant was charged with responsibility for some follow-up and some of the narrative write-up and review. This data-gathering process sometimes left to the assistant the delicate task of probing for important politically sensitive events and critical personal relationships. Because of their relatively superficial exposure to the in-depth XSEL case, the assistants were less well prepared to make the mental contrasts and comparisons with the longitudinal data that generated important insights and pointed to the questions to ask.

Volume of Data

A second, very important, shortcoming of this design is the overwhelming volume of data generated—a hazard of all qualitative research, as Miles and Huberman (1984) point out. Although, as noted below, more disciplined data gathering would have helped, it is difficult to identify critical data in a real-time longitudinal study while one is in the midst of the research. Consequently, my files are full of notes, presentations made partway through the research, and questionnaire responses to several small-scale surveys that for various reasons I have not yet fully analyzed, much less rendered into publishable form. A certain amount of this thrashing about is probably inherent in any real-time, in-depth study, and in fact in any case study. However, the interplay between the retrospective and the real-time studies fostered an exploratory attitude because of the pattern-matching opportunities mentioned above. Many of the small-scale surveys undertaken represented short-lived forays to investigate some particular issues that surfaced in the retrospective studies but could be investigated in depth only in real time (e.g., the impact of intentionally varied training approaches on users' expectations about the technology).

Shortcomings Attributable to Operationalization

The problems noted above may be inescapable attributes of the dual methodology described in this chapter and may be only ameliorated at best by foreknowledge. The difficulties described below are traceable to minor, perhaps suboptimal, choices I made throughout the research about where and how to focus my efforts. A different researcher might not have encountered them.

Structuring the Data Collection

As noted above, the XSEL study generated a vast amount of data but not necessarily a comparable amount of information. I made many attempts to impose some discipline and structure on the data-gathering process: questionnaires administered to trainees before and after using XSEL for the first time, to members of the User Design Group, and to the systems managers controlling the computers on which XSEL ran. The compilation of these small data sets, which was often inspired by frustration with the relatively superficial perspective provided by the retrospective studies, did generate deeper understanding of the innovation implementation process. However, with hindsight I do not believe the insights they provided were worth the time and effort expended on their careful design and execution. The numbers of people interviewed were really too small (10-30) for hypothesis testing. These data sets were subsequently overshadowed by the two much larger surveys (the three annual nationwide surveys of the sales representatives and the 1986 telephone survey of sales unit managers)—data-collection efforts that produced publishable quantitative data. Therefore, much of the effort spent in carefully structuring these small sample surveys had low payoff. Unstructured interviews could probably have yielded information of comparable worth.

In contrast, the process of moving back and forth between the longitudinal and the retrospective cases in building theory, as described earlier, might have been more valuable had the approach been more structured. For instance, in subsequent comparative cases (conducted 1987-1989, after the research reported here), I was much more careful about interviewing people in exactly comparable organizational positions or roles than I was in the research described herein.

Deciding on the Unit of Observation

A large problem in the XSEL study was my indecision over what should be the unit of observation. Were the comments of individual users in the User Design Group meetings relevant, or should I instead track only the major outcomes of those meetings as critical events or decisions? (See Levinson 1985, for examples of this latter approach.) The indecision was in large part responsible for the accumulation of data at a level of detail that later proved to be unnecessary.

In the retrospective cases, time had sifted many data for me, in that informants focused on events and decisions they regarded as significant. It was important in the in-depth study, therefore, to select a level of observation that had some meaningful parallels in the retrospective studies. Some detailed individual observations could be aggregated to identify trends, a decision, or an event, but individual comments by people with only ephemeral roles in the innovation process were often useless, and, unless they had a significant effect (which a few did), could not be paralleled in the retrospective studies. In most cases, the event or decision point about which the comment was made was the appropriate unit of observation. It might have been useful, therefore, to conduct a few more of the retrospective studies as references, before beginning the longitudinal XSEL study. The cost of such a strategy would have been to lengthen the total period of research.

Rationale for Choice of Cases

Another operational shortcoming was that my selection of complementary retrospective cases was driven almost entirely by a desire for more generalizability, within the constraints described earlier, so as to control for certain variables. Yin (1984) advocates selecting each additional case in a research program to address some very specific aspect of theory inadequately addressed in the previous cases. This approach suggests a much more painstaking sequential selection process than the one I followed, and would be especially appropriate if the researcher's theory is more fully developed at the outset than mine was.

CONCLUSION

Under what circumstances might the research methodology described above be useful? There are at least three factors to consider: the research topic, researchers' skills and preferences, and the availability of research sites. The methodology described here is suited for exploration and hypothesis generation rather than hypothesis testing. Whereas that statement is generally true of case studies, it is particularly relevant for this dual methodology, because one of its principal strengths is the synergy obtained from observing phenomena through both the wide-angle lens of the multiple-site study and the close-up lens of the longitudinal. There are, of course, opportunities for hypothesis testing embedded within the studies, but the overall design is most compatible to theory building. It also seems particularly suited to studying process because of the opportunities for exploring dynamics both as historical patterns in the retrospective studies and as evolving patterns in the real-time study.

Because researchers have differing skills, it behooves us to consider the match between researchers and methodology. In recent years the research case study has gained both rigor and respectability. Noted experimental researcher Donald Campbell may have precipitated the trend by recanting his previous "dogmatic disparagement" (Campbell 1975, p. 191). However, recognition that case studies can be rigorous has not necessarily led to a concomitant realization of the skills needed to interview and then analyze case data successfully. The necessary interviewing skills might be compared with those of an investigative reporter. One needs to keep previous interviewee responses in mind while simultaneously probing with the current informant; one needs to be very aware of the significance of what is left unsaid as well as what is said, and so on. Analysis of the data requires a high tolerance for initial ambiguity, as one iterates toward clarity. Finally, these methods require sustained effort over long periods of time, therefore one must really enjoy fieldwork.

Certain field conditions must prevail for success. The longitudinal study requires the up-front commitment of an organization for extended cooperation. Yet the study sponsor can leave the organization, initial findings may threaten powerful individuals, or the company's fortunes may suffer such a blow that outsiders are no longer welcome. One longitudinal site alone therefore would be rather risky for a doctoral thesis; the combined methodology advocated here lessens that risk somewhat, but one would still be well advised to plan for research output as the study proceeds—not just at the end.

Moreover, this methodology can require that the researcher spend almost as much time and effort on setting organizational expectations and on fostering and maintaining his or her relationship with the organization as on the actual data gathering. For instance, organizations accustomed to the quick turnaround of information available from surveys should be forewarned that the kind of research design outlined above does not yield immediate results. Organizations nevertheless expect some interim reports and feedback. In a very production-oriented business environment, a researcher who is a useful source of information in some way is more likely to be visible and to be kept informed when events occur that affect the study. Therefore, some researchers regularly send papers and other information that could be useful to the managers who are cooperating in the study. (Of course, any information sent to current or prospective informants can constitute an intervention, therefore one needs to be alert to the potential for biasing future responses.) As these examples may suggest, the labor intensity of this methodology can hardly be overstated.

Although the research methodology described herein evolved in the field, it was mostly designed before implementation. Its principal and innovative feature, the simultaneous use of retrospective case studies and a real-time longitudinal study, was a conscious choice made almost at the very outset of the research. As organizational studies continue to move from art toward science, we need many such methodological variants so that we can prevent our tools from dictating and limiting the nature of our insights. Campbell, Daft, and Hulin (1982) note, "Theories that are at least in part based on experience, that take account of the ecology of organizational behavior, and that are intended to function as heuristics seem to be in the shortest supply" (p. 146). The development of such practice-oriented theories necessitates both the refinement of existing field research methodologies and the development of new ones.

Appendix:
Examples of Measures of Dependent Variable

The following is a *partial* list of questions mailed to all project developers and users (responses were discussed over the telephone).

IN THE FOLLOWING QUESTIONS, I WILL REFER TO:
PROJECT _____ DEVELOPERS _____
USER ORGANIZATION _____

1. To what extent do you feel this project met the objectives set for it? (CIRCLE ONE NUMBER FOR EACH CATEGORY OF OBJECTIVE)

	Totally Failed to Meet	Failed Somewhat	Met	Surpassed
Technical objectives	1	2	3	4
Business objectives	1	2	3	4
Budget	1	2	3	4(came in under)
Time schedule	1	2	3	4(finished early)

2. Overall, how would you rate the success of this project? (CIRCLE THE NUMBER THAT BEST REFLECTS YOUR OPINION)

Total Failure		Partial Success		Total Success
1	2	3	4	5

3. AT THE TIME IT WAS INTRODUCED TO USERS, how far along was this technology on the scale below? (CIRCLE ONE)

Still an Unproven Concept	Concept Feasibility Demonstrated	Laboratory Prototype	Production Prototype	Production Model; Some "Bugs" Remaining	Ready for Use in Production
1	2	3	4	5	6

4. To what extent would this technology (if successfully implemented) give the company a proprietary advantage?

Not at All		Somewhat		A Great Deal
1	2	3	4	5

Acknowledgments

The research reported in this chapter was supported by the Division of Research, Harvard Business School. I gratefully acknowledge the helpful comments of George Huber, Andrew Van de Ven, Arie Lewin, and two anonymous reviewers.

References

Anderson, Rolph E. (1973), "Consumer Dissatisfaction: The Effect of Disconfirmed Expectancy on Perceived Product Performance," *Journal Marketing Research,* 10, 38-44.

Barley, Stephen R. (1986), "Technology as an Occasion for Structuring: Evidence From Observations of CT Scanners and the Social Order of Radiology Departments," *Administrative Science Quarterly,* 31, 78-108.

Bourgeois, L. J. and Kathleen M. Eisenhardt (1988), "Strategic Decision Processes in High Velocity Environments: Four Cases in the Microcomputer Industry," *Management Science,* 34, 816-835.

Bower, Joseph (1970), *Managing the Resource Allocation Process: A Study of Corporate Planning and Investment,* Boston: Harvard Graduate School of Business.

Burns, T. and G. M. Stalker (1961), *The Management of Innovation,* London: Tavistock.

Campbell, Donald T. (1975), "Degrees of Freedom and the Case Study," *Comparative Political Studies,* 8, 2, 178-193.

Campbell, Donald T., and D. W. Fiske (1959), "Convergent and Discriminant Validation by the Multitrait-Multimethod Matrix," *Psychological Bulletin,* 56, 81-105.

Campbell, John P., Richard L. Daft, and Charles L. Hulin (1982), *What to Study: Generating and Developing Research Questions,* Beverly Hills, CA: Sage.

Eisenhardt, Kathleen M. (1989), "Building Theories From Case Study Research," *Academy of Management Review,* 14, 532-550.

Franz, C. R., and Daniel Robey (1984), "An Investigation of User-Led System Design: Rational and Political Perspectives," *Communications of the ACM,* 27, 1202-1217.

Huber, George (1985), "Temporal Stability and Response-Order Biases in Participant Descriptions of Organizational Decisions," *Academy of Management Journal,* 28, 943-950.

Jaikumar, Ramchandran, and Roger Bohn (1986), "The Development of Intelligent Systems for Industrial Use: A Conceptual Framework," *Research on Technological Innovation, Management and Policy,* 3, 169-211.

Kimberly, John R., and Michael Evanisko (1981), "Organizational Innovation: The Influence of Individual, Organizational, and Contextual Factors on Hospital Adoption of Technological and Administrative Innovations," *Academy of Management Journal,* 24, 689-713.

Leonard-Barton, Dorothy (1987a), "Implementing Structured Software Methodologies: A Case of Innovation in Process Technology," *Interfaces,* 17, 3, 6-17.

Leonard-Barton, Dorothy (1987b), "The Case for Integrative Innovation: An Expert System at Digital," *Sloan Management Review,* 29 (October/November), 7-19.

Leonard-Barton, Dorothy (1988a), "Implementation as Mutual Adaptation of Technology and Organization," *Research Policy,* 17 (October), 251-267.

Leonard-Barton, Dorothy (1988b), "Implementation Characteristics in Organizational Innovations," *Communication Research,* 15, 603-631.

Levinson, Eliot (1985), "Turning Cases Into Data: Implementation Path Analysis: A Method for Studying Implementation of Information Technology," *Office: Technology and People,* 2, 287-304.

McGrath, Joseph (1982), "Dilemmatics: The Study of Research Choices and Dilemmas," in Joseph McGrath, Joanne Martin, and Richard A. Kulka, *Judgment Calls in Research,* Beverly Hills, CA: Sage.

McGrath, Joseph, Joanne Martin, and Richard A. Kulka (1982), *Judgment Calls in Research,* Beverly Hills, CA: Sage.

Miles, Matthew B., and A. Michael Huberman (1984), *Qualitative Data Analysis: A Sourcebook of New Methods,* Beverly Hills, CA: Sage.

Moch, Michael K., and Edward V. Morse (1977), "Size, Centralization and Organizational Adoption of Innovations," *American Sociological Review,* 42, 716-725.

Oliver, Richard L. (1977), "Effect of Expectation and Disconfirmation on Postexposure Product Evaluations: An Alternative Interpretation," *Journal of Applied Psychology,* 62, 480-486.

Pettigrew, Andrew (1979), "On Studying Organizational Cultures," *Administrative Quarterly,* 23, 570-581.

Rogers, Everett M. (1983), *Diffusion of Innovations* (3rd ed.), New York: Free Press.

Sears, David O., and Jonathan L. Freedman (1974), "Selective Exposure to Information: A Critical Review," in Wilbur Schramm and Donald F. Roberts (Eds.), *The Process and Effects of Mass Communication,* Urbana: University of Illinois Press.

Selltiz, Claire, Lawrence S. Wrightsman, and Stuart W. Cook (1976), *Research Methods in Social Relations* (3rd ed.), New York: Holt, Rinehart & Winston.

Stone, E. (1978), *Research Methods in Organizational Behavior,* Glenview, IL: Scott, Foresman.

Tversky, Amos, and Daniel Kahneman (1986), "Rational Choice and the Framing of Decisions," *Journal of Business,* 59, 4, Part 2, 5251-5278.

Van de Ven, Andrew (1986), "Central Problems in Management of Innovations," *Management Science,* 32, 590-607.

Van Maanen, John (1988), *Tales of the Field: On Writing Ethnography,* Chicago: University of Chicago Press.

Venkatraman, N. (1989), "The Concept of Fit in Strategy Research: Towards Verbal and Statistical Correspondence," *Academy of Management Review,* 14, 423-444.

Yin, Robert K. (1984), *Case Study Research: Design and Methods,* Beverly Hills, CA: Sage.

3

Building Theories
From Case Study Research

KATHLEEN M. EISENHARDT

This chapter describes the process of inducting theory using case
studies—from specifying the research questions to reaching closure.
Some features of the process, such as problem definition and construct validation, are similar to hypothesis-testing research. Others,
such as within-case analysis and replication logic, are unique to the
inductive, case-oriented process. Overall, the process described here
is highly iterative and tightly linked to data. This research approach
is especially appropriate in new topic areas. The resultant theory is
often novel, testable, and empirically valid. Finally, frame-breaking
insights, the tests of good theory (e.g., parsimony, logical coherence), and convincing grounding in the evidence are the key criteria
for evaluating this type of research.

Development of theory is a central activity in organizational research. Traditionally, authors have developed theory by combining observations from previous literature, common sense, and experience. However, the tie to actual
data has often been tenuous (Perrow 1986, Pfeffer 1982). Yet, as Glaser and
Strauss (1967) argue, it is the intimate connection with empirical reality that
permits the development of a testable, relevant, and valid theory.

This chapter appeared originally as "Building Theories From Case Study Research," by Kathleen
M. Eisenhardt, in *Academy of Management Review,* vol. 14, no. 4, October 1989, pp. 532-550.
Copyright © 1989 by the Academy of Management. Reprinted by permission.

This chapter describes building theories from case studies. Several aspects of this process are discussed in the literature. For example, Glaser and Strauss (1967) detail a comparative method for developing grounded theory, Yin (1981, 1984) describes the design of case study research, and Miles and Huberman (1984) codify a series of procedures for analyzing qualitative data. However, confusion surrounds the distinctions among qualitative data, inductive logic, and case study research. Also, there is a lack of clarity about the process of actually building theory from cases, especially regarding the central inductive process and the role of literature. Glaser and Strauss (1967) and more recently Strauss (1987) have outlined pieces of the process, but theirs is a prescribed formula, and new ideas have emerged from methodologists (e.g., Yin 1984, Miles and Huberman 1984) and researchers conducting this type of research (e.g., Gersick 1988, Harris and Sutton 1986, Eisenhardt and Bourgeois 1988). Also, it appears that no one has explicitly examined when this theory-building approach is likely to be fruitful and what its strengths and weaknesses may be.

This chapter attempts to make two contributions to the literature. The first is a road map for building theories from case study research. This road map synthesizes previous work on qualitative methods (e.g., Miles and Huberman 1984), the design of case study research (e.g., Yin 1981, 1984), and grounded theory building (e.g., Glaser & Strauss, 1967) and extends that work in areas such as a priori specification of constructs, triangulation of multiple investigators, within-case and cross-case analyses, and the role of existing literature. The result is a more nearly complete road map for executing this type of research than has existed in the past. This framework is summarized in Table 3.1.

The second contribution is to position theory building from case studies into the larger context of social science research. For example, the chapter explores strengths and weaknesses of theory building from case studies, situations in which it is an attractive research approach, and some guidelines for evaluating this type of research.

BACKGROUND

Several pieces of the process of building theory from case study research have appeared in the literature. One is the work on grounded theory building by Glaser and Strauss (1967) and, more recently, Strauss (1987). These authors have detailed their comparative method for developing grounded theory. The method relies on continuous comparison of data and theory, beginning with data collection. It emphasizes both the emergence of theoretical categories solely from evidence and an incremental approach to case selection and data gathering.

TABLE 3.1 Process of Building Theory From Case Study Research

Step	Activity	Reason
Getting started	Definition of research question	Focuses efforts
	Possibly a priori constructs	Provides better grounding of construct measures
	Neither theory nor hypotheses	Retains theoretical flexibility
Selecting cases	Specified population	Constrains extraneous variation and sharpens external validity
	Theoretical, not random, sampling	Focuses efforts on theoretically useful cases—i.e., those that replicate or extend theory by filling conceptual categories
Crafting instruments and protocols	Multiple data-collection methods	Strengthens grounding of theory by triangulation of evidence
	Qualitative and quantitative data combined	Synergistic view of evidence
	Multiple investigators	Fosters divergent perspectives and strengthens grounding
Entering the field	Overlap data collection and analysis, including field notes	Speeds analyses and reveals helpful adjustments to data collection
	Flexible and opportunistic data-collection methods	Allows investigators to take advantage of emergent themes and unique case features
Analyzing data	Within-case analysis	Gains familiarity with data and preliminary theory generation
	Cross-case pattern search using divergent techniques	Forces investigators to look beyond initial impressions and see evidence through multiple lenses
Shaping hypotheses	Iterative tabulation of evidence for each construct	Sharpens construct definition, validity, and measurability
	Replication, not sampling, logic across cases	Confirms, extends, and sharpens theory
	Search evidence for "why" behind relationships	Builds internal validity
Enfolding literature	Comparison with conflicting literature	Builds internal validity, raises theoretical level, and sharpens construct definitions
	Comparison with similar literature	Sharpens generalizability, improves construct definition, and raises theoretical level
Reaching closure	Theoretical saturation when possible	Ends process when marginal improvement becomes small

More recently, Yin (1981, 1984) has described the design of case study research. He has defined the case study as a research strategy, developed a typology of case study designs, and described the replication logic that is essential to multiple case analysis. His approach also stresses bringing the concerns of validity and reliability in experimental research design to the design of case study research.

Miles and Huberman (1984) have outlined specific techniques for analyzing qualitative data. Their ideas include a variety of devices such as tabular displays and graphs to manage and present qualitative data, without destroying the meaning of the data through intensive coding.

A number of active researchers also have undertaken their own variations and additions to the earlier methodological work (e.g., Gersick 1988, Leonard-Barton 1988, Harris and Sutton 1986). Many of these authors acknowledge a debt to previous work, but they have also developed their own "homegrown" techniques for building theory from cases. For example, Sutton and Callahan (1987) have pioneered a clever use of a resident devil's advocate, the Warwick group has added triangulation of investigators (Pettigrew 1988), and my colleague and I (Bourgeois and Eisenhardt 1988) have developed cross-case analysis techniques.

Finally, the work of others such as Van Maanen (1988) on ethnography, Jick (1979) on triangulation of data types, and Mintzberg (1979) on direct research has provided additional pieces for a framework of building theory from case study research.

As a result, many pieces of the theory-building process are evident in the literature. Nevertheless, at the same time, there is substantial confusion about how to combine them, when to conduct this type of study, and how to evaluate it.

THE CASE STUDY APPROACH

The case study is a research strategy that focuses on understanding the dynamics present within single settings. Examples of case study research include Selznick's (1949) description of TVA, Allison's (1971) study of the Cuban missile crisis, and Pettigrew's (1973) research on decision making at a British retailer. Case studies can involve either single or multiple cases and numerous levels of analysis (Yin 1984). For example, Harris and Sutton (1986) studied 8 dying organizations, Bettenhausen and Murnighan (1986) focused on the emergence of norms in 19 laboratory groups, and Leonard-Barton (1988) tracked the progress of 10 innovation projects. Moreover, case studies can employ an embedded design, that is, multiple levels of analysis within a single study (Yin 1984). For example, the Warwick study of competitiveness and strategic change within major U.K. corporations (Pettigrew 1988) was conducted at two levels of analysis—industry and firm—and the Mintzberg and Waters (1982) study of Steinberg's grocery empire examined multiple strategic changes within a single firm.

Case studies typically combine data-collection methods such as archival searches, interviews, questionnaires, and observations. The evidence may be qualitative (e.g., words), quantitative (e.g., numbers), or both. For example, Sutton and Callahan (1987) relied exclusively on qualitative data in their study of bankruptcy in Silicon Valley, Mintzberg and McHugh (1985) used qualitative data supplemented by frequency counts in their work on the National Film Board of Canada, and Eisenhardt and Bourgeois (1988) combined quantitative data from questionnaires with qualitative evidence from interviews and observations.

Finally, case studies can be used to accomplish various aims: to provide description (Kidder 1982), test theory (Pinfield 1986, Anderson 1983), or generate theory (e.g., Gersick 1988, Harris and Sutton 1986). The interest here is in this last aim, theory generation from case study evidence. Table 3.2 summarizes some recent research using theory building from case studies.

BUILDING THEORY FROM CASE STUDY RESEARCH

Getting Started

An initial definition of the research question, in at least broad terms, is important in building theory from case studies. Mintzberg (1979) notes, "No matter how small our sample or what our interest, we have always tried to go into organizations with a well-defined focus—to collect specific kinds of data systematically" (p. 585). The rationale for defining the research question is the same as it is in hypothesis-testing research. Without a research focus, it is easy for the researcher to become overwhelmed by the volume of data. For example, Pettigrew and his colleagues (see Pettigrew 1988) defined their research question in terms of strategic change and competitiveness within large British corporations, and Leonard-Barton (1988) focused on technical innovation of feasible technologies. Such definition of a research question within a broad topic permitted these investigators to specify the kind of organization to be approached, and, once there, the kind of data to be gathered.

A priori specification of constructs can also help to shape the initial design of theory-building research. Although this type of specification has not been common in theory-building studies to date, it is valuable because it permits researchers to measure constructs more accurately. If these constructs prove

TABLE 3.2 Recent Examples of Inductive Case Study Research

Study	Description of Cases	Research Problem	Data Sources	Investigators	Output
Burgelman (1983)	6 internal corporate ventures in 1 major corporation	Management of new ventures	Archives interviews Some observation	Single investigator	Process model linking multiple organizational levels
Mintzberg and McHugh (1985)	1 National Film Board of Canada, 1939-1975, with 6 periods	Formulation of strategy in an adhocracy	Archives Some interviews	Research team	Strategy-making themes, "grassroots" model of strategy formation
Harris and Sutton (1986)	8 diverse organizations	Parting ceremonies during organizational death	Interviews Archives	Research team	Conceptual framework about the functions of parting ceremonies for displaced members
Eisenhardt and Bourgeois (1988)	8 micro-computer firms	Strategic decision making in high-velocity environments	Interviews Question-naires Archives Some observation	Research team Tandem interviews	Mid-range theory linking power, politics, and firm performance
Gersick (1988)	8 project groups with deadlines	Group development in project teams	Observation Some interviews	Single investigator	Punctuated equilibrium model of group development
Leonard-Barton (1988)	10 technical innovations	Internal technology transfer	Interviews Experiment Observation	Single investigator	Process model
Pettigrew (1988)	1 high-performing and 1 low-performing firm in each of 4 industries	Strategic change and competitive-ness	Interviews Archives Some observation	Research teams	In progress

NOTE: Examples were chosen from recent organizational writing to provide illustrations of the possible range of theory building from case studies.

important as the study progresses, then researchers have a firmer empirical grounding for the emergent theory. For example, in a study of strategic decision making in top management teams, Bourgeois and Eisenhardt (1988) identified several potentially important constructs (e.g., conflict, power) from the literature on decision making. These constructs were explicitly measured in the interview protocol and questionnaires. When several of these constructs did emerge as related to the decision process, there were strong, triangulated measures on which to ground the emergent theory.

Although early identification of the research question and possible constructs is helpful, it is equally important to recognize that both are tentative in this type of research. No construct is guaranteed a place in the resultant theory, no matter how well it is measured. Also, the research question may shift during the research. At the extreme, some researchers (e.g., Gersick 1988, Bettenhausen and Murnighan 1986) have converted theory-testing research into theory-building research by taking advantage of serendipitous findings. In these studies, the research focus emerged after the data collection had begun. As Bettenhausen and Murnighan (1986) write: "We observed the outcomes of an experiment on group decision making and coalition formation. Our observations of the groups indicated that the unique character of each of the groups seemed to overwhelm our other manipulations" (p. 352). These authors proceeded to switch their research focus to a theory-building study of group norms.

Finally, and most important, theory-building research is begun as close as possible to the ideal of no theory under consideration and no hypotheses to test. Admittedly, it is impossible to achieve this ideal of a clean theoretical slate. Nonetheless, attempting to approach this ideal is important because preordained theoretical perspectives or propositions may bias and limit the findings. Thus investigators should formulate a research problem and possibly specify some potentially important variables, with some reference to extant literature. However, they should avoid thinking about specific relationships between variables and theories as much as possible, especially at the outset of the process.

Selecting Cases

Selection of cases is an important aspect of building theory from case studies. As in hypothesis-testing research, the concept of a population is crucial, because the population defines the set of entities from which the research sample is to be drawn. Also, selection of an appropriate population controls extraneous variation and helps to define the limits for generalizing the findings.

The Warwick study of strategic change and competitiveness illustrates these ideas (Pettigrew 1988). In this study, the researchers selected cases from a population of large British corporations in four market sectors. The selection of four specific markets allowed the researchers to control environmental variation, while the focus on large corporations constrained variation due to size differences among the firms. Thus specification of this population reduced extraneous variation and clarified the domain of the findings as large corporations operating in specific types of environments.

However, the sampling of cases from the chosen population is unusual when building theory from case studies. Such research relies on theoretical sampling (i.e., cases are chosen for theoretical, not statistical, reasons; Glaser & Strauss 1967). The cases may be chosen to replicate previous cases or extend emergent theory, or they may be chosen to fill theoretical categories and provide examples of polar types. Although the cases may be chosen randomly, random selection is neither necessary nor even preferable. As Pettigrew (1988) notes, given the limited number of cases that can usually be studied, it makes sense to chose cases such as extreme situations and polar types in which the process of interest is "transparently observable." Thus the goal of theoretical sampling is to choose cases that are likely to replicate or extend the emergent theory. In contrast, traditional, within-experiment hypothesis-testing studies rely on statistical sampling, in which researchers randomly select the sample from the population. In this type of study, the goal of the sampling process is to obtain accurate statistical evidence on the distributions of variables within the population.

Several studies illustrate theoretical sampling. Harris and Sutton (1986), for example, were interested in the parting ceremonies of dying organizations. In order to build a model applicable across organization types, these researchers purposefully selected diverse organizations from a population of dying organizations. They chose eight organizations, filling each of four categories: private, dependent; private, independent; public, dependent; and public, independent. The sample was not random, but reflected the selection of specific cases to extend the theory to a broad range of organizations. Multiple cases within each category allowed findings to be replicated within categories. Gersick (1988) followed a similar strategy of diverse sampling in order to enhance the generalizability of her model of group development. In the Warwick study (Pettigrew 1988), the investigators also followed a deliberate, theoretical sampling plan. Within each of four markets, they chose polar types: one case of clearly successful firm performance and one unsuccessful case. This sampling plan was designed to build theories of success and failure. Finally, the Eisenhardt and Bourgeois (1988) study of the politics of strategic decision making illustrates theoretical sampling during the course of research. A theory linking the centralization of power to the use of politics in top management teams was built and then extended to consider the effects of changing team composition by adding two cases, in which the executive teams changed, to the first six, in which there was no change. This tactic allowed the initial framework to be extended to include dynamic effects of changing team composition.

Crafting Instruments and Protocols

Theory-building researchers typically combine multiple data-collection methods. Although interviews, observations, and archival sources are particularly common, inductive researchers are not confined to these choices. Some investigators employ only some of these data-collection methods (e.g., Gersick 1988 used only observations for the first half of her study), or they may add others (e.g., Bettenhausen and Murnighan 1986 used quantitative laboratory data). The rationale is the same as in hypothesis-testing research. That is, the triangulation made possible by multiple data-collection methods provides stronger substantiation of constructs and hypotheses.

Of special note is the combining of qualitative with quantitative evidence. Although the terms *qualitative* and *case study* are often used interchangeably (e.g., Yin 1981), case study research can involve qualitative data only, quantitative data only, or both (Yin 1984). Moreover, the combination of data types can be highly synergistic. Quantitative evidence can indicate relationships that may not be salient to the researcher. It also can keep researchers from being carried away by vivid, but false, impressions in qualitative data, and it can bolster findings when it corroborates those findings from qualitative evidence. The qualitative data are useful for understanding the rationale or theory underlying relationships revealed in the quantitative data or may suggest directly theory that can then be strengthened by quantitative support (Jick 1979). Mintzberg (1979) describes this synergy as follows:

> For while systematic data create the foundation for our theories, it is the anecdotal data that enable us to do the building. Theory building seems to require rich description, the richness that comes from anecdote. We uncover all kinds of relationships in our hard data, but it is only through the use of this soft data that we are able to explain them. (p. 587)

Also of special note is the use of multiple investigators. Multiple investigators have two key advantages. First, they enhance the creative potential of the study. Team members often have complementary insights that add to the richness of the data, and their different perspectives increase the likelihood of their capitalizing on any novel insights that may be in the data. Second, the convergence of observations from multiple investigators enhances confidence in the findings. Convergent perceptions add to the empirical grounding of the hypotheses, whereas conflicting perceptions keep the group from premature closure. Thus the use of more investigators builds confidence in the findings and increases the likelihood of surprising findings.

One strategy for employing multiple investigators is to make the visits to case study sites in teams (e.g., Pettigrew 1988). This allows the case to be viewed from the different perspectives of multiple observers. A variation on this tactic is to give individuals on the team unique roles, which increases the chances that investigators will view case evidence in divergent ways. For example, interviews can be conducted by two-person teams, with one researcher handling the interview questions while the other records notes and observations (e. g., Eisenhardt and Bourgeois 1988). The interviewer has the perspective of personal interaction with the informant, while the note taker retains a different, more distant, view. Another tactic is to create multiple research teams, with teams being assigned to cover some case sites but not others (e.g., Pettigrew 1988). The rationale behind this tactic is that investigators who have not met the informants and have not become immersed in case details may bring a very different and possibly more objective eye to the evidence. An extreme form of this tactic is to keep some member or members of the research team out of the field altogether by exclusively assigning to them the role of resident devil's advocate (e.g., Sutton and Callahan 1987).

Entering the Field

A striking feature of research to build theory from case studies is the frequent overlap of data analysis with data collection. For example, Glaser and Strauss (1967) argue for joint collection, coding, and analysis of data. While many researchers do not achieve this degree of overlap, most maintain some overlap.

Field notes, a running commentary to oneself and/or the research team, are an important means of accomplishing this overlap. As described by Van Maanen (1988), field notes are an ongoing stream-of-consciousness commentary about what is happening in the research, involving both observation and analysis—preferably separated from one another.

One key to useful field notes is to write down whatever impressions occur, that is, to react rather than to sift out what may seem important, because it is often difficult to know what will and will not be useful in the future. A second key to successful field notes is to push thinking in these notes by asking questions, such as, What am I learning? and How does this case differ from the last? For example, Burgelman (1983) kept extensive idea booklets to record his ongoing thoughts in a study of internal corporate venturing. These ideas can be cross-case comparisons, hunches about relationships, anecdotes, and informal observations. Team meetings, in which investigators share their thoughts and emergent ideas, are also useful devices for overlapping data collection and analysis.

Overlapping data analysis with data collection not only gives the researcher a head start in analysis but, more important, allows researchers to take advantage of flexible data collection. Indeed, a key feature of theory-building case research is the freedom to make adjustments during the data-collection process. These adjustments can be the addition of cases to probe particular themes that emerge. Gersick (1988), for example, added several cases to her original set of student teams in order to observe transition point behaviors among project teams more closely. These transition point behaviors had unexpectedly proved interesting, and Gersick added cases in order to focus more closely on the transition period.

Additional adjustments can be made to data-collection instruments, such as the addition of questions to an interview protocol or questions to a questionnaire (e.g., Harris and Sutton 1986). These adjustments allow the researcher to probe emergent themes or to take advantage of special opportunities that may be present in a given situation. In other situations adjustments can include the addition of data sources in selected cases. For example, Sutton and Callahan (1987) added observational evidence for one case when the opportunity to attend creditors' meetings arose, and Burgelman (1983) added interviews with individuals whose importance became clear during data collection. Leonard-Barton (1988) went even further by adding several experiments to probe her emergent theory in a study of the implementation of technical innovations.

These alterations create an important question: Is it legitimate to alter and even add data-collection methods during a study? For theory-building research, the answer is yes, because investigators are trying to understand each case individually and in as much depth as is feasible. The goal is not to produce summary statistics about a set of observations. Thus if a new data-collection opportunity arises or if a new line of thinking emerges during the research, it makes sense to take advantage by altering data collection, if such an alteration is likely to better ground the theory or to provide new theoretical insight. This flexibility is not a license to be unsystematic. Rather, this flexibility is controlled opportunism in which researchers take advantage of the uniqueness of a specific case and the emergence of new themes to improve resultant theory.

Analyzing Within-Case Data

Analyzing data is the heart of building theory from case studies, but it is both the most difficult and the least codified part of the process. Because published studies generally describe research sites and data-collection methods but give little space to discussion of analysis, a huge chasm often separates data from conclusions. As Miles and Huberman (1984) note, "One cannot ordinarily follow how a researcher got from 3600 pages of field notes to the final conclusions, sprinkled with vivid quotes though they may be" (p. 16). However, several key features of analysis can be identified.

One key step is within-case analysis. The importance of within-case analysis is driven by one of the realities of case study research: a staggering volume of data. As Pettigrew (1988) describes, there is an ever-present danger of "death by data asphyxiation." For example, Mintzberg and McHugh (1985) examined more than 2,500 movies in their study of strategy making at the National Film Board of Canada—and that was only part of their evidence. The volume of data is all the more daunting because the research problem is often open-ended. Within-case analysis can help investigators cope with this deluge of data.

Within-case analysis typically involves detailed case study write-ups for each site. These write-ups are often simply pure descriptions, but they are central to the generation of insight (Gersick 1988; Pettigrew 1988) because they help researchers to cope early in the analysis process with the often enormous volume of data. However, there is no standard format for such analysis. Quinn (1980) developed teaching cases for each of the firms in his study of strategic decision making in six major corporations as a prelude to his theoretical work. Mintzberg and McHugh (1985) compiled a 383-page case history of the National Film Board of Canada. These authors coupled narrative description with extensive use of longitudinal graphs tracking revenue, film sponsorship, staffing, film subjects, and so on. Gersick (1988) prepared transcripts of team meetings. Leonard-Barton (1988) used tabular displays and graphs of information about each case. Abbott (1988) suggested using sequence analysis to organize longitudinal data. In fact, there are probably as many approaches as there are researchers. However, the overall idea is to become intimately familiar with each case as a stand-alone entity. This process allows the unique patterns of each case to emerge before investigators push to generalize patterns across cases. In addition, it gives investigators a rich familiarity with each case, which in turn accelerates cross-case comparison.

Searching for Cross-Case Patterns

Coupled with within-case analysis is cross-case search for patterns. The tactics here are driven by the reality that people are notoriously poor processors of information. They leap to conclusions based on limited data (Kahneman and Tversky 1973), they are overly influenced by vividness (Nisbett and Ross 1980) or by more elite respondents (Miles and Huberman 1984), they ignore basic statistical properties (Kahneman and Tversky 1973), or they sometimes inadvertently drop disconfirming evidence (Nisbett and Ross 1980). The danger is that investigators reach premature and even false conclusions as a result of these information-processing biases. Thus the key to good cross-case comparison is to counteract these tendencies by looking at the data in many divergent ways.

One tactic is to select categories or dimensions, and then to look for within-group similarities coupled with intergroup differences. Dimensions can be suggested by the research problem or by existing literature, or the researcher can simply choose some dimensions. For example, in a study of strategic decision making, Bourgeois and Eisenhardt (1988) sifted cases into various categories, including founder-run versus professional management, high versus low performance, first- versus second-generation product, and large versus small size. Some categories, such as size and product generation, revealed no clear patterns, but others, such as performance, led to important patterns of within-group similarity and across-group differences. An extension of this tactic is to use a 2 × 2 or other cell design to compare several categories at once, or to move to a continuous measurement scale that permits graphing.

A second tactic is to select pairs of cases and then list the similarities and differences between each pair. This tactic forces researchers to look for the subtle similarities and differences between cases. The juxtaposition of seemingly similar cases by a researcher looking for differences can break simplistic frames. In the same way, the search for similarity in a seemingly different pair also can lead to more sophisticated understanding. The result of these forced comparisons can be new categories and concepts the investigators did not anticipate. For example, Eisenhardt and Bourgeois (1988) found that CEO power differences dominated initial impressions across firms. However, this paired comparison process led the researchers to see that the speed of the decision process was equally important (Eisenhardt, 1989). Finally, an extension of this tactic is to group cases into threes or fours for comparison.

A third strategy is to divide the data by data source. For example, one researcher combs observational data, while another reviews interviews, and still another works with questionnaire evidence. This tactic was used in the separation of the analyses of qualitative and quantitative data in a study of strategic decision making (Bourgeois and Eisenhardt 1988, Eisenhardt and Bourgeois 1988). This tactic exploits the unique insights possible from different types of data collection. When a pattern from one data source is corroborated by the evidence from another, the finding is stronger and better grounded. When evidence conflicts, the researcher can sometimes reconcile the evidence through deeper probing of the meaning of the differences. At other times, this conflict exposes a spurious or random pattern, or biased thinking in the analysis. A variation of this tactic is to split the data into groups of cases, focusing on one group of cases initially, and later focusing on the remaining cases. Gersick (1988) used this tactic in separating the analyses of student group cases from her other cases.

Overall, the idea behind these cross-case searching tactics is to force investigators to go beyond initial impressions, especially through the use of structured and diverse lenses on the data. These tactics improve the likelihood of accurate and reliable theory, that is, a theory with a close fit with the data. Also, cross-case searching tactics enhance the probability that the investigators will capture the novel findings that may exist in the data.

Shaping Hypotheses

From the within-site analysis plus various cross-site tactics and overall impressions, tentative themes, concepts, and possibly even relationships between variables begin to emerge. The next step of this highly iterative process is to compare systematically the emergent frame with the evidence from each case in order to assess how well or poorly it fits with case data. The central idea is that researchers constantly compare theory and data—iterating toward a theory that closely fits the data. A close fit is important to building good theory because it takes advantage of the new insights possible from the data and yields an empirically valid theory.

One step in shaping hypotheses is the sharpening of constructs. This is a two-part process involving (1) refining the definition of the construct and (2) building evidence that measures the construct in each case. This occurs through constant comparison between data and constructs so that accumulating evidence from diverse sources converges on a single, well-defined construct. For example, in their study of stigma management in bankruptcy, Sutton and Callahan (1987) developed constructs that described the reaction of customers and other parties to the declaration of bankruptcy by the focal firms. The iterative process involved data from multiple sources: initial semistructured telephone conversations; interviews with key informants, including the firm's president, other executives, a major creditor, and a lawyer; U.S. bankruptcy court records; observation of a creditors' meeting; and secondary source material including newspaper and magazine articles and firm correspondence. The authors iterated between constructs and these data. They eventually developed definitions and measures for several constructs: disengagement, bargaining for a more favorable exchange relationship, denigration via rumor, and reduction in the quality of participation.

This process is similar to developing a single construct measure from multiple indicators in hypothesis-testing research. That is, researchers use multiple sources of evidence to build construct measures, which define the construct and distinguish it from other constructs. In effect, the researcher is attempting to establish construct validity. The difference is that the construct, its definition, and measurement often emerge from the analysis process itself, rather than being specified a priori. A second difference is that no technique like factor analysis is available to collapse multiple indicators into a single construct measure. The reasons are that the indicators may vary across cases (i.e., not all cases may have all measures), and qualitative evidence (which is common in theory-building research) is difficult to collapse. Thus many researchers rely on tables that summarize and tabulate the evidence underlying the construct (Miles and Huberman 1984, Sutton and Callahan 1987). For example, Table 3.3 is a tabular display of the evidence grounding the CEO power construct used by Eisenhardt and Bourgeois (1988), which included qualitative personality descriptions, quantitative scores from questionnaires, and quotation examples. The reasons for defining and building evidence for a construct apply in theory-building research just as they do in traditional, hypothesis-testing work. That is, careful construction of construct definitions and evidence produces the sharply defined, measurable constructs that are necessary for strong theory.

A second step in shaping hypotheses is verifying that the emergent relationships between constructs fit with the evidence in each case. Sometimes a relationship is confirmed by the case evidence, whereas at other times it is revised, disconfirmed, or thrown out for insufficient evidence. This verification process is similar to that in traditional hypothesis-testing research. The key difference is that each hypothesis is examined for each case, not for the aggregate cases. Thus the underlying logic is replication, that is, the logic of treating a series of cases as a series of experiments, with each case serving to confirm or disconfirm the hypotheses (Yin 1984). Each case is analogous to an experiment, and multiple cases are analogous to multiple experiments. This contrasts with the sampling logic of traditional, within-experiment, hypothesis-testing research in which the aggregate relationships across the data points are tested using summary statistics such as F values (Yin 1984).

In replication logic, cases that confirm emergent relationships enhance confidence in the validity of the relationships. Cases that disconfirm the relationships often can provide an opportunity to refine and extend the theory. For example, in the study of the politics of strategic decision making, Eisenhardt and Bourgeois (1988) found a case that did not fit with the proposition that political coalitions have stable memberships. Further examination of this disconfirming case indicated that the executive team in this case had been newly formed at the time of the study. This observation plus replication in another case led to a refinement in the emergent theory to indicate that increasing stabilization of coalitions occurs over time.

At this point, the qualitative data are particularly useful for understanding why or why not emergent relationships hold. When a relationship is supported, the qualitative data often provide a good understanding of the dynamics underlying the relationship, that is, the "why" of what is happening. This is crucial to the establishment of internal validity. Just as in hypothesis-testing research, an apparent relationship may simply be a spurious correlation or

TABLE 3.3 Example of Tabulated Evidence for a Power Centralization Construct

Firm	CEO Decision Description	CEO Power Score	CEO Power Distance[a]	CEO-Dominated Functions	Story Decision Style[b]	Examples[c]
First	Strong Volatile Dogmatic	9.6	3.5	Mkt, R&D, Ops, Fin	Authoritarian	Geoff (chairman) is THE decision maker. He runs the whole show. (VP, Marketing)
Alpha	Impatient Parental Tunes you out	9.6	3.8	Mkt, R&D, Ops, Fin	Authoritarian	Thou shalt not hire w/o presidential approval. Thou shalt not promote w/o presidential approval. Thou shalt not explore new markets w/o presidential approval. (VP, Operations)
Cowboy	Strong Power boss Master strategist	9.1	3.1	Mkt, R&D, Fin	Authoritarian Consensus	The tone of meetings would change depending upon whether he was in the room. If he'd leave the room, discussion would spread out, go off the wall. It got back on focus when he came back. (director, Marketing)
Neutron	Organized Analytic	9.1	2.3	Mkt, Ops, Fin	Authoritarian	If there is a decision to make, I will make it. (president)
Omicron	Easygoing Easy to work with	8.4	1.2	Fin	Consensus	Bill (prior CEO) was a suppressor of ideas. Jim is more open. (VP, Manufacturing)
Promise	People oriented Pragmatic	8.9	1.3	Ops, Fin	Consensus	[My philosophy is] to make quick decisions involving as many people as possible. (president)
Forefront	Aggressive Team player	8.3	1.2	None	Consensus	Art depends on picking good people and letting them operate. (VP, Sales)
Zap	Consensus style People oriented	7.5	0.3	Fin	Consultative	It's very open. We're successful most of the time in building consensus. (VP, Engineering)

SOURCE: Eisenhardt and Bourgeois (1988).
a. Difference between CEO power score and score of next most powerful executive.
b. Authoritarian = decisions made either by CEO alone or in consultation with only one person; consultative = decisions made by CEO in consultation with either most of or all of the team; consensus = decisions made by entire team in a group format.

may reflect the impact of some third variable on each of the other two. Therefore, it is important to discover the underlying theoretical reasons for why the relationship exists. This helps to establish the internal validity of the findings. For example, in her study of project groups, Gersick (1988) identified a midpoint transition in the lives of most project groups. She then used extensive qualitative data to understand the cognitive and motivational reasons why such abrupt and precisely timed transitions occur.

Overall, shaping hypotheses in theory-building research involves measuring constructs and verifying relationships. These processes are similar to traditional hypothesis-testing research. However, these processes are more judgmental in theory-building research because researchers cannot apply statistical tests such as an *F* statistic. The research team must judge the strength and consistency of relationships within and across cases and also fully display the evidence and procedures when the findings are published, so that readers may apply their own standards.

Enfolding Literature

An essential feature of theory building is comparison of the emergent concepts, theory, or hypotheses with the extant literature. This involves asking, What is this similar to? What does it contradict? and Why? A key to this process is to consider a broad range of literature.

Examining literature that conflicts with the emergent theory is important for two reasons. First, if researchers ignore conflicting findings, then confidence in the findings is reduced. For example, readers may assume that the results are incorrect (a challenge to internal validity), or if correct, are idiosyncratic to the specific cases of the study (a challenge to generalizability). Second, and perhaps more important, conflicting literature represents an opportunity. The juxtaposition of conflicting results forces researchers into a more creative, frame-breaking mode of thinking than they might otherwise be able to achieve. The result can be deeper insight into both the emergent theory *and* the conflicting literature, as well as sharpening of the limits to generalizability of the focal research. For example, in their study of strategy making at the National Film Board of Canada, Mintzberg and McHugh (1985) noted conflicts between their findings for this highly creative organization and prior results at Volkswagenwerk and other sites. In the earlier studies, they observed differences in the patterns of strategic change whereby periods of convergence were long and periods of divergence were short and very abrupt. In contrast, the National Film Board exhibited a pattern of regular cycles of convergence and divergence, coupled with a long-term trend toward greater diversity. This and other conflicts allowed these researchers to establish the unique features of strategy making in an "adhocracy" in relief against "machine bureaucracies" and "entrepreneurial firms." The result was a sharper theory of strategy formation in all three types of organizations.

Similarly, in a study of politics, Eisenhardt and Bourgeois (1988) contrasted the finding that centralized power leads to politics with the previous finding that *decentralized* power creates politics. These conflicting findings forced the probing of both the evidence and conflicting research to discover the underlying reasons for the conflict. An underlying similarity in the apparently dissimilar situations was found. That is, both power extremes create a climate of frustration, which leads to an emphasis on self-interest and ultimately politics. In these extreme situations, the "structure of the game" becomes an interpersonal competition among the executives. In contrast, the research showed that an intermediate power distribution fosters a sense of personal efficacy among executives and ultimately collaboration, not politics, for the good of the entire group. This reconciliation integrated the conflicting findings into a single theoretical perspective and raised the theoretical level and generalizability of the results.

Literature discussing similar findings is important as well because it ties together underlying similarities in phenomena normally not associated with each other. The result is often a theory with stronger internal validity, wider generalizability, and higher conceptual level. For example, in her study of technological innovation in a major computer corporation, Leonard-Barton (1988) related her findings on the mutual adaptation of technology and the host organization to similar findings in the education literature. In so doing, Leonard-Barton strengthened the confidence that her findings were valid and generalizable because others had similar findings in a very different context. Also, the tie to mutual adaptation processes in the education setting sharpened and enriched the conceptual level of the study.

Similarly, Gersick (1988) linked the sharp midpoint transition in project group development to the more general punctuated equilibrium phenomenon, to the literature on the adult midlife transition, and to strategic transitions within organizations. This linkage with a variety of literature in other contexts raises the readers' confidence that Gersick had observed a valid phenomenon within her small number of project teams. It also allowed her to elevate the conceptual level of her findings to the more fundamental level of punctuated equilibrium, and strengthened their likely generalizability to other project teams. Finally, Burgelman (1983) strengthened the theoretical scope and validity of his work by tying his results on the process of new venture development in a large corporation to the selection arguments of population ecology. The result again was a higher conceptual level for his findings and enhanced confidence in their validity.

Overall, tying the emergent theory to existing literature enhances the internal validity, generalizability, and theoretical level of theory building from case study research. While linking results to the literature is important in most research, it is particularly crucial in theory-building research because the findings often rest on a very limited number of cases. In this situation, any further corroboration of internal validity or generalizability is an important improvement.

Reaching Closure

Two issues are important in reaching closure: when to stop adding cases, and when to stop iterating between theory and data. In the first, ideally, researchers should stop adding cases when theoretical saturation is reached. (Theoretical saturation is simply the point at which incremental learning is minimal because the researchers are observing phenomena seen before; Glaser and Strauss 1967.) This idea is quite similar to ending the revision of a manuscript when the incremental improvement in its quality is minimal. In practice, theoretical saturation often combines with pragmatic considerations, such as time and money, to dictate when case collection ends. In fact, it is not uncommon for researchers to plan the number of cases in advance. For example, the Warwick group planned their study of strategic change and competitiveness in British firms to include eight firms (Pettigrew 1988). This kind of planning may be necessary because of the availability of resources and because time constraints force researchers to develop cases in parallel. Finally, although there is no ideal number of cases, a number between 4 and 10 cases usually works well. With fewer than 4 cases, it is often difficult to generate theory with much complexity, and its empirical grounding is likely to be unconvincing, unless the case has several minicases within it, as did the Mintzberg and McHugh study of the National Film Board of Canada. With more than 10 cases, it quickly becomes difficult for researchers to cope with the complexity and volume of the data.

In the second closure issue, where to stop iterating between theory and data, again, saturation is the key idea. That is, the iteration process stops when the incremental improvement to theory is minimal. The final product of building theory from case studies may be concepts (e.g., Mintzberg and Waters's 1982 deliberate and emergent strategies), a conceptual framework (e.g., Harris and Sutton's 1986 framework of bankruptcy), or propositions or possibly mid-range theory (e.g., Eisenhardt and Bourgeois's 1988 mid-range theory of politics in high velocity environments). On the downside, the final product may be disappointing. The research may simply replicate prior theory, or there may be no clear patterns within the data. The steps for building theory from case studies are summarized in Table 3.1.

COMPARISON WITH OTHER LITERATURE

The process described here has similarities with the work of others. For example, I have drawn upon the ideas of theoretical sampling, theoretical saturation, and overlapped coding, data collection, and analysis from Glaser and Strauss (1967). Also, the notions of case study design, replication logic, and concern for internal validity have been incorporated from Yin (1984). The tools of tabular display of evidence from Miles and Huberman (1984) were particularly helpful in the discussion of building evidence for constructs.

However, the process described here has important differences from previous work. First, it is focused on theory building from cases. In contrast, with the exception of Glaser and Strauss (1967), previous work has centered on other topics, such as qualitative data analysis (e.g., Miles 1979, Miles and Huberman 1984, Kirk and Miller 1986), case study design (Yin 1981, 1984, McClintock, Brannon, and Maynard-Moody 1979), and ethnography (Van Maanen 1988). To a large extent, Glaser and Strauss (1967) focus on defending building theory from cases, rather than on how actually to do it. Thus, although these previous writings provide pieces of the process, they do not provide (nor are they intended to provide) a framework for theory building from cases as developed here.

Second, the process described here contributes new ideas. For example, the process includes a priori specification of constructs, population specification, flexible instrumentation, multiple investigators, cross-case analysis tactics, and several uses of literature. Their inclusion plus their illustration using examples from research studies and comparison with traditional, hypothesis-testing research synthesizes, extends, and adds depth to existing views of theory-building research.

Third, particularly in comparison with Strauss (1987) and Van Maanen (1988), the process described here adopts a positivist view of research. That is, the process is directed toward the development of testable hypotheses and theory that are generalizable across settings. In contrast, authors such as Strauss and Van Maanen are more concerned that a rich, complex description of the specific cases under study evolve; they appear less concerned with development of generalizable theory.

DISCUSSION

The process of building theory from case study research is a strikingly iterative one. Although an investigator may focus on one part of the process at a time, the process itself involves constant iteration backward and forward between steps. For example, an investigator may move from cross-case comparison, back to redefinition of the research question, and out to the field to gather evidence on an additional case. Also, the process is alive with tension between divergence into new ways of understanding the data and convergence onto a single theoretical framework. For example, the process involves the use of multiple investigators and multiple data-collection methods as well as a variety of cross-case searching tactics. Each of these tactics involves viewing evidence from diverse perspectives. However, the process also involves converging on construct definitions, measures, and a framework for structuring the findings. Finally, the process described here is intimately tied with empirical evidence.

Strengths of Theory Building From Cases

One strength of theory building from cases is its likelihood of generating novel theory. Creative insight often arises from the juxtaposition of contradictory or paradoxical evidence (Cameron and Quinn 1988). As Bartunek (1988) argues, the process of reconciling these contradictions forces individuals to reframe perceptions into a new gestalt. Building theory from case studies centers directly on this kind of juxtaposition. That is, attempts to reconcile evidence across cases, types of data, and different investigators, and between cases and literature, increase the likelihood of creative reframing into a new theoretical vision. Although a myth surrounding theory building from case studies is that the process is limited by investigators' preconceptions, in fact just the opposite is true. This constant juxtaposition of conflicting realities tends to "unfreeze" thinking, and so the process has the potential to generate theory with less researcher bias than theory built from incremental studies or armchair, axiomatic deduction.

A second strength is that the emergent theory is likely to be testable with constructs that can be readily measured and hypotheses that can be proven false. Measurable constructs are likely because they have already been measured during the theory-building process. The resulting hypotheses are likely to be verifiable for the same reason. That is, they have already undergone repeated verification during the theory-building process. In contrast, theory that is generated apart from direct evidence may have testability problems. For example, population ecology researchers borrowed the niche concept from biology. This construct has proven difficult to operationalize for many organizational researchers, other than its originators. One reason may be its obscure definition, which hampers measurability: "that area in constraint space (the space whose dimensions are levels of resources, etc.) in which the population outcompetes all other local populations" (Hannan and Freeman 1977, p. 947). One might ask, How do you measure an area in constraint space?

A third strength is that the resultant theory is likely to be empirically valid. The likelihood of valid theory is high because the theory-building process is so intimately tied with evidence that it is very likely that the resultant theory will be consistent with empirical observation. In well-executed theory-building research, investigators answer to the data from the beginning of the research. This closeness can lead to an intimate sense of things—"how they feel, smell, seem" (Mintzberg, 1979). This intimate interaction with actual evidence often produces theory that closely mirrors reality.

Weaknesses of Theory Building From Cases

However, some characteristics that lead to strengths in theory building from case studies also lead to weaknesses. For example, the intensive use of empirical evidence can yield theory that is overly complex. A hallmark of good theory is parsimony, but given the typically staggering volume of rich data, there is a temptation to build theory that tries to capture everything. The result can be theory that is very rich in detail, but lacks the simplicity of overall perspective. Theorists working from case data can lose their sense of proportion as they confront vivid, voluminous data. Because they lack quantitative gauges such as regression results or observations across multiple studies, they may be unable to assess which are the most important relationships and which are simply idiosyncratic to a particular case.

Another weakness is that building theory from cases may result in narrow and idiosyncratic theory. Case study theory building is a bottom-up approach such that the specifics of data produce the generalizations of theory. The risks are that the theory describes a very idiosyncratic phenomenon or that the theorist is unable to raise the level of generality of the theory. Indeed, many of the grounded case studies mentioned earlier resulted in modest theories. For example, Gersick (1988) developed a model of group development for teams with project deadlines, Eisenhardt and Bourgeois (1988) developed a mid-range theory of politics in high velocity environments, and Burgelman (1983) proposed a model of new product ventures in large corporations. Such theories are likely to be testable, novel, and empirically valid, but they do lack the sweep of such theories as resource dependence, population ecology, and transaction cost. They are essentially theories about specific phenomena. To their credit, many of these theories tie into broader theoretical issues, such as adaptation, punctuated equilibrium, and bounded rationality, but ultimately they are not theories about organization in any grand sense. Perhaps "grand" theory requires multiple studies—an accumulation of both theory-building and theory-testing empirical studies.

Applicability

When is it appropriate to conduct theory-building case study research? In normal science, theory is developed through incremental empirical testing and extension (Kuhn 1970). Thus the theory-building process relies on past literature and empirical observation or experience as well as on the insight of the theorist to build incrementally more powerful theories. However, there are times when little is known about a phenomenon, current perspectives seem inadequate because they have little empirical substantiation, or they conflict with each other or common sense. Or, sometimes, serendipitous findings in a theory-testing study suggest the need for a new perspective. In these situations, theory building from case study research is particularly appropriate because theory building from case studies does not rely on previous literature or prior empirical evidence. Also, the conflict inherent in the process is likely to generate the kind of novel theory that is desirable when extant theory seems inadequate. For example, Van de Ven and Poole (1990) argue that such an approach is especially useful for studying the new area of longitudinal change processes. In sum, building theory from case study research is most appropriate in the early stages of research on a topic or to provide freshness in perspective to an already researched topic.

Evaluation

How should theory-building research using case studies be evaluated? To begin, there is no generally accepted set of guidelines for the assessment of this type of research. However, several criteria seem appropriate. Assessment turns on whether the concepts, framework, or propositions that emerge from the process are "good theory." After all, the point of the process is to develop or at least begin to develop theory. Pfeffer (1982) suggests that good theory is parsimonious, testable, and logically coherent, and these criteria seem appropriate here. Thus a strong theory-building study yields good theory (that is, parsimonious, testable, and logically coherent theory) that emerges at the end, not the beginning, of the study.

Second, the assessment of theory-building research also depends upon empirical issues: strength of method and the evidence grounding the theory. Have the investigators followed a careful analytic procedure? Does the evidence support the theory? Have the investigators ruled out rival explanations? Just as in other empirical research, investigators should provide information on the sample, data-collection procedures, and analysis. Also, they should display enough evidence for each construct to allow readers to make their own assessments of the fit with theory. Although there are no concise measures such as correlation coefficients or *F* values, nonetheless thorough reporting of information should give confidence that the theory is valid. Overall, as in hypothesis testing, a strong theory-building study has a good, although not necessarily perfect, fit with the data.

Finally, strong theory-building research should result in new insights. Theory building that simply replicates past theory is, at best, a modest contribution. Replication is appropriate in theory-testing research, but in theory-building research, the goal is new theory. Thus a strong theory-building study presents new, perhaps frame-breaking, insights.

CONCLUSIONS

The purpose of this chapter has been to describe the process of theory building from case studies. The process, outlined in Table 3.1, has features that range from selection of the research question to issues in reaching closure. Several conclusions emerge.

Theory developed from case study research is likely to have important strengths, such as novelty, testability, and empirical validity, which arise from the intimate linkage with empirical evidence. Second, given the strengths of this theory-building approach and its independence from prior literature or past empirical observation, it is particularly well suited to new research areas or research areas for which existing theory seems inadequate. This type of work is highly complementary to incremental theory building from normal science research. The former is useful in early stages of research on a topic or when a fresh perspective is needed, whereas the latter is useful in later stages of knowledge. Finally, several guidelines for assessing the quality of theory building from case studies have been suggested. Strong studies are those that present interesting or frame-breaking theories that meet the tests of good theory or concept development (e.g., parsimony, testability, logical coherence) and are grounded in convincing evidence.

Most empirical studies lead from theory to data. Yet the accumulation of knowledge involves a continual cycling between theory and data. Perhaps this chapter will stimulate some researchers to complete the cycle by conducting research that goes in the less common direction from data to theory, and equally important, perhaps it will help others become informed consumers of the results.

Acknowledgments

I appreciate the helpful comments of Paul Adler, Kenneth Bettenhausen, Constance Gersick, James Frederickson, James Jucker, Deborah Myerson, Dorothy Leonard-

Barton, Robert Sutton, and the participants in the Stanford NIMH Colloquium. I also benefited from informal conversations with many participants at the National Science Foundation Conference on Longitudinal Field Research Methods for Studying Organizational Processes, Austin, Texas, September 1988.

References

Abbott, A. (1988), "Workshop on Sequence Methods, presented at the National Science Foundation Conference on Longitudinal Research Methods for Studying Organizational Processes, Austin, TX, September.

Allison, G. (1971), *Essence of Decision,* Boston: Little, Brown.

Anderson, P. (1983), "Decision Making by Objection and the Cuban Missile Crisis," *Administrative Science Quarterly,* 28, 201-222.

Bartunek, J. (1988), "The dynamics of personal and organizational reframing," in R. Quinn and K. Cameron (Eds.), *Paradox and Transformation: Towards a Theory of Change in Organization and Management* (pp. 137-162), Cambridge, MA: Ballinger.

Bettenhausen, K., and J. K. Murnighan (1986), "The Emergence of Norms in Competitive Decision-Making Groups," *Administrative Science Quarterly,* 30, 350-372.

Bourgeois. L. J., and K. M. Eisenhardt (1988), "Strategic Decision Processes in High Velocity Environments: Four Cases in the Microcomputer Industry," *Management Science,* 34, 816-835.

Burgelman, R. (1983), "A Process Model of Internal Corporate Venturing in a Major Diversified Firm," *Administrative Science Quarterly,* 28, 223-244.

Cameron, K., and R. Quinn (1988), "Organizational Paradox and Transformation," in R. Quinn and K. Cameron (Eds.), *Paradox and Transformation* (pp. 1-18), Cambridge, MA: Ballinger.

Eisenhardt, K. M. (1989), "Making Fast Strategic Decisions in High-Velocity Environments," *Academy of Management Journal,* 32, 543-576.

Eisenhardt, K. M., and L. J. Bourgeois (1988), "Politics of Strategic Decision Making in High Velocity Environments: Toward a Mid-Range Theory," *Academy of Management Journal,* 31, 737-770.

Gersick, C. (1988), "Time and Transition Work Teams: Toward a New Model of Group Development," *Academy of Management Journal,* 31, 9-41.

Glaser, B. G., and A. L. Strauss (1967), *The Discovery of Grounded Theory: Strategies for Qualitative Research,* Chicago: Aldine.

Hannan, M., and J. Freeman (1977), "The Population Ecology of Organizations," *American Journal of Sociology,* 82, 929-964.

Harris, S., and R. Sutton (1986), "Functions of Parting Ceremonies in Dying Organizations," *Academy of Management Journal,* 29, 5-30.

Jick, T. (1979), "Mixing Qualitative and Quantitative Methods: Triangulation in Action," *Administrative Science Quarterly,* 24, 602-611.

Kahneman, D., and A. Tversky (1973), "On the Psychology of Prediction," *Psychological Review,* 80, 237-251.

Kidder, T. (1982), *Soul of a New Machine,* New York: Avon.

Kirk, J., and M. Miller (1986), *Reliability and Validity in Qualitative Research,* Beverly Hills, CA: Sage.

Kuhn, T. (1970), *The Structure of Scientific Revolutions* (2nd ed.), Chicago: University of Chicago Press.

Leonard-Barton, D. (1988), "Synergistic Design for Case Studies: Longitudinal Single-Site and Replicated Multiple-Site," paper presented at the National Science Foundation Conference on Longitudinal Research Methods for Studying Organizational Processes, Austin, TX, September.

McClintock, C., D. Brannon, and S. Maynard-Moody (1979), "Applying the Logic of Sample Surveys to Qualitative Case Studies: The Case Cluster Method," *Administrative Science Quarterly,* 24, 612-629.

Miles, M. B. (1979), "Qualitative Data as an Attractive Nuisance: The Problem of Analysis," *Administrative Science Quarterly,* 24, 590-601.

Miles, M. B., and A. M. Huberman (1984), *Qualitative Data Analysis: A Sourcebook of New Methods,* Beverly Hills, CA: Sage.

Mintzberg, H. (1979), "An Emerging Strategy of 'Direct' Research," *Administrative Science Quarterly,* 24, 580-589.

Mintzberg, H., and A. McHugh (1985), "Strategy Formation in an Adhocracy," *Administrative Science Quarterly,* 30, 160-197.

Mintzberg, H., and J. Waters (1982), "Tracking Strategy in an Entrepreneurial Firm," *Academy of Management Journal,* 25, 465-499.

Nisbett, R., and L. Ross (1980), *Human Inference: Strategies and Shortcomings of Social Judgment,* Englewood Cliffs, NJ: Prentice Hall.

Perrow, C. (1986), *Complex Organizations* (3rd ed.), New York: Random House.

Pettigrew, A. (1973), *The Politics of Organizational Decision Making,* London: Tavistock.

Pettigrew, A. (1988), "Longitudinal Field Research on Change: Theory and Practice," paper presented at the National Science Foundation Conference on Longitudinal Research Methods for Studying Organizational Processes, Austin, TX, September.

Pfeffer, J. (1982), *Organizations and Organization Theory,* Marshfield, MA: Pitman.

Pinfield, L. (1986), "A Field Evaluation of Perspectives on Organizational Decision Making," *Administrative Science Quarterly,* 31, 365-388.

Quinn, J. B. (1980), *Strategies for Change,* Homewood, IL: Dow-Jones Irwin.

Selznick, P. (1949), *TVA and the Grass Roots,* Berkeley: University of California Press.

Strauss, A. (1987), *Qualitative Analysis for Social Scientists,* Cambridge: Cambridge University Press.

Sutton, R., and A. Callahan (1987), "The Stigma of Bankruptcy: Spoiled Organizational Image and Its Management," *Academy of Management Journal,* 30, 405-436.

Van de Ven, A. H., and M. S. Poole (1990), "Methods for Studying Innovation Development in the Minnesota Innovation Research Program," *Organization Science,* 1, 313-335.

Van Maanen, J. (1988), *Tales of the Field: On Writing Ethnography,* Chicago: University of Chicago Press.

Yin, R. (1981), "The Case Study Crisis: Some Answers," *Administrative Science Quarterly,* 26, 58-65.

Yin, R. (1984), *Case Study Research,* Beverly Hills, CA: Sage.

4

Longitudinal Field Research on Change

Theory and Practice

ANDREW M. PETTIGREW

This chapter reveals the author's theory of method for conducting longitudinal field research on change. The chapter also discusses a range of practical problems in carrying out time-series research in organizational settings. The practical problems include dealing with time in longitudinal research; issues of site selection; choices about data collection and degrees of involvement; the importance of clarifying research outputs, audience, and presentation; and the handling of problems of complexity and simplicity associated with longitudinal comparative case study research on change. The chapter concludes with a discussion of some of the ethical issues involved in longitudinal field research and the managerial issues that arise in a community of researchers.

The purpose of this chapter is to reveal my theory of method for conducting longitudinal field research on change. In attempting this task, I follow the example of writers such as Glaser and Strauss (1967) and Strauss (1987), who have made explicit a great deal of the tacit knowledge acquired through practicing empirical research. This chapter is not, therefore, written by a methodologist for other methodologists. Rather, it is an attempt to codify and

---

This chapter appeared originally in *Organization Science,* vol. 1, no. 3, August 1990, pp. 267-292.

organize learning from experience in the hope that such experience may be of value to other scholars seeking to conduct longitudinal studies of change processes. Although I have been carrying out such empirical inquiries for a score or more years (e.g., Pettigrew 1973a, 1973b, 1975, 1979, 1985a, 1987b), little of this practical experience has been distilled and communicated to others. In writing this distillation now, I recognize that even the willing reflective practitioner probably knows more than can be said (Schön 1983). What is presented here is bound to be partial. My hope is that it may also be illuminating, both for myself and for other interested scholars.

I have made one previous attempt to present my theory of method (Pettigrew 1985b). This chapter is an attempt to build on that 1985 statement by incorporating some of the learning from the program of research now under way at the Centre for Corporate Strategy and Change (CCSC), University of Warwick. Since 1985, the building of a program of research at the CCSC has allowed the broadening and deepening of the mid-1980s statement of contextualist longitudinal research on change. Pulling together an interdisciplinary team of full-time and experienced researchers has allowed us to make empirical progress. The research includes inquiries into competitiveness and strategic change; the study of linkages among changes in business environment, business strategy and structure, and human resource policies and practices in the firm; and also major change in the provision of services in the British National Health Service (NHS). Comparative and longitudinal research is complete and/or under way in more than 100 organizations in eight industries in the private sector, and also in the NHS (e.g., Pettigrew, Hendry, and Sparrow 1989, Pettigrew, McKee, and Ferlie 1988a, 1988b, Whipp, Rosenfeld, and Pettigrew 1989, Sparrow and Pettigrew 1988c).

The analytic cornerstone of the CCSC research is the view that theoretically sound and practically useful research on change should explore the contexts, content, and process of change together with their interconnections through time. The focus is on changing, catching reality in flight, and in studying long-term processes in their contexts, a return to embeddedness as a principle of method. *Context* refers to the outer and inner context of the organization. *Outer context* includes the economic, social, political, and sectoral environment in which the firm is located. *Inner context* refers to features of the structural, cultural, and political environment through which ideas for change proceed.

The overall research challenge in our work is to link the content, contexts, and processes of change over time to explain the differential achievement of change objectives. Theoretically, the CCSC's approach challenges rational, linear theories of planning and change where actions are seen as ordered and sequenced in order to achieve rationally declared ends and where actors behave mechanistically and altruistically in the pursuit of organizational goals. Instead, the task is to explore the complex, haphazard, and often contradictory ways that change emerges and to construct a model that allows for an appreciation of conflicting rationalities, objectives, and behaviors. There is an explicit recognition that change is multifaceted, involving political, cultural, incremental, environmental, and structural, as well as rational, dimensions. Power, chance, opportunism, and accident are as influential in shaping outcomes as are designs, negotiated agreements, and master plans (Pettigrew 1985a). The conventional split between policy formulation and implementation is also questioned, and these processes are not viewed as discrete or chronological but as interactive and muddled (Quinn 1980).

This chapter is divided into three sections. The first briefly outlines the contextualist theory of method guiding our research on change. The second reveals some of the range of practical problems faced in the implementation of our methodological approach. Here the focus is on the practical problems of dealing with time in longitudinal research: issues of site selection; choices about data collection and degrees of involvement; the importance of clarifying research outputs, audience, and presentation; and finally handling the problems of complexity and simplicity associated with longitudinal comparative case study research on change. The third and final section points to the lessons from the theory and practice of our method for future longitudinal field research on change processes. Particular focus is given in this final section to the ethical issues involved in longitudinal field research and to the managerial considerations involved in leading a community of researchers.

CONTEXTUALISM AS A THEORY OF METHOD

One reason for the success of books such as those by Burrell and Morgan (1979) and Morgan (1986) is that these authors help to make explicit the various ontological and theoretical assumptions guiding much of organizational analysis. From time to time there is a requirement for empirical researchers to make clear the theory of method that guides their inquiries. The theory of method informing my research on change is contextualism, as proposed initially by the philosopher Stephen Pepper (1942).

I have provided an introduction to contextualism and a broad review of the literature on change elsewhere (Pettigrew 1985a, 1985b, 1985c, 1985d). In those earlier publications, I argue that with a few limited noteworthy exceptions (Berg 1979, Kervasdoue and Kimberly 1979), much research on organization change has been ahistorical, aprocessual, and acontextual in character. In this respect, the area of organization change merely reflects the biases inherent in the social sciences generally and in the study of organizations in particular. There are remarkably few studies of change that actually allow the change process to reveal itself in any kind of substantially temporal or contextual manner. Where the change is treated as the unit of analysis, the focus is on a single event or a set of discrete episodes somehow separate from the immediate and more distant antecedents that give those events form, meaning, and substance. Such episodic views of change not only treat innovations as if they had a clear beginning and a clear end but also, where they limit themselves to snapshot time-series data, fail to provide data on the mechanisms and processes through which changes are created. Studies of transformation are, therefore, often preoccupied with the intricacies of narrow changes rather than the holistic and dynamic analysis of changing.

The suggestion made here is that one way to respond to the above weaknesses in the literature on change is to encourage a form of research that is contextualist and processual in character (Pettigrew 1985b). A contextualist analysis of a process such as change draws on phenomena at vertical and horizontal levels of analysis and the interconnections between those levels through time. The *vertical level* refers to the interdependence between higher or lower levels of analysis upon phenomena to be explained at some further level, for example, the impact of a changing socioeconomic context on features of intraorganizational context and interest group behavior. The *horizontal level* refers to the sequential interconnectedness among phenomena in historical, present, and future time. An approach that offers both multilevel or vertical analysis and processual, or horizontal, analysis is said to be contextualist in character.

In summary, the key points to emphasize in analyzing change in a contextualist mode are as follows: first, the importance of embeddedness, studying change in the context of interconnected levels of analysis; second, the importance of temporal interconnectedness, locating change in past, present, and future time; third, the need to explore context and action, how context is a product of action and vice versa; and finally, the central assumption about causation in this kind of holistic analysis, that causation of change is neither linear nor singular—the search for a simple and singular grand theory of change is unlikely to bear fruit. Explanations of change are bound to be holistic and multifaceted. Beware of the myth of the singular theory of social or organizational change. Look for continuity and change, patterns and idiosyncrasies, the actions of individuals and groups, the role of contexts and structures, and processes of structuring. Give history and social processes the temporal space to reveal their deep-seated continuities and often idiosyncratic untidiness. Arguments over the true or single source of change, although interesting and worthwhile in the sharpening of academic minds and egos, are ultimately pointless. For the analyst interested in the theory and practice of changing, the task is to identify the variety and mixture of causes of change and to explore through time some of the conditions and contexts under which these mixtures occur.

Our first assumption of contextualism is that target changes should be studied in the context of changes at other levels of analysis. Thus explanations of the changing relative competitive performance of firms should be linked to sectoral and economic change (Pettigrew and Whipp 1990). A source of change is the asymmetries between levels of context, where processes at different levels of analysis are often observed to have their own momentum, rates, paces, and trajectories. Thus the rate and trajectory of change in an industrial sector characterized by significant boundary changes may be much faster than the sensing and adjustment pathways of individual firms to the regrouping of the sector. The relative slowness of the sensing and adjustment process of firms, and their failure to recognize that the bases of competition may have changed in that sector, is a key factor explaining their loss of competitive performance (Pettigrew and Whipp 1990). Equally well, the analyst of change has to recognize that activities at some levels of context may be more visible and rapid than at other levels, and thus in the short term sources of change may appear unidirectional, whereas in the longer term a multidirectional pattern may appear.

Our second background assumption about contextualism is the importance of revealing temporal interconnectedness. There is a search to catch reality in flight. Antecedent conditions shape the present and the emerging future. The human resource inheritance of many firms may affect the rate and pace of business strategy change if the business change requires significant adjustments in the knowledge base of the firm (Pettigrew, Hendry, and Sparrow 1989). Thus history is not just an event in the past but is alive in the present and may shape the future. However, history is to be understood not just as events and chronology; there may be deeper pathways if the analyst searches for structures and underlying logics. But in the search for deeper structures, beware of the dangers of determinism. Our approach makes no assumption of predetermined timetables, of ordered and inevitable sequences or stages. Trajectories of change are probabilistic and uncertain because of changing contexts.

Our third background assumption relates to the role of context and action. Here the key starting point is that it is not a question of nature or nurture, or context or action, but context and action. Context is not just a stimulus environment but a nested arrangement of structures and processes where the subjective interpretations of actors perceiving, comprehending, learning, and remembering help shape process. Thus processes are both constrained by contexts and shape contexts, in the direction of either preserving or altering them. In the past, structural analyses emphasizing abstract dimensions and contextual constraints have been regarded as incompatible with processual analyses stressing action and strategic conduct. Here an attempt is being made to combine these two forms of description and analysis, first of all by conceptualizing structure and context not just as a barrier to action but as essentially involved in its production (Giddens 1979, Ransom, Hinings, and Greenwood 1980) and second by demonstrating how aspects of structure and context are mobilized by actors and groups as they seek to obtain outcomes important to them (Pettigrew 1985a, Pettigrew, McKee, and Ferlie 1988a, 1988b, Ferlie and Pettigrew 1990).

Finally, our holistic and multifaceted treatment of change makes certain causal assumptions. Causation is neither linear nor singular. There is no attempt to search for the illusory single grand theory of change, or indeed of how and why a single independent variable causes, or even affects, a dependent or outcome variable. Changes have multiple causes and are to be explained more by loops than by lines—"the shifting interconnectedness of fused strands," as Mancuso and Ceely (1980) put it. Thus in our competitiveness research, five key features distinguished our high-performing automobile, investment banking, insurance, and book publishing firms from their lesser-performing competitors. But the real issue explaining relative competitive performance was not just the isolation of these five features of environmental assessment, human resources as assets and liabilities, managing strategic and operational change, leading change, and coherence, but the convergent interactions and interconnected loops among the five features in the firm over time.

The analyst of change will know how difficult it is to take our background assumptions of contextualism into the practice of field research. The principal aim of the next section is to describe and discuss some of the practical issues we encounter in conducting longitudinal research in organizational settings.

PRACTICING LONGITUDINAL RESEARCH
IN ORGANIZATIONAL SETTINGS

To conduct the kind of research outlined in the previous section, we have undertaken longitudinal research by means of the comparative case study method. Our case studies involve comparisons between firms in the same industrial sector and between firms in different sectors, and sometimes, as in our human resource work, we make direct sector to sector comparisons. Time is captured in our work through a combination of retrospective and real-time analysis. Thus far, the retrospective element can provide us with up to a 20-year time series, whereas for reasons of funding we have been restricted to a real-time analysis of up to 3 years. In earlier work on strategic change in ICI (Pettigrew 1985a), a real-time analysis of 10 years was achieved that was complemented by 20-plus years of retrospective data, but this is an ideal rarely to be accomplished in organizational analysis. The kind of intensive comparative analysis practiced in the CCSC means that a practical load for two senior and experienced full-time staff is 10 case studies over a 3-year period. Our research strategy is resource intensive, intellectually challenging, and highly demanding of the social and political skills of the Centre staff.

Given all the variants of longitudinal research sketched by Kimberly (1976), Miller and Friesen (1982), and others, why have we adopted the comparative case study method? The simple answer is that the longitudinal comparative case method best suits the research topic we are pursuing, the contextualist mode of analysis we adopt, and the broad research objectives we have in mind. The longitudinal comparative case method provides the opportunity to examine continuous processes in context and to draw in the significance of various interconnected levels of analysis. Thus there is scope to reveal the multiple sources and loops of causation and connectivity so crucial in identifying and explaining patterns in the process of change.

But what are some of the practical problems of implementing a research strategy incorporating the longitudinal comparative case method and underpinned by a contextualist theory of method? Five major research implementation issues are as follows:

1. Truth is the daughter of time.
2. Comparative method and the choice of research sites.
3. Observation and verification—issues of data collection and degree of involvement.
4. Research outputs, audience, and presentation.
5. Routes to reality and structured understanding.

Truth Is the Daughter of Time

For the practitioner of longitudinal research, issues of time are critical and pervasive. How does the choice of the time series influence the perspective of the researcher? When does the process begin and end? When is the appropriate moment to make assessments about outcome evaluation? Is time just events and chronology, or is time a socially constructed phenomenon that influences behavior? Are there varying time cycles at levels of analysis beyond the focal level of investigation? Does the appreciative system of the researcher change over time, and therefore is what the researcher is capable of thinking and saying conditional on when pen is put to paper?

First, there is the crucial issue of time and perspective. Time sets a frame of reference for what changes are seen and how those changes are explained. In the microevents that surround our particular lives and in the daily trumpetings of the media change has an ever-present illusion of reality. The more we look at present-day events, the easier it is to identify change; the longer we stay with an emergent process and the further back we go to disentangle its origins, the more we can identify continuities. Empirically and theoretically, change and continuity are a matter of time. Any adequate empirical inquiry into change has to be capable of revealing the temporal patterns, causes, and movements from continuity to change and vice versa. To do this we have chosen to collect longitudinal data, which allows us to explore the present in relation to the past and the emerging future.

But when does a change process begin and end, especially where the unit of analysis is the continuous process in context and not the change episode or project? When does the field researcher start and stop collecting data? Does one stop peeling the layers from the onion only when the vapors inhibit all further sight? There are, of course, no absolute and simple answers to such questions. Pragmatically, judgments will be made in the light of the themes and research questions being pursued, the empirical setting of the research, the nature and quality of researcher-subject relationship in any site, and funding or other resource constraints. An example is perhaps in order. In Hardy's (1985) research on factory closures a judgment had to be made concerning when the process of closure began. One choice point was when the senior management announced the closure. Another was when the senior management agreed to stop investing in the factory in question. The latter choice point preceded the closure announcement by around five years in one of Hardy's cases. With the management pursuing a conscious long-term strategy of allowing the factory to wither on the vine, it was not a difficult choice to begin the data collection at the earlier of the two options. A researcher's theoretical framework suggests other justifications for beginning and ending data collection. The framework may focus on major social dramas or breakpoints (Pettigrew 1985a, Tushman and Romanelli 1985) in a firm's history that indicate the end or beginning of periods of continuity or change. A contextual analysis would suggest that these breakpoints may have been preceded by major disjunctures at higher levels of analysis (e.g., the sector or economy), and this may provide the rationale for choice.

The issue of when to conclude the data collection and analysis is closely linked to the problem of when to make judgments about outcome evaluations in a change process. The time-series data on the birth, evolution, impact, and fate of internal consultancy groups reported in Pettigrew (1975, 1985a) illustrates how judgments of impact and fate are sensitive to time and the vagaries of shifting internal and external contexts. Judgments about impact are conditioned not only by the time point of observation, but also by the subjective interpretations of actors involved in and around the change process. Often contradictory accounts are obtained from different respondents.

Where this occurs, one approach used in the Centre is to expose alternative accounts rather than accord one privileged status. We thereby obtain and present a pluralist analysis where different versions of reality are revealed by the range of actors who operate with a variety of interests and perceptions. In our experience, the effect of publicly revealing different versions of reality is to diffuse tension rather than to exacerbate it. Recognizing differences can have the effect of respecting differences and gives people the confidence to articulate minority positions. Such revealed pluralism can trigger discussion at the feedback workshops provided by Centre staff to groups of respondents, who can then offer additional confirmatory or disconfirmatory information. Where the research teams are confident about the balance of empirical evidence and there is a strong link between that evidence and their theoretical framework, the researchers' interpretation can predominate, but only after the description and analysis of respondents' competing versions of reality.

Questions of evaluation are also linked to core problematics such as the meaning of "change" in the research. In our health service research, Ferlie and Pettigrew (1988) argue this apparently simple concept can reveal various facets of change. There is the *speed* of health service change question: How quickly has the health authority changed its pattern of service? There is the *quantity* of service change question: What have been the changes in inputs such as hospitals, beds, staff, and number of new facilities? There is the *quality* of service change question: To what extent have there been developments of new roles, new working practices and attitudes? Finally, there is the *process* of service change question as experienced by the members of the organization: Has the change been driven through, but at the cost of wrecked relationships, leaving the health authority unable to contemplate further change? Different theories of change will lead a researcher to focus on different facets of change. Thus Miller and Friesen (1982) have described quantum and piecemeal changes, Pettigrew (1985a) revolutionary and evolutionary eras, and Tushman and Romanelli (1985) periods of convergence and reorientation. In the final analysis, change is what the researcher defines it to be in his or her theoretical framework. Thus it behooves researchers to define explicitly what change means in their research design.

Related to the core question of what change means in longitudinal research is the equally important issue of the meaning of time in temporal analysis. As Elchardus (1988) argues, "Time is increasingly recognised as an issue in its own right and not just a secondary factor that becomes relevant when the question of social change is raised" (p. 36). For a citizen such as me whose grand passion is antiquarian horology, it is easy to assume a single means of time reckoning: clock time. But as Whipp (1988) reminds us, "Time is more diverse and necessarily social and subjective" (p. 211). Time is not just "out there" as neutral chronology, it is "in here" as a social construction.

In certain kinds of organizations there are socially constructed time frames built around, for example, the design and development cycle of a car, or the long process of taking an idea for a new drug from the laboratory to the marketplace. An important implication of this duality of time (time as chronology and time as a social construction) is that we have to study events and the social constructions of those events in the context of the important time cycles that help to provide the implicit rhythm of particular social systems.

A social construction of time suggests that it be conceived as more than just a chronology of events. We follow Ladurie (1979) in seeking to tame the event, "the long sequence of simple and uncomplicated events." Instead, events are seen as stepping-stones in the search for the study of structures, "the persistent patterns of the long term" (p. 111). Or as Morgan (1986) puts it, "We need to try and understand how the discrete events that make up our experience of change . . . are generated by a logic unfolded in the process of change itself" (p. 267). What is critical is not just events, but the underlying logics that give events meaning and significance. Understanding these underlying logics in the process of change is the goal, and this requires data on events, interpretations of patterns in those events, when they occur in socially meaningful time cycles, and the logics that may explain how and why these patterns occur in particular chronological sequences.

Lerner and Kauffman (1985) as well as Abbott (1990) remind us there is the added complication that there may be different temporal patterns in the process occurring at different levels in a contextualist analysis; what they call the nonequivalent temporal metric across levels of analysis. The firm may be changing more quickly or more slowly than the sectors of which it is a part. Furthermore, Lerner and Kauffman use an example from developmental psychology to illustrate the general point that time may have different meanings at different levels of analysis. Thus infant neuromuscular change can be detected in weeks, but social-institutional change may take years to reveal itself. Thus it may be difficult to detect the influence of changes at one level on another—a perennial problem for the longitudinal researcher using a contextualist mode of analysis.

Finally, there is the issue of time and the appreciative systems of the researcher. Collecting and analyzing comparative and longitudinal data on change processes is a highly complex social and intellectual task. There are times when one feels overwhelmed by detail. Later in the process one may feel a temporary, often illusory, sense that order is prevailing. There are indeed patterns, not only in this case but across these cases in quite different contexts. At some point in time the painful process of writing must begin and end. When one puts pen to paper will influence what one can see and say. However, there is, of course, no ideal time to write up research. I make this point here to reaffirm this aspect of the subjective side of social science. The actual choice point is going to be influenced by social science judgments about quality and quantity of evidence and theoretical interpretation. That choice is also going to be bounded by pragmatic considerations about the sequencing of work and the requirements of funding bodies. Truth is indeed the daughter of time.

Comparative Method
and the Choice of Research Sites

There is an intentional or design component in the process of choosing and gaining access to research sites, but the practicalities of the process are best characterized by the phrase *planned opportunism.* From the perspective of the CCSC, one can identify a longer-term planning activity where the issue of the research strategy of the Centre is linked to matters of academic and practitioner relevance, funding strategies, and explicit network building to open up site options. At the level of short-term planning for individual research projects, there are clear decision rules that can be invoked to inform the choice of research sites. The short-term decision rules bound up with research design are dependent upon the success of the longer-term planning activity, and vice versa.

The selection of research sites is shaped by the choice of research topics and questions being posed, together with the language with which the research domain is expressed. In this sense, any longer-term planning is possible only insofar as a research area is fundable. Like it or not, funding decisions are very much a product of a jointly intellectual, social, and political process. Topic areas rise and fall in their academic and practitioner salience and relevance. In saying this I make no simple dichotomy between academic salience and practical relevance. The most jugular practical problems contain within them the most theoretically challenging research questions. Thus in Mrs. Thatcher's Britain it was no accident that our Centre featured the language of corporate strategy and change. Topic choice, funding, the selection of sites, and realizing access are all interconnected.

Another feature of long-term planning relates to the settings where it is hoped particular access will be sought. In which sectors, public or private, is the research to be pursued? Is the geographic focus to be the United Kingdom, Continental Western Europe, or the Pacific Basin? Relationships have to be built to underpin research topics that require new settings. Network building is a critical activity for any serious group of empirical researchers. Every research center needs a foreign policy that guides relationships with key stakeholders in the environments in which the center operates. Everyone working in a research center is a critical factor in the foreign policy. Research performance is a confluence of topic selection, intellectual creativity and surefootedness, entrepreneurial energy, the quality and nature of a center's networks, skill in negotiating access to critical sites, and a broad-based and well-executed dissemination strategy.

The short-term planning aspect of site selection is more easily linkable to what we call *research design*. Here again a judicious mixture of forethought and intention, chance, opportunism, and environmental preparedness plays its part. However, experience suggests that the decision rules elaborated below may help to guide choice.

1. Go for extreme situations, critical incidents, and social dramas.

The rationale here is straightforwardly pragmatic. If the phenomena to be observed have to be contained within a single or relatively small number of cases, then choose cases where the progress is *transparently observable*.

The point of studying a sequence of social dramas longitudinally is that they provide a transparent look at the growth, evolution, transformation, and conceivably decay of an organization over time. In an earlier publication, I noted that each drama provides a clear point of data collection, an important practical consideration in such an extended stream of time, events, people, and processes (Pettigrew 1979). Furthermore, each drama can act as an in-depth case study within the overall case study and thereby provide a dramatic glimpse into the current workings of the social system. The longi-tudinal study of a sequence of dramas allows varying readings to be taken of the development of the organization, of the impact of one drama on succes-sive and even consequent dramas, and of the kinds of mechanisms that lead to, accentuate, and regulate the impact of each drama.

As the point about mechanisms of transformations implies, dramas pro-vide consequence and meaning in relation to routines. The quality and analytic impact of the study of dramas can be only as good as the researcher's understanding of the relative routines with which each drama is interspersed. In this sense the routines provide the contextual backdrop for the foreground drama, and the researcher becomes interested in the interactive effect between context and foreground and the mechanisms and processes of transformation from routine to drama and new routine and further drama. Examining the dramas affords the researcher the opportunity to study continuous process. Thus in a study of a school, the focus on continuous process related to questions of organizational goals, their emergence and transformation, and to changes in systems of beliefs, power relationships, and culture (Pettigrew 1979).

Sometimes social dramas and the public inquiries they produce offer social scientists their first opportunity to look inside a previously shielded social system. Thus the bank rate scandal in Britain in 1957 and the published inquiry reports that followed it provided Wilson and Lupton (1959) with an opportunity to research and publish one of the first studies of the interlocking family connections and directorates in the City of London. Perrow (1984) was quick to use the Three Mile Island accident to develop thinking about disasters.

A variant of the critical case is the choice of a highly visible case. By and large, social scientists have not studied the elite and powerful groups in the societies where they practice their skills. Access to and publication of significant research results about an elite institution can have significant positive knock-on effects. The publication of the Imperial Chemical Industries study of strategic change (Pettigrew 1985a) has opened many doors for the CCSC.

Theoretical propositions may also guide the choice of research settings. Thus theoretical writing and empirical inquiry on organizational politics suggests a relationship between high levels of political activity and nonprogrammed innovative activity (Pettigrew 1973a, Hickson et al. 1986). If you want to observe politics in action, choose cases where there are consequential and structurally complex decisions being made.

2. Go for polar types.

If one is interested, as we are, in the links between the capability of firms to manage strategic and operational change and their relative competitive performance, then one needs to select sites that illustrate high and low performance. Measuring relative competitive performance is not a straightforward matter, but by treating competitiveness as a multilevel and dynamic phenomenon (Whipp, Rosenfeld, and Pettigrew 1989), one can structure site selection to pursue the research question one has in mind.

An important guideline for choosing polar types is to select cases that disconfirm patterns from early case studies. In a program of research driven initially by a strong series of hunches that in turn are reinforced by early data collection, a sound strategy is to build in space for later cases that can be used for purposes of disconfirmation. Chains of evidence should be challenged by chains of possible falsification (see, for example, Yin 1984, Whipp, Pettigrew, and Sparrow 1989).

3. Go for high experience levels of the phenomena under study.

The pragmatic logic here is similar to that which is explained under the extreme situation decision rule above, though there is not the implication of any necessary transparent drama suddenly revealing a social system. The site selection of our human resources work and our AIDS research is guided by this decision rule. Thus in the human resources work we have chosen longitudinal cases where there is evidence of recent business environment and business strategy change occasioning some degree of concern for and activity in changing human resource and practices. In the AIDS research, where the phenomenon under study did not exist as an organizational fact in the United Kingdom until 1983, we are choosing research sites where there is experience of hospital-based services, community-based services, or health promotion activity.

4. Go for more informed choice of sites and
increase the probabilities of negotiating access.

This last suggestion is not so much a decision rule as a general tactical recommendation that we have developed by learning from doing. Faced with the situation where one wishes to focus on a particular industry sector, where there is a requirement to choose sites that meet one or another of the three decision rules mentioned above, and where one needs the kind of intensive access necessary for longitudinal work, do a low-cost study of the key players in the sector first. In the British context, where there are strongly established norms about privacy, it is easier to "cold call" firms for two or three 1½-hour interviews than it is to persuade firms to grant long-term access. A low-cost survey of the key players in a sector can provide researchers with an empirically formed view of the problems, prospects, and a range of experiences in a sector. Early publications at the sector level of analysis may then result. The low-cost survey may also help to establish a network of relationships in a sector fairly quickly, and may allow more informed choices to be made about sites on the basis of theoretical ideas and empirical trends. Finally and crucially, in our experience the survey has dramatically increased the success rate in negotiating access into preferred longitudinal sites.

The other critical practical consideration that stands alongside the choice of sites is, How many sites? Again, there is no absolute answer to this question. An *n* of 1 can be adequate if the treatment of the case material is sufficiently generic (see Miller and Friesen 1982, p. 1016, for a development of this point) or if the quality and nature of the findings are suitably unique or in other ways strong. In our experience, reasonably high standards of input and output can be sustained if each experienced full-time researcher conducts no more than four to six cases over a three-year period. There can be some flexing of these numbers and standards if distinctions are made between major (intensive) cases and minor (less intensive) cases. The significant loss on the minor cases compared with the major ones will be a weakening of data richness and interpretation of how and why the change occurs (the process and the contexts), while there may be approximate equivalence of standards on what (content) change occurred.

Observation and Verification—
Issues of Data Collection and Degree of Involvement

Skill in the field is critical to the success of any endeavor based on the longitudinal comparative case study method. Yin (1984) and others have commented on some of the kinds of skills required of good fieldworkers. These include asking and interpreting apposite questions, listening, being adaptive and flexible, being knowingly unbiased, and having a firm grasp of the issues being studied. In addition to these requirements, the long-distance fieldworker needs the social and political skills to develop and maintain credibility with a wide range of respondents from different levels and functions inside and outside the focal organization, and in the case of the Centre's work, the skills to run research-in-action workshops (discussed later).

This is clearly too big a subject to dwell on here. I can only highlight some of the key features of our data-collection procedures. General issues of fieldwork in case study research have been adequately dealt with by Van Maanen (1983, 1988), Yin (1984), and Burgess (1984).

Our aims are to collect data that are *processual* (an emphasis on action as well as structure over time), *comparative* (a range of studies in various sectors), *pluralist* (describe and analyze the often competing versions of reality seen by actors in change processes), *historical* (take into account the historical evolution of ideas and actions for change as well as the constraints within which decision makers operate), and *contextual* (examine the reciprocal relations between processes and contexts at different levels of analysis). This means producing case studies and not just case histories—going beyond chronology to develop analytic themes. It also means collecting data at different levels of analysis (demonstrating how actors mobilize features of economic and sectoral contexts to legitimate or delegitimate ideas for change and continuity at organizational levels).

What does this imply for fieldwork? A triangulated methodology is used to gather different types of data that can be used as cross-checks. The aim of the triangulated approach is to draw on the particular and different strengths of various data-collection methods. Interviews can provide depth, subtlety, and personal feeling. Interviews may also be staged occasions where feeling and evocation are high and factual detail low. Documents can provide facts but are subject to dangers of selective deposit and survival. Direct observation provides access to group processes and can confront the researcher with discrepancies between what people have said in interviews and casual conversations and what they actually do. Crucially, data collection is concerned with observation and verification, and in longitudinal field studies these are iterative processes. One observes, follows themes and trails, identifies patterns, has those patterns disconfirmed or verified by further data, and the process moves on.

Thus, for example, in our health service work (McKee and Pettigrew 1988a) this can involve the following:

- *In-depth interviews with key informants:* Informants are selected because of their lead positions in the organization or in the change process under analysis; they include those affected by the changes as well as the initiators of change and come from different elites and interest groups internal and external to the focal organization (on average, 50 interviews per case). Interviews are tape-recorded. Interview pro formas are discussed in each research team, tested in the field, and then modified as appropriate.

- *Documentary and archive data:* These data include the minutes of relevant meetings, strategy and policy documents, and secondary quantitative material on activity levels, deaths, and discharges, as well as memos and correspondence.

- *Observational and ethnographic material:* This material includes observations made during attendance at formal meetings and planned site visits to meet staff and visit facilities, as well as informal, chance meetings, conversations, and extensive time spent living and working within the organization.

Fieldwork can involve two or three days a week over a five-month period, with intermittent contact thereafter. The balance among the three sources of data mentioned above varies from project to project. In terms of the sequencing of data collection, the pattern is for the *what* of change, the chronology to be established first, often using archival data and interviews; and then further interviewing, observation, secondary data collection, and informal questioning to reveal the *how* and *why* of changes, drawing on variables at different levels of analysis.

At this stage in the Centre's development we have not found it desirable or necessary to create standardized decision rules to inform the compilation of different data sets. The Centre maintains standards by requiring researchers to collect different forms of data and by testing interpretations in project meetings, early case study writing, and ultimately by presentations made to respondents in research-in-action workshops and academic gatherings. Research is a craft process conducted by professionals with varying backgrounds and experience, and a wise manager seeking commitment respects differences in personal work styles and balance in using data sources within a climate where such differences are openly discussable and their consequences revealed.

Managing the degree of involvement with the research site is a crucial issue for any field researcher. It is also an important area for strategic clarity for a research center. If you are working with a system for three years, you cannot play the role of the brusque, detached scientist. Research is a social process, not just a technical task. Equally, one should not become overinvolved and "go native." Researchers are in the perspective business. They must seek and listen to different versions of reality. Individuals in senior management may be able to intellectualize their actions in a language and style most comfortable to management researchers, but those on the receiving end of a major business or health care change have the power of feelings behind what may seem a less articulate and conceptual presentation. The researcher has the privilege and benefit of listening to all sides of a drama. With that privilege comes the scientific and ethical responsibility to present all significant views before offering the researcher's perspective.

The fact that we work in three-person project teams and meet regularly as project teams and as a center helps enormously to balance detachment and involvement and to inhibit tendencies to overidentify with particular interpretations or interests. Our comparative methodology also helps us to achieve perspective on individual case studies.

Research is also a reciprocal activity. People engage in it for a variety of motives. Time spent clarifying motives and expectations at the front-end process of negotiating access can save heartache and friction later. We have a standard "contract" about entry that is explicitly reciprocal. We have access to study the topic we define, and all publications are shown to the organization prior to publication. Respondents have an opportunity to correct errors of fact and to ensure we do not divulge commercially sensitive information. Editorial control remains with the research team. In fact, the process is not as stark as that. Practices vary from researcher to researcher at the Centre, but wiser souls manage the release of interpretations toward the end of the research process so that final case study reports do not inflict massive surprise on respondents.

One mechanism we offer as reciprocity for access is a research-in-action workshop. Each workshop is designed to meet the particular requirements of a given case, but by and large each involves presenting a full case study report to key power figures prior to the workshop, preparing an executive summary before the workshop for all the workshop participants, and running a one-day interactive feedback workshop for 10 to 15 key people in the organization during which an analysis of the past and present development of the organization is explicitly linked to the future strategic concerns of that organization.

The workshops offer important opportunities for further data collection precisely when the research team feels confident about identifying and presenting patterns in the process under analysis. New facts may spin out of these occasions. If the participants are carefully chosen with pluralism in mind, a charged situation may develop, and new interpretations may flow from the dynamics of the meeting. But the real value of such occasions, from an observation and verification standpoint, derives from the level of discourse they stimulate. Looking at archival material, one may see elements of fact and interpretation. Conducting interviews, one can probe beyond the what of change and get into the subtleties of why and how. In a workshop situation, reviewing facts, interpretation, and overall patterns in the process, there is an interactive dialogue at a richer and higher level than is normally possibly from data gathering with individual respondents. This richer mixture can add considerably to the iterative process of observation, verification, and validation at this later stage in the process of discovery.

Caution, however, must be taken not to conduct these workshops too early, for doing so may have obtrusive effects on subsequent actions and responses of organizational participants who are influenced by the researchers' perspective and framework at these workshops. Even descriptive reports that, for example, describe the sequence of events the researchers have observed to occur (with minimal interpretation or analysis) can have an impact in reconstructing a new or revised social reality for organizational participants. However, the trade-offs for this and other possible "Hawthorne effects" are significant gains of achieving validation and new data, deepening understanding of changes, and achieving a broader pluralistic perspective. The workshops are also an important arena for the personal development of Centre staff.

Research Outputs, Audience, and Presentation

Researchers experienced in comparative case study research (e.g., Glaser and Strauss 1967, Strauss 1987, Van de Ven, Angle, and Poole 1989) all emphasize the iterative and at times untidy character of the research process. The research may begin with only a broad definition of the research problem that is sharpened by a complex and evolving mixture of literature analysis; data collection; internal discussion and memo writing among the research team; the uncovering of themes, patterns, and propositions; followed by more data collection and more polished and structured thematic writing, as cross-case analysis occurs. Our approach to field research acknowledges such activities and processes. Indeed, they will be explored further below. Here, however, I want to point to the role of research outputs, audience, and presentation in the inductive process of moving from field observations to more abstract and general theories. However, clarifying research outputs is not just a technical requirement to aid the process of moving from the

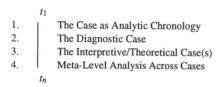

Figure 4.1. Varieties of Research Output From Longitudinal Comparative Case Study Work

particular to the general. Being specific about the form and audience for research outputs is also a crucial part of the social process of motivating research staff and respondents through extended periods of data collection and analysis.

The obvious may be stated at the outset. Researchers need to be clear about the *varieties* of research output achievable within their mode of operation, the *sequencing* with which those outputs are deliverable over time, the *audiences* for which the outputs are intended, and the most suitable form of *presentation* for each audience.

Figure 4.1 sets out some of the varieties of research output possible from longitudinal comparative case study work. It also suggests through the vertical line running from time t_1 to t_n what forms of output may be deliverable at what points in time in the research process.

Clarifying the nature of research output in an interdisciplinary research center using longitudinal comparative case study research is a nontrivial issue. Conducting longitudinal field research can be an arduous task for researchers and host organizations. For the researcher, motivation can seep away as the volume of inputs increases and the delayed gratification of outputs recedes ever into the future. Achieving successful outputs of the 1 and 2 variety is a very important motivational consideration along the way to the "higher-level" outputs implied in varieties 3 and 4.

But what are these four levels of output? Level 1 refers to the case as an analytic chronology. The requirement here is to lay out the narrative, to tell the story, but to tell the story across levels of analysis. So the story of Jaguar Cars between 1960 and 1988 is interwoven with the corresponding development of the European and world auto industry and the changing fortunes of the U.K. economy and political scene over the same period. Throughout the presentation there is an explicit attempt to interpret and explain the changing competitive performance of Jaguar Cars in terms of features of the inner context of the focal firm as well as changes in the outer context of Jaguar Cars. An analytic chronology is more like Strauss's (1987) case study than his case history. The case history is characterized by temporal presentation.

The case study features "analytic abstractions for purposes of presenting theory" (Strauss 1987, p. 218). Our analytic chronologies reach toward theory presentation but are prepared to get on top of the data, to clarify sequences across levels of analysis, suggest causal linkages between levels, and establish early analytic themes. Such case studies are a psychological marker of progress and a necessary prelude to the cross-case analysis and more explicit pattern formation that follows.

The diagnostic cases are produced for the research-in-action workshops with our case study firms. These cases contain all of the features of the analytic chronologies, but in addition contain a listing and analysis of the organization's current strategic concerns. Such diagnostic cases also assist the iterative process of inductive pattern generation and theory building. The strategic concerns identified and discussed at the workshops have an implied prescriptive tone, but they are obviously closely linked back to the patterns in the data. The discipline of producing an executive summary of these diagnostic cases also forces closure in the pattern recognition process much in the same way as Strauss's (1987) description of using memos between members of his research team.

Interpretive theoretical cases move the analysis and writing beyond the analytic chronologies. There is now a more explicit attempt to interpret the narrative but also to link emerging conceptual and theoretical ideas inductively derived from the case to both stronger analytic themes within the case and wider theoretical debates in the literature. A further twist is given to the generalizing process by linking the empirical findings in the case to other published empirical data. Published examples of level 3 and 4 outputs in our work include Sparrow and Pettigrew (1988c), Whipp, Rosenfeld, and Pettigrew (1989), Ferlie and Pettigrew (1990), Rosenfeld, Whipp, and Pettigrew (1989), and Hendry, Pettigrew, and Sparrow (1989).

Level 4 outputs involve cross-case analysis. The goal is broad thematic presentation, linking the theoretical and empirical findings across cases to wider bodies of literature. In some of our writing—for example, the book reporting our findings on competitiveness and strategic change (Pettigrew and Whipp 1990)—there is no attempt to preserve case integrity. The chapters of the competitiveness book are organized entirely around major concepts and themes, such as environmental assessment and coherence. The case study appears only to illustrate and draw out the subtleties of broad themes and theoretical developments. In our other book-length publications, mini-cases are interwoven with thematic presentation (e.g., Pettigrew, Hendry, and Sparrow 1989), whereas in our health care research on change, comparative case study chapters are linked to chapters that are more explicitly thematic and conceptual in character (Pettigrew, Ferlie, and McKee 1992).

Thus far the pattern in the Centre is for level 1 outputs to be written for ourselves as part of the process of sharing, learning, and pattern recognition.

Shortened versions of level 1 outputs have been produced for practitioner journals. See, for example, the *Personnel Management* series featuring our human resources work (Hendry and Pettigrew 1987, Sparrow and Pettigrew 1988a, 1988b) as well as our series on health care change published in the *Health Service Journal* (Pettigrew, McKee, and Ferlie 1989, McKee and Pettigrew 1988b, Ferlie and Pettigrew 1988). Here we have learned that publishing a series of short articles in the same widely read practitioner journal can have a significantly greater impact than spreading case writing around a series of journals. Level 3 and 4 outputs can be produced only alongside other research demands into the second and third year of a three-year project. The major meta-level publications are to be in book form and will appear in the fourth and subsequent years.

In this section I have emphasized the role of different research outputs in assisting the inductive process of pattern recognition and theory building. I now turn to discussion of the final implementation issue to be addressed, the routes to reality and structured understanding in longitudinal comparative case study work.

Routes to Reality and Structured Understanding

Anyone who has carried out longitudinal field research or who has worked in an interdisciplinary team using the comparative case study method, or who has tried to assist doctoral students through such a research process, will know that the central problem is dealing with complexity; first of all, capturing the complexities of the real world, and then making sense of it. For some there is no release from the overwhelming weight of information, from the task of structuring and clarifying, from the requirement for inductive conceptualization. The result is death by data asphyxiation—the slow and inexorable sinking into the swimming pool that started so cool, clear, and inviting and now has become a clinging mass of maple syrup.

Rather than dwelling on the causes of complexity, or the process that leads to the overwhelming of the researcher by data, I shall use this section of the chapter to highlight some of the pathways for avoiding data asphyxiation. I call these routes to reality and structured understanding and offer them as a source of encouragement for scholars prepared to take the risk of conducting longitudinal and comparative field research in organizational settings. Many of the routes have been implicitly mentioned earlier in the chapter; I collect them together here to provide summary emphasis.

Before listing and discussing some of the routes to structured understanding consciously used at the CCSC, however, I need to offer a general characterization of the overall process of capturing and making sense of the complexities of longitudinal comparative case study data. Elements of the process have been described by other authors. Van Maanen (1988) denotes a process of searching for rich and complex descriptions, building them up using the skills of an investigative detective and then ordering and presenting ideas in a finely honed narrative. Strauss (1987) is also concerned with capturing complex descriptions, but he is more explicit than Van Maanen (1988) in how this is to be carried out. Like Huberman and Miles (1983), Strauss (1987) is particularly strong on the operational elements of simplifying complex data through techniques of data reduction and display, but as a consequence Strauss underplays the importance of some of the more strategic elements of the process, such as making explicit the researcher's meta-analytic framework and the character of generic propositions being sought. I will now discuss some of these more strategic elements.

The overall process of capturing a complex reality and structuring it involves cycles of expanding complexity and simplification. Periods of increasing complexity and openness are necessary to gain appreciation of the richness of the subject matter being investigated. However, the tension produced by such complexity requires periods of reduction and simplification that in turn require further verification through more data collection and then additional simplification through framework building and pattern recognition. The recent reporting of the Minnesota Innovation Research Program (Van de Ven, Angle, and Poole 1989) confirms the Centre's overall characterization of the iterative process of structured understanding of longitudinal field research.

Table 4.1 lists some of the routes to structured understanding that researchers at the CCSC have consciously used. This list of 10 routes is by no means complete, and I invite all colleagues to add to it from their "learning by doing." As the list is incomplete, it may also be idiosyncratic—research is after all a craft activity, the merging of skills, knowledge, and the person around an intellectual problem. However, the list also has a systemic and generalizable quality about it—the categories are sufficiently broad to be capable of interpretation and application to many particular situations. Crucially, the list covers many of the key activities in the research process—from objectives, the fundamentals of the front end of the process, to outputs, the goal of attempts at discovery. I belabor this point about the scope of the list to emphasize that the problems of data overload and the requirement for structured understanding are not reducible just to questions of data reduction and display (Huberman and Miles 1983). Operational elements such as clarity about unit of analysis, coming to terms with time, identifying analytic themes, and techniques of data reduction and display are important. However, success in such operational matters will also be conditional on attention to more strategic considerations, such as clarity of research goals, explicitness of the researcher's theory of method, meta-level analytic framework and generic propositions, and the varieties and sequencing of research output.

TABLE 4.1. Some Routes to Structured Understanding in Longitudinal and Comparative Field Research

---

1. Being clear about research objectives
   Building on strengths
   Awareness of limitations
2. Being clear about the unit of analysis and study questions
3. Coming to terms with time
4. Making explicit one's theory of method
5. Making explicit one's meta-level analytic framework
6. Making explicit the character of the generic propositions one is seeking
7. Identifying analytic themes that cut across the data
8. Using techniques of data reduction and display
9. Making prescriptive statements as an aid to analytic generalization
10. Making explicit the varieties and sequencing of research output

---

Being clear about research objectives is crucial for any social scientist. Such goals include the following:

1. precision of measurement

2. generality over actors and situations

3. realism of context

4. theoretical and conceptual development

5. contribution to particular and general questions of policy and practice

Given the limited character of our knowledge of change in organizational settings, and in particular how so much change research is acontextual, ahistorical, and aprocessual (Pettigrew 1985a, 1987a, 1987b), the time is ripe for intensive and contextually sensitive studies of changing. We thus give primacy to realism of context and theoretical and conceptual development as research goals, and by the very nature of the research process we engage in and the kinds of data we collect, thereby create some of the circumstances to pose and answer questions of policy and practice. Given that the contextualist explicitly works toward goals 3, 4, and 5, research of a contextualist character should be evaluated principally around those three criteria. The emphasis given to goals 3, 4, and 5 does not, of course, preclude the use of measurement; indeed, the generation of apposite measures—that is, measures invented and sensitively linked to the subtleties and nuances of a particular context or contexts—is an important consideration for the style of research described here.

Having clear research goals and recognizing the strengths and limitations of one's preferred research approach is one way of setting a strategic framework around research. Strategic focus also derives from explicitness about theory of method and meta-level analytic framework. Our contextualist theory of method has been stated in earlier work (e.g., Pettigrew 1985b, 1985d) and has been further elaborated previously in this chapter. Our meta-level analytic framework—the exploration of change through time by means of the interconnected analysis of contexts, content, and process—is the critical basis for intellectual coherence in the Centre. The framework offers analytic structure at a broad level but no overrestrictive theoretical web, and plenty of space to adjust research designs and study questions as researchers move from one content area of change to another. Furthermore, it provides intellectual space for teams of talented interdisciplinary researchers.

Focused understanding at a strategic level also emanates from the generic propositions guiding the research. Our generic propositions are deduced from our meta-level analytic framework. In the dialogue between researcher and researcher over the development of analytic themes and general propositions, requests for prescriptive statements may help simplification. If, for example, the intellectual task is to begin to specify the characteristics of so-called receptive and nonreceptive contexts for change, researchers may clarify the variables at play by asking, What features of intraorganizational context would one have to change in order to increase or decrease the degree of change receptivity in that particular setting?

Finally and crucially, strategic focus is provided on particular research projects, and indeed across the work of an interdisciplinary research center, through the researchers' explicitness about the varieties and sequencing of research output. This has already been discussed in detail elsewhere in this chapter. Our goal is to produce meta-level articles and books that are strong on empirical patterning across cases and on theoretical elaboration, but we know we cannot go from chronology to meta-level analytic writing in one leap. Indeed, carefully sequenced additive writing is a crucial part of the iterative inductive and deductive process described in this chapter.

Turning to more operational mechanisms for structuring understanding, I again refer to the exceptionally clear and pragmatic writing on this topic found in Huberman and Miles (1983), Miles and Huberman (1984), and Strauss (1987). Techniques of data reduction and display are crucial mechanisms for structuring and thereby simplifying data. Pattern reduction is a critical intellectual process for all engaged in longitudinal comparative case study work.

Of course, pattern reduction is not just something that occurs during and after data collection. As I have emphasized, no qualitative researcher starts with his or her mind a blank, waiting for it to be filled with evidence. In our view, comparative case study work does not rely on induction alone. A crucial link between the deductive element of specifying theories of method, meta-level analytic framework, and the character of generic propositions and the inductive elements of data reduction, display, and theoretical elaboration is the creation and use of the interview pro forma.

We use pro formas, flowcharts of chronology, matrices, graphs, tables, lists of factors with assessments of relative importance—all the unexceptional sorting and classifying tools of a researcher. A key feature of Strauss's (1987) craft is the use of intrateam memos, both to suggest early interpretations of chronology and to point to emerging conceptual frameworks and draw together theoretical ideas. We use a similar approach. Pro formas are explicitly linked to the starting meta-level analytic framework. They are operationalized through team discussion and debate, and are tested and refined in the field in early data collection. Such pro formas would operationalize the context, content, process framework and link it to the specific themes of that study. Care would be taken to verify "what"-level information, by this stage probably established from archival analysis, but to move out from the what or chronology of change to begin to build up a picture of the why and how of change. For the interested reader, some of the detail of one of our pro formas is published in Pettigrew, Whipp, and Rosenfeld (1989).

LESSONS FOR FUTURE
LONGITUDINAL RESEARCH ON CHANGE

Longitudinal research in the social sciences has always been a minority taste. In the particular field of organization analysis, by and large academic careers have not accommodated processual research on the what, why, and how of organizations in action.

However, there has been some charting of longitudinal strategies in the social sciences. Encouraged by the then (British) Social Science Research Council, Wall and Williams (1970) have offered a useful review of the literature up to the late 1960s. More recently, Goldstein (1979) and then Tuma and Hannan (1984) have set out some of the theoretical and practical problems of conducting longitudinal studies of development and change. In the narrower fields of organizational analysis and business strategy, the reviews by Kimberly (1976) and Miller and Friesen (1982) have also proved useful, as has the work of Boruch and Pearson (1988) on longitudinal surveys.

Although published longitudinal research in organizations is still unusual, such research appears to be increasing, and there is variety in what is being studied and how it is being carried out and reported. Empirically, the 1980s brought us time-series studies of processes of strategic change (Pettigrew 1985a, Edstrom 1986, Johnson 1987, Child and Smith 1987). Whipp and

Clark (1986) have produced longitudinal studies of the design innovation process. Topics such as ideologies (Engwall 1985), decision making (Lucas 1987), political processes (Feldman 1987), and organizational structure and strategy (Mintzberg and Walters 1982) have all attracted longitudinal research. Although the above-reported studies have tended to use single or comparative case studies, often using historical or historical and real-time data, other studies have used repeated surveys (Brousseau 1978) and quasi-experiments (Wall et al. 1986).

In among this encouraging diversity of work, this chapter has drawn out some of the learning from a major program of research on change using longitudinal comparative case studies. I have emphasized here the need to conceptualize the research process accurately and realistically. I have portrayed research as an iterative process involving phases of observation, induction, deduction, verification, and further observation. Complexity reduction has been portrayed as a multilayered process, a question of clarifying overall research goals, units of analysis, and study questions. But deeper than that, intellectual clarity and explicitness about theory of method are necessary, together with making available a meta-level analytic framework to guide the research. Finally, attention should be devoted to the importance of time in longitudinal research, the decision rules that inform our choice of research sites, how and why we structure research outputs, and some of the methods of data reduction and display used in our research.

There are two final and crucial practical issues to signal where lessons may be learned from our experience. The first relates to ethical considerations in conducting longitudinal field research; second are the managerial considerations involved in leading a community of researchers.

Ethical Considerations

More than 40 years ago, in a paper titled "The Strengths of Industrial Sociology," George Homans (1949) wrote that "people who write about methodology often forget that it is a matter of strategy, not of morals. There are neither good nor bad methods but only methods that are more or less effective under particular circumstances in reaching objectives on the way to a distant goal" (p. 330). Homans is, of course, quite right in one respect: The choice of methodology is contingent on the problems and questions under study and the state of development of any body of knowledge. Choices will also be bounded by budget and time constraints, the vagaries of site selection, and individual differences between members of a research team and the individuals in research sites to whom they have to relate. Although I doubt Homans ever meant to imply as such, it would be wrong to suggest that the contingent and strategic aspect of choice of method indicates that such choices are amoral. There are many ethical considerations posed by the kind of fieldwork advocated in this chapter. These ethical questions relate particularly to the front end of the research—how expectations and contracts are set between the grant-awarding body and researchers, among researchers, and between researchers and respondents. There are also major ethical issues raised by the gathering and use of highly sensitive information about long-term processes of strategic choice and change.

Searching for lessons from experience cannot be just a strategic or tactical exercise. But neither should one be drawn into the kind of moral imperatives Homans may have been trying to avoid. A theme of this chapter has been that research is a craft activity; it is not just the application of a formal set of techniques and rules. A craft activity involves the application of skills, knowledge, and the person in varying settings. Within these settings, individual judgments are made in the context of a wider system of collective rules and communication. Even if the methods advocated in this chapter had all been codified and written down (and there is much productive work to be done in that direction), craft skills would still be required to interpret and apply such codifications according to the particular nuances and subtleties of each research project and site. Strauss (1987) is very clear on this: There are no simple general rules that can be applied in a standardized fashion.

Researchers are clearly engaged in a craft process with ethical requirements. They are also in the perspective business. Given that we have contextually deep and longitudinally rich data from our research sites, we try to negotiate the right to use the proper names of our host organizations. Individuals' names have been used in research publications, but we also preserve the anonymity of respondents through the use of pseudonyms. There have been occasions when the future intentions of individuals have been edited out of publications to protect their career interests. However, as I have attempted to show in previous work (Pettigrew 1973a, 1985a), being in the perspective business does not imply producing sanitized accounts of decision-making or change processes. The moral basis of what we do is linked to key issues such as free choice of participation for all respondents, respect for all persons and points of view, clear contracting at the front end of research assignments, and an open and reciprocal relationship between the researchers and their host organizations.

Reciprocity is a guiding factor in our work. Social scientists have no insuperable right to be granted access to any institution or anyone in it. Longitudinal research makes great demands on a research team; it may make greater demands on the host organization. Offering to reciprocate for access by running a research-in-action workshop is not only a sound instrumental act that can increase researchers' probabilities of entry and a wise technical way for researchers to test the validity of their interpretations, it is also a clear sign of respect that researchers can make toward their new partners. We are open and clear about reciprocity when we contract with our host organizations. We also make explicit agreements about publication, confidentiality, and consent of participation.

All publications are forwarded to the host research organization prior to publication. This is to ensure that we do not make factual errors or divulge information of commercial value to competitors. We are also careful to respect information that has been passed to us for background understanding and with the proviso that it may not be used publicly in an attributable or nonattributable fashion. We listen to and respect comments that may disagree with our interpretations of events, but retain editorial control. Even with the high-level and often highly sensitive information that we have and often seek to publish, there have been few cases of major disagreements over interpretation. This is because we rarely surprise host organizations with contentious material, but release and discuss interpretations as they are being fashioned.

Confidentiality is an important issue within the Centre. All duplicate research materials are stored in a central and locked location. These data are made available only to members of the research team on the particular project from which the data are derived. Requests for access beyond the original research team are considered on a case-by-case basis. On one occasion, tape-recorded interviews were made available to a researcher employed by one of our host organizations to prepare a business history of that firm. Tapes were made available only after consent was given by the individual respondents involved, and the tapes were retained on the Centre premises for scrutiny by the business historian concerned.

Informed consent is, of course, a multilayered moral issue. Consent for access is negotiated in relation to a particular set of expectations. However, individuals can and should have rights of noncooperation with our research teams. This is respected. Much of our interview material is tape-recorded, and this is obviously done only with consent. Practices vary, but some of our research staff make it absolutely clear the respondent is in control of the tape recorder and may turn it off at any time. For some of our respondents, no such prompting is necessary.

Managing a Community of Researchers

Finally, I turn to some of the issues that arise in managing a community of researchers. Here the reader may detect tentativeness, not only because of the natural dangers of abstracting lessons from one research center located in the particular academic culture of a U.K. university business school, but also because so little seems to have been written by other researchers on this topic. One of the few papers I could find tangentially relevant to the theme of managing a community of researchers is by Angle and Hudson (1986). This paper reports data from the research group on the Minnesota Innovation Research Program and deals rather more with the motives for academics joining collective research endeavors than with the problems of managing those who elect to join.

Having expressed such tentativeness, I would like to raise six issues: leadership and coherence, standard setting and productivity, team building, motivation and rewards, personal development, and the need for a research center to have an effective foreign policy.

But a word or two about the structure and financial base of the CCSC to put these six issues into context. The Centre is a freestanding research organization within Warwick Business School, University of Warwick. The director of the Centre is a professor within the Warwick Business School and is the only permanent tenured member of the Centre. The other professional staff are all experienced academics, and most have Ph.D.s. The professional staff are on two- and three-year contracts. The most senior staff have rolling contracts that extend beyond their initial appointments, but would be terminated eventually if the Centre got into financial difficulties. The Centre receives no direct financial assistance from the university and has to generate all its financial requirements from research grants, contracts, and other forms of sponsorship. The CCSC generated £2.5 million between 1985 and 1990, and as of 1990 was composed of a group of 10 professional and 2 administrative/secretarial staff.

Leadership and coherence are critical requirements for most organizations. They are especially important for an interdisciplinary research center in the social sciences that has to generate and maintain a strong funding base. Central to the issue of coherence is the existence of an academically strong and policy-relevant research idea (in our case, the study of corporate strategy and change), together with a product champion for that idea. As I have argued elsewhere (Pettigrew 1987a, 1987b, 1987c), strategic change cannot be effectively studied bounded by the myopias of any particular discipline. The Centre, therefore, has recruited individuals with doctorates in organizational analysis, modern history, social policy, sociology, and psychology. But with an interdisciplinary topic and a multidisciplinary team, incoherence beckons. Here we have found our meta-level analytic framework to be crucial. The context-context-process framework offers a guiding general outline for our work that can be used to study different content areas of change in a theoretically nonrestrictive manner. With elements of a common language, and bringing the strengths of particular disciplinary backgrounds, small teams of individuals can operationalize, fashion, and develop our meta-level framework according to the intellectual themes and organization settings of different empirical projects.

The size of a research center obviously has impacts on leadership and coherence. The Centre staff have discussed this issue, and our prevailing view is that once an interdisciplinary group grows beyond 12 or 15 professional staff, subgroup formation may well begin to weaken overall teamwork and collective consciousness. A group of 15 also implies more projects and a greater distancing of the director from individual sites and project work, and ever greater pressures in the spheres of fund-raising and administration. One way of dealing with the administrative problem is to provide greater administrative support to the director (now a requirement for all large Economic and Social Research Council centers in the United Kingdom). At the CCSC we have decided to deal with the likely problems of size by keeping our group within the 10- to 12-person range.

Managing a balance between intellectual diversity and coherence is one thing; blending in different personalities and styles is another. This potential problem may be managed by ensuring that team members help to recruit their colleagues, and by giving each project team space to develop its own modus operandi at the early stages of new projects. Because individuals become very dependent on one another for the success of individual projects, selection decisions are critical. We know that skills of inductive conceptualism are critical in case study work, but so are writing skills of a high order. However, fieldwork will not be completed without equivalent social and political skills, and these requirements have to be blended in to provide complementary assets across a project team and a research center. It may be obvious, but selection decisions are pervasively important.

Standard setting is a task for all the senior members of the Centre. They are the role models for others and, through quiet and sensitive watching, as well as through joint fieldwork assignments, senior members of staff can provide clarity about expectations and behavior. Best practices about how to write a case study, how to negotiate access, or how to preserve academic freedom while reflecting the concerns of respondents are discussed explicitly in Centre meetings and in bilateral conversations. Standards concerning quantity and quality of research output are influenced by many interested parties. The director's role is to create a culture of high performance where individuals recognize, identify, and are rewarded for success. This can be done through public recognition of successes and through formal processes of promotion.

Team building is easier where the leader can choose his or her own team and where the pattern of everyday work requires team effort. However, as we all know, teams do not necessarily always develop out of the settings that demand them. Team building is a subtle and changing issue and hard to articulate briefly. We encourage team building in the Centre and project team levels and find these two levels of team working need one another. Project teams do develop their own modi operandi and create their own space and successes. This, in a Centre of our size, assists rather than detracts from an overall sense of identity with the larger Centre team. However, we have regular meetings, social gatherings, and joint centerwide conferences that all build and maintain a sense of teamwork. We have also found that two of our Centre secretaries have played an invaluable role in binding the Centre together, and this role has been recognized and encouraged.

The motivational calculus in a research center emanates from the framework and context provided by the elements discussed above. Intellectual creativity is aided by identification with a clear and broad research idea and an analytic structure that helps to operationalize that idea. If the research idea is being successfully championed in and outside the university, and at least partially self-selected teams can see their contributions linked to those successes, there is a productive context to build on. Possible drains on motivation and energy in a center devoted to longitudinal research are the long process of data collection and the possible delays in publication, with their consequential effects on academic career advancements. This problem has been discussed and managed in the Centre in three ways: first, by clarifying a range of outputs from longitudinal research linked to what can be realistically produced at different phases of the work; second, by demonstrating that sound academic and practitioner publications can be delivered during and not just at the end of longitudinal work; and third, by agreeing and arranging that more junior research staff get primacy in dual- or multiple-authorship situations during the research contract, while principal investigators get their rewards in publications toward the end of the project life cycle.

Explicit attention has been given in the Centre to the personal development of staff. For some this has meant extending their role into entrepreneurial and project management tasks. For others it has meant working on two or more related projects at the same time. For some staff, personal development has meant promotion inside and outside the university. Presentational skills have been a key focus for personal development. The Centre's program of conferences and research-in-action workshops have been a demanding and confidence-building source of personal development for all Centre staff.

Finally, no research center can survive and flourish without a permeable boundary and an effectively implemented "foreign policy" to manage relationships across that boundary. The director's role here is critical; he or she must serve as fund-raiser, network builder, listener, and marketer of the center's services. But environmental assessment and action have to be collective endeavors, explicit and welcome parts of everyone's role. This is accepted in the Centre. Everyone in the Centre has grown up in an academic generation in the United Kingdom where quality, relevance, mutuality, and self-sufficiency have become rising values and necessary prerequisites of success. But exhortation and acceptance of rising values are not sufficient. Operationally, our "foreign policy" involves creating a senior advisory board of academics and policy makers, a consortium of 10 organizations to provide financial support for the Centre over a five-year period, plus designated liaison roles for each Centre staff member with specified organizations. But as we all know, no customer service strategy can rely entirely on selling. Ultimately, success depends on the delivery of outputs respected by the key stakeholders in the Centre's environment. That means working with, and indeed helping to create, the many and varied standards faced by academic research centers in the management field in the late 1980s and the 1990s. In that process the quality of human talent available is paramount. But if the necessary conditions for an effective management research center are likely to involve a judicious mixture of a strong research idea, a talented staff, leadership and coherence, and sound organization, high on the list of sufficient conditions must be the energy and commitment of the whole team.

Acknowledgments

This is a shortened and modified version of a paper presented to the National Science Foundation Conference on Longitudinal Research Methods for Studying Organizational Processes, Austin, Texas, September 1988. I am grateful to Chris Bennett of the CCSC for his assistance in compiling elements of the literature for the paper, and to my other Centre colleagues Lorna McKee, Paul Sparrow, and Richard Whipp for their helpful comments on earlier drafts. I would also like to acknowledge the thoughtful criticisms of Andrew Van de Ven and the anonymous reviewers of earlier versions of this chapter.

References

Abbott, A. (1990), "A Primer on Sequence Methods," *Organization Science,* 1, 375-392.
Angle, H. L., and R. L. Hudson (1986), *The Minnesota Innovation Research Program: Collective Action in an Individualist Culture?* (Discussion Paper 57, Strategic Management Research Centre), Minneapolis: University of Minnesota.
Berg, P. O. (1979), *Emotional Structures in Organizations: A Study of the Process of Change in a Swedish Company,* Lund: Student Literature.
Boruch, R. F., and R. W. Pearson (1988), "Assessing the Quality of Longitudinal Surveys," *Evaluation Review,* 12, 3-58.
Brousseau, K. R. (1978), "Personality and Job Experience," *Organizational Behavior and Human Performance,* 22, 235-252.
Burgess, R. G. (1984), *In the Field: An Introduction to Field Research,* London: Allen & Unwin.
Burrell, G., and G. Morgan. (1979), *Sociological Paradigms and Organizational Analysis,* London: Heinemann.

Child, J., and C. Smith (1987), "The Context and Process of Organizational Transformation: Cadbury Limited in Its Sector," *Journal of Management Studies,* 24, 565-594.

Edstrom, A. (1986), "Leadership and Strategic Change," *Human Resource Management,* 25, 581-606.

Elchardus, M. (1988), "The Rediscovery of Chronos: The New Role of Time in Sociological Theory," *International Sociology,* 3, 1, 35-59.

Engwall, L. (1985), "Organizational Drift as a Response to Resource Dependence," Working Paper, Department of Business Administration, University of Uppsala, Sweden.

Feldman, S. P. (1987), "The Crossroads of Interpretation: Administration in Professional Organization, *Human Organization,* 46, 2, 95-102.

Ferlie, E., and A. M. Pettigrew (1988), "AIDS: Responding to Rapid Change," *Health Service Journal* (December 1), 1422-1424.

Ferlie, E., and A. M. Pettigrew (1990), "Coping With Change in the NHS: A Frontline Districts Response to AIDS," *Journal of Social Policy,* 19, 191-220.

Giddens, A. (1979), *Central Problems of Social Theory,* London: Macmillan.

Glaser, B. G., and A. L. Strauss (1967), *The discovery of grounded theory: Strategies for qualitative research,* Chicago: Aldine.

Goldstein, H. (1979), *The Design and Analysis of Longitudinal Studies,* London: Academic Press.

Hardy, C. (1985), *The Management of Organizational Closure,* Aldershot: Gower.

Hendry, C., and A. M. Pettigrew (1986), "The Practice of Strategic Human Resource Management," *Personnel Review,* 15, 5, 3-9.

Hendry, C., and A. M. Pettigrew (1987), "Banking on HRM to Respond to Change," *Personnel Management* (November), 29-32.

Hendry, C., A. M. Pettigrew, and P. R. Sparrow (1989), "Linking Strategic Change, Competitive Performance and Human Resource Management: Results of a UK Empirical Study," in R. M. Mansfield (Ed.), *New Frontiers of Management,* London: Routledge.

Hickson, D. J., R. J. Butler, D. J. Cray, G. R. Mallory, and D. C. Wilson (1986), *Top Decisions: Strategic Decision Making in Organizations,* Oxford: Basil Blackwell.

Homans, G. C. (1949), "The Strategy of Industrial Sociology," *American Journal of Sociology* 54, 330-339.

Huberman, A. M., and M. B. Miles (1983), "Drawing Valid Meaning From Qualitative Data: Some Techniques of Data Reduction and Display," *Quality and Quantity,* 17, 281-339.

Johnson, G. (1987), *Strategic Change and the Management Process,* Oxford: Basil Blackwell.

Kervasdoue, J., and J. R. Kimberly (1979), "Are Organization Structures Culture Free?" in G. England et al. (Eds.), *Organizational Functioning in a Cross-Cultural Perspective,* Kent, OH: Kent State University Press.

Kimberly, J. R. (1976), "Issues in the Design of Longitudinal Organizational Research," *Sociological Methods and Research,* 4, 321-347.

Ladurie, E. Leroy (1979), "The Event and the Long Term in Social History: The Case of the Chouan Uprising," in E. Leroy Ladurie, *The Territory of the Historian,* London: Harvester.

Lerner, R. M., and M. B. Kauffman (1985), "The Concept of Development in Contextualism," *Developmental Review,* 5, 309-333.

Lucas, R. (1987), "Political-Cultural Analysis of Organizations," *Academy of Management Journal,* 12, 144-156.

Mancuso, J. C., and S. G. Ceely (1980), "The Self as Memory Processing," *Cognitive Therapy and Research,* 4, 1, 1-25.

McKee, L., and A. M. Pettigrew (1988a), "The Management of Change in the NHS: Bromsgrove and Redditch DHA," Unpublished Research Report, CCSC, University of Warwick.

McKee, L., and A. M. Pettigrew (1988b), "Managing Major Change," *Health Service Journal* (November 17), 1358-1360.

Miles, M. B., and A. M. Huberman (1984), *Qualitative Data Analysis: A Sourcebook of New Methods,* Beverly Hills, CA: Sage.

Miller, D., and P. M. Friesen (1982), "The Longitudinal Analysis of Organizations: A Methodological Perspective," *Management Science,* 28, 1013-1034.

Mintzberg, H., and J. Walters (1982), "Tracking Strategy in the Entrepreneurial Firm," *Academy of Management Journal,* 25, 465-499.

Morgan, G. (1986), *Images of Organization,* Beverly Hills, CA: Sage.

Pepper, S. C. (1942), *World Hypotheses,* Berkeley: University of California Press.

Perrow, C. (1984), *Normal Accidents: Living in High Risk Technologies,* New York: Basic Books.

Pettigrew, A. M. (1973a), *The Politics of Organizational Decision Making,* London: Tavistock.

Pettigrew, A. M. (1973b), "Occupational Specialization as an Emergent Process," *Sociological Review,* 21, 255-278.

Pettigrew, A. M. (1975), "Strategic Aspects of the Management of Specialist Activity," *Personnel Review,* 4, 5-13.

Pettigrew, A. M. (1979), "On Studying Organizational Cultures," *Administrative Science Quarterly,* 24, 570-581.

Pettigrew, A. M. (1985a), *The Awakening Giant: Continuity and Change in ICI,* Oxford: Basil Blackwell.

Pettigrew, A. M. (1985b), "Contextualist Research: A Natural Way to Link Theory and Practice," in E. E. Lawler (Ed.), *Doing Research That Is Useful in Theory and Practice,* San Francisco: Jossey-Bass.

Pettigrew, A. M. (1985c), "Examining Change in the Long-Term Context of Politics and Culture," in J. M. Pennings (Ed.), *Organizational Strategy and Change,* San Francisco: Jossey-Bass.

Pettigrew, A. M. (1985d), "Contextualist Research and the Study of Organizational Change Processes," in E. Mumford et al. (Eds.), *Research Methods in Information Systems,* Amsterdam: North Holland.

Pettigrew, A. M. (1987a), "Theoretical, Methodological, and Empirical Issues in Studying Change: A Response to Starkey," *Journal of Management Studies,* 24, 420-426.

Pettigrew, A. M. (1987b), "Context and Action in the Transformation of the Firm," *Journal of Management Studies* 24, 649-670.

Pettigrew, A. M. (Ed.) (1987c), *The Management of Strategic Change,* Oxford: Basil Blackwell.

Pettigrew, A. M., E. Ferlie, and L. McKee (1992), *Shaping Strategic Change: Making Change in Large Organizations—The Case of the NHS,* London: Sage.

Pettigrew, A. M., C. Hendry, and P. R. Sparrow (1989), *Training in Britain: Employers' Perspectives on Human Resources,* London: Her Majesty's Stationery Office.

Pettigrew, A. M., L. McKee, and E. Ferlie (1988a), "Understanding Change in the NHS," *Public Administration,* 66, 297-317.

Pettigrew, A. M., L. McKee, and E. Ferlie (1988b), "Wind of Change Blows Through the NHS," *Health Service Journal* (November 3), 1296-1298.

Pettigrew, A. M., L. McKee, and E. Ferlie (1989), "Strategic Change in the NHS: The Role of Context and Action," *Health Service Journal* (February 12), 200-203.

Pettigrew, A. M., and R. Whipp (1990), *Managing Change for Competitive Success,* Oxford: Basil Blackwell.

Pettigrew, A. M., R. Whipp, and R. Rosenfeld (1989), "Competitiveness and the Management of Strategic Change Processes: A Research Agenda," in P. K. M. Tharakan and A. Francis (Eds.), *The Competitiveness of European Industry: Country Policies and Company Strategies,* London: Routledge.

Quinn, J. B. (1980), *Strategies for Change: Logical Incrementalism,* Homewood, IL: Irwin.

Ransom, S., C. R. Hinings, and R. Greenwood (1980), "The Structuring of Organization Structures," *Administrative Science Quarterly,* 25, 1-18.

Rosenfeld, R., R. Whipp, and A. M. Pettigrew (1989), "Processes of Internationalization: Regeneration and Competitiveness," *Economia Aziendale,* 7 (April), 21-47.

Schön, D. A. (1983), *The Reflective Practitioner: How Professionals Think in Action,* London: Temple Smith.

Sparrow, P. R., and A. M. Pettigrew (1987a), "Britain's Training Problems: The Search for a Strategic Human Resources Management Approach," *Human Resource Management,* 26, 1, 109-127.

Sparrow, P. R., and A. M. Pettigrew (1988a), "Contrasting HRM Responses in the Changing World of Computing," *Personnel Management,* 20, 2, 40-45.

Sparrow, P. R., and A. M. Pettigrew (1988b), "How Halfords Puts Its HRM Into Top Gear," *Personnel Management,* 20, 6, 30-34.

Sparrow, P. R., and A. M. Pettigrew (1988c), "Strategic Human Resource Management in the UK Computer Supplier Industry," *Journal of Occupational Psychology,* 61, 1, 25-42.

Strauss, A. L. (1987), *Qualitative Analysis for Social Scientists,* Cambridge: Cambridge University Press.

Tuma, N. B., and M. J. Hannan (1984), *Social Dynamics,* Orlando, FL: Academic Press.

Tushman, M., and E. Romanelli (1985), "Organizational Evolution: A Metamorphosis Model of Convergence and Reorientation," in L. L. Cummings and B. M. Staw (Eds.), *Research in Organizational Behavior* (Vol. 7), Greenwich, CT: JAI.

Van de Ven, A. H., H. L. Angle, and M. S. Poole (1989), *Research on the Management of Innovation: The Minnesota Studies,* New York: Ballinger/Harper & Row.

Van Maanen, J. (Ed.) (1983), *Qualitative Methodology,* Beverly Hills, CA: Sage.

Van Maanen, J. (1988), *Tales of the Field: On Writing Ethnography,* Chicago: University of Chicago Press.

Wall, T. D., N. J. Kemp, P. R. Jackson, and C. W. Clegg (1986), "Outcomes of Autonomous Work Groups: A Long-Term Field Experiment," *Academy of Management Journal,* 29, 280-304.

Wall, T. D., and H. L. Williams (1970), *Longitudinal Studies and the Social Sciences,* London: Heinemann.

Whipp, R. (1988), "A Time to Every Purpose: An Essay on Time and Work," in P. Joyce (Ed.), *The Historical Meanings of Work,* Cambridge: Cambridge University Press.

Whipp, R., and P. Clark (1986), *Innovation and the Auto Industry,* London: Frances Pinter.

Whipp, R., A. M. Pettigrew, and P. R. Sparrow (1989), "New Technology, Competition and the Firm: A Framework for Research," *International Journal of Vehicle Design,* 10, 453-469.

Whipp, R., R. Rosenfeld, and A. M. Pettigrew (1989), "Culture and Competitiveness: Evidence From Mature UK Industries," *Journal of Management Studies,* 26, 561-585.

Wilson, C. S., and T. Lupton (1959), "The Bank Rate Tribunal: The Social Background and Connections of Top Decision Makers," *Manchester School of Economic and Social Studies,* 27, 30-51.

Yin, R. K. (1984), *Case Study Research: Design and Methods,* Beverly Hills, CA: Sage.

5

Studying Changes in
Organizational Design and Effectiveness

Retrospective Event Histories
and Periodic Assessments

WILLIAM H. GLICK

GEORGE P. HUBER

C. CHET MILLER

D. HAROLD DOTY

KATHLEEN M. SUTCLIFFE

This chapter describes assumptions, rationales, and trade-offs involved in designing the research methodology used in a longitudinal study of the relationships among changes in organizational contexts, designs, and effectiveness. The basic research question concerns when, how, and why different types of organizational change occur. Given this research question and a desire to develop and test generalizable theory about changes in organizational design and effectiveness, the authors conducted a longitudinal study of more than 100 organizations. Data concerning the changes were obtained through four interviews spaced 6 months apart with the top manager in each organization. Each interview provided a short-term retrospective event history over the preceding 6-month interval. In aggregate, the four interviews provided a 24-month event history for each organi-

This chapter appeared originally in *Organization Science,* vol. 1, no. 3, August 1990, pp. 293-312.

zation. Additionally, periodic assessments of the state of the organization's context, design, and effectiveness were collected with two questionnaires spaced one year apart. Finally, in each organization, the top manager's personal characteristics were assessed after all other data were obtained. This chapter examines the alternatives, advantages, and disadvantages of the research design decisions. With some hindsight, the authors also offer some suggestions for future researchers with similar goals of developing and testing generalizable explanations of change processes in organizations.

Top managers are preoccupied by change, both the changes that they must react to, such as new and important threats and opportunities, and the changes that they initiate as a result of their values and aspirations. To increase effectiveness, improve efficiency, gain market share, or simplify the organizational design, managers are constantly creating new programs, streamlining procedures, evaluating proposed courses of action, and encountering new opportunities in their organizations' environments. All of these activities involve change.

We designed the research methodology described in this chapter to aid in our investigation of changes in organizations, particularly the important changes that grasp the attention of the organization's top manager. What types of changes occur? What types of changes occur most frequently? When and how do these different types of changes occur? In other words, what are the antecedent conditions, causes, and consequences of changes across a variety of organizational forms, contexts, and internal processes? Our goals in this investigation were to build and to test theories to answer these research questions. The overall research program chosen to achieve this goal was a multi-investigator set of longitudinal studies of Changes in Organizational Design and Effectiveness (CODE). This chapter focuses on the central study in the program. The dependent variables of primary interest in the central CODE study were attributes of changes (e.g., types of changes and frequency of changes) and attributes of change processes (e.g., causes of changes, consequences of changes, and sequences of changes). To understand more fully these attributes of changes and change processes, we investigated their relationships with characteristics of the organization, such as its environment, performance, technology, strategy, and design.

Our primary purposes in this chapter are (1) to describe the research methodology for the central study, (2) to discuss the trade-offs that shaped the methodology, and (3) to evaluate these choices with the advantage of some hindsight. These purposes are addressed in turn in the four major sections of the chapter, which are organized around the key features of the methodology: (1) the management and conduct of the overall research program and the central study, (2) the field sites, (3) the retrospective event histories, and (4) the assessments of organizational, contextual, and top manager characteristics.

MANAGEMENT AND CONDUCT OF
THE CODE RESEARCH PROGRAM

Trade-Offs Decided Prior to Funding

Thorngate (1976, p. 126) and Weick (1979, pp. 35-142) note that it is impossible for a theory to be "simultaneously accurate, general, and simple." Given the basic research questions, our biases, and the interests of the funding agency, the focus of the research was on developing and testing *generalizable theory* about the changes that are likely to affect or occur in any organization. This focus obviously precluded our addressing alternative research questions, such as questions about the rich details of the processes related to one or a few types of organizational changes (see Barley 1990, Leonard-Barton 1990, Van de Ven and Poole 1990). The resultant relatively positivist focus and research question also precluded research designs involving very intensive examination of a limited number of cases. Thus, even before submitting the research proposal, we made the first trade-off that shaped the methodology, sacrificing some depth in order to gain breadth.

Another major issue that had to be resolved prior to submission of the research proposal was the matter of choosing a design that would be satisfactory with respect to the following criteria: (1) the efficiency of data-collection techniques; (2) the time span of the data; (3) the efficiency and ease of coordinating the research project; (4) the need to recruit and maintain participation of a large number of field sites; (5) the desire to discover new types of changes, antecedents, and consequences; and (6) the desire to develop new theory about the antecedents and consequences of different types of change in different contexts. The first two criteria argue for archival data collection over a long period of time to capture both rapid and evolutionary changes in organizational design and effectiveness. The last two criteria, however, prevented complete reliance on archival or survey data-collection techniques because of the need for richer, more detailed information. Because theory development often can be facilitated by the interaction of multiple, independent researchers, and because the use of multiple researchers also facilitates the recruitment and maintenance of multiple field sites, the last three criteria argued for the inclusion of multiple researchers. The inherent difficulties of coordinating among multiple researchers, however, obviously run counter to the third criterion.

After considering the trade-offs among these criteria, we adopted a design that emphasizes a series of interviews in a large number of field sites by several researchers. Four additional researchers at different universities collaborated in the research program. All collaborators took responsibility for theory development for their local studies and data collection for both their local studies and the central study. (The central study is hereafter referred to simply as the study.) Each local study reflected the respective collaborator's research interest, but was required to be related also to the central study theme of organizational change. In order to draw upon an even larger base of methodological and substantive expertise, we also included six consultants in the research program (see Table 5.1).

Choices Made During the Study

The overall CODE research program was scheduled for five years beginning September 1, 1985. During the first year, the principal investigators initiated literature reviews and theory-building efforts to guide the subsequent empirical research. The products of these efforts include Daft and Huber (1987), Huber (1990, 1991), Huber and Daft (1987), Huber and McDaniel (1986), and Huber, Miller, and Glick (1990). This work identified many variables relevant to changes in organizational design and effectiveness that would be of interest to both the research and practitioner communities. These reviews also revealed a lack of maturity in the field's understanding of change. Thus we decided that in addition to addressing some a priori issues, the research would be designed to develop a database that could be used in the future in the development of post hoc theories about the relationships among many dimensions of change, design, and effectiveness.

During the second year, we designed the central study and conducted pretests of the interview instrument, the interview administration and coding procedures, and the organizational assessment questionnaire. Also during that year, the collaborating researchers began designing their studies and establishing their field sites. All central study instruments and the respective protocols for administering them were circulated among the researchers and consultants for feedback before being finalized.

A trade-off unique to large-scale research projects involves reaching a compromise between encouraging each collaborator to do something unique and insisting on uniform adoption of a single theoretical model. This trade-off stimulated a lively debate during the second year of our project. Arguing

TABLE 5.1 CODE Research Program Contributors

Dr. George P. Huber, Principal Investigator, University of Texas at Austin	Dr. William H. Glick, Co-Principal Investigator, University of Texas at Austin

Collaborating Researchers	*Consultants*
Dr. Kim S. Cameron, University of Michigan	Dr. William W. Cooper, University of Texas at Austin
Dr. Richard L. Daft, Texas A&M University[b]	Dr. Arie Y. Lewin, Duke University
Dr. Kenneth Bettenhausen, Texas A&M University	Dr. Peter S. Monge, University of Southern California
Dr. Alan D. Meyer, University of Oregon	Dr. John W. Slocum, Southern Methodist University
Dr. Charles A. O'Reilly, University of California	Dr. Andrew Van de Ven, University of Minnesota
	Dr. Karl E. Weick, University of Texas at Austin[b]

Research Associates[a]	
Joan Boothe, University of California, Berkeley	Aneil Mishra, University of Michigan
Geoffrey Brooks, University of Oregon	Doug Orton, University of Michigan[b]
D. Harold Doty, University of Texas at Austin[b]	Richard Snyder, University of California, Berkeley
Sarah Freeman, University of Michigan[b]	Kathleen M. Sutcliffe, University of Texas at Austin
James B. Goes, University of Oregon	Beverly B. Tyler, Texas A&M University
C. Chet Miller, University of Texas at Austin[b]	

a. Added after the study began.
b. This researcher has changed affiliations since this list was made; affiliations shown are those in effect at the time the contributor joined the research study.

in favor of greater consensus on theoretical perspectives are the criteria of economies of scale, standardization, ease of identifying the main contribution of the research project, the potential to stimulate a very creative theory-building process among a group of collaborators, and the potential to make a single, large research contribution. The advantages of encouraging multiple perspectives include greater diversity of final theories, reduced need for coordination, more contributions, each collaborator's ability to pursue his or her own interests, and the possibility of enlisting in the collaborative project established researchers with interesting research agendas. Given the field's limited understanding of change processes in organizations and the geographic dispersion of the collaborators, we decided against adopting a unified theoretical perspective for the project.

During the third, fourth, and fifth years, the four interviews were conducted and all questionnaires were administered. The interview data suggested that detailed information was also needed about the top manager. Thus
an additional questionnaire was designed and administered during this period. Also during the fifth year, additional data coding schemes were developed and employed, and all researchers focused on interpreting their results
and publishing the result of their studies.

In addition to frequent coordination contacts by telephone and electronic
and postal mail, the researchers, consultants, and some research associates
met annually for a one-day coordination meeting. Many of the ideas discussed in this chapter were brought into sharper perspective through informal
exchanges at these meetings and subsequent interactions. Myriad problems
were preempted or solved using these coordination procedures. Nevertheless, despite our coordination efforts, lack of uniformity crept into data-collection procedures and resulted in the need to discard and replace some data.
In retrospect, additional efforts at coordination probably would have reduced
this problem. Our insufficient coordination was the result of our partially
incorrect beliefs that protocols and related communications would provide
sufficient training for all interviewers and that all researchers would adhere
tightly to the protocol. Also, we believed that more frequent coordination
meetings would detract from the time and enthusiasm directed at developing
and testing theories. Consequently, although we seriously considered additional meetings for focusing the research questions, interviewer training, and
final discussion of the research design, we decided against them. Hindsight
suggests that additional coordination, especially meetings related to interviewer training, should have been undertaken.

FIELD SITE SELECTION AND RETENTION

Number of Field Sites

Data were collected from 153 diverse organizations. Complete data sets—
that is, four interviews, two organizational/context questionnaires, and the
top manager characteristics questionnaire—were collected from more than
100 organizations.[1] Two related arguments contributed to the decision to
study this relatively large number of field sites rather than to focus on a
limited number of case studies. First, as indicated earlier, the goal of the
research was to develop theories that would be generalizable across a variety
of organizational forms, contexts, and processes. Given this goal, statistical
power considerations suggested a bare minimum of 15 observations to detect
very large effects with better than a 50/50 probability (Cohen 1988). Tests

of more complex contingency hypotheses required sample sizes in excess of 100 (Cohen 1988, Dragsow and Kang 1984).

A second reason for studying a large number of field sites was the underlying assumption that any change in organizational design and effectiveness is likely to be determined by a plethora of factors (Katz and Kahn 1978, Weick 1979). Multiple processes and events may increase the probability of a change, but any single event or process may fail to have the expected effect due to countervailing forces. Thus, given an overdetermined system, it is impossible to specify the necessary and sufficient conditions for any change in organizational design and effectiveness (Markus and Robey 1988, Mohr 1982). Antecedents could be necessary *or* sufficient, but might not be both. In addition, the marginal impact of any process or effect is often a function of the levels or changes in other factors, levels or changes that may not be known or recognized for their importance. Thus causal determinants of change are not wholly predictable in their effects because other unmeasured determinants of change might be changing simultaneously.

There are two possible ways to handle the methodological complications implied by overdetermination and the consequent inability to specify fully the necessary and sufficient conditions for changes in organizations. The first approach is very idiographic and emphasizes context-dependent descriptions of the processes of change (Markus and Robey 1988, Mohr 1982). The second approach is more nomothetic and treats all causal explanations as probabilistic rather than deterministic statements. This approach is based on the following assumptions: (1) Changes and outcomes of changes in organizations are overdetermined, (2) countervailing forces may obscure a true effect, and (3) countervailing forces occur at random. Thus any causal effect is a probabilistic rather than deterministic event. Given our nomothetic research goals, we adopted the second approach. The methodological implication of adopting this approach is that inferences should be based on large samples and statistical criteria rather than detailed observations of a single case.

Variation Among Field Sites

The focus of the study was on understanding the nature of a broad variety of changes and change processes that might occur in a variety of organizations. This focus is based on the nomothetic assumption that many of the antecedents and consequences of organizational change are important across a broad variety of organizations. Thus we chose to study a heterogeneous set of field sites. The set of field sites includes organizations ranging in size from 16 to 6,000 employees, with a mean of 1,024 and median of 304, and includes multiple industries in both service and manufacturing sectors. Heterogeneity was constrained only by the requirement that each organization (1) have primary responsibility for its strategy and design, (2) include at least two managerial levels, and (3) have an external constituency independent of any parent organization.

Despite our general acceptance of the nomothetic assumption of generalizability, however, we included homogeneous clusters of organizations in the set of field sites. The homogeneous clusters enable development of limited-domain or middle-range theories (Pinder and Moore 1980; Weick 1974). The study includes (for example) sizable clusters of hospitals, electronics manufacturers, financial services, business schools, new organizations, organizations in declining manufacturing industries, profit-oriented organizations, and not-for-profit organizations.

This combination of overall heterogeneity and within-cluster homogeneity allows us to test both nomothetic and idiographic assumptions (Duncan 1972, Hambrick 1982). A limited domain theory developed or initially validated within one cluster can be tested further in the larger, heterogeneous set of organizations or in other clusters from the larger set. To the extent that theories developed in one context generalize across clusters or to other clusters, it will be possible to support more nomothetic, less idiographic assumptions. Alternatively, a theory developed or initially validated in the heterogeneous set of organizations can be tested within clusters to examine the assumption that the theory can be generalized to specific homogeneous clusters.

This decision to use field sites that in aggregate were heterogeneous but clustered into homogeneous sets involved a trade-off. First, it resulted in the loss of an opportunity to sample randomly from a *theoretically* defined and *theoretically* relevant population of organizations. This loss is important because it weakens the generalizability of the results to an unknown degree. We believe, however, that the final set of field sites is sufficiently heterogeneous and representative of the population of organizations to support most assertions of generalizability. Second, this trade-off created several problems in the development of instruments useful in a variety of contexts. Simple terms such as *customers, financial backers,* and *organizational performance* are interpreted differently in different contexts, such as banks, hospitals, business schools, and manufacturing firms. (In one religious organization, the main criterion of performance was the number of souls saved.) Despite these disadvantages, the considerations above led to an early decision to study field sites that were heterogeneous overall, but homogeneous within clusters.

Selecting and Recruiting Field Sites

To assure maximal generalizability of results, field sites should be randomly sampled from a known population of organizations. Further, the boundaries of the population should be defined based on theoretical consid-erations. In addition to generalizability, however, researchers also must contend with the two practical considerations of limited resources and potentially unwilling participants.

To make the greatest use of travel and time budgets, we and our collabo-rators selected and recruited field site organizations that were located in nearby geographic areas, typically in cities near our universities. If the researcher had good rapport with the contact person at the field site after one or two face-to-face interviews, telephone interviews were used occasionally to conserve additional time and travel expenses.

Besides the matter of limited travel and time budgets, a second practical consideration was that each organization's top manager had to be willing to commit to multiple interviews and questionnaires over a two-year period. By using nearby field sites, we increased the likelihood that the top managers would participate in the research, because we could interview them face-to-face and because they were helping researchers from local universities rather than distant rivals. The final set of field sites was geographically dispersed throughout the United States, with large clusters in Central California, the San Francisco Bay Area, central Texas, southeast Texas, Virginia, and parts of the midwestern states of Michigan, Ohio, and Illinois.

The purposeful selection of field sites resulted in some loss of generalizabil-ity of the results due to the lack of random sampling from a theoretically defined population. We believe, however, that the loss in generalizability is limited by the heterogeneity of the total set and the ability to test assumptions of generalizability across clusters. The heterogeneity of the field sites reflects more closely the population of strategic business units that are the focus of most organizational theories than do the more homogeneous sets of field sites used in most empirical organizational research.

Retaining Field Sites

Unlike participants in cross-sectional interview studies, our key inform-ants were required to provide four interviews over an 18-month period and to complete two seven-page questionnaires spaced a year apart and one one-page questionnaire at the end of the 18 months. Believing that whatever motivations led to initial cooperation would likely diminish across time, we worked to retain as many of the organizations as possible across the entire study. We cultivated the informant at each field site by taking one or more of the following steps: (1) making it easy for the informant to participate by scheduling interviews at his or her convenience; (2) asking for and using a limited amount of the informant's time; (3) guaranteeing confidentiality; (4) maintaining a personal relationship through phone calls, letters, and personal visits; (5) promising (and providing) clear rewards to the informant, such as personalized feedback and copies of the papers and book at the end of the project; (6) focusing the fixed amount of researcher time and energy on a limited number of informants; (7) using semipersonalized letters describing the relevance of the study to the practice of management before the first interview and again with each organizational profile assessment questionnaire; (8) developing personal rapport with each participant by engaging in "common interest" conversation before the interview began; and (9) personally mailing to participants journal articles or other materials of professional interest. (When such mailings occurred, care was taken so that their content was unlikely to affect data provided by the informants in the future.) These procedures seem to be effective; we estimate at the time of this writing that attrition due to controllable causes will be less than 10%, that attrition due to uncontrollable causes (such as acquisition and bankruptcy) will be 10%, and that attrition due to turnover of the key informant (and subsequent noninterest of the new top manager) will also be 10%.

Summary

We selected field site organizations to reflect the heterogeneous population of organizations by including a heterogeneous set of homogeneous clusters. We used this approach in order to obtain variety in the nature and antecedents of change and thereby to develop interpretations of organizational actions that were both contextually valid within clusters and generalizable across clusters. Each cluster of organizations within a single domain provides specificity for validating explanations related strictly to that domain. The heterogeneity of the total set is compatible with more nomothetic assumptions about the phenomena of interest, and yet allows us to test more specific, idiographic assumptions about the limits of generalizability.

RETROSPECTIVE EVENT HISTORIES

The primary methodology for obtaining information about the changes in the field sites organizations was to develop a 24-month retrospective event history (Tuma and Hannan 1984) obtained from a series of four structured interviews with the top manager in each organization. The interview procedure focused the top manager's attention on relevant changes by soliciting the retrospective report after the manager had reviewed two lists headed "generic examples of organizational design changes" and "generic examples of organizational nondesign changes" (see Table 5.2).[2] The top manager was placed in the role of key informant (Bagozzi and Phillips 1982, Phillips 1981,

TABLE 5.2 Generic Examples of Organizational Changes

Design Changes

a. Important changes in the responsibility or resources of top management team members (i.e., of the CEO or of any manager who reports to either the CEO or to the chief operating officer)
b. Important changes in responsibility or resources at the other levels in the organization
c. Important additions or eliminations of a major organizational unit
d. Important changes in the way that your organization interacts with its customers, clients, or parent organization, such as introducing electronic funds transfer or the solicitation of orders by phone
e. Important changes in the way that you produce your product or service, such as a change in equipment, techniques, or sequencing of activities
f. Important changes in administrative procedures such as changing control or incentive systems
g. Important changes in internal coordination or communication procedures, such as introducing electronic mail or teleconferencing

Nondesign Changes

a. Important changes in the performance of either the whole organization or an important subunit (e.g., changes in costs, client complaints, personnel turnover, sales)
b. Important changes in the organization's external environment (e.g., changes in competitors, regulators, or suppliers)
c. Important changes in the organization's externally directed strategy (e.g., changes in products, markets, emphases, relations with important outsiders)
d. Important changes in the organization's internally directed goals, philosophy, or culture (e.g., the decision to focus on human resource development, cost control, employee participation)
e. Important changes in specific personnel or in staffing levels (e.g., additions, deletions, transfers, reassignments) not mentioned previously

Seidler 1974) and asked to take 10 to 20 minutes to describe briefly the important design and nondesign changes that occurred at his or her organization during the six months preceding the interview. Example changes included the departure of specific, key personnel; a doubling in sales volume; addition of new product lines; major reorganizations or reassignments of people and resources; and change in governmental regulations. The manager was also asked to identify the dates that these changes occurred, unless the changes were actually ongoing processes, such as a demographic trend, in which case he or she was asked the date when a critical level of change was noted, or, if this was not possible, to label the change as "ongoing."

After listing the changes, the manager was asked to identify the three most important design and three most important nondesign changes and the factors leading to these six important changes. Although different top managers may have used different criteria in assigning importance, we felt that the inter-viewers would be less qualified to make this assessment than would the top managers. The disadvantage of this protocol design is that some of the variation across organizations may be attributed to the differences in criteria applied by the top managers rather than any real differences in importance of the different types of changes.

This retrospective event-history methodology reflected a series of trade-offs. The three most important judgment calls were (1) selecting the method to assess change, (2) using the organization's top manager as the sole key informant about the organization, and (3) defining the characteristics of the change to be coded. The following subsections describe alternative method-ologies, the nature of the trade-offs, and the alternative that we selected in making each of these judgment calls.

Selecting the Method to Assess Change

Researchers interested in organizational change are very often absent when important changes occur. Thus a major challenge to researchers study-ing organizational change and change processes is to get data consistently on events and processes that may occur while the researchers are not present.

Alternative Methodologies to Assess Change

We considered four alternative methods to assess change: (1) direct observation, (2) records compiled by organizational members, (3) panel designs, and (4) retrospective reports. One approach for investigating change requires researchers to be immersed in the organizations in order to be more likely to observe changes directly. Given the obvious time demands, this approach is most compatible with small-sample research. Change processes that occur either *simultaneously* or *unpredictably* in different organizational subunits cannot be studied using direct observation unless multiple observers are used in each organization. Our interest in understanding a broad variety of changes, including unpredictable changes that may occur simultaneously, precluded the use of this approach.

A second approach to studying change is to rely on an organizational member to make the observations and record the data as changes occur, or shortly thereafter. The records can be compiled in a special log provided by the researcher or in archival sources that are regularly used by the organiza-tion. Logs are useful tools for capturing change processes, but many top managers are not willing to keep logs of changes for research purposes across an extended period of time (such as two years). Archival sources are also useful for studying change, but these sources are rarely sufficiently detailed or consistent across time or organizations to fulfill our research goal.

A third approach to examining change is analogous to time-lapse photography; change processes can be inferred by researchers who look for differences across a series of snapshots taken at fixed time intervals. For example, panel designs assess change processes by estimating change between static assessments; they do not capture directly the critical change events. Panel designs are most effective when the time lapses between the static assessments are very short. Shortened time intervals lose less information about the sequencing of events and improve the continuous time estimates of dynamic processes (Tuma and Hannan 1984). Panel designs are very useful in many organizational contexts (Monge 1990), but if any of the causal processes occur in shorter periods than the intervals between panels of data collection, it is impossible to estimate accurately the relationships among the variables (Cook and Campbell 1979, Monge et al. 1984). Given the fast pace of many changes in organizational design and effectiveness, a panel design would have required weekly or monthly interviews. This would have been prohibitively expensive, given our decision to study a large number of organizations, and would have caused many top managers to refuse to participate across the period of the study.

Retrospective reports from key informants, a fourth approach to capturing change, was adopted as the primary method for obtaining information about important events and processes. Every six months the top manager was asked to report the important changes that occurred over the previous six months and the dates when these changes occurred. The factors that led to the six most important of these listed changes were also elicited in the interview and, in the subsequent interview six months later, the consequences of these six most important changes were elicited. This series of four interviews provided retrospectively reported changes for a retrospective event history spanning 24 months. The sequencing of these reported changes and the open-ended nature of the retrospective reports provided a rich base of data and stimulated insights into the unique changes in each organization.

Advantages and Disadvantages of Retrospective Reports

A key advantage of the retrospective reports is that the time intervals between events are much shorter than the intervals between interviews. It is important to recognize that the data from the four interviews are not analogous to four snapshots of static conditions at 6-month intervals; rather, they are four reasonably fresh and timely reports of events and their causes and consequences across a 24-month period. The actual dates of changes are obtained with direct questions rather than being a consequence of the frequency and timing of data collection, as would be the case in a panel design.

A second advantage of retrospective reports is that the top manager describes directly the key events and processes of change. Organizational participants often attend to different characteristics of organizations and describe these characteristics and their relationships using terms different from those used by organizational scientists (Blackburn and Cummings 1982, McGuire 1986). We involved organizational participants in the theory development process (as recommended by Beyer and Trice 1982) by relying on open-ended retrospective reports. The top managers described the important changes and their antecedents in their own terminology. Thus we expect our theory development to be more grounded in the experiences and terminology of top managers.

A disadvantage of asking open-ended questions and relying on the top managers' terminology is that their terminology may be imprecise or may be inconsistent across top managers. Thus our interpretations of their open-ended responses may be inaccurate or depend on the verbal skills of the top managers. This creates problems as the open-ended responses are recorded and then coded by the interviewer and other researchers using the data. As we discovered new types of changes or later decided to code additional characteristics of the changes, the open-ended responses had to be reinterpreted by someone who had never visited any of the field sites. Given our reliance on the top managers' terminology, the validity of our coding interpretations undoubtedly suffered, particularly when the coder did not have all of the rich cues that are available in the actual interview.

A second disadvantage of asking open-ended questions about recent changes is that the responses may be associated with errors of recall; for example, informants may selectively neglect some events that are important or focus on trends that are actually unimportant but are temporarily conspicuous to the informant. If too many truly important events are omitted, the theoretical explanations will be inaccurate and will lack descriptive relevance. If nonimportant events are included, they may be falsely accepted as important possible antecedents of other changes in organizational design and effectiveness. Errors of recall can result from strong cognitive processes such as rationalization, self-presentation, simplification, attribution, and simple lapses of memory (Wolfe and Jackson 1987). And, of course, more recent changes are more likely to be recalled. Although errors of recall are important problems with retrospective event histories, the magnitude of these problems was minimized in the study by the following procedural safeguards: (1) The interview was explicitly focused on "important" changes, which tend to be recalled more reliably; (2) all key informants were top managers who, by virtue of their positions, tended to be involved with or close observers of the important events and processes about which they reported; and (3) the questions were restricted to changes that occurred relatively recently (within the previous six months). Each of these safeguards tends to minimize errors of recall (Huber 1985, Huber and Power 1985) and was used in the interviews.

Selecting the Key Informant(s)

A second judgment call in the retrospective event-history methodology involved selecting the person(s) to provide the event history from each organization. The use of retrospective reports implied that the interviewee should be placed in the role of key informant, supplying descriptive information about the organization, rather than in the role of a respondent, reacting to questions about his or her perceptions (Glick 1985, Houston and Sudman 1975, Phillips 1981, Seidler 1974). This key informant role was most appropriate given the research questions.

The top full-time manager in each organization was selected as the single key informant for describing changes in that organization.[3] The choice of the top full-time manager to be the sole key informant was based on (1) criteria for selecting informants, and (2) criteria for choosing to use single versus multiple informants.

Criteria for Selecting Key Informants

The main criteria used to select key informants were (1) the expected validity of their descriptions and assessments of the phenomena and (2) the anticipated extent of cooperation in providing these data across the duration of the study. These criteria implied that the best key informants for the study would be (1) knowledgeable about the widest possible variety of important changes and their relative importance, (2) knowledgeable about the antecedents and consequences of these changes, (3) able to articulate the important changes and their antecedents accurately, and (4) willing to report accurately (see Glick 1985, Houston and Sudman 1975, Huber and Power 1985, Phillips 1981, Seidler, 1974).

Any organizational member was a potential key informant because of his or her knowledge about some events. Every organizational member, however, was also relatively ignorant about other events due to the reward structure, the pattern of specialized information flows in organizations, and individual and organizational limits in information processing. Of the potential informants, the top manager was the most likely to be knowledgeable about a broad variety of important changes both within and outside the organization, as argued by Snow and Hrebiniak (1980) and Zajac and Shortell (1989) and as found by Hambrick (1981; also see Aguilar 1967,

Mintzberg 1975, Zajonc and Wolfe 1966). The top manager also was most likely to be able to assess the relative importance of changes from an organizational point of view and, therefore, to report only the changes that were most important to the organization. Other informants in more specialized product or functional positions were likely to emphasize changes that were primarily relevant to their positions (Dearborn and Simon 1958, Ireland et al. 1987). Selective perception and exposure to different information lead more specialized or less central managers to report more peripheral events (see Houston and Sudman 1975, Phillips 1981). Finally, variations in knowledge about the intentions of change initiators (Hax and Majluf 1988) were also likely to result in different reported antecedents if informants holding a variety of organizational positions were used. By selecting the top manager as the sole key informant, we avoided these threats to the validity of the reports, but by doing so we undoubtedly obtained data that are biased in the direction of an overreporting of factors linked to the top manager.

Given the attributes of desirable key informants, one alternative to selecting the top manager as the key informant in all organizations was to select the most knowledgeable, articulate, and cooperative informant from each organization, regardless of position. Although in some organizations this selection rule might provide better informants than the top manager, we believed that it would be difficult to apply across a large number of organizations. We also believed that it would result in the introduction of different biases associated with the informants' positions (Dearborn and Simon 1958, Ireland et al. 1987, Zajonc and Wolfe 1966). Thus this selection rule would confound real differences among organizations with the biases associated with the informants.

It is important to note that by consistently selecting the top manager as the key informant from the same position in each organization, we controlled for the several biases that are associated with the top manager position (Glick 1985, Seidler 1974). That is, report biases that are associated with the top manager position are present in all of the reports and, therefore, are not a source of cross-organizational variance in reports concerning changes and their antecedents and consequences.

Choosing Between Single and Multiple Informants

Although our treatment of the top manager as a key informant was consistent with obtaining the most valid retrospective reports possible, the use of a single key informant did not respond to frequent calls for multiple informants (Bagozzi and Phillips 1982, Huber and Power 1985, Phillips 1981, Seidler 1974, Williams, Cote, and Buckley 1989). An important advantage of using multiple informants is that the validity of information provided by any informant can be checked against that provided by other informants. By selecting a single informant, we traded off the opportunity to test the validity of the reports.

A second, more important, advantage of using multiple informants is that the validity of the data used by the researcher can be enhanced through the resolution of discrepancies among different informants' reports. Researchers typically resolve discrepancies by using a heuristic to compute a composite score for the organization or through face-to-face discussions among the informants (Wolfe and Jackson 1987). With continuous or equal interval-level data, the most common heuristic is a simple averaging across inform-ants. With categorical data, such as the types of reported changes and their antecedents, discrepancies must be resolved by more elaborate heuristics, such as ignoring any changes mentioned by less than two informants.

But using multiple informants rather than a single informant also has important disadvantages: (1) Organizations tend to decline to participate or to continue participating in the study because they incur greater costs, especially when asked to volunteer the time of multiple informants to supply seemingly redundant factual information as a validity check on the most informed informant's report; (2) informants tend to decline to participate, or to put forth substandard efforts, when they are one of several informants rather than the special key informant; (3) informants decline to participate or withhold information for fear of breaches of confidentiality in subsequent interviews with other informants; (4) the researchers' time and other resources are absorbed with the additional interviews rather than employed to access additional single informant field sites; and, most important, (5) the larger the number of informants, the less well qualified is the average informant. Given the importance of generalizability to our study, the potential self-selection and loss of organizations and informants were also important.

After considering all of these issues and considering our prior decision to study a large number of organizations, we made the judgment call to use the top manager as the sole key informant from each organization.

Defining the Attributes of Changes to Be Coded

The third major judgment call involved the process of reducing open-ended descriptions of changes into a parsimonious set of attributes for theory testing and building. The retrospective reports of recent changes were solic-ited with open-ended questions that encouraged top managers to describe the changes in their own words. Some of the attributes to be coded were defined a priori, whereas others were developed and applied post hoc. The diverse descriptions of changes from the top managers provided an extremely rich data set for both deductive and inductive theory development. Four examples of the attributes that have been coded are described below.

Nominal Type of Change

Top managers were asked to describe recent design and nondesign changes for their organizations. These two types of changes were separated in the interview; the interviewer provided the top manager with separate lists of generic design and nondesign changes (Table 5.2) and asked first for descriptions of design changes and then for descriptions of nondesign changes. Occasionally, the informants described nondesign changes when the interviewer was recording design changes, and vice versa. The initial coding of the changes identified each change as a design or nondesign change. Changes were subsequently coded into the subcategories suggested in the lists of generic examples (Table 5.2).[4] This coding system was applied both to the reported changes and to the reported antecedents of the most important changes.

Reaction Versus Proaction as Impetus for Change

In accord with the "reactive" system-structure paradigm (Astley and Van de Ven 1983), we initially expected antecedents of the most important changes to be other recent or expected design or nondesign changes. We did not anticipate that many of the reported antecedents would reflect a proactive nature of organizations. Early in our interviewing efforts, however, we discovered that many of these antecedents were long-standing aspirations or changes in aspiration levels rather than actual or expected changes. For example, some top managers reported that recent changes were changes that they had always wanted to introduce, but were unable to pursue or accomplish until recently. Other top managers reported that recent changes were the consequence of their attention and action on an existing, well-known opportunity. In some cases, these change-inducing shifts in aspiration levels were prompted by ideas from consultants, professional meetings, or reading of management literature.

Given a large number of these proactive changes, after the first round of interviews we had the interviewers code all factors leading to changes either as (1) an actual, observable change that had occurred or that, at the time of the decision to make the change, was expected to occur, or as (2) an increase or decrease in aspiration level or a long-standing aspiration or policy that was not satisfied. This distinction between reactive and proactive changes is supported in Hrebiniak and Joyce's (1985) theoretical model of the causes of strategic actions.

Distinguishing Discrete Events From Ongoing Processes

At the extreme, changes can occur either as discrete events or as relatively ongoing dynamic processes. For changes that occur as discrete events, observers can date the events and examine the sequencing of changes to learn about the causal processes connecting different types of changes. Ongoing dynamic processes, however, are more difficult to locate in a temporal sequencing, and intertwined causes and effects render causal inference problematic (Meyer 1982). For example, the AIDS epidemic is having profound effects on health care providers, but these effects cannot be linked to specific events or critical junctures. Further, the causation is circular, because health care providers are undertaking changes designed to control the AIDS epidemic.[5]

Between the extremes of very discrete events and ongoing processes, change also may occur as a moderately discrete event. For example, change may occur as an accelerating process with a clear inflection point in the trend line. Change may occur as a slow process that evolves over months or years, rather than minutes. The speed of a change may also vary across time. Alternatively, an ongoing change may reach a specific threshold level that triggers a decision point for a top manager. The length and intensity of a change process can vary considerably. Thus, to distinguish accurately among the variety of changes, research methodologies must represent each change as a series of observations to capture the complete trend line with inflection points, fluctuations in speed, threshold levels, and absolute beginning and end points of the change process. Although accuracy is enhanced, simplicity is ignored by this much detail.

Our approach to representing change and distilling the change sequences strongly favors simplicity by classifying each change as either a relatively discrete event or an ongoing process. Relatively discrete events were dated by the month in which they were first observed or crossed a threshold level. If we had decided to study fewer organizations or fewer changes for each organization, we would have preferred a more fine-grained assessment of the trend line of the change processes.

Relative Importance of Changes

Some key informants listed changes that appeared to be relatively unimportant, or at least of a nature that the key informants in other organizations did not list. For example, when a major shift in organizational structure was made, some informants listed changes about reporting relationships of lower-level personnel. Other informants did not bother to mention these lower-level changes. In some cases, we suspected that this omission of lower-level changes was an artifact of the interview protocol's limiting the description of design and nondesign changes to a maximum of 20 minutes. In very dynamic organizations, time limits caused the informant not to have time to get to the lower-level changes. In more stable organizations, informants had plenty of time to describe mundane, lower-level changes. To control for these apparent differences in reporting behaviors, all 1,110 changes from the first-round interviews were coded by two people as "strategically important," "important, but not strategically important," and "not important." Interrater reliabilities are 0.74 and 0.85 for single and multiple raters, respectively (ICC[1,1] and ICC[1,k]; Shrout and Fleiss 1979).[6] Subsequent interview rounds were coded by a single rater. By coding the relative importance of changes, we controlled for differences in reporting behaviors by deleting unimportant changes or by differentially treating changes based on their relative strategic importance. Thus we can avoid testing theories of important or strategic change with data about less strategic changes.

Summary

After considering many trade-offs, we selected retrospective reports by the top manager as the primary method for developing and testing theories about the nature and antecedents of important changes. We attempted to minimize the errors of recall by interviewing the top managers every 6 months and asking about recent, important changes. Our decision to use the top manager as the sole key informant was based on our belief that the top manager was the person most knowledgeable about the broad variety of changes that occur within and across the organization.

The outcome of the four interviews was a 24-month event history for each of well over 100 organizations with comparable data on thousands of important organizational changes. The open-ended descriptions of these changes were coded with multiple coding schemes to characterize the nature of changes and their antecedents. To understand these changes further and to develop theories about change processes, we collected additional information about these organizations concerning their designs, contexts, and leaders, as described below.

ASSESSMENTS OF ORGANIZATIONAL, CONTEXTUAL, AND TOP MANAGER CHARACTERISTICS

To enhance our understanding of reported changes, we assessed a large number of organizational and contextual variables for each organization after both the first and third retrospective event-history interviews.[7] These variables were related to multiple dimensions of structure, process, technology, strategy, environment, and performance. We also assessed the characteristics of the top manager of each organization after the final retrospective event-history interview.[8] These characteristics included demographic variables, work histories, and personality variables. The organization, contextual, and top manager characteristics were assessed with questionnaires that were hand delivered or mailed to the key informants. Completed questionnaires were returned by mail to the researchers.

Selecting the Key Informant for the Questionnaire

The top manager was selected to complete both types of questionnaires for all of the same reasons described above concerning the selection of the key informant for the retrospective event history, especially the expectation that the top manager would be the most knowledgeable and qualified informant (Hambrick 1981, Snow and Hrebiniak 1980, Zajac and Shortell 1989). It also was easier to continue using the top manager after we had developed a good rapport during the interviews. This decision to again use the top manager as the key informant was not without cost. A consequence of the decision is that data from the interviews would be more correlated with data from the questionnaires than if different key informants had provided the two types of data (Glick, Jenkins, and Gupta 1986). The problem with the single-informant procedure is that top managers may provide answers on the various data-collecting media that are cognitively consistent and reflect their own cognitive maps of how organizations operate. To the extent that the cognitive maps of most top managers overemphasize some causal connections, the common methods variance may bias the relationships between variables assessed in the interviews and variables assessed with the questionnaires.

We attempted to minimize the problem of common methods variance by employing different methods for collecting information from the informant. Specifically, the methods for obtaining the retrospective report data and the questionnaire data differed in three ways: (1) The interview questions were open-ended (e.g., "Please list . . ."), whereas the mailed questionnaire items were closed-ended (e.g., "To what extent is . . . ," with forced-choice or numeric responses); (2) the interview response mode was oral in a social context, whereas the questionnaire response mode was written in private; and (3) the time interval between the interview and completion of the questionnaire was long enough for informants to forget the specifics of the interview before completing the questionnaire, with an expected procedural minimum of one week and an allowed maximum of three months. The mean interval was approximately one month. Despite these efforts to minimize common methods variance, however, the top managers' cognitive maps may have influenced the observed patterns of relationships to some unknown degree. In retrospect, we believe that choosing to use a single informant for the retrospective reports was a good decision. On the other hand, it would have been useful to have sent the organizational assessment questionnaires to multiple informants in order to have collected more independent measures of the consequences of changes, and of the effectiveness of the organizations with the questionnaires. Although the top manager was the best informant for assessing the changes and most other information, in retrospect we believe that multiple informants should have been used for some outcome measures to eliminate single-source bias in predicted relationships.

Characteristics Assessed in the Questionnaires

The main purpose of the questionnaire about organizational and contextual characteristics was to enhance our understanding of changes in organizational design and effectiveness. For example, the questionnaires asked for information about the organization's effectiveness, external environment, strategy, internal functioning, goals, technology, and size. The specific variables and measures used in the questionnaires were identified through reviews of the theoretical and empirical literatures, as noted earlier.

A variety of empirical studies have demonstrated that the top manager's characteristics are important determinants of organizational change or effectiveness (e.g., Gupta and Govindarajan 1984, Meyer and Goes 1988, Miller, Kets de Vries, and Toulouse 1982). After the last of the four interviews, our key informants completed a questionnaire on which they provided information on their ages, educations, work histories, and six personality characteristics.

Validity and Reliability of
CODE Study Questionnaire Measures

The validity and reliability of the questionnaire measures are partial consequences of four critical judgment calls described earlier: (1) The key informant, the top manager, was selected as the most knowledgeable about his or her organization; (2) a single informant was questioned rather than multiple informants; (3) the set of field sites was selected to be heterogeneous in terms of the key variables in the study; and (4) the questionnaires were designed to assess these variables in terminology that is meaningful to top managers in a broad variety of organizations. To the extent that these judgment calls were appropriate, we expected the factor analyses and reliability statistics to support our a priori measures. After a few of the a priori measures were deleted due to disconfirming evidence from one or more of the analyses, the mean Cronbach's alpha interitem scale reliability for the first-round organizational assessment questionnaire was 0.72. Following revision of the questionnaire for the second round, the mean reliability was 0.74. The mean reliability for the top manager questionnaire also was 0.61. Overall, these results support the validity and reliability of our measures and the four judgment calls described above.

As a further assessment of these judgment calls, in the 36 organizations selected by the University of Texas research group, multiple informants were asked four of the same organizational effectiveness questions that were asked of the top managers. These additional informants were members of top management teams who reported to the top managers or chief operating officers. Averaging across all informants within each organization provided a reliable organization-level score. The mean rater reliabilities (ICC[1,k]; see Glick 1985, Shrout and Fleiss 1979) for the four items were 0.71, 0.68, 0.74, and 0.63, respectively.[9] These mean rater reliabilities indicated that the average scores varied substantially across organizations on all four dimensions of effectiveness. This supports our belief that the set of organizations in the University of Texas local study was moderately heterogeneous. Heterogeneity was even greater among the set of field sites in the overall study.

Our decision to question the top manager as the sole key informant in most field sites is more difficult to evaluate. Although we can estimate the interrater reliability of a single rater with ICC(1,1),[10] this estimate applies to the reliability of an informant randomly selected from the set of actual informants. As argued earlier, the top manager is a more qualified informant than the other members of the top management team. The multiple informants from the University of Texas local study occupied diverse positions with different functional and product line responsibilities that exposed them to different information, reward structures, and so on. Thus our estimates of the interrater reliability of a single rater can be interpreted only as lower-bound estimates of the accuracy of the top managers' assessments. In our local study of 36 organizations, the interrater reliabilities for a single randomly selected top management team member, ICC(1,1) (Glick 1985, Shrout and Fleiss 1979), are 0.30, 0.26, 0.33, and 0.23 on the four dimensions of effectiveness. These values indicated that randomly selecting a single informant from the top management team would not provide reliable measures of effectiveness.

In addition to the distinction between the top manager and other top management team members, it is likely that even stronger positional effects are associated with the dramatic differences among top management team members' job titles. We cannot separate, however, the differences among these other positions because the titles vary considerably across organizations. Therefore, we can conclude that the top managers will be more accurate than suggested by the reported ICC(1,1), but we cannot determine how much more accurate. Selecting the key informant from a single position controls for all systematic differences among positions. By consistently selecting the top manager from each organization as the key informant, we control for the moderate positional effects that we estimated above, and for an undetermined amount of variance associated with differences among other top management team positions.

SUMMARY AND CONCLUSION

Our goal in undertaking the CODE study was to understand better the nature, frequency, antecedents, and consequences of a broad variety of changes in organizations, particularly as these changes affect organizational effectiveness. This relatively positivist goal had several implications that led us to adopt a methodology that involved more independent observations than have been used in the other longitudinal studies described in this volume.

To learn about the variety of ways in which organizational designs, contexts, and leaders can affect how and when different types of changes occur, we had to make numerous trade-offs. First, despite the potential for coordination problems, top-grade researchers from several universities were included as collaborators to contribute data, insights, and theory. Second, rather than focus on a small number of changes or organizations, we collected data about a large number of changes in each of more than 100 organizations. This set of organizations was heterogeneous, yet clustered in subsets that are relevant to our theories. The heterogeneous clusters allow development of middle-range theories within clusters as well as tests of generalizability across the heterogeneous set. Third, retrospective reports of the most important, recent changes in the organizations were obtained in semiannual interviews. These reports provide retrospective event histories that include information on the timing of changes in much greater detail than is possible with a panel design. Fourth, the top manager was selected as the key informant for each organization. The top manager is likely to be more knowledgeable than other informants about a broader variety of changes. By consistently selecting an informant from the same position in each organization, we controlled for a number of report biases that are likely to be associated with an informant's position in the organization due to specialized information flows and biased information processing. Fifth, only one key informant was used in each organization. This minimized the loss of field sites (and thus the compromising of generalizability) and avoided the inclusion of reports from less knowledgeable informants. As a consequence, however, we did not gain the potential advantages of multiple informants, such as the reduction of common methods variance, the testing of reliability, and the increase in validity gained by the resolution of discrepancies among multiple reports. Sixth, multiple attributes of the reported changes were coded to distill the diverse descriptions of specific changes into relatively simple and general (Weick 1979) descriptions of the changes. Seventh, assessments of organizational, contextual, and top manager characteristics were obtained with questionnaires completed by the top manager. The use of the same informant for the interview and the questionnaires might confound our results with common methods variance, but this potential confounding is limited by the use of different methods for collecting information from the informant and the collection of different types of data at different occasions. We accepted as a trade-off the threat to internal validity due to common methods variance from a single informant to avoid the reductions in internal and external validity that would result from the use of less knowledgeable informants or from the loss of field sites that would not provide multiple informants.

All research methodologies reflect necessary trade-offs among the desirable theory characteristics of generality, accuracy, and simplicity (Thorngate 1976, Weick 1979). Some methodologies, however, achieve lower scores on all characteristics, whereas stronger methodologies achieve higher aggregate scores across all three dimensions. In the CODE study methodology, we sought *generality* by acquiring and using data from a relatively large variety of organizations and organizational contexts. We sought *accuracy* by developing and comparing theories created within and for specific contexts or domains—that is, specific industries and environments. We also sought accuracy by obtaining data on a variety of contingency variables. Finally, we sought *simplicity* by creating a database sufficiently large that events and variables that might possibly be antecedents, causes, or consequences of organizational change and change processes could be tested for inclusion using inferential statistics. Less important and nonsignificant factors can be dropped to develop simplicity in the final theories. Still, the trade-offs we made in establishing the CODE study methodology resulted in more generality, but less accuracy, than is found in the more ethnographic methods typically used to study organizational changes and change processes.

Acknowledgments

This research was supported by a research contract from the Basic Research Office of the Army Research Institute for the Behavioral and Social Sciences to the first two authors. We thank Alan Meyer and Andrew Van de Ven for their helpful comments on earlier drafts of the manuscript, and the helpful comments on our presentation from participants in the National Science Foundation Conference on Longitudinal Field Research Methods for Studying Organizational Processes, Austin, Texas, September 1988.

Notes

1. At the time of this writing, additional data were still being collected. The completed data set will have complete information on approximately 120 organizations.

2. The interview instruments, protocols, and coding instructions are described in CODE Study Technical Reports 01, 05, 10, and 11, which are available from the first author.

3. In roughly 10% of the organizations, the top position on the organizational chart was occupied by an individual with substantial or primary responsibilities in nonadministrative capacities, and most administrative issues were handled by a full-time professional administrator. In these cases, we interviewed the professional administrator. In several cases, the CEO explicitly told us that the professional administrator was the most knowledgeable individual for our study.

4. These subcategories are defined more precisely in CODE Technical Reports 01 and 05, which are available from the first author.

5. This vivid example of the difficulty of disentangling causal effects from ongoing processes was provided by Alan Meyer, one of the collaborators on this study.

6. The interrater reliability of a single rater, ICC(1,1) (Glick 1985, Shrout and Fleiss 1979), is analogous to an item reliability statistic, whereas the interrater reliability of the mean, ICC(1,k), is similar to an interitem scale reliability statistic, such as Cronbach's alpha. ICC(1,k) is an estimate of the interrater reliability of the *average* of the two raters for each coded change. ICC(1,1) is an estimate of the interrater reliability of the rating from a *single* rater randomly selected from the pair of actual raters. Both ICC(1,k) and ICC(1,1) are functions of the within and between coded change variances and the number of informants (raters) per coded change. Given an acceptable individual rater reliability for the coding task (0.74), only a single rater coded the subsequent changes.

7. The questionnaires used to assess organizational and contextual variables are included with full documentation in CODE Study Technical Reports 02 and 06, which are available from the first author.

8. The questionnaire to assess top manager characteristics is included with full documentation in CODE Study Technical Report 09, which is available from the first author.

9. As described in note 6, interrater reliability of the mean, ICC(1,k), is analogous to an interitem scale reliability statistic, such as Cronbach's alpha (Glick 1985, Shrout and Fleiss 1979). In the University of Texas local study, there were an average of 5.9 key informants for each of the 36 field sites.

10. As described in note 6, the interrater reliability of a single rater, ICC(1,1), is analogous to an item reliability statistic (Glick 1985, Shrout and Fleiss 1979).

References

Aguilar, F. J. (1967), *Scanning the Business Environment,* New York: Macmillan.

Astley, W. G., and A. Van de Ven (1983), "Central Perspectives and Debates in Organization Theory," *Administrative Science Quarterly,* 28, 245-273.

Bagozzi, R. P., and L. W. Phillips (1982), "Representing and Testing Organizational Theories: A Holistic Construal Process," *Administrative Science Quarterly,* 27, 459-489.

Barley, S. R. (1990), "Images of Imaging: Notes on Doing Longitudinal Field Work," *Organization Science,* 1, 220-247.

Beyer, J., and H. Trice (1982), "The Utilization Process: A Conceptual Framework and Synthesis of Empirical Literature," *Administrative Science Quarterly,* 27, 591-622.

Blackburn, R., and L. L. Cummings (1982), "Cognitions of Work Unit Structure," *Academy of Management Journal,* 25, 836-854.

Cohen, J. (1988), *Statistical Power Analysis for the Behavioral Sciences* (2nd ed.), Hillsdale, NJ: Lawrence Erlbaum.

Cook, T. D., and D. T. Campbell (1979), *Quasi-experimentation: Design and Analysis Issues for Field Settings,* Chicago: Rand McNally.

Daft, R. L., and G. P. Huber (1987), "How Organizations Learn: A Communication Framework," in S. B. Bacharach and N. DiTomaso (Eds.), *Research in the Sociology of Organizations* (Vol. 5, pp. 1-36), London: JAI.

Dearborn, D. C., and H. A. Simon (1958), "Selective Perception: A Note on the Departmental Identifications of Executives," *Sociometry,* 21, 140-144.

Drasgow, F., and T. Kang (1984), "Statistical Power of Differential Validity and Differential Prediction Analyses for Detecting Measurement Nonequivalence," *Journal of Applied Psychology,* 69, 498-508.

Duncan, R. B. (1972), "The Characteristics of Organizational Environments and Perceived Environmental Uncertainty," *Administrative Science Quarterly,* 17, 313-326.

Glick, W. H. (1985), "Conceptualizing and Measuring Organizational and Psychological Climate: Pitfalls in Multi-Level Research," *Academy of Management Review,* 10, 601-616.

Glick, W. H., G. D. Jenkins, Jr., and N. Gupta (1986), "Method Versus Substance: How Strong Are Underlying Relationships Between Job Characteristics and Attitudinal Outcomes?" *Academy of Management Journal,* 29, 441-464.

Gupta, A. K., and V. Govindarajan (1984), "Business Unit Strategy, Managerial Characteristics, and Business Unit Effectiveness at Strategy Implementation," *Academy of Management Journal,* 27, 25-41.

Hambrick, D. C. (1981), "Strategic Awareness Within Top Management Teams," *Strategic Management Journal,* 2, 263-279.

Hambrick, D. C. (1982), "Environmental Scanning and Organizational Strategy," *Strategic Management Journal,* 3, 159-174.

Hax, A. C., and N. S. Majluf (1988), "The Concept of Strategy and the Strategy Formation Process," *Interfaces,* 18 (May-June), 99-109.

Houston, M. J., and S. Sudman (1975), "A Methodological Assessment of the Use of Key Informants," *Social Science Research,* 4, 151-164.

Hrebiniak, L. G., and W. F. Joyce (1985), "Organizational Adaptation: Strategic Choice and Environmental Determinism," *Administrative Science Quarterly,* 30, 336-349.

Huber, G. P. (1985), "Temporal Stability and Response-Order Biases in Participant Descriptions of Organizational Decisions," *Academy of Management Journal,* 28, 943-950.

Huber, G. P. (1990), "A Theory of the Effects of Advanced Information Technologies on Organizational Design, Intelligence, and Decision Making," *Academy of Management Review,* 15, 47-71.

Huber, G. P. (1991), "Organizational Learning: The Contributing Processes and the Literatures," *Organization Science,* 2, 88-115.

Huber, G. P., and R. L. Daft (1987), "The Information Environments of Organizations," in F. M. Jablin, L. L. Putnam, K. H. Roberts, and L. W. Porter (Eds.), *Handbook of Organizational Communication* (pp. 130-164), Newbury Park, CA: Sage.

Huber, G. P., and R. R. McDaniel (1986), "The Decision Making Paradigm of Organizational Design," *Management Science,* 32, 572-589.

Huber, G. P., C. C. Miller, and W. H. Glick (1990), "Developing More Encompassing Theories About Organizations: The Centralization-Effectiveness Relationship as an Example," *Organization Science,* 1, 11-40.

Huber, G. P., and D. J. Power (1985), "Retrospective Reports of Strategic-Level Managers: Guidelines for Increasing Their Accuracy," *Strategic Management Journal,* 6, 171-180.

Ireland, R. D., M. A. Hitt, R. A. Bettis, and D. A. DePorras (1987), "Strategy Formulation Processes: Differences in Perceptions of Strength and Weakness Indicators and Environmental Uncertainty by Managerial Level," *Strategic Management Journal,* 8, 467-485.

Katz, D., and R. L. Kahn (1978), *The Social Psychology of Organizations* (2nd ed.), New York: Wiley.

Leonard-Barton, D. (1990), "A Dual Methodology for Case Studies: Synergistic Use of a Longitudinal Single Site With Replicated Multiple Sites," *Organization Science,* 1, 248-266.

Markus, M. L., and D. Robey (1988), "Information Technology and Organizational Change: Causal Structure in Theory and Research," *Management Science,* 34, 583-598.

McGuire, J. B. (1986), "Management and Research Methodology," *Journal of Management,* 12, 5-17.

Meyer, A. D. (1982), "Adapting to Environmental Jolts," *Administrative Science Quarterly,* 27, 515-537.

Meyer, A. D., and J. B. Goes (1988), "Organizational Assimilation of Innovations: A Multilevel, Contextual Analysis," *Academy of Management Journal,* 31, 897-923.

Miller, D., M. E. R. Kets de Vries, and J. Toulouse (1982), "Top Executive Locus of Control and Its Relationship to Strategy-Making, Structure, and Environment," *Academy of Management Journal,* 25, 237-253.

Mintzberg, H. (1975), "The Manager's Job: Folklore and Fact," *Harvard Business Review,* 53, 49-61.

Mohr, L. B. (1982), *Explaining Organizational Behavior,* San Francisco: Jossey-Bass.

Monge, P. R. (1990), "Theoretical and Analytical Issues in Studying Organizational Processes," *Organization Science,* 1, 406-430.

Monge, P. R., R. V. Farace, E. M. Eisenberg, K. I. Miller, and L. L. White (1984), "The Process of Studying Process in Organizational Communication," *Journal of Communication,* 34, 1, 22-43.

Phillips, L. A. (1981), "Assessing Measurement Error in Key Informant Reports: A Methodological Note on Organizational Analysis in Marketing," *Journal of Marketing Research,* 18, 395-415.

Pinder, C. C., and Moore, L. F. (1980), "The Inevitability of Multiple Paradigms and the Resultant Need for Middle-Range Analysis in Organizational Theory," in C. C. Pinder and L. F. Moore (Eds.), *Middle-Range Theory and the Study of Organizations* (pp. 87-100), Boston: Martinus Nijhoff.

Seidler, J. (1974), "On Using Informants: A Technique for Collecting Quantitative Data and Controlling Measurement Error in Organization Analysis," *American Sociological Review,* 39, 816-831.

Shrout, P. E., and J. L. Fleiss (1979), "Intraclass Correlations: Uses in Assessing Rater Reliability," *Psychological Bulletin,* 86, 420-428.

Snow, C. C., and L. G. Hrebiniak (1980), "Strategy, Distinctive Competence, and Organizational Performance," *Administrative Science Quarterly,* 25, 317-336.

Thorngate, W. (1976), "Possible Limits on a Science of Social Behavior," in L. H. Strickland, F. E. Aboud, and K. J. Gergen (Eds.), *Social Psychology in Transition* (pp. 121-139), New York: Plenum.

Tuma, N. B., and M. Hannan (1984), *Social Dynamics: Models and Methods,* New York: Academic.

Van de Ven, A. H., and M. S. Poole (1990), "Methods for Studying Innovation Development in the Minnesota Innovation Research Program," *Organization Science,* 1, 313-335.

Weick, K. E. (1974), "Middle Range Theories of Social Systems," *Behavioral Science,* 19, 357-367.

Weick, K. E. (1979), *The Social Psychology of Organizations* (2nd ed.), Reading, MA: Addison-Wesley.

Williams, L. J., J. A. Cote, and M. R. Buckley (1989), "Lack of Method Variance in Self-Reported Affect and Perceptions at Work: Reality or Artifact?" *Journal of Applied Psychology,* 74, 462-468.

Wolfe, J., and C. Jackson (1987), "Creating Models of the Strategic Decision Making Process via Participant Recall: A Free Simulation Examination," *Journal of Management,* 13, 123-134.

Zajac, E. J., and S. M. Shortell (1989), "Changing Generic Strategies: Likelihood, Direction, and Performance Implications," *Strategic Management Journal,* 10, 413-430.

Zajonc, R., and D. Wolfe (1966), "Cognitive Consequences of a Person's Position in a Formal Organization," *Human Relations,* 19, 139-150.

6

Methods for Studying
Innovation Development in the
Minnesota Innovation Research Program

ANDREW H. VAN DE VEN

MARSHALL SCOTT POOLE

This chapter describes the methods being used by the Minnesota Innovation Research Program to develop and test a process theory of innovation that explains how and why innovations develop over time and what developmental paths may lead to success or failure for different kinds of innovations. After a background description of the longitudinal field research, this chapter focuses on the methods being used to examine processes of innovation development. These methods pertain to the selection of cases and concepts, observing change, coding and analyzing event data to identify process patterns, and developing theories to explain observed innovation processes. The authors believe these methods are applicable to other studies that examine a range of temporal processes, including organizational start-up, growth, decline, and adaptation.

In their extensive review of the innovation literature, Tornatsky et al. (1983) point out that although many studies have examined the antecedents to or consequences of innovation, very few have directly examined how and why

This chapter appeared originally in *Organization Science,* vol. 1, no. 3, August 1990, pp. 313-335.

innovations emerge, develop, grow, or terminate over time. Yet an appreciation of the temporal sequence of activities in developing and implementing new ideas is fundamental to the management of innovation. Innovation managers need to know more than the input factors required to achieve desired innovation outcomes. They are centrally responsible for directing the innovating process within the proverbial black box between inputs and outcomes. To do this, the innovation manager needs a road map that indicates how and why the innovating journey unfolds, and what paths are likely to lead to success or failure.

In other words, the innovation manager needs a *process theory* that explains innovation development.[1] From a developmental perspective, such a process theory focuses on explaining the temporal order and sequence of steps that unfold as an innovative idea is transformed and implemented into a concrete reality. A process theory may produce some fundamental "laws of innovating" useful for explaining how a broad class of processes, sequences, and performance conditions unfold along the innovation journey. A process theory may also identify certain paths more likely to be effective under certain developmental conditions. Empirical verification of a process theory could make a major contribution to improving the capabilities of managers, entrepreneurs, and policy makers to innovate.

Since 1983, researchers at the University of Minnesota have been engaged in a longitudinal field research program with the objective of developing such a process theory. The Minnesota Innovation Research Program (MIRP) consists of longitudinal field studies of 14 different technological, product, process, and administrative innovations in public and private sectors (see Figure 6.1). The 14 studies were undertaken by different interdisciplinary research teams (in total consisting of 15 faculty and 19 doctoral students from eight different academic departments and five schools at the University of Minnesota). While the program accommodates individual requirements of each innovation, MIRP researchers adopted a common framework and methodology to compare and integrate findings across all innovations. This common framework is based on the definition that the process of innovation is the invention and implementation of new *ideas,* which are developed by *people,* who engage in *transactions* with others over time within an institutional *context,* and who judge *outcomes* of their efforts and act accordingly.

Beginning with historical baseline data collected in 1984, when the innovations began in their natural field settings, these core concepts were repeatedly measured over time throughout their developmental period. As of February 1990, most of the innovations were either terminated or implemented, and fieldwork had thus largely concluded. MIRP researchers are now concentrating on analyzing their longitudinal data in order to determine

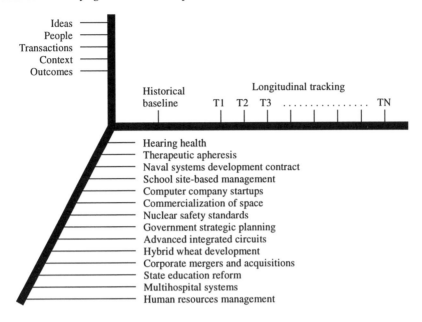

Figure 6.1. The Minnesota Innovation Research Program

how and why the innovations developed over time and what paths led to successful and unsuccessful outcomes.

The first section of this chapter provides a brief overview of the MIRP research design and longitudinal data-collection methods used to track the innovations (see details in Van de Ven, Angle, and Poole 1989). It provides a useful background for addressing problems of analyzing data collected in the field, which will be the major focus of the second part of the chapter.

The kind of fieldwork discussed in the first section often represents the highly visible and "extroverted" period of a longitudinal study, as researchers engage in many stimulating interactions with many diverse people and organizations to collect field data. Over time, these interactions grow into many rewarding interpersonal bonds of acceptance and friendship, and these sometimes result in researchers losing their objectivity and "going native." Funding and institutional support for longitudinal research tends to peak during this period. It is often the most labor-intensive period of a longitudinal study, when the research team swells with additional research assistants and coinvestigators engaged in data collection, and when growing research administration tasks often remove the principal investigator too far from direct field observation. It is also the period when organizational participants and research supporters are most anxious to receive feedback and learn of the study's findings. The ability to provide this feedback first requires data analysis, and by the time results become apparent it is often too late; interest in research findings by organizational participants and research supporters wanes with time. As a consequence, the mobilization of ongoing support and participation in a longitudinal field research study requires researchers to develop an extensive set of craft skills. In their contributions to this volume, Pettigrew (Chapter 4), Barley (Chapter 1), and Leonard-Barton (Chapter 2) address these skills very well.

However, as with all seasons of work, there is a time for planting and a time for harvesting. Indeed, our experience has been that over the duration of a longitudinal study, nearly every hour of fieldwork requires an equal hour of homework, with the latter occupying increasing proportions of time in the autumn of the research. Using MIRP as an example, this chapter will focus on how researchers might spend their hours more creatively and efficiently in performing this homework. This homework tends to represent the less visible, more "introverted," less socially rewarding, yet often more technically complex and creative "backroom" work of longitudinal research. Researchers must often support this homework "out of their own hides," because funding and resources to support it are seldom adequate and difficult to obtain. In addition, whereas data collection in the field can often be programmed and divided among research team members, significant research findings cannot be "manufactured" in this way. Instead, systematic and creative data analysis often involves a sequential set of tasks best performed by one or two individuals, who can increase their probabilities of learning and generating significant insights by performing all these tasks from beginning to end.

Unfortunately, little attention has been devoted to the development of systematic and efficient ways to do this data analysis and to report homework. As a consequence, data collected in most field studies remain grossly underanalyzed. It is ironic that after researchers invest such intensive and longitudinal efforts in collecting rich field data, they spend relatively little time and effort doing the homework needed to harvest their studies' bounty. Tragically, the archived files of far too many researchers are overflowing with underanalyzed, unused, and decaying data, as they flee to the next field research opportunity to collect another set of data (we ourselves are no exception).[2] The central purpose of this chapter is to emphasize the need for more systematic and efficient homework procedures to analyze longitudinal data that can (1) decrease the growing waste and opportunities lost from underanalyzed data, and (2) increase our capabilities to develop and test process theories of organizational change and development in longitudinal data (particularly on qualitative events observed over time).

BACKGROUND OVERVIEW OF MIRP FIELDWORK

As the field research work began, MIRP researchers adopted five methodological guidelines to study innovation processes. They pertain to (1) sample selection, (2) real-time process observation, (3) selection of core concepts for observing innovation processes, (4) identification and comparison of alternative models to explain observed processes, and (5) the addressing of problems of measurement and sequence analysis to test alternative process models. These methodological guidelines represent basic decisions and steps that need to be addressed in almost any field study of organizational change processes.

1. Sample a wide variety of innovations in order to enrich the range of insights and enhance generalizability. Since the project's inception, MIRP researchers were interested in developing a broad strategic orientation to the management of innovation, as opposed to the functionally defined and technically oriented perspective that has pervaded prior studies of innovation. We therefore adopted a broad definition of the population of innovations to study, including both technical innovations (new technologies, products, and services) and administrative innovations (new procedures, policies, and organizational forms) in public, private, and not-for-profit organizational settings in the United States and abroad. Through an involved sampling and negotiation process (described in Van de Ven and Angle 1989), access was obtained to conduct longitudinal studies of innovations in areas dealing with agriculture, industry, electronics, health care, education, nuclear power, government, and public-private sector partnerships (see Figure 6.1).

Critics have questioned the wisdom of this heterogeneous sampling of innovations, for it may result in attempts to compare apples with oranges. Our response is that we will never know the limits where valid comparisons end and where invalid comparisons begin unless we empirically examine the broadest possible range of cases to which our definition of innovation applies. After all, the comparative method is perhaps the most general and basic strategy for generating and evaluating valid scientific knowledge. This strategy involves the selection of comparison groups that differ in the scope of the population and conceptual categories of central interest to the research. As Kaplan (1964, p. 52) points out, scientific knowledge is greatly enhanced when we divide the subject matter into concepts and cases that "carve at the joints" over the widest possible ranges, types, conditions, and consequences. In this way we can develop and evaluate the limits of many important propositions about the subject matter.

2. Study the innovation process throughout its entire life, from beginning to end. Most studies of innovation or change to date have been retrospective case histories, conducted after outcomes were known. However, it is widely recognized that prior knowledge of the success or failure of an innovation invariably biases a study's findings. While historical analysis is necessary for examining many questions, and concerted efforts can be undertaken to minimize bias, it is generally better to initiate historical study before the outcomes of an innovation become known. It is even better to observe the innovation process throughout its unfolding. This approach maximizes the probability of discovering short-lived factors and changes that exert important influence. As Pettigrew (1985) notes, "The more we look at present-day events, the easier it is to identify change; the longer we stay with an emergent process and the further back we go to disentangle its origins, the more likely we are to identify continuities." Appreciating this dilemma requires that investigators carefully design their studies in order to observe changes that are relevant to the purposes and users of their research. Because the purpose of MIRP is to understand the management of innovation, we decided to frame the research from the innovation manager's temporal and contextual perspective. This involved gaining access to study innovation projects as early as possible, and to focus observations primarily on the actions and perceptions of managers over time while they were engaged in developing their innovations—without knowing how the innovation journeys might unfold or if they would be successes or failures.

Once access was obtained to study specific innovations from fall 1983 to mid-1984, case histories and baseline data were obtained on each innovation. These provided an understanding of the institutional context and the historical events that led to the status of each innovation at the time longitudinal tracking began. A variety of data-collection instruments were developed and used to observe the innovations as they developed in the ensuing years, including schedules for on-site observations, interviews, questionnaires, and archival records. These instruments are presented and evaluated in Van de Ven and Chu (1989), and some were initially tested by Van de Ven and Ferry (1980).

3. Develop a core set of constructs to guide and unify different field studies of innovation, and gather "rich" longitudinal data on these concepts. Implicitly or explicitly, study of any change or innovation process requires a set of categories or variables to describe innovation development. Because study of development processes in organizations is at an embryonic stage, these core concepts are best viewed as "sensitizing categories" for conducting an exploratory grounded theory kind of research (Glaser and Strauss 1967). As should be expected, different categories will produce very different substantive results.

Based on the MIRP definition of the innovation process, five sensitizing categories were adopted in the study of innovation development: ideas, people, transactions, context, and outcomes (see Figure 6.1). These concepts

TABLE 6.1 A Comparison of the Conventional Wisdom and MIRP Observations

	Literature Implicitly Assumes	*But We See This*
Ideas	One invention, operationalized.	Reinvention, proliferation, reimplementation, discarding, and termination.
People	An entrepreneur with fixed set of full-time people over time.	Many entrepreneurs, distracted, fluidly engaging and disengaging over time in a variety of organizational roles.
Transactions	Fixed network of people/firms working out details of an idea.	Expanding and contracting network of partisan stakeholders diverging and converging on ideas.
Context	Environment provides opportunities and constraints on innovation process.	Innovation process constrained by and creates multiple enacted environments.
Outcomes	Final result orientation; a stable new order comes into being.	Final result may be indeterminate; multiple in-process assess-ments and spin-offs; integration of new orders with old.
Process	Simple, cumulative sequence of stages or phases.	From simple to multiple progressions of divergent, parallel, and convergent paths, some of which are related and cumulative, others not.

SOURCE: Van de Ven and Angle (1989, p. 11).

were selected because they constitute the central factors of concern to innovation managers (Van de Ven 1986). The process of innovation consists of motivating and coordinating *people* to develop and implement new *ideas* by engaging in *transactions* (or relationships) with others and making the adaptations needed to achieve desired *outcomes* within changing institutional and organizational *contexts*. These concepts were used and operationalized differently depending upon the type of innovation being studied, the data-collection methods employed, and the substantive focus of the investigators (see Van de Ven, Angle, and Poole 1989).

As is typical in grounded theory research, assumptions and definitions of these concepts changed substantially and become progressively clearer with field observations over time. Table 6.1 compares the starting assumptions of these concepts drawn from the literature at the time (summarized in the left-hand column) with how MIRP researchers came to view them as a result of their field studies (in the right-hand column). The latter disclosed a different reality from the rather orderly and naive conceptions of the former.

Innovation ideas were found to proliferate into many ideas. There is not only invention, but there is re-invention as well, with some ideas being discarded as others are reborn. There are many persons involved in innovation, but most of these
are only partially included in the innovation effort, as they are distracted by very
busy schedules as they perform many other roles unrelated to the innovation. The
network of stakeholders involved in transactions is constantly being revised. This
"fuzzy set" epitomizes the general environment for the innovation, as multiple environments are "enacted" by various parties to the innovation. Rather than a simple, unitary and progressive path, we see multiple tracks, spin-offs, and the like,
some of which are related and coordinated, and others of which are not. Rather
than a single after-the-fact assessment of outcome, we see multiple, in-process assessments. The discrete identity of the innovation may become blurred as the new
and the old are integrated. (Van de Ven and Angle 1989, pp. 14-15)

Based on these field observations, MIRP researchers progressively refined
the definitions and measures of their core concepts.

*4. Compare and test alternative innovation process theories and models (as
opposed to a single model).* The MIRP field studies quickly demonstrated
that innovation processes are exceedingly complex, and far beyond the
explanatory capabilities of any single process theory found in the literature.
Moreover, MIRP researchers feared that efforts to develop a single process
theory grounded in the data would produce either an untestable theory or a
self-fulfilling prophesy. As Mitroff and Emshoff (1979), among others, have
observed, when scholars and practitioners have only a single perspective or
theory, they tend to twist and rationalize facts to fit their model. It is generally
better to develop and juxtapose alternative theories, and then determine
which theory better explains the data.

Thus MIRP researchers decided to adopt a comparative theory development and testing approach—that is, to apply alternative models to the data
and successively evaluate them in comparison with one another. At the least,
this would reduce complexity, because it is very difficult to analyze a large
array of field data without conceptual guidance. This strategy emphasizes
that testing a process theory is not based on Platonic criteria of an ideal
theory, which may never be found. Instead, it is based on the relative
explanatory power of alternative theories that are available or can be developed
to explain the phenomena. This comparative theory approach is consistent
with the principle that knowledge advances by successive approximations
and comparisons of competing alternative theories.

However, evaluating alternative process models or theories is not merely
a matter of identifying and testing them, any more than evaluating a theory
of structure is merely a matter of conceiving types of structures and testing

them. Between conception and test are the intervening tasks of defining constructs, finding indicators, developing propositions about innovation development, and using appropriate methods of sequence analysis. These intervening tasks constitute MIRP's last methodological guideline: *Address problems of measurement and sequence methods in order to identify process patterns in temporal data.* Undertaking this guideline brings us to MIRP's current research agenda, which we will now discuss.

METHODS FOR MEASUREMENT AND SEQUENCE ANALYSIS

Consider the challenge confronting MIRP researchers who followed the above guidelines in tracking the development of an innovation. Over three to five years of real-time field study of an innovation, they collected quantitative and qualitative data with a survey questionnaire completed every six months by innovation participants, conducted interviews with key innovation managers every six months, attended and made direct observations of regularly scheduled (monthly or bimonthly) innovation team meetings, and maintained study diaries in which they recorded and filed notes on frequent informal discussions with innovation managers, organizational memos and reports, and stories in trade journals and newspapers about the innovation.

Confronted with such an array of raw data, how do we transform them into a form useful for developing and testing process theories of innovation development? As stated before, a theory of development consists of statements about the temporal sequence of events that explain an observed stream of incidents or occurrences as innovations unfold. To make such a theory operational, and hence testable, it is important to distinguish between an *incident* (a raw datum) and an *event* (a theoretical construct). Whereas an incident is an empirical observation, an event is not directly observed; it is a conceptual construct in a model that explains the pattern of incidents. For each event one can choose any number of incidents as indicators that the event has happened. *Measurement* deals with the problem of selecting reliable and valid indicators of each event. But a good process model of innovation development does more than simply define its component events; it strings them together in a particular temporal order and sequence to explain how and why innovations unfold over time. *Sequence analysis* deals with methods to evaluate the degree to which event indicators conform with the model.

We will now discuss specific methods being used and contemplated by MIRP researchers to deal with problems of measurement (tasks 1-4 below) and sequence analysis (tasks 5-7 below). These tasks are interrelated, but we will discuss them in the following order:

1. Define a qualitative datum, and enter raw data into incidents.
2. Evaluate the reliability and validity of incidents.
3. Code incidents into qualitative event constructs.
4. Evaluate the reliability and validity of coded events.
5. Transform qualitative codes into quantitative categories.
6. Analyze temporal relationships in event sequence data.
7. Analyze temporal patterns or phases in event sequence data.

As this list suggests, MIRP is dealing with a common set of measurement and sequence analysis problems that almost any field study of the temporal sequence of events in an organizational change must address. Therefore, we believe that other researchers will benefit by borrowing from the following measurement and sequence analysis those methods that look promising and avoiding the others. Because some of the methods for these tasks are in developmental stages, we will not be able to indicate how well they work. We provide examples for others to make them clear.

Defining a Datum: An Incident

In quantitative survey data, the datum is typically assumed to be sufficiently clear to require no explicit treatment. However, we have found that this is not so with qualitative data, where it is important to define a datum, which is the basic element of information that is entered into a data file for analyzing temporal event sequences in the development of innovations.

In survey research, a *quantitative datum* is commonly regarded to be (1) a numerical response to a question scaled along a distribution (2) about an object (the unit of analysis) (3) at the time of measurement, which is (4) entered as a variable (along with other variables on the object) into a record (or case) of a quantitative data file, and (5) is subsequently recoded and classified as an indicator of a theoretical construct. In comparison, MIRP researchers defined a *qualitative datum* as (1) a bracketed string of words capturing the basic elements of information (2) about a discrete incident or occurrence (the unit of analysis) (3) that happened on a specific date, which is (4) entered as a unique record (or case) in a qualitative data file, and (5) is subsequently coded and classified as an indicator of a theoretical event.

As these definitions indicate, while similar in most respects, the basic element of information on a qualitative datum is a bracketed string of words about a discrete incident, whereas in a quantitative datum the element of information is a number scaled along a predetermined distribution of a variable. Raw words, sentences, or stories collected from the field cannot be entered into a qualitative data file until they are bracketed into a datum(s).

Obviously, explicit decision rules are needed to bracket raw words, and should reflect the substantive purposes of the research.

In the case of MIRP, the decision rule used to bracket words into a qualitative datum was the definition of an incident that occurred in the development of an innovation. Following guideline 3 above, an *incident* was defined as a major recurrent activity or whenever changes were observed to occur in any one of the five core concepts in the MIRP framework: innovation ideas, people, transactions, context, and outcomes. When each incident was identified, the bracketed string of words required to describe it included date of occurrence, the actor(s) or object(s) involved, the action or behavior that occurred, the consequence (if any) of the action, and the source of the information.

As with any decision rule, some further subjective judgments are involved in defining innovation incidents in an operationally consistent manner. In particular, interpretations among MIRP researchers varied on the level of specificity and the temporal duration of incidents. Some MIRP investigators used fine-grained definitions of incidents, whereas others adopted more coarse-grained definitions. A fine-grained perspective of incidents was often associated with short units of time—on the order of days or weeks; coarse-grained definitions often included incidents of long temporal duration—perhaps months or years.

Many of these differences were found to result from unique temporal laws that govern the rates of development of various kinds of innovations, and the differing research questions associated with these rates. For example, two MIRP researchers (Knudson and Ruttan 1989) found that the rate of hybrid wheat development is governed by biological laws that require several decades in order to move from basic research through technology development to market introduction. They observed that hybrid wheat's innovation process has been following this "biological time clock" since the late 1950s. In MIRP studies of biomedical innovations by Polley and Van de Ven (1989) and Garud and Van de Ven (1989), the rate of development appears to be governed by an "institutional regulation time clock," in which the design, testing, and commercial release of cochlear implants and therapeutic apheresis innovations entailed extensive review and approval steps by the U.S. Food and Drug Administration, sometimes lasting five years. Finally, rates of development of other innovations, such as new company start-ups (Venkataraman and Van de Ven, 1989) and some new administrative programs (Roberts and King 1989, Bryson and Roering 1989), are more rapid and appear to be limited only by entrepreneurial time and attention. As a consequence, theories and methods used to track developmental processes must be adapted to be consistent with the temporal laws of development and the corresponding granularity of incident detail appropriate to different types of innovations being examined.

If different innovation studies are viewed as different data points for examining the same model, as McPhee discusses in Chapter 7 of this volume, procedures for adjusting to or normalizing these variations in incident specificity and duration between different kinds of innovations may be needed to make process comparisons. We have not yet developed operational procedures to deal with this problem. Instead, at this early stage of data representation, we have focused primarily on developing procedures that produce a consistent tabulation of the temporal duration and specificity of incidents that occurred over time within each innovation. Once that is achieved, statistical process comparisons can be made between innovations of comparable incident duration and specificity. We anticipate that McPhee's suggestions on different approaches to comparing innovation studies will be highly useful in our future work.

By adopting the preceding conventions and decisions rules, MIRP researchers developed a chronological listing of all the incidents observed in the development of an innovation and entered them into a qualitative data file. Each incident represents a datum that is entered as a unique record into a qualitative data file for each innovation. Table 6.2 shows an example of a few incidents in such a data file. A variety of database software programs can be used; we are using Rbase System V software to organize and manage the qualitative data files.

Reliability and Validity of
Transforming Raw Data Into Incidents

Obviously, it is important to establish the reliability of classifying raw data into incidents. An equally important, though often neglected, issue is the validity of this bracketing procedure (Folger, Hewes, and Poole 1984, Poole, Folger, and Hewes 1987). Researchers often assume that the meaning of incidents is clear and that establishing reliability is equivalent to showing clear meaning of codings. However, attaining reliability among coders simply indicates that the meaning of incidents is clear to the particular group of researchers who designed the coding system. Of course, this does not mean the classifications correspond to the way participants see them. Thus it is important to distinguish between classifications meaningful to researchers and those meaningful to organizational participants. These two types of classifications may not overlap, and researchers must be clear about what sorts of claims they make about the meaning of their codings. It is necessary to test empirically whether researchers' classifications are consistent with practitioners' common perceptions of events. If the evidence indicates inconsistency, then no claims about the meaning of events to the participants are valid. Researchers can still sustain claims about the meaning of the incident

TABLE 6.2   Example of Innovation Incidents in Qualitative Data File for One
MIRP Study

INCIDENT NUMBER: 312 INCIDENT DATE: 06/01/87
INCIDENT: MN firm executive states he will not support TAP beyond 1988. The MN
firm has been investing about $4M per year in TAP, and the MA firm is only spending
between $1 and 1.5M. The MN executive thinks the MA firm should contribute more.
SK met with JB and offered several options such as donating modules, writing a check
for $1M, or taking less royalties. JB will see if the MA firm is still interested.

DATA SOURCE: Phone calls with SK and JB, 6/1/87.
CORE MIRP CODES: Outcome-negative Context-internal Context-external Transaction,
Contraction

INCIDENT NUMBER: 313 INCIDENT DATE: 06/01/87

INCIDENT: June SBU meeting canceled.

DATA SOURCE: Phone call with SK 6/1/87.
CORE MIRP CODES: Context-internal Contraction

INCIDENT NUMBER: 314 INCIDENT DATE: 06/18/87

INCIDENT: Emergency meeting conducted of MN firm's core TAP team to discuss restructuring finances as a result of recent internal management review. Items for discussion included 10-15% across-the-board budget reductions, omission of diagnostics,
assumption of improved electronics by 1/1/88, 70% of sales by 1995 will come from tu-
besets manufactured outside of the MI firm, and no significant research beyond LDL
and immune complex.

DATA SOURCE: Internal memo of 6/10/87 and 6/18/87 meeting notes.
CORE MIRP CODES: Transaction Idea-core Context-internal

INCIDENT NUMBER: 315 INCIDENT DATE: 06/25/87

INCIDENT: Joint administrative review of TAP by MN and MA firm executives. MN executive suggests bringing in a third partner to reduce financial burden. He suggests that
TAP be spun off into a joint venture with a third partner. No conclusion reached. The
MA firm executive asks, "Why has my partner blinked?" He questions if the MN firm
is really committed to TAP. The MN firm executive states that it is just an issue of financing and additional opportunities for investment.

DATA SOURCE: AHV notes of 6/25/87 administrative review meeting.
CORE MIRP CODES: Transaction Context-internal Context-external Outcome-negative

INCIDENT NUMBER: 316 INCIDENT DATE: 08/03/87

INCIDENT: SK begins contacting outside firms in search of an investment partner. Nine
types of investors identified.

DATA SOURCE: SK phone call 8/3/87.
CORE MIRP CODES: Transaction Context-external

from their theoretical position, but no claims about the "social reality" of the event are appropriate.

Two basic procedures were used to enhance the reliability and validity of the incidents entered into the qualitative data file. First, the entry of incidents from raw data sources into a data file was performed by at least two researchers. Consensus was required among these researchers on a consistent interpretation of the decision rules used to identify incidents. Second, the resulting list of incidents was reviewed by the innovation's key managers. They were asked to indicate if any incidents that occurred in the development of their innovations were missing or incorrectly described. Based on this feedback, revisions in the incident listings were made if they conformed to the decision rules for defining each incident. Typically, these two steps resulted in a more complete listing of incidents about an innovation's development.

However, it is important to recognize that the resulting list of incidents does not represent the population of occurrences in the development of an innovation. Even with real-time field observations, it is not humanly possible to observe and record all possible incidents that happened over time. Thus, as is well established in classical test theory of item sampling (Lord and Novick 1968), the incidents represent a sample of indicators of what happened over time as an innovation developed.

Coding Incidents Into Event Constructs

As they stand, the incident listings are not particularly useful for analysis, because each incident is just a qualitative indicator of what happened in the development of an innovation over time. The next step in representing the data is to code the incidents into theoretically meaningful events. A common problem with many coding systems is that they reduce rich qualitative data to a single dimension of meaning. For example, a failure to get renewed funding for an innovation may influence the development of the idea behind the project, it may also result in layoffs of innovation personnel, and it may signal a change in the relationship of the innovation to external resource controllers. If we code this incident as an event of the termination of an idea, we omit other dimensions of meaning. To avoid this problem, incidents may be coded on several dimensions of an event. For example, we might code the incident on four event dimensions: a negative outcome (resource cut), a change in the core innovation idea, people leaving, and a change in transactions (relations with resource controllers).

One way to organize these multidimensional data into a format to analyze change processes is to array them on multiple tracks that correspond to conceptually meaningful categories. The procedure of coding incidents along several event tracks evolved in Poole's (1983a, 1983b) studies of decision development in small groups. Poole argued that previous models of group decision development—which commonly posited a rational decision process of three to five stages—were too simple. He was interested in testing the hypothesis that decisions did not follow a fixed sequence of phases, but instead could follow several different paths. He also believed that the previous practice of coding only one dimension of group behavior, such as task process, was responsible for previous findings supporting the single-sequence models. To examine a richer model of group development, he developed a three-track coding system: One track coded the impact an incident had on the process by which the group does its work (in this case, an incident was a member's statement), a second coded the same incident in terms of its effect on group relationships, and a third track indexed which of several topics the incident referred to. By coding an incident on several conceptually relevant dimensions simultaneously, Poole was able to derive a richer description of group processes than had been gained in previous studies.

MIRP adopted Poole's idea of coding each innovation incident according to multiple dimensions or constructs of events. Consistent with the MIRP definition of innovation process, a coding scheme was adopted that captures key dimensions of changes in innovation ideas, people, transactions, context, and outcomes in an observed incident. Table 6.3 summarizes this coding scheme.

Within each conceptual track a number of more specific codings are possible, depending on the particular questions being addressed by the researchers. For example, in their MIRP study Ring and Rands (1989) coded incidents in terms of more refined dimensions of transactions in order to examine their model of formal and informal transaction processes, whereas Garud and Van de Ven (1989) expanded the context track into a number of dimensions to examine their model of industry emergence. Thus the coding scheme can be tailored to meet the needs and interest of individual MIRP study teams.

Assessing Reliability and Validity of Coding Scheme

A number of steps can be taken to enhance the reliability and validity of coding incidents into indicators of event constructs. First, operational definitions and coding conventions were drafted for event constructs. Periodically, meetings were conducted with researchers and other colleagues to evaluate the construct validity of these definitions—that is, the extent to which operational definitions appeared to be logical and understandable indicators of the constructs under consideration.

From prior research (Van de Ven and Ferry 1980), we learned that a useful way to conduct these meetings is to begin with an overall presentation of the

TABLE 6.3 Illustration of Coding Tracks on Core MIRP Dimensions

People track _____	
Ideas track _____	
Transactions _____	
Context track _____	
Outcomes track _____	
TIME ─┼─	

People track: a coding of the people/groups involved in an incident, the roles and activities they perform at a given point in time.

Ideas track: a coding of the substantive ideas or strategies that innovation group members use to describe the content of their innovation at a given point in time.

Transactions track: the informal and formal relationships among innovation group members, other firms, and groups involved in the incident.

Context/environmental track: a coding of the exogenous events outside of the innovation unit in the larger organization and industry/community that are perceived by innovation group members to affect the innovation.

Outcomes track: when incidents provide evidence of results, they are coded as representing either positive (good news or successful accomplishment), negative (bad news or instances of failure or mistakes), and mixed (neutral or ambiguous news indicating elements of both success and failure).

conceptual model being studied. Then, participants are handed written definitions of each construct in the model and the suggested indicators to be used to measure each construct. Participants can then be asked to "suggest better indicators for measuring this construct as defined previously." Often using a nominal group technique format (see Delbecq, Gustafson, and Van de Ven 1975), the reviewers are provided a brief period to think and respond to the questions in writing. Then a general discussion ensues, during which group opinions are obtained. The qualitative written comments from these review sessions are especially helpful in sharpening the norms of correspondence (Kaplan 1964) between definitions of constructs and even indicators, and in clarifying ambiguities in decision rules for coding event indicators.

An operating norm of MIRP is that the actual coding of incidents into event constructs is performed independently by two or more MIRP researchers. This permits us to compute interrater reliability as a basic criterion to evaluate the reliability of the coding procedures. Following these procedures, 85%, 93%, and 91% agreements between coders have been obtained thus far in coding event indicators for three innovations.

In addition to obtaining comments from other researchers and theorists, it is also useful to assess whether the researchers' dimensions of events correspond to those of innovation participants (for methods of doing this, see Folger, Hewes, and Poole 1984). Although not necessary for purposes of testing theories, it is useful to determine the interpretive adequacy of our theoretical classifications. If our categories map events in ways that correspond to how participants see them, our findings can support claims about the social phenomenological processes of innovation.

Transforming Coded Incidents
Into Bit-Maps for Time-Series Analysis

As Abbott (1990) suggests, new analytic methods are needed to identify the sequence, order, and causal relationships among coded innovation events. Use of these methods requires the transformation of an innovation's chronological listing of coded incidents into dichotomous indicators of event constructs. Such a transformation of qualitative codes into quantitative dichotomous variables permits the application of various statistical methods in examining time-dependent patterns of relation among the event constructs.

Theoretically, it is possible to exhaust the information contained in a text with binary oppositions. A dichotomous indicator uses 1 to represent the presence and 0 the absence of a certain code of the qualitative incident. The choice of a particular set of indicators depends on the substantive problem of interest; we have described in the previous section the event indicators chosen to code the innovation incidents. With the indicators chosen, each coded construct of an incident is transformed into a dichotomous variable of 1 (change occurred) or 0 (no change occurred) in a different column of a row (an incident) in the incident data file. Then all the rows (incidents) in the file are mapped into a matrix of 1s and 0s, which we call a *bit-map*.

Table 6.4 illustrates a partial bit-map data file for the first 30 of 253 incidents in the development of one MIRP innovation. In such a bit-map, the chronological listing of qualitative events is time dependent, meaning that the sequential order of the rows is crucial and should be taken into account when information is to be extracted, although the columns are interchangeable. A method that returns the same results when the rows of an event sequence bit-map are interchanged is not appropriate for identifying dynamic patterns, because the information contained in the temporal order of the incidents is not used.

Analysis of Temporal Relationships in Bit-Map Data

The above transformation of qualitative codes into quantitative bit-map data files sets the stage for an examination of temporal relationships and patterns among dimensions in the development of innovations. Sequence analysis is the family of methods concerned with the problem of determining the temporal order among events (Abbott 1984). Analogous to analysis of

TABLE 6.4 Partial Bit-Map of Innovation Incidents in One MIRP Study

Variables[a]	
num:	Incident number
date:	Incident date
days:	Number of days from 01/01/68 (the first incident)
ic:	Idea-core [68]
ir:	Idea-related [4]
pe:	People [49]
tr:	Transaction [165]
ci:	Context—internal [8]
ce:	Context—external [22]
op:	Outcome—positive [58]
on:	Outcome—negative [59]
om:	Outcome—mixed [7]

Incident num	*date*	*days*	*ic*	*ir*	*pe*	*tr*	*ci*	*ce*	*op*	*on*	*om*
1	01/01/68	1	1	0	0	0	1	0	0	0	0
2	01/01/68	1	0	0	0	1	0	0	0	0	0
3	01/01/68	1	0	0	0	0	0	1	0	0	0
4	01/01/68	1	0	0	0	0	0	1	0	0	0
5	01/01/68	1	1	0	0	1	0	0	0	0	0
6	01/01/68	1	1	0	0	1	0	0	0	1	0
7	01/01/74	2193	1	0	1	0	0	0	0	0	0
8	01/01/74	2193	0	0	1	0	0	0	0	0	0
9	12/01/78	3988	0	0	1	0	0	0	0	0	0
10	10/01/79	4292	1	0	1	1	0	0	0	0	0
11	10/07/79	4298	1	0	0	1	0	0	0	0	0
12	01/01/80	4384	0	0	0	0	0	1	0	0	0
13	01/04/80	4387	1	0	0	0	0	0	0	0	0
14	01/08/80	4391	0	0	0	1	0	0	0	1	0
15	01/12/80	4395	1	0	0	0	0	0	1	0	0
16	04/01/80	4475	1	0	0	0	0	0	0	0	0
17	04/07/80	4481	0	0	0	1	0	0	1	0	0
18	05/01/80	4505	0	0	0	1	0	0	0	0	0
19	10/01/80	4658	1	0	0	0	0	0	0	1	0
20	10/07/80	4664	0	0	0	1	0	0	1	0	0
21	11/01/80	4689	0	0	1	1	0	0	0	1	0
22	11/07/80	4695	1	0	0	0	0	0	0	0	0
23	11/15/80	4703	0	0	0	1	0	0	0	1	0
24	11/21/80	4709	0	0	0	1	0	0	0	1	0
25	12/01/80	4719	1	0	1	1	0	0	0	0	0
26	12/11/80	4729	0	0	0	1	0	0	0	1	0
27	12/15/80	4733	0	0	0	1	0	0	1	0	0
28	12/21/80	4739	1	0	0	0	0	0	1	0	0
29	01/01/81	4750	0	0	1	1	0	0	0	0	0
30	03/01/81	4809	0	0	0	1	0	0	1	0	0

a. numbers in brackets represent the frequency of 1s.

variance, which determines differences or correlations between spatial orders (variables), sequence analysis examines similarities and differences between temporal orders (discrete events).

The bit-map data files can be analyzed with a variety of statistical methods to identify substantively interpretable time-dependent patterns (or lack thereof) of relationships among innovation dimensions that are coded as 1s and 0s. In particular, in this section we discuss the use of (1) chi-square tests and log-linear models to examine probabilistic relationships between categorical independent and dependent variables, (2) Granger causality and vector autoregression to identify possible causal relationships between bit-map variables, and (3) time-series regression analysis on incidents aggregated into fixed temporal intervals to test specific process models. These methods focus on detecting bivariate relationships between coded event variables. In the next section we discuss a multivariate technique we call phase analysis, used to identify and compare developmental patterns or stages in the temporal sequence data.

Other statistical methods are also being explored to examine the temporal duration and sequence among coded events. For example, *renewal theory* can be used to examine whether the duration between two consecutive events in the development of an innovation is distributed according to some known probabilistic distribution, such as the exponential or the more general Weibull distribution. In addition, a "hazard rate" can be computed for each variable of a bit-map if the occurrence of a change on the variable, represented by the value 1, is considered as the occurrence of an event itself.

In an experimental effort to identify causal relations among dichotomous variables in the bit-map data, we are currently analyzing bit-map data of several MIRP studies. The purpose is to investigate possible causal relationships, including vicious cycles, among changes in the five MIRP constructs as innovations develop over time. A preliminary cross-correlation analysis, conceptually based on the notion of Granger causality and vector autoregression (Freeman 1983), shows that changes in ideas and, to a lesser degree, in people are significantly associated with later changes in transactions, whereas the reverse is not true. Whereas statements like these are in themselves substantively interesting, other models, such as the lagged log-linear model, are also being explored. Relationships identified in an innovation will be compared with those in other innovations in order to determine if the findings replicate in other innovations and settings.

The use of sequential information implies that the values (1 or 0) of some variables at a certain time period may have impact on the values of the same or other variables at a later period. For example, changes in an innovation idea may lead to changes in people (a layoff of employees) and transactions (reduced business relationships). Since both causes and effects may take more than the varying time lapse between the occurrence of individual incidents, a researcher may be interested in the aggregate relationships between variables—for instance, between the monthly counts of 1s (changes) in innovation ideas, people, and transactions. Regression analysis of time series provides systematic methods for going beyond "subjective eyeballing" to examine causal relationships in the coded event sequence data.

In order to apply regular time-series regression analysis, it is necessary to aggregate the event sequence data into fixed temporal intervals. Three considerations are involved in aggregating the coded events into fixed temporal intervals: (1) what interval is most appropriate, (2) how to weight the importance of events, and (3) what computational procedures to employ.

First, the major substantive consideration is the expected time duration for relationships between variables to take effect. For example, if the time needed for an action or event to take effect is a matter of weeks, aggregation of sequential data into monthly counts could result in the true (weekly) causal links being overlooked or misspecified. On the other hand, other events (e.g., administrative reviews by resource controllers) often occur in semiannual cycles, and detecting empirical consequences of such events with weekly count data may produce too much "noise" and may not be possible. In general, the interval chosen should be guided by the substantive theory being examined and the developmental time clock (discussed earlier) of the innovations being analyzed.

A second consideration in aggregating event sequence data is the assumption that each occurrence has the same weight or importance. This is certainly a strong assumption, but any weighting scheme is arbitrary in some sense. We have chosen not to weight the importance of events because doing so could bias the results before statistical analysis has demonstrated the importance of certain temporal relationships. Instead, we are relying on a qualitative interpretation of the importance of events after quantitative data analysis has established relationships among coded events.

The third issue, involving aggregating the event sequence data into fixed-interval count data, was handled by use of SELAGGR, a computer software program that performs selection and aggregation operations for raw event sequence data files (Lin 1989).

The analysis of an event sequence bit-map of one MIRP innovation to test a stimulus-response model of trial-and-error learning illustrates findings produced by time-series regression analysis. The model argues that actions and outcomes are reciprocally connected: People do more of what is believed to lead to success and less of what is believed to lead to failure. Based on this model, incidents in an innovation's development are coded in terms of expanding versus contracting actions and positive versus negative outcomes. Figure 6.2 presents a graph of the monthly frequency of these coded expanding-contracting actions and positive-negative outcomes. The expanding-contracting

Figure 6.2. Plot of Expanding-Contracting Actions With Positive-Negative Outcomes Event Time Series in Development of Therapeutic Apheresis Innovation

time series consists of the number of monthly events coded in terms of actions that expanded or continued (totaling 197 events) minus the monthly number of contracting or shifting events (totaling 128 events) from the previous courses of action that the innovation unit was pursuing over an eight-year period. Two-thirds (66%) of the total 325 events represented expansions or continuations of prior actions. Similarly, the positive-negative outcomes time series consists of 81 incidents that contained evidence of changes in outcomes, 46 (or 57%) of which were judged negatively, while 35 were judged to represent positive outcomes for the innovation.

Three temporal periods are reflected in this graph: (1) an initial gestation period from September 1980 to October 1983, (2) a start-up period of mostly expanding activities from November 1983 to September 1986, followed by (3) an ending contraction period of mostly contracting activities and negative outcomes from October 1986 to July 1988, when the innovation's development was terminated. As the graph suggests, very different patterns of associations were found from regression analysis between the actions and outcomes event time series in the gestation, expansion, and contraction periods. (1) Actions and outcomes were unrelated in the gestation period, suggesting that no trial-and-error learning occurred. (2) During the expansion period negative outcomes significantly predicted subsequent expansions of actions, while actions had no effect on subsequent outcomes. These results suggest a faulty learning process of escalating commitments to failing courses of action during the expansion period. (3) Actions and outcomes were strongly positively correlated (+0.84) during the contraction period, mutually predicting each other over time as the trial-and-error learning model predicted. Unfortunately, in this case, evidence for trial-and-error learning did not occur until it was too late. Resource controllers terminated the innovation in July 1988 before it could be implemented.

Analyzing Developmental Patterns or Phases in Temporal Data

The above coding of incidents into event constructs also sets the stage for the examination of multivariate patterns in temporal sequence data. In particular, we will introduce a technique, called phase analysis, to identify and compare developmental phases in the temporal sequence data. This method can be used to both develop and test models that incorporate theoretical hypotheses about development. One advantage of the method is that it is designed to evaluate more than one process model. As our fourth MIRP guideline (above) suggests, comparison testing of alternative models provides useful ways to uncover the nature of developmental processes and to learn about the relative strengths and weaknesses of alternative models to explain the order and sequence of events.

One example will illustrate the sorts of comparative tests that can be conducted with phase analysis procedures. One MIRP research team reviewed the literature showing that most process models of innovation specify a simple unitary sequence of phases of development (Schroeder et al. 1986). For example, the innovation process is typically viewed as a sequence of separable stages (e.g., invention, development, elaboration, and diffusion) sequentially ordered in time and linked with transition routines to make adjustments between stages. This sequence is presented as though it is logically or *historically necessary,* and is presumed to be the path the "typical" innovation follows. Although many process theories take this form, it is certainly not the only possible theory of development. For example, we have alternatively proposed an *accumulation model* of development that argues that for an innovation to succeed it must acquire certain prerequisites—funding, support, champions, a good design—but that these prerequisites may be acquired in any order (Poole and Van de Ven 1989). This model does not preordain a set of phases the innovation must pass through in a certain order; it is a clear alternative to the historical necessity model.

The two models lead to different predictions about the phases of innovation development. With the historical necessity model, we would expect definite phases, occurring in a certain order, and a relatively similar developmental path for different innovations. With the accumulation model we would expect different innovations to follow different paths (since the model permits events to accumulate in different sequences), with no definite order in phases, and somewhat more complex developmental paths than the historical model would predict. Using the phase analysis procedures to be described below, these two models can be tested and evaluated comparatively.

The phase analysis method requires one to define discrete phases of innovation activity conceptually and then analyze their sequences and properties. A phase is a period of unified and coherent activity that serves some innovation function. Therefore, a phase is defined by a meaningful set of co-occurring activities on coded constructs or tracks of events. So one phase for the five MIRP tracks might be "concept refinement," indicated by a change in some innovation idea, occurring at a meeting of three experts (people) engaged in discussion and conflict (transactions) during a period of low resources (context) and resulting in high tension and morale (outcomes). The phase would be indicated by the co-occurrence of this pattern (change in idea, experts, discussion and conflict, low resources, high tension and high morale) in a consecutive series of events.

In general, phases can be defined in terms of conceptually coherent patterns on any number of coded constructs or tracks. We might be interested only in defining phases on a single track, or we might want to define phases using more conceptual tracks. Obviously, definition of a phase gets progressively harder as we add more conceptual tracks. In addition, a given phase might have several different conceptually coherent coded patterns. For example, "concept refinement" might be indicated by two patterns: (1) change in idea, experts, discussion and conflict, low resources, high tension and higher morale; and (2) and change in idea, experts, discussion and conflict, influx of resources, high tension and higher morale. Either of these patterns would be recoded into the phase designation "concept refinement."

Figure 6.3 illustrates this procedure. Part A shows sample codes for a very simple scheme with three conceptual tracks. For the sake of example, let us call Track 1 "ideas," with specific codes for introduction of a new idea (1a),

A. Track Codes

   Track 1 codes: 1a, 1b, 1c, 1d

   Track 2 codes: 2a, 2b, 2c

   Track 3 codes: 3a, 3b

B. Phase Indicators (Ordered triples of track codes)

   Phase A indicators: (1a, 2a, 3a), (1c, 2a, 3a), (1d, 2a, 3a), (1a, 2c, 3a)
                         (1c, 2c, 3a), (1d, 2c, 3a), (1a, 2a, 3b)

   Phase B indicators: (1b, 2a, 3a), (1b, 2b, 3a), (1b, 2c, 3a), (1b, 2a, 3b)
                         (1b, 2b, 3b), (1b, 2c, 3b)

   Phase C indicators: (1a, 2b, 3a), (1c, 2b, 3a), (1d, 2b, 3a), (1a, 2b, 3b)
                         (1c, 2b, 3b), (1d, 2b, 3b), (1a, 2c, 3b)

   Nonmeaningful
       indicators (∅):   (1c, 2a, 3b), (1d, 2c, 3b), (1c, 2c, 3b), (1c, 2a, 3b)

C. Track Data Recoded into Phases

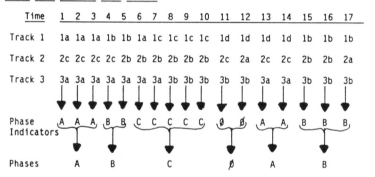

Time	1	2	3	4	5	6	7	8	9	10	11	12	13	14	15	16	17
Track 1	1a	1a	1a	1b	1b	1a	1c	1c	1c	1c	1d	1d	1d	1d	1b	1b	1b
Track 2	2c	2c	2c	2c	2b	2b	2b	2b	2b	2b	2c	2a	2c	2c	2b	2b	2a
Track 3	3a	3a	3a	3a	3a	3a	3a	3b	3b	3b	3b	3b	3a	3a	3b	3b	3b

Phase Indicators: A A A B B C C C C C ∅ ∅ A A B B B

Phases: A   B   C   ∅   A   B

Figure 6.3. A Sample Data Set Illustrating Phasic Recoding

adaptation of an idea (1b), actions that maintain the existence of an idea or prevent its rejection by the organization (1c), and termination of an idea (1d). We will call Track 2 the "people" track, and code the particular types of people involved in an activity at a given time: technical experts (2a), resource controllers (2b), or both experts and resource controllers (2c). Track 3 is a "context" track, and is coded 3a if the innovation has a low level of resources available to it and 3b if it has a high level of resources. Taken together, the three types of codes indicate certain phases of group activity.

Part B represents indicators for each phase, that is, patterns of codes across tracks. There are three phases, each indicated by several patterns. The phases are Creation (A), Adoption (B), and Rejection (C). The phases are indexed by coded patterns, and more than one pattern may indicate a given phase. So, for example, Creation is indicated by the coded pattern (1a, 2a, 3a), which is an event in which an idea is introduced (coded as 1a on track 1) by resource controllers (coded as 2a on track 2) under conditions of low resources (coded as 3a on track 3). Creation is also indicated by (1a, 2b, 3b), an event in which experts introduce an idea when there are lots of resources available. Both of these events could plausibly signify idea creation. Basically, the phase indicators in Part B are a key that enables us to reduce the three tracks to single phase codes.

Note that there are some combinations of codes that do not make sense: an event in which there is termination of an idea by technical experts with high resources committed to the project (1d, 2b, 3b) does not signify a phase that is meaningful for this analysis—the combination of termination by low-level members while major resources have been committed seems implausible. So it is consigned to a class titled "nonmeaningful indicators." This extra category keeps phases from becoming self-fulfilling prophecies; we will not always have coherent or understandable activities, and it is important to avoid force-fitting phases onto incidents that are not coherent.

Part C shows how the coded patterns are recorded into phase markers, which are then parsed into phases. In this illustration the event data yielded a sequence A-B, which then dissolved into a short period of unorganized activity (indicated by 0) and reemerged into a B sequence; there was a short period of creation, then adoption, then a short period in which rejection was attempted, followed by a new period of adoption (and perhaps solidification). Changes in these patterns of phase indicators signal a shift in a phase. Notice also that there was a single occurrence of phase A in the midst of the first phase B that was "smoothed" into that phase. Rules for partitioning phase indicators into phases are summarized in Poole and Roth (1989a), and Michael Hohmes has written a computer program (available from the authors) for parsing indicators into phase maps. This method of defining phases results in a very detailed diagram that can generate phases of different lengths. This makes this procedure very sensitive to differences among groups and avoids the problems with earlier methods of identifying phase patterns (Poole 1981).

Once phase maps are developed, the next step is to identify meaningful patterns from the maps. We have focused on two kinds of patterns that can serve as variables in tests of developmental models: (1) the type of developmental path and (2) structural properties of developmental sequences.

The first pattern is the *type of sequence* a given developmental path represents. Several researchers have advanced typologies of developmental sequences (Van den Daele 1969, 1974, Poole and Roth 1989a). Here we will mention some rudimentary methods for developing topologies or for determining whether a given developmental path fits a previously identified type.

The most common method is to make up charts of the developmental path and sort them into sets. Miles and Huberman (1984) provide a number of useful examples for developing data displays. This works well when there are only a few types of sequences and where the data are well understood. However, with complex data there is a danger that important distinctions will be missed or that types that differ only due to "error" will be distinguished. Recent methodological advances suggest more systematic ways of developing topologies. Pelz (1985) shows how the nonparametric statistic, gamma, can be used to establish the sequencing of phases and their degree of overlap. Abbott (1984, 1990) outlines a number of methods for statistical derivation of developmental typologies.

A number of *structural properties* of sequences are also of interest, including cycles and breakpoints. A recurrent pattern of behavior is called a *cycle*. Cycles are identified when repetitions occur within tracks over time. *Breakpoints* are of key importance to understanding change processes because they represent transitions between cycles of activities. They indicate the pacing of activities within tracks and possible linkages between tracks of activities. Poole (1983a) and Mintzberg, Raisinghani, and Théorêt (1976) suggest four types of breakpoints: normal breakpoints or topical shifts, delays, internal disruptions, and external interrupts.

When breakpoints interrupt cycles within a single track, this suggests that the track is loosely coupled with other tracks. On the other hand, when breakpoints occur simultaneously in several tracks, those tracks are likely to be highly interdependent, and the rupture may presage major events or shifts in developmental activity. Thus, when cyclical breaks in multiple tracks occur in some coherent fashion, phases or stages similar to those in classical models may be found. However, at other points, there may be no relationship in the cyclical breaks between tracks, and therefore no recognizable phases. In this case, each track is analyzed in its own right, but the entire ensemble of tracks does not yield a coherent analysis.

Phase analysis allows us to test different models of development insofar as those models make predictions about the types of sequences that should result or about the properties of sequences, such as the pattern of breakpoints or the existence of cycles. For example, as mentioned above, most traditional models of innovation posit a single sequence of phases, whereas functional models would predict multiple sequences. Phase mapping and analysis can be used to determine which of these two predictions holds for a given sample. Moreover, typologies and structural properties can be used as independent variables to test the effects of various innovation processes on outcomes, or as dependent variables to assess the impact of context or input factors on innovation processes.

CONCLUDING DISCUSSION

We have introduced in this chapter the fieldwork methods adopted by the Minnesota Innovation Research Program to study how and why innovations develop over time. Five operating guidelines to study innovation processes have been discussed pertaining to (1) sample selection, (2) real-time process observation, (3) selection of core concepts for observing innovation processes, (4) identification and comparison of alternative models to explain observed processes, and (5) the addressing of problems of measurement and sequence analysis to test alternative process models. These methodological guidelines represent basic decisions and steps that need to be addressed in most any field study of organizational change processes. Our description of how they were addressed by MIRP researchers provides a concrete example of key issues involved in field research work to study organizational change processes.

The major part of this chapter has focused on the homework tasks of measurement and sequence analysis in longitudinal qualitative data collected in the field studies. We have emphasized that more systematic and efficient procedures for analyzing longitudinal data are needed for two reasons: (1) so that researchers can more fully analyze data collected in field research and thereby more fully harvest a study's bounty, and (2) so that we can increase our capabilities to develop and test process theories of organizational change and development in longitudinal data. We have indicated that the basic operational question deals with how we might represent longitudinal data in a fashion that permits systematic and rigorous analysis of event sequence data. To answer this question, we suggest four steps (1-4 below) dealing with measurement and three steps (5-7 below) for sequence analysis.

1. Define the qualitative datum as an incident, bracket raw data collected from the field into incidents, and enter this information into a qualitative incident data file.

2. Evaluate the reliability and validity of classifying raw data into incidents by (a) achieving consensus and consistent interpretations of decision rules among at least two researchers performing this task, and (b) asking organizational participants to review the chronological list of incidents that occurred in their innovation or change effort.

3. Code each incident in terms of the presence or absence of theoretical event constructs, and add these codes to the incident data file.

4. Evaluate the reliability and validity of the event coding scheme by following conventional procedures for establishing construct validity and interrater reliability of measures.

5. Transform the qualitative codes into dichotomous variables or a bit-map event sequence data file, which permits time-series analysis of process theories of organizational change or development.

6. Analyze temporal relationships between variables in the event sequence data file using a variety of statistical time-series procedures appropriate to the theoretical question at hand. Enrich the interpretation of statistical results by reading and content analyzing the relevant sequence of incidents in the qualitative data file (developed in steps 1-3 above).

7. Analyze developmental patterns or phases in organizational change or innovation by defining and examining coherent patterns of activity among temporal events in the incident data file.

These steps and methods are the children of necessity, in the sense that they are evolving in our struggles with MIRP longitudinal field data. Of course, researchers will need to modify and extend these methods to meet the particular circumstances of their own studies. However, we believe they have wide applicability and can also serve a heuristic function by encouraging researchers to think differently about qualitative longitudinal data.

One might draw the conclusion that the methods proposed here may overquantify qualitative data. This conclusion may be the inadvertent result of our objective in this chapter to introduce some systematic new methods that overcome the limitations in most research reports of relying exclusively on subjective eyeballing and anecdotal information in qualitative data. However, in practice our objective is to combine the special information that quantitative and qualitative data provide to understand organizational change processes. After all, quantitative data, by themselves, provide only a skeletal configuration of structural regularities, often devoid of life, flesh, and soul. Qualitative data, by themselves, are like amoebas; although rich with life, they are squishy, soft, and absent of apparent structure. Only by combining quantitative and qualitative data in a balanced way do we come to understand the richness of life in its varied regularities.

Acknowledgments

Support for the Minnesota Innovation Research Program has been provided by a grant to the Strategic Management Research Center at the University of Minnesota from the Program on Organization Effectiveness, Office of Naval Research (code 4420E), under contract No. N00014-84-K-0016. In addition, we gratefully recognize support to undertake specific studies in the program from 3M, IBM, Honeywell, Control Data, CENEX, Dayton-Hudson, First Bank System, Bemis, Dyco Petroleum, ADC Telecommunications, Farm Credit Services, Hospital Corporation of America, the Federal Reserve Bank of Minneapolis, the Bush Foundation, McKnight Foundation, the Minnesota Agricultural Experiment Station, and the University of Minnesota. Without this broad base of support, this longitudinal research would not have been possible.

Notes

1. Our developmental view of process should not be confused with two other common usages of the term *process* in the literature, where it refers either to (1) the underlying logic that explains a causal relationship between independent and dependent variables in a variance theory, or (2) a category of concepts of organizational actions, such as rates of communications, work flows, decision-making techniques, or methods for strategy making. While these concepts or mechanisms may be at work to explain an organizational result, they do not describe how these variables or mechanisms unfold or change over time.

2. With a few exceptions (Van de Ven 1980a, 1980b, Van de Ven, Walker, and Liston 1979, Van de Ven and Walker 1984), most of the longitudinal data that Van de Ven invested seven years collecting on the start-up and development of early childhood organizations in Texas from 1973 to 1980 remain unexamined. Best intentions notwithstanding, a relocation to Minnesota and the launching of MIRP interrupted the harvesting of this study's rich longitudinal data. Poole has transcriptions of codings and field notes on hundreds of group decision-making sessions collected over 10 years, which have yet to be analyzed in depth. Some results are reported in Poole and Roth (1989a, 1989b).

References

Abbott, A. (1984), "Event Sequence and Event Duration: Colligation and Measurement," *Historical Methods,* 17, 192-204.

Abbott, A. (1990), "A Primer on Sequence Methods," *Organization Science,* 1, 375-392.

Bryson, J. M., and W. D. Roering (1989), "Mobilizing Innovation Efforts: The Case of Government Strategic Planning," in A. H. Van de Ven, H. L. Angle, and M. S. Poole (Eds.), *Research on the Management of Innovation: The Minnesota Studies* (pp. 583-610), New York: Ballinger/Harper & Row.

Delbecq, A., D. Gustafson, and A. Van de Ven (1975), *Group Techniques for Program Planning: A Guide to Nominal Group and Delphi Processes,* Glenview, IL: Scott Foresman.

Folger, J. P., Hewes, D. E., and Poole, M. S. (1984), "Coding Social Interaction," in B. Dervin and M. Voight (Eds.), *Progress in Communication Sciences* (Vol. 5), Norwood, NJ: Ablex.

Freeman, John (1983), "Granger Causality and the Time Series Analysis of Political Relationships," *American Journal of Political Science,* 27, 337-358.

Garud, R., and A. H. Van de Ven (1989), "Technological Innovation and Industry Emergence: The Case of Cochlear Implants," in A. H. Van de Ven, H. L. Angle, and M. S. Poole (Eds.), *Research on the Management of Innovation: The Minnesota Studies* (pp. 489-532), New York: Ballinger/Harper & Row.

Glaser, B. G., and A. L. Strauss (1967), *The Discovery of Grounded Theory: Strategies for Qualitative Research,* Chicago: Aldine.

Kaplan, A. (1964), *The Conduct of Inquiry: Methodology for Behavioral Science,* New York: Chandler.

Knudson, M. K., and V. W. Ruttan (1989), "The Management of Research and Development of a Biological Innovation," in A. H. Van de Ven, H. L. Angle, and M. S. Poole (Eds.), *Research on the Management of Innovation: The Minnesota Studies* (pp. 465-488), New York: Ballinger/Harper & Row.

Lin, T. (1989), *SELAGGR: A Selection and Aggregation Program for Bit-Map Data* (Technical Report), Minneapolis: Strategic Management Research Center, University of Minnesota.

Lord, F. M., and M. R. Novick (1968), *Statistical Theories of Mental Test Scores,* Reading, MA: Addison-Wesley.

Miles, M. B., and A. M. Huberman (1984), *Qualitative Data Analysis: A Sourcebook of New Methods,* Beverly Hills, CA: Sage.

Mintzberg, H., D. Raisinghani, and A. Théorêt (1976), "The Structure of 'Unstructured' Decision Processes," *Administrative Science Quarterly,* 21, 246-275.

Mitroff, I., and J. Emshoff (1979), "On Strategic Assumption Making: A Dialectical Approach to Policy and Planning," *Academy of Management Review,* 4, 1-12.

Pelz, D. C. (1985), "Innovation Complexity and the Sequence of Innovating Stages," *Knowledge: Creation, Diffusion, Utilization,* 6, 261-291.

Pettigrew, A. (1985), *The Awakening Giant: Continuity and Change in ICI,* Oxford: Basil Blackwell.

Polley, D., and A. H. Van de Ven (1989), "Therapeutic Apheresis Program Joint-Venture Case," in A. H. Van de Ven, H. L. Angle, and M. S. Poole (Eds.), *Research on the Management of Innovation: The Minnesota Studies* (pp. 261-276), New York: Ballinger/Harper & Row.

Poole, M. S. (1981), "Decision Development in Small Groups I: A Comparison of Two Models," *Communication Monographs,* 48, 1-24.

Poole, M. S. (1983a), "Decision Development in Small Groups II: A Study of Multiple Sequences in Decision Making," *Communication Monographs,* 50, 206-232.

Poole, M. S. (1983b), "Decision Development in Small Groups, III: A Multiple Sequence Model of Group Decision Development," *Communication Monographs,* 50, 321-341.

Poole, M. S., J. P. Folger, and D. E. Hewes (1987), "Analyzing Interpersonal Interaction," in M. E. Roloff and G. R. Miller (Eds.), *Interpersonal Processes,* Newbury Park, CA: Sage.

Poole, M. S., and J. A. Roth (1989a), "Decision Development in Small Groups IV: A Typology of Decision Paths," *Human Communication Research,* 15, 323-356.

Poole, M. S., and J. A. Roth (1989b), "Decision Development in Small Groups V: Test of a Contingency Model," *Human Communication Research,* 15, 549-589.

Poole, M. S., and A. H. Van de Ven (1989), "Toward a General Theory of Innovation Processes," in A. Van de Ven, H. L. Angle, and M. S. Poole (Eds.), *Research on the Management of Innovation: The Minnesota Studies* (pp. 637-662), New York: Ballinger/Harper & Row.

Ring, P., and G. Rands (1989), "Transaction Processes in 3M-NASA Relations," in A. Van de Ven, H. L. Angle, and M. S. Poole, *Research on the Management of Innovation: The Minnesota Studies* (pp. 337-366), New York: Ballinger/Harper & Row.

Roberts, N. C., and P. J. King (1989), "The Process of Public Policy Innovation," in A. H. Van de Ven, H. L. Angle, and M. S. Poole (Eds.), *Research on the Management of Innovation: The Minnesota Studies* (pp. 303-336), New York: Ballinger/Harper & Row.

Schroeder, R., A. Van de Ven, G. Scudder, and D. Polley (1986), "Managing Innovation and Change Processes: Findings From the Minnesota Innovation Research Program," *Agribusiness,* 2, 501-523.

Tornatsky, L. G., J. D. Eveland, M. G. Boylan, W. A. Hetzner, E. C. Johnson, D. Roltman, and J. Schneider (1983), *The Process of Technological Innovation: Reviewing the Literature,* Washington, DC: National Science Foundation.

Van den Daele, L. D. (1969), "Qualitative Models in Development Analysis," *Developmental Psychology,* 1, 303-310.

Van den Daele, L. D. (1974), "Infrastructure and Transition in Developmental Analysis," *Human Development,* 17, 1-23.

Van de Ven, A. H. (1980a), "Problem Solving, Planning and Innovation: Part I, Test of the Program Planning Model; and Part II, Speculations for Theory and Practice," *Human Relations,* 33, 711-740, 757-779.

Van de Ven, A. H. (1980b), "Early Planning, Implementation, and Performance of New Organizations," in J. R. Kimberly and R. H. Miles (Eds.), *The Organizational Life Cycle* (pp. 83-134), San Francisco: Jossey-Bass.

Van de Ven, A. H. (1986), "Central Problems in the Management of Innovation," *Management Science,* 32, 590-607.

Van de Ven, A. H., and H. L. Angle (1989), "An Introduction to the Minnesota Innovation Research Program," in A. Van de Ven, H. L. Angle, and M. S. Poole (Eds.), *Research on the Management of Innovation: The Minnesota Studies* (pp. 3-30), New York: Ballinger/Harper & Row.

Van de Ven, A. H., H. L. Angle, and M. S. Poole (Eds.) (1989), *Research on the Management of Innovation: The Minnesota Studies,* New York: Ballinger/Harper & Row.

Van de Ven, A. H., and Y. Chu (1989), "A Psychometric Assessment of the Minnesota Innovation Survey," in A. H. Van de Ven, H. L. Angle, and M. S. Poole (Eds.), *Research on the Management of Innovation: The Minnesota Studies* (pp. 55-104), New York: Ballinger/Harper & Row.

Van de Ven, A. H., and D. L. Ferry (1980), *Measuring and Assessing Organizations,* New York: Wiley.

Van de Ven, A. H., and G. Walker (1984), "The Dynamics of Interorganizational Coordination," *Administrative Science Quarterly,* 29, 598-621.

Van de Ven, A. H., G. Walker, and J. Liston (1979), "Coordination Patterns Within an Interorganizational Network," *Human Relations,* 32, 19-36.

Venkataraman, S., and A. H. Van de Ven (1989), "Qnetics New Business Creation Case," in A. H. Van de Ven, H. L. Angle, and M. S. Poole (Eds.), *Research on the Management of Innovation: The Minnesota Studies* (pp. 228-243), New York: Ballinger/Harper & Row.

7

Alternate Approaches to Integrating Longitudinal Case Studies

ROBERT D. McPHEE

In dealing with a large set of longitudinal case studies, researchers often assume that they can and should seek a single set of variables and explanatory theory to deal similarly with all the cases. This chapter describes three approaches to the problems of cross-case integration and comparison. It also describes a set of comparative methods that can be used to diagnose case study data sets, to see which integrative approach is best.

The problem of integrating findings of numerous studies by multiple researchers or research teams has become a central problem for social science. The quantitative technique of meta-analysis was developed mainly to rectify the logical flaws and dissatisfying results of traditional reviews of conflicting literature (Hunter, Schmidt, and Jackson 1982). The same problem has been noted by researchers favoring qualitative methods (Miles and Huberman 1984, Strauss 1987, Ragin 1987), and at least one team of authors has attempted to develop an integrative technique, analogous to meta-analysis, for ethnographic studies (Noblit and Hare 1988). Finally, it should be noted that the problem of *integrating* study results is closely related to the problem of *comparative* research. Comparative research admits that cases differ, but

This chapter appeared originally in *Organization Science,* vol. 1, no. 4, November 1990, pp. 393-405.

tries to find more general grounds on which to compare and reach overall conclusions about them. But then how do we avoid the problems of mixing apples and oranges, such as looking for "orange cores" or rejecting perfectly good apple theories because they do not apply to oranges? Researchers have done extensive work on these *problems of comparability*, and a variety of authors have focused on methods of comparing cases (see Hammel 1980). Such problems arise in the course of typical comparative research and literature reviews, but they take on special importance for large-scale research programs where different researchers are involved in the study of different cases.

The problem of comparison is not a new challenge. In anthropology, the "comparative approach" was announced more than a hundred years ago by E. B. Tylor, and immediately more quantitatively oriented methodologists began to raise problems with it. Hammel's (1980) conclusion, after reviewing the anthropological experience, is that "definition of the problem and consistency of observation and classification are paramount. Reliable comparisons cannot be made between data sets that are not governed by *similar* theoretical intent, techniques of collection, and types of classification" (p. 153, emphasis added). This view may be unduly pessimistic. It also raises several practical questions: *How* "similar" must the intent, data-collection techniques, and classification systems be? For qualitative studies in particular, how can we describe their similarity? And, if they are *not* extremely similar, what can we do?

My purposes in this chapter are twofold. First, I want to explain an important distinction among three alternative approaches to the comparison of longitudinal studies. I will use three major research programs described in this volume as examples of the approaches: the CODE program described by Glick et al. (Chapter 5), the CCSC studies described by Pettigrew (Chapter 4), and the MIRP program described by Van de Ven and Poole (Chapter 6). All three programs involve rather large samples of cases, with information being gathered by a variety of researchers or teams, so in each case the merger or comparison of the cases is a potential issue. Second, I want to suggest some comparative methods that are useful for diagnosing sets of longitudinal case studies, to suggest which integrative or comparative approach is appropriate.

THE THREE APPROACHES TO COMPARISON

Suppose our research question is, What sequence of events typically occurs in the emergence and adoption of a successful organizational innovation? Also suppose that we have a number of case studies tracking the

TABLE 7.1 The Three Approaches to Integrating Longitudinal Case Studies

Dependent Variables or Core Concepts	Independent Variables or Explanatory Concepts	
	Same	*Different*
Same	*Different data points:* The case studies can all be subsumed under the same theoretical model.	*Different explanations:* The case studies portray different causal or developmental paths to the same basic type of phenomenon.
Different	[Not a coherent approach: merely different descriptions of the same thing.]	*Different images:* The case studies involve different, incommensurable, but comparable types of phenomena.

development of different innovations. Our first reaction might be, Of course the case studies can be compared and collated to derive a model of the typical sequence of events. But I believe that there are really three important possibilities, as indicated in Table 7.1. First, the various case studies may indeed be *different data points,* all fitting the same model of innovation emergence. Second, the cases may correspond to *different explanations.* Here, we might identify several alternate sets of conditions for successful innovation or stages for the emergence of innovations. Third, the cases may correspond to fundamentally *different images* (see Morgan 1986). The studies that we initially collected under the label "innovations" might actually be so different that we gain more understanding by studying their contrasts.[1]

As Table 7.1 indicates, one way of thinking of this distinction is in terms of independent and dependent variables. Cases are different *data points* when they are described well by a single set of variables. Different *explanations* require different independent variables, different explanatory accounts for cases that still appear to be essentially the same. But cases that fit different *images* are essentially different, at least in subtle respects, and may require different dependent variables to capture the typal differences.

This distinction can be illustrated using an example from baseball. We might seek, in a comparison among baseball players, to answer the question, What set of activities (the independent variables) makes a baseball player excellent offensively (the dependent variable)? We might try to account for players' offensive performance by finding a single index of activities for every player—perhaps batting average or RBI total, or some composite of those. Then we would have a single model, with the different players being different data points. (We could test a model like this by seeing whether the index—the independent variable—predicted subjective ratings of offensive performance.) On the other hand, we might argue that there can be *different explanations* for offensive greatness. For instance, a great leadoff batter would have a good batting average and draw lots of walks; a good cleanup batter would have high RBI and home-run totals. The activities (or independent variables) making them good performers would be different. Note that offensive greatness in this instance still has one meaning—the player's contribution to total runs scored or team victories, say. But players in different batting positions would contribute in different ways. Last, we might argue that good offensive performance is partly a matter of "team style." Some great teams have consisted of speedy, "hungry" players who get on base, steal, hit and run, and so on. Even a Babe Ruth, who had many strikeouts each year, might disrupt that kind of attack by being called out so often, more than he helped through home runs. His strikeouts might even demoralize the rest of the team. Yet on a "power team" he would be invaluable. Such team styles are *different images* of performance. One player, doing the same things in the same lineup spot, might be rated very differently on teams with two different styles. We can say that "good offensive performance" *means* subtly different things, or denotes different *phenomena*—is a different dependent variable—on the two teams.

A manager might choose one style over another due to his or her own preferences and the players on hand, but there would be no one "best style." And so there would be no one "right way" to rate performance: People could legitimately argue whether Ty Cobb was better than Babe Ruth, and players could justifiably choose to emulate either one.

There is no one right answer about which of the three *approaches* to baseball offense is best, either. In part, the approach we pick may be based on our goals or values. If we are arbitrators trying to decide a player's general fair market value, the first approach, using fully general criteria of effectiveness, may be unavoidable: We *must* decide how the player performs relative to others, often regardless of lineup differences. Yet such an approach may be counterproductive if we are managers choosing one player to lead off— that choice demands a particular model for "leadoff performance" that would be a poor "explanation" for "cleanup performance." And if we move to manage a different team, we might find that our model is inappropriate for the new team's style, and demands revision in a "different image." Good players on the old team may seem and/or be less effective on the new.

But it is also important to remember that the right approach depends partly on the nature of the cases we are dealing with. If all the players have roughly similar *profiles* of skills, and differ only in overall skill *level,* then the first approach is best. If team styles do differ greatly, the third approach becomes more salient.

Let me mention one other more or less parallel example for my distinction, well known in organizational science: the distinctions among universal models (Likert's System 4, Peters and Waterman's principles of excellence), contingency models based on continuous situational variables (Burns and Stalker, Galbraith), and configurational models (Mintzberg, Miller and Friesen). The first asserts a universal model for all organizations; the second, a universal criterion of situational fit or information-processing sufficiency, which can be achieved in a variety of ways (so that there are multiple explanations of how to organize to process information). The third can be read as positing a variety of images for organizations, each with its own standards of excellence and distinct meanings: *Participative management* means something very different in a machine bureaucracy than in an adhocracy, for instance.

The point of this chapter is that the same distinction holds true for *studies*: The right approach to comparison or integration depends on the nature of the specific case studies involved. We could say that a case study is a description of an object using a set of concepts. So if a study's concepts, as applied to its object in one study, are substantially different from those of another study, the two often should not be treated under one conceptual model.

The three approaches to integration are reviewed in more detail below.

Different Data Points

Cases that can be integrated as different data points all fall under the same conceptual and explanatory model. Differences among cases are explained as the results of the same *kinds* of determining conditions and events, which differ in degree. For instance, suppose we have two case studies of innovation, one based on a suggestion by a powerful research lab member, the other on a suggestion by the company president. Differences in the resources devoted to these innovations might be explained by differences in the power of their sponsors.

An easy and familiar way to contrast the three approaches is in terms of a standard quantitative research model, a linear regression equation. The first situation is the one to which a regression equation is well adapted. Different cases are different points on a regression line, probably with different values for various independent variables (such as power) and, consequently, for the dependent variable (resources devoted to innovation, in the example above). The treatment of cases by Miles and Huberman (1984) in developing integrated causal process models that explain and integrate processes observed in all their sample of cases is a good example of this approach.

The Changes in Organizational Design and Effectiveness (CODE) program of studies may be seen as another example of this approach. It includes data on a broad array of changes experienced in organizations, along with data on many contextual independent variables, and the investigators plan construction of a model that will explain change types and change frequencies across organizations. In one respect, Glick et al. (Chapter 5) really do not treat their sample as a homogeneous set of data points. They explicitly recognize that models may vary among different clusters of organizations, and they plan to explore cluster-level models as well as overall models. But in other respects the changes are treated as a homogeneous sample (with varying attributes).

The key challenge in integrating cases under a single model is one of calibration—making sure that cases with different values for the model's general variables or categories really do belong on the same dimension in the order they appear to have. So in the example of two innovations mentioned earlier, we need a way to evaluate the power of a company president *relative* to that of a "powerful" lab member—the descriptive term *powerful* may mean different things or may be hard to compare across studies. Similarly, one of the CODE change categories is "Important changes in responsibility or resources at other levels [than the top management team] in the organization." A CEO in a multisite organization might report different changes corresponding to this category than a CEO in a single-site organization, simply because different sorts of changes are possible and/or noticeable. The outcome of this approach to comparison is a general model that sums up the comparison among cases.

Different Explanations

Where cases correspond to different explanations, they deal with the same *kinds* of phenomena or processes, but demand quite different explanatory models. Just as there can be two or more alternative routes to a destination, so there might be two models for product innovation emergence—either a laboratory worker has an idea and sells it to successive levels of decision makers, or a powerful sponsor such as the company president has an idea and forces the company to develop and implement it. Determinants of resources devoted to the innovation in the first case, such as initial results and slack resources, might be completely irrelevant in the second case.

If cases call for different explanations, any single explanatory regression equation is invalid. In different kinds of cases, we would need different regression models involving the same dependent variable (resources) but quite different sets of independent variables and regression weights. If we know of a keying variable (perhaps "inventor rank" in our example) that determines which set of independent variables and regression weights will indeed explain the innovation, we might be able to combine the models into one equation with interactive terms. But there might be no known or measurable keying factor.

The studies of organizational change conducted by Andrew Pettigrew and his colleagues at the Centre for Corporate Strategy and Change seem to be good examples of this second approach to study integration or comparison. Pettigrew is willing to include studies of all sorts of change in the research domain he considers, but adopts a meta-level posture of contextualism in the conduct of each study. In his contextualist stance and in his earlier research practice, Pettigrew commits himself to complex historical narrative explanations of the various organizational changes he observes. Unique events with great explanatory significance in one narrative may have no analogues in other contexts. A concrete research example is Pettigrew's (1985) study of organizational development in different ICI divisions, where the fate of OD is treated as a single kind of context-dependent phenomenon, but the specific relevant contextual factors and their impacts vary from case to case. Whereas Pettigrew reports general themes (e.g., that performance problems are motivating preconditions of change), he also notes major variations on those themes (e.g., that the most successful changes he observed began in times of good performance, which served as a hindrance overcome by other factors; pp. 459ff.).

This approach assumes that there is still no deep conceptual problem involved in comparison or integration across such cases. The cases are merely different, and no general model or simple "covering law" for them exists at present. Instead, to integrate them we produce an explanatory typology—a single map containing alternate paths to the terminal event. The key challenge of this approach involves distinguishing between "minor" case differences and differences reflecting different models, and determining the exact relations that hold among different models.

Different Images

A much more radical difference is present when the different cases correspond to *different images*. The cases are seen to differ not just in degree or in explanatory account required, but in kind. *What is being studied* differs from one set of cases to another, and that difference demands a corresponding difference in *conceptual frame*. All variables or concepts involved in describing and explaining the case outcomes may be incommensurable (Kuhn 1970) from case to case. A telling sign of different images is that the main *dependent* variables—the facts that need to be explained—themselves differ, either obviously or subtly in meaning, from case to case.

The term *different images* is suggested by Gareth Morgan's *Images of Organization* (1986), which valuably conveys the conceptual discords between one image and another. But such images, in the context of this chapter, should not be thought of as mere conceptual frames, any one of which can be applied to any case studied. Instead, images here are descriptions that have emerged in a dialectic of research and analysis between researcher and "object" of study. Such emergent concepts are a common outcome of ethnographic methods and grounded theory, but quantitative studies also require creative and adaptive model building, operationalizations, and so on that have theoretical significance. The concepts that make up the image have case-specific meanings and relations, so the image that emerges in case study has substantive significance—the fact that *it* emerged says something about the case (as well as about the researcher).

An example of different images might be two cases of product innovation where one of the cases occurs in a heavily regulated industry—a new drug, for instance (see Van de Ven and Poole, Chapter 6). In an unregulated industry, the power of an innovation's sponsor might affect the resources devoted and thereby the speed of development of an innovation. In the highly regulated drug industry, where time-consuming steps of testing are spelled out by regulations, sponsor power might have little direct effect on speed of product introduction, but might affect subtler variables, like the degree to which safety tests "cut corners" or are biased in favor of concluding the drug to be safe. Even if the innovations are identical, we might justly conclude that the case studies involved two different *images* of innovations, between which any comparison would involve a potentially troublesome interpretive and translative process.

As in the case of different models, no single regression equation would be able to describe all the cases validly. In this situation, however, the dependent variable of the equation also might be different from image to image. Often this difference would be subtle, and would correspond to different causal processes from case to case, and to different theoretical networks involving the dependent variable. A good example of this situation is the metatheory generated out of the MIRP studies described by Van de Ven and Poole (Chapter 6; for the metatheory, see Poole and Van de Ven 1989). They describe three different "process motors" that characterize different kinds of innovation processes. Each kind of process involves a different expected sequence of stages and different determinants of progress from stage to stage.

The key challenges in this approach are to find and characterize the various natural kinds or images of cases, to assign cases to images correctly, and to explore the relations among the different images. (Of course, an object may shift logical type and force the researcher to recognize its change in nature; see the example of Gouldner 1954 and the discussion of this kind of change by Poole and Van de Ven 1989.) A typology of images must avoid two dangers. If the analysis produces too many images, it will not be useful for drawing comparative conclusions. But if there are too few images, so that each contains substantially unlike cases, then the typology will mask important differences. A successful analysis based on the "different images" approach will at least provide revealing contrasts among the different types, which were perhaps once all treated as alike. There is also the possibility that, as in Poole and Van de Ven's analysis, a metatheory will emerge that can explain the differences among images and transitions from one image to another.

But a common tendency is to assume or impose a single image and even a single explanation as a basis for integration of qualitative studies. If a single model is imposed, the integrator seeks to measure or code all cases on general or second-level variables. Researchers may deal with differences in explanation as residual or by seeking a synthetic model. They often deal with differences in image by analyzing each theory into elemental propositions, putting these pieces together into a more general pattern, and interpreting discrepant concepts in accord with the needs of the general pattern. If, for instance, we design a multisite qualitative study, we often include coordinating structures and processes that will result in a single conceptual scheme being used at all sites (Strauss 1987, Miles and Huberman 1984).

Because researchers tend to prefer a single image to encompass an array of case studies, I review below some reasons for allowing or even preferring multiple images in a single empirical domain. There are two sorts of reasons: Different images are often unavoidable, and they can be valuable.

Image-level differences in case analyses are sometimes unavoidable because of the nature of qualitative methods and the nature of the cases themselves. Case studies in all three of the research programs that are the focus of this chapter involve more or less open-ended exchanges between researchers and informants about the array of changes or innovation developments experienced in the organization. Inevitably, the interacting parties negotiate an understanding about what events are or are not worthy of report and follow-up. In this negotiation process, relatively idiosyncratic understandings may emerge, and the researchers may alter their notions of change or types of change.

Another argument for case comparisons not based on a single explanation or image is presented by Bonnell (1980) in her account of different approaches to comparison. In comparison "mediated by concepts," comparisons serve to deepen understanding of a concept by uncovering similarities and differences across cases. These reveal both the general properties of the concept and the variety of ways it can work and be related to other phenomena. Universal concepts such as "class" and "authority" (or "innovation" and "change") are so general that they require typological specification before they can be applied to cases, and the types, to be useful, must be so spatio-temporally bound that integrated theory across unlike domains is impossible—only contrastive analysis can be done. Bonnell cites Bendix's statement that "comparative analysis should sharpen our understanding of the *contexts in which more detailed causal inferences can be drawn*" (pp. 168-169, emphasis added).

On both these grounds, differences in images are not always necessary. Some sets of case studies fit a single image or explanation, but some other sets cannot be collapsed into a homogeneous sample or domain, and that possibility is not under the control of the synthesist or team principal investigator.

There are also real advantages to programs that create different theories grounded in contrasting databases. For instance, some of the advantages that emerged due to interaction among diverse images of innovations in the MIRP project include a high level of creativity, at multiple levels of generality and with multiple foci; the likelihood that each study is a highly valid expression of the specific nature of the phenomenon studied; criticism and productive suggestions from one theory to another, aimed at evolving conceptual convergencies and issues; and a special impetus to attend to plural theoretic ideas in further theory construction.

DIAGNOSTIC METHODS

But is there any way to tell when to try to integrate a sample of cases as different data points and when to contrast them as requiring different explanations or different images? The factors that make one approach better than another may be subtle and rooted in different senses of concepts or variables involved in different studies. In this section I will discuss four general methods to aid the comparative analysis of qualitative case studies. I call them *diagnostic* because they can provide evidence about which approach—different data points, different explanations, or different images—we should use in comparative analysis. Each of the methods takes advantage of the longitudinal nature of each case description—the fact that there is a sequence of ordered information about the case, within which internal comparisons can be drawn.

The methods I will describe include creation of glossaries, a set of concordances, a set of chronologies, and systematic cross-study comparison of the studies from an outside standpoint. I will discuss the diagnostic value of each method and give examples of its use for the three exemplary multistudy research programs discussed above. Table 7.2 summarizes how these methods diagnose approach differences.

TABLE 7.2　Implications of Diagnostic Methods for the Three Approaches to Study Comparison and Integration

Methods	Approaches		
	Different Data Points	Different Explanations	Different Images
Glossaries or codebooks	Concepts with very similar meanings and substructures	Explanatory concepts or independent variables with varying meanings or substructures	Core concepts or dependent variables with different meanings or substructures
Concordances (case time)	Concepts appearing in roughly equivalent places in all case histories	Explanatory concepts distributed differently in various case histories	Core concepts distributed differently in various case histories
Chronologies (research team time)	Converging concepts toward a general model	Diverging explanatory concepts, but converging core concepts	Diverging core and explanatory concepts toward rival images
Cross-study comparisons	Similar use of conceptual structures across studies, as shown by teams' cross-evaluations and independent recoding	Divergent uses of explanatory concepts, but not core concepts—competing explanations perceived	Divergent uses of core concepts as well as explanatory concepts—basic interpretive differences perceived

Glossaries or Codebooks

The creation of a glossary or codebook is actually a method used for coordinating the various studies of MIRP (Van de Ven, Angle, and Poole 1989). The various team members on that project compiled a list of key concepts and variables, together with definitions and rules for applying them. A useful adaptation of this device would be a collected glossary containing both shared concepts and concepts developed in particular case studies, with definitions. If possible, different terms for the same concept, and different meanings for the same terms, would be recorded here too. Finally, the glossary should indicate the *substructure* of the more abstract concepts—not just the definition of a concept such as "authority," but the types or features of authority that have their own names elsewhere in the glossary.

It is this last feature that captures the diagnostic value of a glossary. In two different case studies, the same concept might have two different names—power and authority, for instance. But if those terms have different substructures—if the types and features distinguished in one study do not match up well with those of the second study—then the two probably cannot be treated as different data points under a single model. For instance, "power" in one study might have a large substructure of concepts and a number of definitional linkages to other concepts, whereas "authority" in the other study might have a rather simple conceptual development. In that case, integration of the studies as data points for a single model might be unwise, because to treat the two studies in a parallel way, the factor of power in the first study might have to be oversimplified and slighted. So the glossary has substantive significance. It is not just a list of definitions, but an indicator of the range of concepts required to map the complexity of the phenomenon being studied. If the concepts are explanatory or independent variables, then the best approach may be to create different explanations of the phenomenon. And if the concepts describe the central phenomenon itself, or are dependent variables, then the best approach may be the acceptance of different images.

For example, researchers for the CODE program asked organization CEOs about changes, then coded them using a 12 specified categories of design and nondesign changes. A set of glossaries could record the interpretations of these categories related to questionnaire items used by CODE research. For instance, each researcher's glossary could indicate whether increased reliance on "informal, unwritten rules" (a questionnaire item) is a change in "the way you produce your product or service," "administrative procedures," "internal coordination or communication procedures," or "goals, philosophy, or culture" (these are four alternate change categories for coding CEO accounts). Then changes on the questionnaire item could supplement the interview data and might signal different senses or images of structural change across cases.

Another example can be drawn from Pettigrew's work on ICI. Glossaries for the four divisions he studied might have entries for pressures toward organizational development emanating from corporate headquarters, whereas the glossary for the headquarters' OD effort would have no such entry for downward pressure. This kind of difference would confirm that the contexts of the various units studied were different and would support the search for different explanations for change across the divisions.

Concordances

A concordance is a record of where, in the description or analysis of a case study, a term or concept is used. Concordances are common tools in literary criticism; a concordance of, say, Shakespeare's work would give the exact lines in which he uses specific words or phrases throughout his plays. In longitudinal case study analysis, a concordance might indicate how many events in an event history are relevant to a certain concept, and where they are concentrated in the history. It might be constructed through computerized keyword analysis (as has been done in the case of MIRP). Such concordances capture some of the concrete distributional aspects of the data records. They can be compared—at the extreme, in a two-way matrix by chi-square—to identify important study differences.

Such comparisons can be used diagnostically to help decide whether cases represent different data points, explanations, or images. If events corresponding to explanatory concepts cluster in different stages of two case studies, or differ in the order in which they have impact, we probably should develop multiple explanatory models. And if the phenomenon itself, and its features or dependent variables, is distributed differently across stages of a process, the phenomenon itself may need to be treated as multiple in kind, demanding different images.

For instance, in the CODE studies researchers might find certain pairs of categories (perhaps "changes in goals, philosophy, or culture" and "changes in administrative procedures") reported simultaneously or even linked by informants, in organizations experiencing low internal and external turbulence, whereas the two occur independently in highly turbulent organizations. Such a finding might lead the CODE researchers to conclude that there are *two images* of value change, one strongly linked to formal implementation and the other independent of the formal structure. They might then develop a second-order coding scheme to capture and try to explain these distinct types of change.

MIRP's computerized keyword analysis, as mentioned above, could also easily be adapted for concordance construction. The varied distribution of keywords across various periods or stages of the innovation process could even be tested for differences using a chi-square statistic.

Analysis Chronologies

For each case, a *chronology* of data record and theory development should be created. In part, this general prescription is drawn from an insight of Aaron Cicourel expressed in his classic essay titled "Three Models of Discourse Analysis: The Role of Social Structure" (1980). Cicourel, in criticizing three models, makes a point that goes beyond his well-known examination of the conditionality of social scientific research. He notes that *how* a conceptual scheme or set of variables is applied and elaborated in a study is a *finding* of that study and usually an unintended consequence of the particular research history of the case. To understand the basis of, the justification for, the scheme itself, we need not a theoretic rationalization or empirical illustration, but a record, even a diary or internal "chronology," of the process of its emergence and adaptation in the course of observation and analysis. In qualitative analysis, the case description and its analysis are most often presented as finished products, with no report of the experience-driven evolution of categories and case description to their final state (an evolution illustrated in Strauss 1987).

So a chronology traces not the location of a concept in "case time" (a concordance does that), but its process of emergence in "research team time," as recorded by the researchers observing themselves. Such chronologies could be useful at several levels of analysis. At the *data record* level, they could be constructed at the same time as the field notes or event history, to reflect the experience and formulations that shape those texts. Alternatively, in a *retrospective* chronology team members could recall or find, and summarize, the key problems and decisions involved in data record construction: what concerns, and examples, caused the most trouble in "reaching consensus" about the sequence of events, events to concentrate on, event labels, and other seemingly descriptive but latently theory-relevant matters.

At the level of concepts, members can construct real-time or retrospective chronologies, for each case, of how concepts and categories were elaborated and coding decisions and rules made. A similar analysis can be made of broader theoretic integration—when in a case problems of consistency among explanations of different events became apparent, what stimulated moves toward theoretic closure, and so on.

Chronologies have diagnostic value primarily in indicating the grounds and interests that have led to compatible or apparently incompatible theory development by researchers analyzing different cases. If there is really strong similarity among the cases, and if the researchers are concentrating on similar questions, then the chronologies should reveal a sort of conceptual convergence, as researchers exploring different cases find they cannot do without the full range of concepts of a single general model. On the other hand, if the cases correspond to different models or theories, then the problems or experiences that led the researchers to unique concept development should be real problems for the other models or theories—things that are validly outside the domain of other models or theories. And we should find, rather than a general convergence, a mixed pattern of convergence within sets of cases, sets that diverge from one another.

For instance, in one of the MIRP studies, Ring and Rands developed a special system of subcategories for organizational transactions. A record of the events that led them to their specific distinctions might be used by other teams to decide whether to use the same codes, perhaps altering their meanings to fit new applications, or to introduce new coding categories. If new categories are required, a contrast of the new events requiring change with Ring and Rands's chronology might signal the need for a different explanation or a different image of process phases involving transactions.

In the CCSC studies, too, chronology construction might prove useful. The structure of the various accounts of organizational contexts may be an unintended function of researcher access to certain key decision makers and the specific problems brought to the attention of those informants. Chronologies for the various cases studied could highlight the extent to which central concepts were linked more to the accounts of one informant than another, and perhaps suggest reinterpretations that would render cases more comparable.

Cross-Study Comparisons

The suggestion here is that we should try to get a new, comparable perspective on each study to allow comparison and perhaps even cross-fertilization. We can do this in several ways, all of which require us to adopt a metastance outside the perspective of any single study.

One way is to induce the researchers for each study to go outside their own case focus and perform the comparison for us. Where possible, teams assigned to research on specific cases inside a larger project should perform cross-evaluations of at least one other study's data record and theoretic analysis. Perhaps they should all evaluate the longest record available, and describe ways in which they would have collapsed its accounts, ways in which it seems incomplete, or places where they would have expected or searched for more events, wording differences, and so on. They also could critically analyze, using their own experience and practices, the ways theoretic concepts were applied to construct an explanatory account of the other case.

The diagnostic value of these cross-evaluations lies mainly in the reactions of each team to the others' products. Cases falling under the same model as different data points ought to provoke one of two reactions: recognition of similarity and value in the other analysis or critique of inadequacies of focus or procedure in that analysis. In the case of different explanations or images, cross-evaluation should lead to realization on both sides of substantive differences between the case the team studied and the other case. For example, researchers from different universities who participated in the CODE studies could study each other's data sheets and unitizing/coding practices. They might discover, among the changes recorded and coded by other researchers, events emphasized by other CEOs that some of their own informants ignored or underplayed. Analysis of these differences in CEO importance standards might lead to generation of different explanations or different images for the different cases.

Another example of the value of cross-evaluation would be the MIRP studies. The rather independent investigating teams seem to have evolved quite different interpretations of the five core concepts, with several studies concentrating on detailed development of just a few of the concepts. Cross-evaluations might lead to conceptual critique and development, but also to understanding of the case differences that spawned differences in concept interpretation.

Another way to create a metaperspective to allow study comparisons is to impose an outside conceptual frame or coding system on all of the studies. This would not be a meta*theory* (as in Poole and Van de Ven 1989), but rather an analytic frame that could reveal unnoticed common regularities across varying case studies. To be valuable for comparative purposes, the new coding system must include basic ideas involved in the perspectives of each of the studies—it must go to an underlying or deeper level. Of course, this can require creative work on the part of the person performing the comparison, and may not be possible for some sets of case studies.

But for longitudinal studies, a promising comparison frame might emerge if we focus on *time itself.* It is common to distinguish between "clock time" and "event time," where the latter is time as measured by important events. But we can also look at how time is treated and informally measured by a group as part of our study, and develop substantive concepts to describe it. One way to do that is inductively, by seeing how successive pairs of events in our data record are related. To take an example from a study of a MIRP defense contracting division (USD), the relation of a first event—"appointment of many 'transition teams' (for integration and planning) in USD"—and a second—"USD winning a large Navy fee"—might be coded as relatively unrelated, or as results of opposed causes, or as the second helping to pay for and reinforce the first, or as the second giving prestige and a boost to the first, or as the second showing that the first is not an indicator of bad communication. This maximizes the chance of generating unique and data-fitting process concepts.

Second, to study "time" we might develop concepts that capture the different statuses events can have relative to process. Many process studies end with theories phrased in terms of phases or stages, with different event types falling into and composing each phase. Rather than postulating that events are the *stuff* of phases, we should note that in many studies phase transitions are *created* by events—events cause and bound phases, and even serve as breakpoints (if those are different from phase boundaries). Even when internal to phases, events can have different relations to the underlying state, and so on, inducing the phasic pattern. They may *enact* phase causation, or resist it (be generated by its contradictory character), or *mark* the process (as human temperature does a fever). At this point a generative analysis of the various ways phases work is in order, sensitized by metatheoretic schemes rich in their analysis of real/empirical relations.

These cross-study comparisons have diagnostic value because they can reveal some underlying roots of case difference and similarity. Some cases may seem to require different images because they deal with matters, such as resistance to change, that others ignore but that can be uncovered in the records of those other cases.

CONCLUSION

My main object in this chapter has been to indicate that comparative analysis is more complex than we often realize, and that we are not limited to just one course of action—treating cases as multiple data points. There may often be more theoretical merit, and practical merit as well, in exploring and accepting the possibility of different explanations or different images. The methods discussed here may serve as sources of evidence that one approach is more appropriate than others in integrating a set of studies.

But the methods should not be regarded merely as diagnostic tools. Even after we have chosen an approach to integration of cases, the methods are very useful for improving analytic rigor and balance, validity, and reliability. And they also seem very useful as sources of new theoretic ideas. In a variety of ways, then, these methods help us take advantage of the richness of longitudinal study data.

Acknowledgments

I am very grateful to Andrew Van de Ven and three anonymous reviewers for helpful suggestions. An earlier version of part of this chapter was presented at the National Science Foundation Conference on Longitudinal Field Research Methods for Studying Organizational Processes, Austin, Texas, September 1988.

Note

1. I am aware that in this chapter I take a position relevant to a number of literatures: on idiographic versus nomothetic images of science, on realism, on relativism, on postmodernism, on interpretive and hermeneutic practices. Discussion of these issues is beyond the scope of this chapter.

References

Bonnell, V. (1980), "The Uses of Theory, Concepts, and Comparison in Historical Sociology," *Comparative Studies in History and Society,* 22, 2, 156-173.
Cicourel, A. (1980), "Three Models of Discourse Analysis: The Role of Social Structure," *Discourse Processes,* 3, 101-132.

Gouldner, A. (1954), *Patterns of Industrial Bureaucracy,* New York: Free Press.

Hammel, E. A. (1980), "The Comparative Method in Anthropological Perspective," *Comparative Studies in History and Society,* 22, 2, 145-155.

Hunter, J., F. Schmidt, and G. Jackson (1982), *Meta-Analysis,* Beverly Hills, CA: Sage.

Kuhn, T. (1970), *The Structure of Scientific Revolutions* (2nd ed.), Chicago: University of Chicago Press.

Miles, M. B., and A. M. Huberman (1984), *Qualitative Data Analysis: A Sourcebook of New Methods,* Beverly Hills, CA: Sage.

Morgan, G. (1986), *Images of Organization,* Beverly Hills, CA: Sage.

Noblit, G., and R. Hare (1988), *Meta-Ethnography: Synthesizing Qualitative Studies,* Newbury Park, CA: Sage.

Pettigrew, A. (1985), *The Awakening Giant: Continuity and Change in ICI,* London: Basil Blackwell.

Poole, M. S., and A. H. Van de Ven (1989), "Toward a General Theory of Innovation Processes," in A. H. Van de Ven, H. L. Angle, and M. S. Poole (Eds.), *Research on the Management of Innovation: The Minnesota Studies* (pp. 637-662), New York: Ballinger/Harper & Row.

Ragin, C. (1987), *The Comparative Method: Moving Beyond Qualitative and Quantitative Strategies,* Berkeley: University of California Press.

Strauss, A. L. (1987), *Qualitative Analysis for Social Scientists,* New York: Cambridge University Press.

Van de Ven, A. H., H. L. Angle, and M. S. Poole (Eds.) (1989), *Research on the Management of Innovation: The Minnesota Studies,* New York: Ballinger/Harper & Row.

8

A Primer on Sequence Methods

ANDREW ABBOTT

This chapter considers the technical problem of analyzing sequences
of social events. Examples of such sequences from organizational
behavior include organizational life cycles, patterns of innovation
development, and career tracks of individuals. The methods considered here enable the analyst to find characteristic patterns in such
sequences. Forces shaping those patterns can then be found by more
conventional methods. After a brief definitional section, the chapter
begins with discussion of three types of sequence questions: (1)
questions about whether a typical sequence or sequences exist, (2)
questions about why such patterns might exist, and (3) questions
about the consequences of such patterns. The theoretical foundations
of the first type of question, which is in fact the most important, are
then considered. Having established the legitimacy of the approach
here taken, the chapter then introduces two exemplary data sets with
which to focus discussion. These raise the issue of conceptualization
and measurement of sequence data. Illustrative cases are presented
to show the importance of extreme care in conceiving a sequence to
measure and then choosing indicators for it. The chapter then turns
to methods proper, considering them in several categories. It first
briefly mentions methods not employing "distance measures" between events: permutational techniques, stochastic (e.g., Markov)
models, and durational methods. Most of these do not directly address
sequence questions but can be used to do so if necessary. Turning to
the methods based on event distance, the chapter first considers the
problem of measuring distance between events (1) in terms of
elapsed time, (2) in terms of categories of events, and (3) in terms

This chapter appeared originally in *Organization Science,* vol. 1, no. 4, November 1990,
pp. 375-392.

of observed successions. It then considers methods for unique event sequences (sequences in which no events repeat), proposing the use of multidimensional scaling and illustrating it with an analysis of data on medical organizations. For the separate case of repeating event sequences, the chapter discusses optimal matching methods, which count the number of individual transformations required to change one sequence into another. These methods are illustrated through an analysis of data on musicians' careers. The chapter then briefly considers the problem of finding subsequences common to several longer sequences (or repeated in one longer sequence). It closes with a discussion of assumptions made and caveats required when these types of methods are used.

Like other social scientists, organizational scientists often theorize about sequences of events. Every stage theory, for example, embodies a hypothesis about the typical order of events; the common argument that organizations pass through a characteristic life cycle asserts that a specific series of events—founding, expansion, drift, diversification, and so on—follow in a characteristic order, irrespective of the organization involved. Similarly, every process theory argues for patterned sequences of events. In innovation, for example, we wonder whether the presence of particular kinds of information early in the process makes a difference, or whether certain sequences of implementation bear fruit with particular rapidity. These too are questions about the order and sequence of events and about the effects of that order and sequence on other factors. Such questions are widespread in organization science, as in social science generally. Their importance is clear. If preferable outcomes can be associated with particular sequences of activities, there are obvious application possibilities.

But we have few methods for testing these sequence hypotheses. Statistical techniques in social science generally ignore the order of events. Indeed, they shun the idea of events altogether, preferring to organize inquiries in terms of variables (see Abbott 1983, 1988; Abell 1987). There is good reason for this: The assumption of variables brings tremendous rewards. By assuming that the world is composed of independent entities describable by measured attributes (that is, of cases located in an N space of variables), analysts can apply the powerful mathematics of linear transformations. Moreover, repeated applications of such transformations can represent successive elapsed periods. But every reward has its cost. The variables approach assumes that the past has "no depth"; a case's path to its present

N-space location is not used in predicting its next move. Such an approach, although powerful, leaves us impotent before the kinds of sequence questions mentioned above.

In this chapter I shall briefly remedy this deficiency. I begin with some definitions and a discussion of typical questions that concern us about sequences. I then present some data sets to illustrate these questions and provide a foundation for later discussion. After a short examination of sequence conceptualization and measurement, I then discuss some methods available to address sequence questions directly.

Before beginning, I should locate my approach with respect to other, perhaps more familiar, ones. The repeated linear transformation model I have just defined is a continuous-state, discrete-time Markov generalization of the usual linear model. The methods discussed here differ from that model and its various specifications in that they attend to the paths cases take through *N* space rather than to the pattern the aggregate of cases makes in that space between two given moments. A useful analogy is to think of a school of minnows (cases) swimming in a lake (the variable space). The variables model looks at deformations of the whole school from one time to another; the methods I discuss look at the paths of individual fish over several time periods.

In general, the Markovian methods implicit in the variables approach study sequences only indirectly, by examining their aggregate properties. Such methods cannot be used to analyze regular sequential patterns of the kind discussed in the opening paragraph. This restriction applies as well to event-history methods, the methodological foundation of the current population ecology perspective on organizations, which analyze only one step in a sequence at once (but achieve thereby the advantage of extensive modeling of exogenous effects). It applies also to the simpler Markovian methods on which studies of occupational mobility have generally been based. The methods I discuss here, by contrast, directly analyze whole sequences of events. Like the linear and Markovian models, of course, they forgo other explanatory power to acquire this strength. But since their advantages and disadvantages complement those of other approaches, they offer a useful alternative for analysts interested primarily in sequential patterns.

PRELIMINARY MATTERS

In this chapter I use the word *sequence* to refer to an ordered sample of things.[1] That order may be temporal, as in the order of events in an organization's development, or it may be spatial, as in the order of positions in an organization. (Although in this chapter I deal only with temporal sequences, most of the methods I discuss apply equally well to one-dimensional spatial sequences, another fact that sets these methods apart from Markovian and other stochastic techniques.) The ordering principle of a sequence may be continuous, as in salary hierarchies, or it may be discrete, as in the order of events in a particular episode of innovation. I shall here be mostly concerned with discrete orders, as they are the most commonly intractable type of sequence data. The ordering principle of a sequence sometimes permits ties, as does, for example, the ranking of functional positions across a set of organizations. At other times it does not, as in the temporal order of a set of overall strategic policies.

Since my discussion mostly refers to temporal sequences, I shall refer to the elements in sequences as *events*.[2] The set of all possible events in a set of sequences is the universe; if the number of distinguishable events is finite, that number is the size of the universe. A *sequence data set* is a set of sequences whose elements are drawn from a particular universe. An example would be a collection of histories of particular innovations or a group of organizational histories.

A sequence that samples the universe without replacement is a *nonrecurrent sequence*; the length of such a sequence cannot exceed the size of the universe. It need not necessarily equal that size, if certain events do not happen. A sequence that samples the universe of events with replacement is a *recurrent sequence*. The length of a recurrent sequence has no limit.

SOME SEQUENCE PROBLEMS

We usually entertain certain basic questions about sequence data. These questions are of three kinds: questions about the pattern of the sequences, questions about independent variables that affect those patterns, and questions about the dependent variables affected by the patterns.

The pattern questions begin with the central issue of existence. Is there a typical sequence? Do certain events always occur in a characteristic order? For example, we may have data on histories of innovation and seek the typical pattern of innovation. In some cases, of course, there may be several possible versions of a sequence in a population. There might, for example, be several alternative typical patterns among a set of innovations. These typical pattern(s) questions are supplemented by a second set of pattern questions, which concern the existence of common subsequences. An example of such a common subsequence might be a subset of career events always traversed in the same order. Or perhaps although the whole histories of a set of innovations are not similar, certain subsections of those histories are. Finally, we often wish to know about internal interdependencies in sequences.

Are certain orders of events seldom or never observed? For example, if an organization's morale has monotonically declined for several time periods, does recovery never occur? Such questions concern internal constraints within the sequence pattern. They form a transition to the second general class of questions about sequences, which concern external effects.

Given a set of sequence patterns, we can ask why those patterns are the way they are. There are two particularly important families of questions here. The first concerns the independent variables that influence which of several sequence patterns is observed. Does education, for example, determine the characteristic sequence of career? Does the size of an organization determine the shape of the status rankings we find in it? In each case our basic approach is to classify the careers and rankings, then see what independent variables best predict the classification. But sometimes there exist external constraints that absolutely prevent certain sequence patterns or that otherwise shape sequence data. For example, only a certain number of careers can terminate in executive positions. This fact seriously constrains the possibilities for typical careers. Specifying these constraints complements the discovery of independent effects on sequence pattern.

Finally, we may also be interested in the effects of given sequence patterns on variables. That is, we may be concerned with effects running not to the sequence from some external set of variables, but from the sequence to that external set of variables. Perhaps the most obvious version of this question is the fundamental one of whether the order in which a set of events occurs influences their ultimate outcome. A typical question of this type concerns whether those promoted before acquiring certain kinds of expertise are helped or hindered in their ultimate career success.

Answers to questions about the causes or consequences of sequences generally presuppose answers to questions about the sequence patterns themselves. One must be able to categorize sequences to assess their effects, and one must be able to differentiate sequence types to analyze the effects of independent variables on them. Thus the first questions discussed—the questions about whether there is (are) one or more sequence pattern(s)—are the place where analysis must begin. I shall call these questions the typical-sequence/families-of-sequences (TSFS) questions; they are in fact the central questions of the sequence area.

There are two broad approaches to TSFS questions. They disagree about the ontological status of temporal sequences, although the real cause of debate is usually concealed by a surface disagreement about methods. The older and more established approach is one that does not believe in history. It arises as a defense of the long-established use of Markov models for social processes, particularly for intergenerational social mobility, a practice that goes back to Prais (1955) and Bartholomew (1967). This school maintains (implicitly) that histories are to be viewed as a surface reality generated by an underlying probabilistic process realized at each instant through time. On this argument, while an organizational career appears to be a simple sequence of events, in fact each event in it is the realization of a choice process with parameters and constraints, calculated at succeeding points in time. The entire influence of the past occurs through its determination of the immediate present, which in turn serves (via the process) as the complete determinant of the immediate future. (This is, essentially, the general-general linear model posited above.) This approach holds TSFS questions to be false questions, since they concern not the real regularities in the mechanism of history making, but only the apparent regularities of their results. At the least, the proper approach to TSFS questions is to model the underlying process. Information about the TSFS questions may then emerge, but the questions themselves are not central and analysis based on them is misleading at best.

The other line of argument is implicitly followed by those who insist on the integral quality of temporal sequences as wholes. While this school admits the choice process model for some cases, it finds it unnecessarily restrictive as a general strategy. First, some histories do not arise from choice processes, but are set up as wholes. The manufacture of hybrid integrated circuits may take several hundred steps, but their order is not determined by a choice process running from beginning to end, but rather by an overall design reflecting processing and material constraints. Yet while there is no generating stochastic process, we may nonetheless desire methods that could compare one way of manufacturing hybrid integrated circuits with another.

Second, even where choice processes obviously occur, as in careers, the choosers generally shape their choices by comparison of their own careers with culturally accepted models (in that case, models for full careers). Junior executives trying to decide what move to make next not only compare their present age and status with criterion standards, but also consider the sequence of steps that took them to that present. Thus the choice process assumed by the first school presupposes as an input the actors' full analyses of their own pasts; if that input includes a sequential judgment, we must be able to analyze that judgment to model the choice process effectively. Finally, to the extent stochastic choice models consider any effect of the past order of events on present choice, they themselves presuppose a method for categorizing sequences; such a method must characterize past sequences as a whole.

While the philosophical status of TSFS questions is thus a vexing problem, for the duration of this chapter I shall take the second position, the position that TSFS questions are legitimate and require some methodological examination.[3] Readers who disagree may simply read this chapter as suggesting a useful descriptive technique. Many students of organizations and other areas would like methods for discovering or describing typical sequences or families of typical sequences in "history" data. I shall review these methods by first discussing two illustrative sequence data sets and then considering methods for analyzing them.

TWO EXEMPLARY SEQUENCE DATA SETS

To provide a basis for later discussion, I shall present two simple sequence data sets. One concerns the development of medical institutions in American communities. The other concerns a set of organizational careers in the somewhat less familiar setting of baroque Germany. The two data sets have an important difference. The institutional histories of medicine are conceived as nonrecurrent sequences. The events included are things like the founding of an association or the passage of a licensing law (rather than the simple existence of an association or a law); since a local society or law, once formed, usually remained in place until the present, events do not repeat. In the career data, by contrast, a given individual may occupy a job for several years, leave it for a few more, then return to it again. Here, events are not unique but recurrent.[4]

I begin with the data on medical institutionalization. The question here is whether there is a typical order in which local communities of American doctors built their profession. Which came first, the development of associations, the attempt to control work, the desire to build or control education, the need to develop better knowledge, or the willingness to build organizations for medical work? The underlying theoretical issue is a standard problem in the sociology of professions: Does professionalism mean serving a social function (in which case knowledge and education come first) or does it mean using monopoly to achieve high status (in which case control and organization come first)? The cases are 165 American towns and cities. The observed events are the first occurrences of 10 possible institutions:

- informal feebill (publishing an informal list of prices for services)
- formal feebill (publishing a formal list of prices for services)
- local organization (founding a local medical society)
- long school (founding a school that endured a long time)
- general hospital (founding an enduring general hospital)
- short school (founding a school that endured only briefly)
- medical school library (creating a library in a medical school)
- hospital library (creating a library in a hospital)
- short journal (founding a brief-duration local journal)

- knowledge/information (founding an enduring local journal or a society for knowledge exchange)

The ordering principle in these data is discrete time; we have dates by year. Ties may therefore appear, since events may come in the same year. The "measurement" scheme dates events at their first occurrence, even though there may be reasons for wanting to choose the second or some other occurrence if there are more than one of a given type. This measurement scheme has the advantage of giving us a nonrecurrent sequence, since the first observation of a given event can occur only once. There is no need that every event in the data be observed, and, indeed, in most cases most of the events are not observed. Only in cities such as New York and Philadelphia do we find instances of all these events.

My second exemplary data set concerns the careers of musicians in the courts and towns of eighteenth-century Germany. The empirical question is whether there are common career ladders that successful musicians generally followed. Did one, for example, zigzag up from court position to town position? Did one move gradually through the ranks? Did one advance by changing instruments or by changing the ensemble in which one played? The data here are the careers of 279 musicians active in Germany between 1660 and 1800. The universe of events in this case is not 10 types of organization foundings, but 34 types of jobs. Each job represents a combination of a "sphere of activity" (e.g., court, opera, town) and a position (e.g., *Kapellmeister,* organist, vocalist). The ordering principle is again discrete time, since the data are again by year. Ties are not allowed, because in principle an individual can hold only one job at once. (In fact, many musicians held two, but they are not included in the 279 considered here.) The measurement scheme is simple. Each career has as many "events" as there are years between its beginning and end, and each event is simply the job occupied in the relevant year of the career. The sequences are therefore recurrent, since jobs were often occupied for many years. An illustrative career follows, with the number of years in a job given before the letter M and the identifying number of the job afterward:

6M18   2M50   2M11   5M50   4M8

This musician (W. A. Mozart) spent six years in the job M18 (court *Konzertmeister*), two years in an "other" position, two years as a court organist (M11), 5 more years in an other position (actually freelancing in Vienna), then 4 years as a court composer (M8).

These two data sets illustrate typical sequence data and typical sequence questions. Sometimes we have recurrent events, sometimes nonrecurrent.

Sometimes we seek a single typical pattern, as among the medical institutions, and sometimes families of patterns, as in the musical careers. Before we consider the methods applicable to these questions, however, we must briefly examine the conceptualization of sequence data.

A NOTE ON CONCEPTUALIZATION AND MEASUREMENT

It is easy to think that conceptualization and measurement present no problems with sequence data. After all, we know what a job, or a medical school, is. But consider the medical data in a little more depth. The question is whether there is a typical order in which communities of American doctors built their profession. As I said, the theoretical issue is whether new professions turn first to tasks of monopoly or to tasks of internal exchange. The methodological strategy seems obvious. One measures when the first licensing laws, feebills, and other control measures are created, and one measures when doctors start to exchange knowledge; then one compares the two dates, over some set of locations. But we cannot simply assume that publishing a feebill *is* expressing interest in control or that founding a journal *is* an interest in knowledge formation; feebills often took long effort to hammer out, and individuals often founded journals simply for personal advancement. That is, there is a difference between the general conceptual categories (of interest in control and in forming knowledge) on the one hand, and the particular episodes (of publishing a feebill or founding a journal) on the other. Of course, in standard methods we do not assume indicators *are* concepts—for example, that years of schooling *are* education rather than simply *indicate* education. The same rule applies in sequence methods. We must distinguish between indicators (occurrences) and concepts (events).

But this distinction requires that we put extensive care into the conceptualization and measurement. On the one hand, we must undertake "colligation": making up a basic theoretical "story" of conceptual events and linking them together. This is the equivalent of "conceptualization" in standard methods. On the other, we must employ careful measurement, choosing observed occurrences to indicate that story, assessing the interaction of data limits with the measures we have chosen and weighing the variation of the relation between conceptual events and indicating occurrences throughout the story.

What happens when one ignores these issues? Consider Wilensky's (1964) still extensively cited paper on the development of professions. It asks the same question as I ask above, but about professions in general, rather than about local communities of professionals. Wilensky's data concern the following universe of events across several professions: (the first date of) university schooling, nonuniversity schooling, licensing law, national association, ethics code, and school accreditation. Wilensky found that the events came in this order generally and made up a story about professionalization to fit the order. But consider why the University of Pennsylvania medical school (1765) antedates the founding of the American Medical Association (1847). This happens not because interest in education precedes interest in association, but because there are many medical schools but only one AMA. Even if the theoretical distributions of possible dates of the foundings of medical schools and of the national association exactly coincided, the fact that we date the interest in education by the first element of a large sample (the first of 400-odd actually founded medical schools) and interest in association by the first element of a sample of one (the one national association actually founded) virtually guarantees that we will regard interest in education as coming first. (Note that if we used the last association founding and the last school founding, we would regard association as coming first.) Wilensky's order is in fact largely the order of the sample sizes; the more numerous events are regarded as earlier. Hence the schools, numbering in the hundreds, antedate the licensing laws, numbering in the dozens, which in turn antedate the national professional association and its ethics code, which occur only once. By ignoring colligation and measurement, Wilensky reaches an artifactual conclusion.[5]

I have extensively considered these issues in an earlier paper (Abbott 1984) and so shall simply summarize the basic issues here. The first set of problems are those of colligation, assembling a story that can legitimately be "measured" in a set of data. Wilensky's example illustrates the first and cardinal rule of sequence colligation; one must establish a single social level of action on which all story events must occur. One cannot mix national (AMA) and local (Philadelphia) events. Along with the choice of level of analysis goes the choice of "central subject." Generally, we require that all the events in a given sequence happen to a coherent actor: a developing medical community, a musician, an innovating organization. The second task of colligation is assembling the story itself: deciding what are its essential events and what are the mechanisms believed to propel the story from one to the next. This is the substantive task analogous to establishing the variables model in standard techniques. Once this is accomplished, colligation is completed by a qualitative analysis of the events involved. In particular, one must decide the *duration* of the events involved, because this radically affects one's ability to order the events, both in principle and in practice.

On the basis of firm colligation, one may move to measurement, just as one moves from conceptualization to indication in standard models. In the terms introduced at the beginning of this section, measurement involves choosing occurrences (that is, observed happenings) to indicate events (which are conceptual abstractions). Founding a medical school, in this sense, is an occurrence, while a local medical community's becoming interested in education is an event. Should we, for example, choose the first medical school in a city to indicate that interest, or should we assume that the first school is a fly-by-night proprietary operation (as was often the case) and choose the second? These kinds of choices make up the measurement problem with sequence data. The choice of indicators for a particular event is a function of the shape of the relevant occurrence data, the degree of right-hand censoring (occurrences unobserved because the data series ends), the quality of the data, and numerous other factors. Indication choice lies chiefly between parametric statistics and order statistics. The former are uninfluenced by outliers and less influenced by variations in distribution shape and data quality than are the latter, but are rendered meaningless by substantial right-hand censoring. The order statistics solve the right-hand censoring problem at a cost of susceptibility to outliers, and, as the Wilensky example shows all too clearly, a further cost of producing artifactual results if occurrences are not of theoretically equivalent "importance" across events. There are other indicators—based on rates at which occurrences happen—but they demand very extensive data. Excellent examples of careful colligation and measurement of sequence data are found in the work of Poole (e.g., 1983).[6]

METHODS FOR SEQUENCE DATA

There are a variety of methods available for analyzing sequence data. Although the main methods I give here utilize information on the "distance" between events to answer the typical sequence questions, I shall briefly mention some other methods at the outset. The discussion therefore has four sections. In the first I mention nondistance-based methods. In the second, I turn to the mechanics of interevent distance. This discussion provides the foundation for the third and fourth sections, which concern sequences of nonrecurrent and recurrent events, respectively. I assume throughout the following discussion that we have a sequence data set that is unambiguously colligated and measured, consisting of sequences sampling a known universe such that each event in each sequence has a known temporal location in discrete time. For the duration of the chapter, that is, I assume away conceptualization and measurement problems.

Methods Not Employing Interevent Distances

Sometimes one has nonrecurrent sequences in which every event is observed once and only once. Such data are simply permutations. They are subject to a variety of statistical approaches. The easiest uses the Spearman rank correlation coefficient (or one of its relatives) as a direct measure of the resemblance of one sequence to another.[7] Once such distance measures have been applied to all pairs of sequences in a data set, one may then submit the resulting distance matrix to any standard classification technique (e.g., cluster analysis, multidimensional scaling) to derive families of sequences. A "most typical" sequence may then be found by finding the sequence that minimizes some (possibly weighted) function of the distances to all other sequences. Permutation statistics have problems with extensive ties, however, as they do with missing events.

In the case of recurrent sequences, the standard approach that avoids using event distances is to postulate a generating stochastic process whose random realizations are the observed sequences. I have already mentioned the philosophical foundation for such a model. The only stochastic process widely used for analyzing sequence data is the discrete-time, discrete-state Markov process. The Markov model assumes that the likelihood that an event occurs is conditional only on the immediate predecessor event. A Markov process is completely described by the matrix of these conditional probabilities, the so-called transition matrix. Its elements are easily estimated from the observed proportions (e.g., the percentage of the time event A is followed by event A, event B, and so on). A wide variety of observed sequence properties can be used to test the model. In absorbing chains (chains with a terminal event), the chief such property is length. In regular (endless) chains, one tests the number of times a given event is observed and the mean waiting time between observations of a given event. All these can be directly calculated from matrices related to the transition matrix. For a detailed treatment, the reader may consult Kemeny and Snell (1976).[8]

Sometimes recurrent sequences consist of runs of one or two particularly important states. A good example is marital history, where periods of marriage are interrupted by periods of singleness. In such cases, the duration of a particular state (the length of the run of "marriage events") is of particular interest. This situation has long interested industrial reliability workers, biologists, and others concerned with how long machines, people, marriages, or other such transients endure. A highly sophisticated methodology—the partial likelihood method—addresses that question. The technique allows the analyst to investigate the impact of dozens of external variables on the duration of a particular sequence event. For the full exposition of these models, see Hannan and Tuma (1984). A primer is found in Allison (1984).[9]

Distance Between Events

Many sequence methods begin with measures for the distance between events. Some methods use these distances directly to assemble a typical sequence of the events. Others use them as input to further techniques for assessing sequence resemblance. In either case, interevent distances are calculated first. There are three general ways to measure interevent distance: in terms of time, in terms of categorical resemblance, and in terms of sequential adjacency.

One can, first of all, measure the proximity of two events by averaging the temporal "distance" between them across all cases. One measures the period intervening between A and B in case 1, in case 2, and so on, then creates some kind of (possibly weighted) average over the entire data set. Most often, temporal measures are used with nonrecurrent events, so there is only one possible interevent distance (for any pair of events) per case. Since the calculated means can include varying numbers of cases, there is no necessity that every event be observed in every case.

The major issue with temporal distance is the "meaning" of that distance. In any sequence model (in fact in any over-time model), time is a surrogate for the pacing of causality. Consider the first and last event occurring in a given case and call a case "short" or "long" depending on the relation of its total duration (last event minus first event) to the duration of other cases. If one measures time as real time between pairs of events averaged across all cases, long cases will dominate the overall figure. That is, if one considers time between association and licensing in medical communities, and one or two communities happen to acquire associations a century earlier than we might expect, these figures will have disproportionate influence. A moment's reflection shows that there is implicit here the assumption that cause flows at equal rates at all times in all cases.

We can more easily imagine what this assumption means by considering what happens when we let distance be the logarithm of real time between two events. Now the long cases have less impact. The logarithmic measure embodies an assumption that over the long run, causal rates can fluctuate somewhat between cases that we might regard as in fact equivalent; long-run temporal differences mean little. But in the short run, causal rates are assumed strictly constant across cases; short-run temporal differences are important. This set of assumptions is in many ways more realistic than are the real-time assumptions; the difference between taking 2 years to develop a new process and taking 4 years is considerably more important than the difference between taking 12 years and taking 14.

One might reduce this effect even further by treating distance only in rank-order terms. Although this measure ignores all the continuous-time information, it completely avoids the problems of long cases. Here the causality assumption is that only order matters; duration means little. This is a radical position about causal pacing, but one worth considering in some cases. Finally, one might consider the causal assumption that the ratios of various durations are always the same within cases, but that some cases go through a set of stages more slowly than do others. Distance is standardized, so that the duration between two given events is represented as a fraction of total duration (last event minus first event) within that case. Here, the causal assumption is that there are slow developers and fast developers but the ratios of causal forces (and thus of events) are equivalent across cases. Once on the fast track, always on the fast track; once out of the running, always out of the running.

There is *no possible measure* of time without assumptions about the pacing of causes. To treat clock time as more "real" than other kinds is simply to make the constant causality assumption noted above. Since that is, in many ways, the most restrictive possible assumption about casual pacing, it is in many ways the least desirable for investigation, despite its deceptively natural character.[10]

The second general type of measure for interevent resemblance is direct categorical resemblance. This is particularly useful with recurrent events, where temporal closeness is conceptually problematic. For example, consider the German musician data above. The 34 jobs are actually generated by an array of 15 positions (e.g., composer, organist) across 9 spheres (e.g., court, opera). Each job is a position/sphere combination. (The many 0 cells make $N = 34$, not 135.) We can make interjob distance a function of whether jobs share a sphere, a position, or neither; interjob distance might be set equal to 1 if sphere or position is shared and 2 if neither is. That is, the jobs are categorized under one or more principle of classification, and then "distance" between job is measured in terms of nearness in those hierarchies, just as we reckon distance in kinship. There are many different ways to generate categorical resemblance measures, but all use common properties of the various events to establish distances between them. The problem is a standard classification task.

Finally, one may also measure interevent distance by considering transition rates. In the German musician data, for example, court instrumentalists (M5) commonly became *Konzertmeisters* (M18); the transition probability M5-M18 is fairly high. By suitable transformation, one can use this information as a distance measure between these jobs. Essentially, one treats the matrix of transition probabilities (discussed above) not as a means of testing a Markovian model of sequence generation, but rather as information on the resemblance of events. Like the categorical measures of resemblance, this too will generally be used with recurrent events.

There are theoretical arguments for and against all of these measures, and one or another may be preferable in a particular case. But they give a variety of possibilities for measuring interevent distance. There are, of course, various means for mixing them together: averaging, compounding, and so on. And the resulting composite distances are usually transformed into proximities by some simple technique, such as taking reciprocals or subtracting from constants. The overall result, then, of the measurement of interevent distance is an *event proximity matrix.* This in turn is used for direct analysis.

Techniques for Nonrecurrent Events

Given an interevent proximity matrix, one is ready for analysis. The choices here differ with nonrecurrent and recurrent sequences. Often with nonrecurrent events one is interested in finding a typical sequence, a characteristic order of events. The problem of finding a best one-dimensional sequence given a set of proximity data is called the *seriation problem,* and is simply the one-dimensional version of multidimensional scaling.

Sometimes the seriation problem can be solved by inspection. One aims to rearrange the event proximity matrix so that the proximities increase as one approaches the main diagonal along any row or column (a matrix so arranged is said to be in Robinson form). One lists the proximities from largest to smallest, then proceeds down the ordered list, adding onto the sequence any proximity (i.e., any pair) that does not either involve an interior state of the sequence so far or join the ends of a single "nucleus" (this algorithm is given by Gelfand 1971). If the matrix does not possess a Robinson form, such methods have problems. With the medical institutions data above, for example, I created proximity matrices using all four time measures: real, log, rank, and standardized. The Spearman rank correlations between the four seriations given by this algorithm from those matrices range from -0.152 to 0.758. There are two possible reasons for these low correlations: Either the algorithm itself is overly sensitive to data variations, or the different metrics are indeed effectively embodying different causal pacing assumptions, between which we must then decide.

To rule out the former possibility, one solves the seriation problem with more sophisticated methods, by using multidimensional scaling (MDS) algorithms, which are available in most statistical packages. There are two possible approaches. In the first, one submits the proximity matrix to MDS with dimension constrained to one. This gives a seriation that allows ties and produces interval measure (within the sequence), not merely the rank information of the inspection algorithm. In the second approach, one submits the proximity matrix with dimension set at two. Then one "connects the dots" in the resulting scaling, drawing lines that connect all points linked by proximities greater than a certain threshold. This so-called horseshoe method reflects the fact that one-dimensional patterns often appear as horseshoes in two-dimensional scaling.[11]

Using MDS constrained to one dimension on the data just mentioned gives Spearman rank correlations across the four time measures ranging from

0.867 to 0.976. The equivalent Pearson correlations range from 0.932 to 0.988. Clearly, these results are far more stable; the inspection algorithm has failed because none of the matrices actually has a Robinson form. One can sum the ranks across time measures or use weights based on the interval scores to produce a composite order. Such a composite order, giving the typical development of medical institutions in American communities, is as follows:

1. informal feebill
2. formal feebill
3. local organization
4. long-duration school
5. short-duration journal
6. knowledge/information
7. general hospital
8. short duration school
9. medical school library
10. hospital library

The results conform well with local medical histories. They rather strongly support the power view of professions, since indicators of the control events are earlier than those of the knowledge events. Scientific transformation, indicated by the founding of libraries, is last. However, it is somewhat surprising, in light of the power thesis, that the dominated work site—general hospital—comes late. Note that the ordering leads one to see schooling as something in between a control method (the way the power theorists view it) and a functional necessity (the way the functionalists view it).[12]

If one aims more at finding families of sequences—one perhaps suspects two or three characteristic patterns—one can in principle follow an alternate procedure. (It is possible only when there are no missing data; every case must have generated every event.) In this case, one may bypass the averaging process discussed above, simply transforming the data logarithmically or otherwise as one desires and creating *individual* proximity matrices for each case. These may then be input to a multiway MDS program (such as INDSCAL and ALSCAL), which will create not only a best order, as do standard MDS programs, but also a subject space showing variation between cases.[13]

With sequence analysis, as with analysis generally, one must consider the problem of intercase contagion. In temporal sequences, contagion is most problematic in the case of period events. Certain events may occur at uniform times across cases. The idea of feebills, for example, may have been proposed at a national medical convention and spread to local communities forthwith. In communities well along in their development at that point, feebills would appear late in the sequence, whereas in less well developed communities they would appear early. Any sequence data set presenting serious possibilities for period events should be screened carefully. One may simply consider mean dates and inspect the standard deviations; low standard deviations identify the suspect events. Verified period events should be omitted from the sequence analysis. There may also be a general, systemwide order pattern across all the cases; all events may be period events. In this case, the level of analysis is mistaken, and the larger pattern suffices to cover the particular cases.[14]

Recurrent Events

Sequences of recurrent events have seen massive study in the past 20 years, study stimulated largely by biological problems (for reviews, see Sankoff and Kruskal 1983, Miura 1986). The now-standard techniques are the so-called optimal matching or alignment techniques. These are not stochastic models for events, producing sequences as artifacts. Rather, they are measurement methods, producing a direct measure of dissimilarity between two sequences given a matrix of dissimilarity between sequence elements.

My example here will draw on the data set concerning German musicians. The reader will recall that this data set contains 279 careers, expressed as lists of jobs. The optimal matching algorithm calculates a "distance" between each pair of careers using an algebra of insertion, deletion, and substitution. Thus suppose we have the two careers, (A) 36M5 34M18 and (B) 5M5 1M28 26M18. Musician A spent 36 years as an M5 (court instrumentalist), then 34 years as an M18 (*Konzertmeister*). Musician B spent 5 years as an instrumentalist, then 1 year as a music teacher associated with a court opera (M28), then 26 years as a *Konzertmeister*. The algorithm calculates "distance" between sequences by the number of insertions, deletions, and substitutions required to turn sequence A into sequence B. To go from 36M5 34M18 to 5M5 1M28 26M18 requires that one take sequence A, delete 31M5, add 1M28, and delete 8M18. The result is sequence B. These insertion, deletions, and substitutions have varying "costs," set by the analyst (i.e., in the example we might find it "cheaper" to substitute 1M18 for 1M28 and delete only 7M18 on our way from A to B, if M28 for M18 were an inexpensive substitution). These costs are set ahead of time, by the event proximity matrix derived above. (Event proximities generally depend on categorization here, rather than on time.) Simple dynamic programming guarantees that we find the minimal distance between the two sequences, given the cost array.[15]

Optimal matching produces a distance matrix between sequences them-selves. This matrix can then be used in classification methods as well as in scaling to see the relation between various sequences. That is, one may cluster the data to find families of sequences. One may scale the data to find dimensions of difference. One may apply grouping tests to verify categori-zations of sequences. Optimal matching techniques have been shown to be relatively stable under fairly drastic perturbation of coding rules and of substitution costs (see Forrest and Abbott 1990). The techniques also allow transformations of the underlying time metric, as were used above to embody different causal pacing assumptions. One simply transforms the raw data before input to the algorithm.

To show what can be accomplished with these methods, I offer here a brief discussion of material from earlier work on the German musicians (Abbott and Hrycak 1990). I divided the 279 careers into three subsets. My aim in doing so was to test the different "models" of causal pacing discussed above. Therefore, in one subset, duration was left untransformed; in the second, durations were logarithmically transformed; and in the third, all careers were set to a standardized overall length, and differed only in the ratios of their particular contents. The substitution costs were set by a mixture of direct categorization and transition information. After applying the matching algo-rithms, I applied average linkage clustering to the resulting intercareer distance matrices to produce groups of careers with common patterns. The three panels of Table 8.1 show the results for court musicians in particular. Entries in the table give the number of careers in the group (first column) and the mean intercareer distance within group (second column). At the left is a verbal description of the type of career. For example, the first group has six careers in it, with a mean intercareer distance of 0.309. It consists of a set of short instrumentalist careers measured in real time. One may test these career groupings, using the between- and within-group means of interse-quence distance, to see whether these groupings are effective. I have used jackknife statistics because of problems in the distribution of distances. (These tests include all careers, not just those shown above.) The results for each time metric are shown at the bottom of the table. The high t values show that there are clear groups of careers here.

One can go further still. Seeking an ideal type, one can create a model for each group. The last column of Table 8.1 displays ideal types appropriate to each group. One can then test whether every sequence is closer (in optimal matching terms) to the ideal type characteristic for its group than to any other ideal type. If so, we might think it "correctly classified." At this classification task, the ideal types are enormously successful. Allowing for duplicate careers, the real types correctly place 85 of 88 careers, the log types correctly place 78 of 80 careers, and the standardized types correctly place 84 of 86

TABLE 8.1

Type of Career	Number in Group	Average Distance	Model		
Real Time Measure					
Short instrumentalist	6	0.309	15M5		
Medium instrumentalist	9	0.285	25M5		
Long instrumentalist	5	0.292	50M5		
Short instrumentalist/ Konzertmeister	5	0.325	5M5	30M18	
Instrumentalist/Konzert- meister/administrator	2	0.457	8M5	20M18	23M21
Instrumentalist/other/ Kapellmeister	3	0.491	10M5	10M50	10M14
Standard Time Measure					
Instrumentalist	17	0.037	48M5		
Konzertmeister	4	0.014	50M18		
Short instrumentalist/ Konzertmeister	2	0.418	8M5	27M18	
Long instrumentalist/ Konzertmeister	4	0.128	35M5	12M18	
(Other court?)/ administrator	5	0.486	45M21		
Instrumentalist/Konzert- meister/Kapellmeister	5	0.292	10M5	7M18	29M14
Logarithmic Time Measure					
Short instrumentalist	3	0.121	5M5		
Medium instrumentalist	15	0.195	10M5		
Short instrumentalist/ Konzertmeister	6	0.288	4M5	10M18	
Instrumentalist/Konzert- meister/administrator	3	0.386	3M5	7M18	6M12
Any court/other/ Konzertmeister	2	0.556	5M34	5M50	8M18
Instrumentalist/ Kapellmeister	3	0.356	6M5	9M14	
Any court/Kapellmeister	2	0.519	8M34	8M14	

	Real	Standard	Logarithmic
Average within groups	0.372	0.137	0.387
Average between groups	0.860	0.810	0.825
Jackknife ratio estimate	1.495	1.901	1.434
t value	10.31	13.17	4.57
df	93	91	92

careers. (Careers not falling under any of these types account for the missing careers up to the total of 94, 93, or 92, respectively.) These ideal types allow one to analyze much larger data sets, because they obviate the need for dyadic (relational) data. With the ideal types one no longer has to estimate distances from each sequence to every other sequence, a task that increases with the square of the data set size. One can use pilot data to find "typical sequences," then classify the main data set by using the ideal types as standards, a task that increases only with the product of data set size and the number of ideal-typical sequences. I could therefore, in principle, now classify several thousand careers of German musicians (if I had the data) by using the 20 to 25 ideal types that appear to classify the pilot careers effectively.

Related Techniques and Assumptions

The techniques just discussed mainly concern the first of the basic sequence pattern questions: whether there are typical sequence patterns. One other pattern question is often of interest to organization researchers: the extent of common subsequences. These subsequences may be sought between two different histories, as when we consider whether a certain portion of the development process repeats in every one of a set of innovations. Or we may be interested in a subsequence that repeats within a given innovation's history.

The common subsequence problem is of wide scientific interest, and is particularly important in studies of DNA. The basic analytic technique is simple. Any two sequences within which common subsequences are sought are used to define the rows and columns of a matrix, one sequence element per row (column). The matrix is then filled with ones wherever the row and column element match. Common subsequences then appear as diagonals of ones in the matrix. If there are slight disorderings (for example, a few transpositions in the common subsequence), the regularities will appear as "clouds" of ones around a diagonal rather than as an exact diagonal. Software for performing this analysis is widely available in DNA analysis packages.

I close this section with a brief list of the assumptions made by the techniques I have discussed. They assume, first of all, that sequences are to be treated as wholes, rather than as processes generated from one end to the other. They assume as well that the significance or definition of one event is independent of those of other events (this is a type of no-interaction assumption). In the case of the seriation methods, particularly those using order statistics, they assume equivalent "importance" for different types of occurrences used to indicate different events; results will otherwise be artifactual. Finally, like all over-time sequence methods, they have to assume the independence of one observed sequence from another. (Event-history applications generally assume that independence between different periods within the case as well.) Interdependent time-series analysis is perhaps the lone exception to this last assumption, and there are disagreements about its epistemological standing.

CONCLUSION

This chapter has given a quick sketch of methods for direct analysis of sequential data. It has focused on methods relying on interevent distances, although mentioning those that do not. The basic techniques have concerned two kinds of sequences. In the first, nonrecurrent sequences, we are generally interested in the typical order of some set of events, as in the illustrative data I have used on development of local medical communities. There, the technique of choice is an estimation of interevent distance followed by some form of scaling. In the second type, recurrent sequences, we are again interested in orders of events, but generally are less likely to believe in a "one best order." For example, I expected several different types of careers in the careers of musicians I have used as an example. There the preferable technique is again to estimate interevent distances, but then to use them as input to matching algorithms that calculate intersequence distances, which can in turn be analyzed with standard classification techniques.

I have tried to indicate the relation of these techniques to other forms of over-time analysis. The chief difference lies in their taking histories as wholes rather than as stepwise processes generated by iterated models. There are, in fact, other approaches to holistic sequence analysis. For example, I have ignored Abell's (1984, 1985, 1987) graph-theoretic approach to sequence analysis, the practical details of which are not yet fleshed out. Nor have I discussed Mayhew's early attempts at aggregate-property sequence analysis (Mayhew, Gray, and Mayhew 1971; Mayhew and Levinger 1976). I have also omitted the artificial intelligence approach to the problem (see, e.g., Dietterich and Michalski 1985). I have indeed merely provided outlines of the techniques I describe, which the interested reader will wish to pursue through references provided. Nonetheless, I hope that I have succeeded in my aim to show students of organizations that there do exist serious methods for directly addressing the kinds of life-cycle and process questions that arise so frequently in organizational data.

Acknowledgments

This chapter is based on material prepared for the National Science Foundation Conference on Longitudinal Field Research Methods for Studying Organizational Processes, Austin, Texas, September 1988. I would like to thank the organizers of the conference, and in particular Andrew Van de Ven, for stimulating me to put these thoughts together in one place.

Notes

1. In presenting some definitions, I am not foreshadowing a rigorous exposition, but rather assuring that basic terms are similarly understood by author and reader.

2. In stratification rankings we often call the elements *statuses* and the order itself a *hierarchy*. In other work, I have explicitly distinguished events and occurrences, the former being conceptual, the latter observed (Abbott 1984). In this chapter I use *event* in the usual sense except briefly in the section on conceptualization and measurement.

3. I have briefly considered the philosophical foundations of the choice process model in previous work (Abbott 1983, especially no. 26). I am expanding that treatment in work currently in progress. Among many practitioners of event history analysis, the position has become a dogma forbidding the use of alternative approaches to sequence data. See also Abbott and Hrycak (1990) and Abbott (1990).

4. I should note that the medical institution data *could* be reconceived on a recurrent event basis, a fact I shall later take up. I apologize that neither data set concerns current organizations. But the medical communities develop a life-cycle pattern, as do current organizations, and the German musicians, as organizational employees, follow patterns similar to those of contemporary organizational workers. The distance is smaller than it appears. In any case, since I write here chiefly as an exponent of sequence models, I must use examples from my current work.

5. The mathematical argument showing why the larger of two samples on coincident distributions will most likely contain both a smaller and a larger value than the smaller sample rests on the theory of extremals (see Abbott, 1984, no. 20).

6. The measurement properties of sequence data are largely uninvestigated. In particular, as Scott Poole has pointed out in commenting on this chapter, there is no real work taking effective account of known unreliability in data. My own earlier work simply urges extreme caution, but does not offer positive solutions, although J. Forrest and I (1990, Abbott and Forrest 1986) have investigated the stability of optimal matching under fairly strong perturbations of coding and have found encouraging results. To my reading, those using event-history methods treat the measurement issues I have raised as nonexistent; certainly those using them have never considered the importance of distinguishing conceptual "events" and empirical "indicators," which is obviously the first step toward a measurement theory for sequence data.

7. The Spearman is in fact one of a large class of linear permutation statistics. The interested reader may consult Hubert (1979) for a somewhat technical review.

8. Markov models may be adapted to deal with "deeper" pasts by estimating transition probabilities for all sequences of states two (or more) steps long. Such models are called second- (third-, and so on) order Markov models. Since the number of probabilities to be estimated rises with the square of the nth power of the number of states for each n steps so included, multiorder Markov processes are seldom used for empirical research.

9. In fact, partial likelihood methods are one formalization of a widely dispersed set of methods known variously in various disciplines: reliability or hazard-function methods in industrial engineering, durational methods in economics, life-table methods in biostatistics, and event-history methods in sociology. The essence of partial likelihood is ignoring the absolute size of the general transition rates to focus on factors increasing or decreasing that rate in particular cases.

10. I should note that if one uses untransformed real time as an interevent distance metric, there is no difference between applying the scaling techniques later discussed and looking at the

simple order of means. I thank J. Kadane of Carnegie Mellon University for calling this point to my attention. Some readers have objected to my argument that elapsed real time embodies the most stringent causal pacing assumptions. Unfortunately, space limits prevent my developing this argument here; I intend to return to it in other work.

11. Sources on the MDS approach to seriation are Kendall (1971) and Kruskal (1971). A general primer is found in Kruskal and Wish (1983).

12. The extremely high correlations among the various metrics suggest that while these metrics in principle embody different causal pacing assumptions, the present data are too imprecise to take advantage of those differences.

13. I am grateful to Scott Poole for suggesting the INDSCAL approach; I should also note that these institutionalization data illustrate a special but common case where each nonrecurrent event involves the creation of a structure that endures through later stages. If that is true, one can transform the data into recurrent event data by a simple expedient. Each case becomes described at any given time by a single state (analogous to the jobs of the musicians), which is determined by which of the "institutions" is present or absent at that time. The number of possible states is thus 2 to the power of the number of events, 1,024 in the medical professionalization data (of course most of these will not be observed). The sequence, year by year, of these states then becomes a recurrent event sequence analyzable with recurrent sequence methods.

14. There is also the possibility of spatial contagion among data sequences. Adjacent localities may have followed similar patterns because local news traveled easily or for some other reason. This problem is beyond the current chapter. General sources on spatial autocorrelation are Cliff and Ord (1981) and the many papers of L. J. Hubert on the subject (e.g., Hubert, Golledge, and Costanzo 1981).

15. Optimal matching software is available in most commercially available DNA sequencing programs (see, e.g., Pustell and Kafatos 1986). I have used the Beldings Program Series written by David Bradley at Long Beach State University. Most of the biological programs are oriented to finding similar subsequences in immensely long sequences, and consequently use hierarchical search methods that may make them less useful for social science applications. Technical sources on optimal matching, beyond those cited in text, are Day (1984), Lipman and Pearson (1984), and Wilbur and Lipman (1982, 1984). Illustrative applications can be found in Sankoff and Kruskal (1983). See also Abbott and Forrest (1986).

References

Abbott, A. (1983), "Sequences of Social Events," *Historical Methods,* 16, 4, 129-147.

Abbott, A. (1984), "Event Sequence and Event Duration: Colligation and Measurement," *Historical Methods,* 17, 4, 192-204.

Abbott, A. (1988), "Transcending General Linear Reality," *Sociological Theory,* 6, 169-186.

Abbott, A. (1990), "Conceptions of Time and Events in Social Science Methods," *Historical Methods,* 23, 140-150.

Abbott, A., and J. Forrest (1986), "Optimal Matching Methods for Historical Sequences," *Journal of Interdisciplinary History,* 16, 471-494.

Abbott, A., and A. Hrycak (1990), "Measuring Resemblance in Sequence Data," *American Journal of Sociology,* 96, 144-185.

Abell, P. (1984), "Comparative Narratives," *Journal for the Theory of Social Behavior,* 14, 309-331.

Abell, P. (1985), "Analyzing Qualitative Sequences," in P. Abell and M. Proctor (Eds.), *Sequence Analysis* (pp. 99-115), Brookfield VT: Gower.

Abell, P. (1987), *The Syntax of Social Life*, Oxford: Oxford University Press.

Allison, P. D. (1984), *Event History Analysis*, Beverly Hills, CA: Sage.

Bartholomew, D. J. (1967), *Stochastic Models for Social Processes*, New York: Wiley.

Cliff, A. D., and J. K. Ord (1981), *Spatial Processes: Models and Applications*, London: Pion.

Day, W. H. E. (1984), "Properties of Levenshtein Metrics on Sequences," *Bulletin of Mathematical Biology*, 46, 327-332.

Dietterich, T. G., and R. S. Michalski (1985), "Discovering Patterns in Sequences of Events," *Artificial Intelligence*, 25, 187-232.

Forrest, J., and A. Abbott (1990), "The Optimal Matching Method for Anthropological Data: An Introduction and Reliability Analysis," *Journal of Quantitative Anthropology*, 1, 69-88.

Gelfand, A. E. (1971), "Rapid Seriation Methods in Archeology," in F. R. Hodson, D. G. Kendall, and P. Tautu (Eds.), *Mathematics in the Archeological and Historical Sciences* (pp. 186-201), Edinburgh: Edinburgh University.

Hannan, M. T., and N. B. Tuma (1984), *Social Dynamics*, New York: Academic Press.

Hubert, L. J. (1979), "Comparison of Sequences," *Psychological Bulletin*, 86, 1098-1106.

Hubert, L. J., R. G. Golledge, and C. M. Costanzo (1981), "Generalized Procedures for Evaluating Spatial Autocorrelation," *Geographical Analysis*, 13, 224-233.

Kemeny, J. G., and J. L. Snell (1976), *Finite Markov Chains*, New York: Springer-Verlag.

Kendall, D. G. (1971), "Seriation From Abundance Matrices," in F. R. Hodson, D. G. Kendall, and P. Tautu (Eds.), *Mathematics in the Archeological and Historical Sciences* (pp. 215-252), Edinburgh: Edinburgh University.

Kruskal, J. B. (1971), "Multidimensional Scaling in Archeology," in F. R. Hodson, D. G. Kendall, and P. Tautu (Eds.), *Mathematics in the Archeological and Historical Sciences* (pp. 119-132), Edinburgh: Edinburgh University.

Kruskal, J. B., and M. Wish (1983), *Multidimensional Scaling*, Beverly Hills, CA: Sage.

Lipman, D. J., and W. R. Pearson (1984), "Rapid and Sensitive Protein Similarity Searches," *Science*, 227, 1435-1441.

Mayhew, B. H., L. N. Gray, and M. L. Mayhew (1971), "Behavior of Interaction Systems," *General Systems*, 16, 13-29.

Mayhew, B. H., and R. L. Levinger (1976), "On the Frequency of Oligarchy in Human Interaction," *American Journal of Sociology*, 81, 1017-1049.

Miura, R. M. (1986), *Some Mathematical Questions in Biology: DNA Sequence Analysis*, Providence, RI: American Mathematical Society.

Poole, M. S. (1983), "Decision Development in Small Groups II: A Study of Multiple Sequences in Decision-Making," *Communications Monographs*, 50, 206-232.

Prais, S. J. (1955), "The Formal Theory of Social Mobility," *Population Studies*, 9, 72-81.

Pustell, J., and F. C. Kafatos (1986), "A Convenient and Adaptable Microcomputer Environment for DNA and Protein Sequence Manipulation and Analysis," *Nucleic Acids Research*, 14, 477-488.

Sankoff, D., and J. B. Kruskal (1983), *Time Warps, String Edits, and Macromolecules*, Reading, MA: Addison-Wesley.

Wilbur, W. J., and D. J. Lipman (1982), "Rapid Similarity Searches of Nucleic Acid and Protein Data Banks," *Proceedings of the National Academy of Sciences*, 80, 726-730.

Wilbur, W. J., and D. J. Lipman (1984), "The Context Dependent Comparison of Biological Sequences," *SIAM Journal of Applied Mathematics*, 44, 557-567.

Wilensky, H. C. (1964), "The Professionalization of Everyone?" *American Journal of Sociology*, 70, 137-158.

9

An Empirical Taxonomy of Implementation
Processes Based on Sequences of Events
in Information System Development

RAJIV SABHERWAL

DANIEL ROBEY

A widely accepted and usable taxonomy is a fundamental element
in the development of a scientific body of knowledge. However, the
creation of good empirical taxonomies of implementation processes
is complicated by the need to consider the dynamics of the implementation processes. This chapter addresses this difficulty by using
an optimal matching procedure to measure the pairwise distances
among event sequences occurring in 53 computer-based information
system (IS) implementation projects. Cluster analysis based on these
intersequence distances is used to generate the empirical taxonomy
of implementation processes.

  The resulting taxonomy includes six distinct archetypal processes. One of the process types is labeled *textbook life cycle* (type
4) due to its close resemblance to the detailed, rational approach
commonly prescribed in IS textbooks. The *logical minimalist* process (type 1) follows some of the basic steps of the textbook approach,
but is characterized by little project definition and infrequent assignment of personnel. Whereas both textbook life-cycle and logical
minimalist approaches are external vendors and consultants to some
extent, external dependence is much greater in *traditional off-the-
shelf* (type 2) and *outsourced cooperative* (type 5) processes. The
traditional off-the-shelf process simply involves purchasing the sys-

This chapter appeared originally in *Organization Science,* vol. 4, no. 4, November 1993,
pp. 548-576.

tem from an external vendor, with little system construction or assignment of personnel. In contrast, the outsourced cooperative process consists of joint system development by internally assigned personnel and external vendors. The remaining two process types— *problem-driven minimalist* (type 3) and *in-house trial and error* (type 6)—are both considerably influenced by performance problems. The problem-driven minimalist process is initiated by such problems, with little project definition, and results in a reassignment of organizational roles. The in-house trial-and-error process begins like the textbook life-cycle process, with a clear project definition, but involves frequent system modifications to respond to the performance problems encountered during the project.

This chapter demonstrates how an empirical taxonomy that incorporates the dynamics of event sequences may be developed. The archetypes constituting the taxonomy are related to other implementation process models available in the literature. Some limitations of the study are acknowledged, and its implications for future research and practice are discussed.

The implementation of technological change has always occupied a central place in organization science. The study of implementation focuses upon the identification and classification of organizational processes leading to outcomes of interest, such as the implementation of new production methods, the creation of new services and products, and the development of computer-based information systems (ISs). Each of these types of technological change has become more important in recent years as environmental changes have necessitated frequent and rapid organizational responses (Child 1987, Huber 1984).

For several reasons, ISs provide attractive opportunities for the study of the process of implementation. First, an IS is a complex technical and organizational innovation involving far more than just an adoption decision or hardware installation (Iivari 1986). Second, IS implementation is project oriented—that is, organizations define a specific system as a project and allocate resources for its completion. An IS project can be studied as an identifiable series of events that are intended to lead to some outcome that benefits the organization (Lucas 1981). Third, an IS is often developed through the cooperation of parties both internal and external to the organization (Henderson 1990). Vendors and consultants frequently interact with internal technical staff and managers to produce the IS, thereby increasing the complexity of the process and the number of identifiable stakeholders. Fourth, an IS can be implemented in either large or small organizations. While there may be differences in the ways organizations of different size approach implementation, findings on implementation are apt to be useful for many different organizations. Finally, an IS is usually intended to affect organizational functioning to a significant degree. In fact, the strategic potential of ISs is now well recognized (Harris and Katz 1991, Venkatraman and Zaheer 1990).

IS implementation has been characterized as "an on-going process which includes the entire development of the system from the original suggestion through the feasibility study, systems analysis and design, programming, training, conversion, and installation of the system" (Lucas 1981, p. 14). Therefore, in studying the process of IS implementation, researchers need to consider a large variety of activities. Many are interested in the degree and nature of participation by various stakeholders, including vendors, end users, technical personnel, and management (Doll 1985, Newman and Noble 1990). Also important are the conditions surrounding implementation efforts, such as the availability of slack resources, technical knowledge, and top-management support (Jarvenpaa and Ives 1991, Robbins and Duncan 1988, Zmud 1984). The nature and timing of activities during the implementation process have received less attention. An interest in the *process of implementation*, as distinguished from its antecedents and consequences, requires examination of the sequence of events involved in that process.

In this chapter we offer a taxonomy of implementation processes based on similarities among the sequences of events that occurred during 53 IS implementation projects. To establish the basis for this taxonomy, we first review the major approaches to specifying theoretical models of the implementation process. We then explain the methodology and data analysis, and present a discussion of the empirical taxonomy. The chapter concludes with an examination of the utility of the taxonomy, acknowledgment of some limitations of the study, and suggestions concerning future research needs.

STRATEGIES FOR RESEARCH
ON THE PROCESS OF IMPLEMENTATION

Considerable research has examined the individual, organizational, and technological variables that affect implementation success (e.g., Churchman and Schainblatt 1965, Ives and Olson 1984, Lucas, Ginzberg, and Schultz 1990, Sanders and Courtney 1985, Schultz 1984, Swanson 1988). Such predictors as top-management support for the implementation effort, user-designer relationship, resource availability, and technical quality have been proposed and examined in various studies. Swanson (1988) has compared our current knowledge about the implementation of an IS to a jigsaw puzzle—we can identify the puzzle's pieces, but we lack research evidence on how to solve the puzzle. The state of knowledge is analogous to cooking with a list of ingredients but without the recipe. We need more research on how the ingredients are combined before we can devise a recipe for successful implementation.

One approach to deriving a recipe for implementation is to develop and test models of the implementation process (Markus and Robey 1988, Mohr 1982, Van de Ven 1992). Such models adopt the process itself as the phenomenon of interest, rather than variables describing the antecedents and conditions surrounding the process. Process models embody various assumptions about the progression of events over time and provide theoretical explanations about sequences of events. Families of process theories reflecting different logics, event progressions, and conditions have been identified (Van de Ven 1992).

The process models offered to explain IS and other kinds of implementation may be divided into three broad groups. First, some process models characterize *the overall process* without examining the sequence of activities involved. For example, Bourgeois and Brodwin's (1984) five models of strategic implementation (the commander, change, collaborative, cultural, and crescive models) focus on broad strategic questions and roles for the top executive. Likewise, Alter (1978) has developed six patterns for the implementation of decision support systems based on the degree of user participation and the degree to which the system is imposed on the user. While both of these research efforts are process oriented, the typologies developed do not capture the specific sequences of activities that occur during implementation.

Second, several researchers divide the implementation process into *a priori stages* or *phases*. For example, Huff and Munro (1985) characterize information technology assessment and adoption in terms of six stages: awareness, interest, evaluation, trial, implementation, and diffusion. This assumes that the stages occur in the same order, thus ignoring the possibility of feedback and alternative sequences (Schroeder et al. 1989). Moreover, the stages that characterize this approach often derive from the researchers' logic rather than from empirical observation of events over time. There is no assurance that alternative temporal orders are infeasible. Some problems associated with a priori selection of a stage model are indicated in a study of urban innovations by Pelz and Munson (1982), who found considerable overlap between stages and discovered that the temporal order of events did not fit their model.

The third, and least used, approach emphasizes the value of empirically examining the *sequences of events* that occur over a project's history (Lewin and Minton 1986, Schroeder et al. 1989, Van de Ven 1992). Van de Ven, Angle, and Poole's (1989) research on innovation explicitly adopts a process approach to the collection and analysis of data. Also, Nutt's (1986) taxonomy of implementation tactics describes actions taken by managers in charge of projects and is based on transactions among key stakeholders. Finally, Newman and Robey's (1992) model of user-analyst relationships in IS development is built around episodes and encounters. Unlike the first two approaches, examining sequences of events allows researchers to describe the processes that actually lead to the outcomes of interest—implemented changes in organizations.

In this chapter we adopt the third strategy for process research, seeking to classify the sequences of activities within organizations that produce outcomes of social and technical change. We view the IS development process as a temporal sequence of events through which an IS project progresses. *Events,* the basic elements of such a sequence, are instances of social action relating to the IS development process (Hirschheim, Klein, and Newman 1991). We are primarily concerned with the sequence of events that occurs within an organization in the context of an IS development project. Events that constitute the IS development process (e.g., the specification of user needs) and events that may either affect implementation (e.g., the hiring of a new IS manager) or be affected by it (e.g., the reorganization of the user department) are included. The social unit of analysis is the work organization within which implementation occurs, although our theoretical focus remains on the implementation process rather than on organizational characteristics.

The construction of a taxonomy of implementation processes is an important step toward improving implementation. A taxonomy identifies alternative approaches that may or may not conform to conventional wisdom and standard professional practices. Although "textbook" approaches to system development, such as the system development life cycle or prototyping, are in common use, their advantages over alternatives have not been demonstrated. Indeed, the literature on IS echoes skepticism that standard practices may serve as rational facades for political motives (Hirschheim and Newman 1991, Robey and Markus 1984). Empirical taxonomies can confirm professional practices while offering constructive alternatives to textbook prescriptions. Mintzberg's (1973) study of managerial behavior, for example, succeeded in moving administrative science away from arbitrary principles and introduced a useful, activity-based taxonomy of managerial work. Such a taxonomy can fuel subsequent research on the appropriateness and effectiveness of different types of implementation. Although not examined in our study, these extensions could potentially help improve the implementation process in organizations.

METHOD

Strategy for Data Collection

Each sequence of events represents one data point in this study. Obtaining a large number of sequences would be very demanding for any single research group (Van de Ven and Huber 1990). To lower the resources expended in data collection, some researchers rely on one or two intensive case studies to support their theoretical ideas. We chose to obtain data on a larger number of event sequences by using data collected by hierarchically organized teams of multiple investigators (Eisenhardt 1989, Miles 1979). This approach was used by Smith and Robbins (1982) in their study of parental involvement in schools. They recruited separate field researchers for each of 57 school districts. Although this approach allows for the collection of more data, it may lead to the "hired hand" syndrome and can create data validity problems (Miles 1979).

A variation of the hierarchical team approach keeps some researchers out of the field altogether and uses them to examine the case studies prepared by the field researchers (Eisenhardt 1989, Sutton and Callahan 1987). Several studies employing this approach have used students to collect field data. Notable among these is Mintzberg, Raisinghani, and Théorêt's (1976) study of 25 strategic decision processes. In IS research, Ein-Dor and Segev (1982) used 53 student project teams to study the relationship between organizational context and IS structure.

In this study we used 53 student groups to obtain descriptions of the IS implementation processes in 53 organizations. Students enrolled in a senior-level course on "organizational impacts of information systems" worked in groups of four or fewer members to examine the implementation of an IS. Each group wrote a description of the implementation process, based on interviews with a variety of individuals in the organization studied. All students were majors in management information systems, and a large proportion of them had prior work experience. The written case project, along with its presentation in class, accounted for about half the grade for a three-credit course.

In any research involving multiple field researchers, and especially when student groups are used to collect data, the senior investigators need to ensure that the various teams address common themes in similar ways (Bryman 1988, Miles 1979). In this study, the course instructor discussed the project at length in class and provided detailed prescriptions for it in the course syllabus, including a format for the report and a method for describing the events during the implementation process. The relevant portions of the course syllabus appear in Appendix A. The instructor closely supervised the

TABLE 9.1 Characteristics of Sample Organizations

Industry	Frequency
Finance/accounting	14
Medicine/law/education	8
Distribution	6
Transport/communications	8
Manufacturer/construction	6
Public utilities	8
Others	3
Total	53

Number of Employees	Frequency
10,000 or more	8
1,000 to 9,999	8
500 to 999	11
100 to 499	11
Fewer than 100	15
Total	53

case projects to ensure that the resulting cases could be used for research purposes. More details about this process are provided in Appendix B.

A total of 77 reports were prepared over two years (six consecutive semesters). Despite the efforts to guide the projects, some groups did not produce usable reports. In some cases, a student group was unable to interview a sufficient number of people in the organization to produce a useful description of the process. In other cases, the descriptions and/or sequences of the events were unclear. We excluded 24 project reports for these reasons. We used the remaining 53 reports to obtain the event sequences examined in this chapter. The characteristics of the organizations studied are summarized in Table 9.1.

Together, the 53 reports are based on 260 interviews with 240 different people. The interviews were 30 to 90 minutes long, with an average duration of about one hour. In each case, at least one senior executive, one user, and one IS executive were interviewed. Some groups also analyzed company documentation. A typical report was 5,000 words long, plus tables and figures.

From Cases to Event Sequences

The 53 student reports provided detailed descriptions of the IS development process in each organization, and these descriptions were used to generate the event sequences. To obtain an event sequence for each project, we each independently read each report and identified the sequences of events. We then compared the two lists, producing a single event list for each case.[1] In preparing these event listings, we treated each event as a separate social action. To facilitate this, we developed rules for writing the events as active sentences that did not combine events and that excluded reference to thoughts, worries, and other mental processes. These rules may have excluded some events that actually occurred, but they prevented the recording of any events that had not appeared in the original report (Mintzberg, Raisinghani, and Théorêt 1976).

Reliability of Event Classification

The event sequences for the 53 IS development processes yielded a total of 1,088 events, necessitating a scheme for classifying them into mutually exclusive and cumulatively exhaustive categories. The classification scheme was developed through a number of successively refined versions, as recommended by Bakeman and Gottman (1986). A similar approach was used by Isabella (1990) to classify events in one organization.

An initial categorization scheme of 25 types of events was produced using 43 student reports. A random set of 100 events was used to assess interrater reliability. We each independently classified each of these 100 test events into 1 of the 25 types, and found that we agreed on the event type in only 65 cases. On the basis of these poor results, we developed a more parsimonious classification of 15 types by merging categories that seemed similar and eliminating categories that were infrequently used.

Using the new classification scheme, we each independently classified another random set of 50 events into the 15 categories. This time we agreed on 45 of the 50 events. This level of agreement can be compared with the expected classification agreement due to chance alone, which is 4%. The 90% interrater agreement was compared with the chance classification accuracy of 4% using Cohen's (1960) kappa. The kappa measure (0.896, with a variance of 0.002, producing a z score of 21.861) showed that the agreement between us was significantly greater ($p < 0.0001$) than the agreement expected due to chance alone (Bakeman and Gottman 1986). This procedure assured the reliability of event classification.[2]

One of the authors then classified the 822 events for 43 cases into the 15 types. To assess whether there was any reliability decay (Bakeman and Gottman 1986) in comparison with the interrater reliability assessed for the small random sample, we followed this classification with the selection of another random set of 50 events. Again, we agreed on the event categories in 90% of the cases, and again the kappa measure was significant ($p < 0.0001$). The categorization scheme comprising the 15 categories was therefore considered acceptable, and one of the authors classified the events for the remaining 10 cases using this scheme. Table 9.2 presents the 15 event types and three representative examples of each. The 64 events in category 15, "others," were excluded from the data analysis because they could not be assumed to be similar to one another.

Data Analysis

The data analysis consisted of two distinct stages: computation of intersequence distances and cluster analysis. Each stage involves a number of issues. These issues, and the ways in which they were addressed during data analysis, are summarized in Table 9.3.

Computation of Intersequence Distances

Several researchers have developed taxonomies based on event sequences (e.g., Mintzberg, Raisinghani, and Théorêt 1976, Nutt 1984). The common method involves preparing charts of the individual event sequences and then sorting these charts into sets. This approach relies on the ability of the researchers to make fine distinctions in a well-understood data set. This approach works well for a small number of sequences, but is likely to miss important distinctions when used for many complex sequences (Van de Ven and Poole 1990). For such sequences, *optimal matching* techniques offer a useful way to measure sequence resemblance directly (Abbott 1990, Abbott and Hrycak 1990, Sankoff and Kruskal 1983).

Optimal matching is a dynamic programming technique that measures sequence resemblance when each sequence is represented by a string of well-defined elements, drawn from a relatively small total set (Abbott and Hrycak 1990). In this study, each event sequence is represented using a string of numbers indicating the event types. For example, a sequence SEQ1 comprising submission of proposal (event type 2), approval or authorization (type 3), project definition (type 4), assignment of personnel to the IS project (type 1), physical system construction (type 8), training (type 9), and reassignment of organizational roles (type 14) would be represented by the string 2, 3, 4, 1, 8, 9, 14.

The similarity between any pair of sequences can be conceived in terms of "distance." The distance between SEQ1 and another example sequence (SEQ2), comprising event types 2, 3, 5, 1, 8, 9, 10, 12, may be computed using the number of insertions, deletions, and substitutions required to transform one sequence into the other. One possible way to transform SEQ1 into SEQ2 involves the following four changes: substituting the third event (type 4) with another event (type 5), deleting the last event (type 14), and

TABLE 9.2 The Classification of Events

Event Type	Examples
1. Assignment of personnel to the IS project (includes assignment of personnel by vendors and the creation of a steering committee or task force for the project)	(1) Top management formed a task force with representatives from four key departments. (2) Head of microcomputer systems assigned two programmers from his staff to work on the project. (3) The vendor designated small systems representative to help determine system requirements.
2. Submission of proposal (includes requests for new system or major enhancements, manpower, etc., as well as vendor proposals/presentations)	(1) Accounting manager suggested creation of a database system to keep track of packages and customer information. (2) IS manager proposed that the company's computer system be upgraded. (3) Vendor presented the system to the CEO, user manager, his assistant, and IS personnel.
3. Approval or authorization	(1) Director of finance authorized purchase of the new system. (2) University Management Committee decided to develop the system in-house. (3) Computer services gave user manager permission to buy a canned software package.
4. Project definition (includes definition of system scope, user needs, and broad definition of the system development process)	(1) The IS project team chose to approach the system development using standard structured methodology. (2) The project team members interviewed clerks during work to see how things were done. (3) Vendor analysts studied forms and reports to determine specifications.
5. Seeking technical knowledge/equipment (includes sending request for proposals to vendors and acquiring technical knowledge, but excludes ordering equipment)	(1) Director of advanced systems development sent request for proposals to vendors. (2) User manager called similar organizations in the state to find out about their systems. (3) Accounting professional (part-time MIS head) educated himself on available technology for one year.
6. Assessment of performance (includes feasibility study, system testing, and assessment of vendor products)	(1) Senior VP of operations and VP of operations went to vendors to see new equipment. (2) External auditors reviewed reports for proper balances. (3) IS manager ran tests and programs on new system.
7. Selection of a specific vendor (includes ordering as well as the selection of specific hardware/software vendors)	(1) President, VP, and the vendor's representative decided on the system hardware. (2) Director of advanced systems development selected a software vendor and a hardware vendor. (3) Judge hired a consulting firm to study the civil division to determine if automation was feasible.

(continued)

TABLE 9.2 Continued

Event Type	Examples
8. Physical system construction (includes system design, development, implementation, hardware/software installation, and maintenance)	(1) Program analyst provided the president with logical/physical design of the system. (2) The vendor installed the inventory module. (3) Document Center began transferring manufacturing documents into the system.
9. Training (includes preparing training material and procedures, and system documentation)	(1) IS designed training program for all company employees. (2) Software vendor held a one-week training seminar. (3) Supervisor of revenue accounting gave explanations to data-entry clerks about screens and general procedures.
10. Performance problems (includes complaints about system speed, errors, etc.)	(1) Manufacturing department could not access a needed document that was locked in the system. (2) Passenger Marketing discovered that vendor did not have necessary facilities to process the calls. (3) VP (IS) encountered buffer size error while installing the system.
11. Successful performance	(1) Users were satisfied with system performance during presentations. (2) Various user departments and IS department benefited from the new system. (3) Government checks found that the system was working successfully.
12. Resistance (includes disagreeing with system requirements, development process, etc.)	(1) User manager (director) took all users off the system. (2) Computer services stated that they would not support or maintain canned software. (3) Some judges (users) refused to allow clerks to enter their calendars on the new system.
13. Acceptance/cooperation (includes doing things beyond one's responsibility to ensure system success)	(1) Enrollment Services and bursar's staff supplied details to enable the design to proceed. (2) Production manager used the new system heavily. (3) Supervisor of revenue accounting learned the new system without documentation.
14. Reassignment of organizational roles (includes redesigning user and IS departments, hiring/firing/resignation, etc., but excludes assigning personnel to IS project)	(1) President created an MIS department. (2) Operations manager reduced the number of employees from six to four. (3) The user manager responsible for the system resigned.
15. Others (includes events in external environment and other events that cannot be classified into the above 14 types)	(1) A new government officer started a campaign to automate his department, which concerned the company studied. (2) Software vendor informed the company that it was no longer selling this system and would not support it. (3) IS applied unused portion of the budget to other projects.

TABLE 9.3 An Overview of Data Analysis

Step 1: Computation of Intersequence Distances

Objective: To measure the distances between all possible pairs of event sequences. The distance between two sequences is based on the number of substitutions, insertions, and deletions needed to transform one sequence to the other.

Issues	*Actions Taken*
Assigning values for the substitution costs	Set all substitution costs to 1.00.
Assigning values for the insertion and deletion costs	Examined three alternative cost sets and then set insertion and deletion costs at 0.50 each.
Reducing the effect of different sequence lengths	Standardized by dividing by the length of the longer sequence.

Step 2: Cluster Analysis

Objective: To group the event sequences into meaningful clusters, based on the intersequence distances computed in Step 1.

Issues	*Actions Taken*
Choosing a linkage method	Conducted the analysis using two alternative methods (group average and Ward's), and following the analysis used the results of Ward's method.
Selecting the number of clusters	Examined the fusion coefficients at each agglomerative stage; decided on six clusters.
Testing for the differences among clusters	Compared the mean distance of each sequence from the other sequences within its cluster with the mean distance from the sequences approximating the centroids of the other clusters; the *t* statistic was significant at the 0.01 level.
Interpretation of clusters	(a) Examined the frequencies of each event type in each cluster.
	(b) Examined the event sequence with the smallest mean distance from the other members of the cluster.
	(c) Visually inspected the various sequences within each cluster.
	(d) Based on the above analysis, identified an ideal sequence for each cluster, and then compared the mean distance of each sequence from the ideal sequence for its group with the mean distance from the ideal sequences of the other clusters; the *t* statistic was significant at the 0.001 level.

inserting two events at the end (types 10, 12). If the "cost" of each insertion, deletion, or substitution is assumed to equal one, this procedure would incur a total cost of four, for one substitution, one deletion, and two insertions. An alternative way to transform SEQ1 into SEQ2 involves three changes: substituting the third event (type 4) with another event type (5), substituting the last event (type 14) with another event (type 10), and inserting one event at the end (type 12). This procedure includes two substitutions and one insertion, and would therefore cost only three. In order to compute the closest intersequence distance between SEQ1 and SEQ2, it is necessary to compute the costs of all possible procedures for transforming SEQ1 into SEQ2 and then take the minimum cost method.

The number of alternative procedures for transforming one sequence into another increases proportionately with the product of the lengths of the two sequences, and it would be extremely difficult to compute all possible distances between two long sequences. An optimal matching algorithm provides an effective solution to this computational problem. Such an algorithm is available in the Beldings Program Series, which we used, and in most commercially available DNA sequencing programs.

Three issues are involved in the use of the optimal matching procedure, as shown in Table 9.3. First, it is necessary to assign values for the substitution costs. The cost of substituting an event of one type for an event of another type should reflect the dissimilarity between the two event types. For sequences that include recurring events, this may be done using two approaches, alone or in combination (Abbott 1990). The first approach examines transition rates across events of various types. If one type of event commonly leads to a second type, then the two types would be considered similar and the cost of substituting one for the other would be set at a lower value. This approach is useful if high transition rates imply similarity in the contents of the two event types, as in Abbott and Hrycak's (1990) study of musicians' careers. In our study, however, this assumption is not valid because high transition rates involve very dissimilar events. To illustrate, submission of proposal (event type 2) commonly leads to authorization (type 3), but these two event types are quite dissimilar. The second approach for assigning substitution costs is based on the conceptual similarity between event types. Thus we could classify the 14 event types into, say, three or four broad categories and set substitution costs within each categories at a lower value than substitution costs across categories. We could, for example, set the cost of substituting approval or authorization (type 3) with reassignment of organizational roles (type 14) to 1.0 and set the cost of substituting approval or authorization with physical system construction (type 8) to 1.5. However, because our 15 types of events were created as distinct categories, grouping them into larger categories would seem inconsistent. After evaluating these alternatives, we adopted a more conservative position by electing to assign all substitution costs equal to 1.[3]

The second issue pertaining to the computation of intersequence distance is the assignment of insertion and deletion costs. One constraint that these costs should satisfy is that their sum should equal or exceed the substitution cost. Otherwise, the substitution cost would be meaningless, because a deletion followed by an insertion would always be a less costly way of substituting. We decided not to preselect one set of insertion and deletion costs but chose to examine the effects of three alternative sets on the intersequence distances and the clusters produced. This analysis, presented below in the results section, led us to set both insertion and deletion costs to 0.50.

The third issue is the reduction of the effect of different sequence lengths. The length of the sequences obviously influences the number of transformations required. A single substitution is relatively more important in a short sequence than it is in a long sequence. To compensate, we standardized by dividing the number of transformations required by the length of the longer sequence (Abbott and Hrycak 1990). This procedure reduces the effect of drastic variations in length. However, the information about length is not lost because it is reflected in the insertion and deletion costs; if two sequences differ in length, more insertions or deletions would be needed to transform one sequence into the other.

Cluster Analysis

The primary objective of this study was to develop an empirical taxonomy of implementation processes based on intersequence distances. For this purpose, cluster analysis is an appropriate technique (Lorr 1983, Harrigan 1985, Ulrich and McKelvey 1990). Four methodological issues arise in the use of cluster analysis: choosing a linkage method, selecting the number of clusters, testing for differences among clusters, and interpreting clusters. Our actions taken to resolve each of these issues are summarized in Table 9.3 and discussed below.

Joining methods, which agglomerate individual observations into small groups based on highest resemblance and then successively join small groups into larger groups until one large group is obtained, are commonly used for cluster analysis (Ulrich and McKelvey 1990). Several linkage techniques are available, with group-average linkage and Ward's (1963) method being the most popular (Punj and Stewart 1983, Ulrich and McKelvey 1990). We conducted the cluster analysis using both of these linkage methods in order to arrive at the most interpretable cluster solution. The clusters obtained using Ward's method, as detailed in the results section, proved to be more interpretable.

The second issue is the selection of the number of clusters. We examined the fusion coefficients at each agglomerative stage for each linkage method to determine this number (Hartigan 1975, Ulrich and McKelvey 1990).

Third, to test for the differences among clusters, we compared within-group distance with across-group distance in the following way. We computed the mean distance of each sequence from the other sequences within its cluster. Then, for each cluster, we considered the sequence with the smallest mean distance from the other members of the cluster to be an approximation to the cluster centroid. We performed a *t* test comparing the mean distance of each sequence from the other sequences within its cluster with its mean distance from the sequences approximating the centroids of the other clusters.[4]

Finally, we based the interpretation of clusters on four assessments. First, we examined the frequencies of occurrence of each event type in each cluster, and compared these frequencies with those predicted by chance. Second, for each cluster, we examined the sequence that represented an approximation to the cluster centroid, obtained through the procedure described above. Third, we visually inspected the various sequences within each cluster. This technique is considered suitable when each cluster has a small number of cases (Abbott and Hrycak 1990). Fourth, based on the sequences approximating cluster centroids and the visual inspection of cluster members, we prepared an "ideal type" for each cluster. These ideal types are hypothetical sequences that best represent the clusters. We also examined the mean distances of these ideal types from the actual sequences. The distance of each sequence from the ideal type for its cluster was compared with the average distance from the ideal types for the other clusters using a *t* test.

RESULTS

Computation of Intersequence Distances

We computed the intersequence distances using optimal matching. As mentioned earlier, we set the substitution cost to 1.0 and examined the effects of three alternative sets of insertion/deletion costs: (1) insertion cost = 0.0, deletion cost = 1.0^5; (2) insertion cost = 0.5, deletion cost = 0.5; and (3) insertion cost = 1.0, deletion cost = 1.0.

Cost set 1 produced clusters with sequences of dissimilar length, whereas cost set 3 led to sequences clustering with sequences of very similar length. This behavior of cost sets 1 and 3 may be explained as follows. The insertion and deletion costs, when compared with substitution costs, determine the relative importance given in optimal matching to two kinds of information contained within the event sequences. One kind of information concerns the structure of each sequence, indicating the nature and the relative order of the events constituting the sequence. This information is captured by the total substitution cost. The second kind of information concerns the length of the sequence—that is, the number of events making up the sequence. This information is captured by the total cost of insertions and deletions.

With cost set 1, we can transform from the smaller to the longer sequence without incurring any insertion/deletion cost, as unit insertion cost is zero. Thus this cost set completely disregards the sequence length information. With cost set 3, if two sequences differ greatly in length, they are unlikely to cluster together even if they are similar in structure. For example, transforming a sequence of 5 events into another of 25 events would require 20 insertions, and even after the length of the longer sequence is divided (which partially corrects for length variations), they would be distant by 0.80 even if the shorter sequence is completely contained within the longer sequence. Thus cost set 3 results in sequences of similar length clustering together.

Cost set 2 falls in between cost sets 1 and 3. It does not completely disregard length information, and it does not result in sequences clustering together with other sequences of similar length. As a result, it produces clusters that are based on both structure and length. Therefore, we selected cost set 2, with both insertion and deletion costs equaling 0.50, for the analysis.

Cluster Analysis

Major jumps in fusion coefficients occur for the six-cluster and seven-cluster solutions in the case of group-average-linkage method and for the six-cluster solution in the case of Ward's methods. However, the six-cluster solution using group-average-linkage method produced some very small clusters; three of the six clusters had five or fewer members. The six-cluster solution using Ward's method also produced better results in terms of the ratio of within-group distance to between-group distance (Harrigan 1985, Ulrich and McKelvey 1990), so we selected this method for the empirical taxonomy.

Table 9.4 presents the event sequences constituting each cluster. Comparison of the mean distance from the other sequences within the same cluster with the mean distance from the sequences approximating cluster centroids of the other clusters produced a t statistic of 2.42, significant at the 0.01 level. This result indicates that the within-group distances are less than the across-group distances and that the six clusters are distinct.

The frequency of occurrence of each event type in each cluster, and the frequencies predicted by chance,[6] are given in Table 9.5. The chi-square

TABLE 9.4 The Event Sequences

No.	Sequence of Events
Ideal 1	
1: 13	2 3 7 8 9 8
2:	2 3 5 7 12 8 8 9 12 13 8
3: 4	2 6 12 12 7 12 5 14 10 13 2 3 8 10 5 1 12 12 9 8
4: 5	2 3 7 2 5 3 14 14 3 3 9 8
5:	3 7 8 13 9 8
6:	2 3 7 8 13 9 8
7: 8	2 4 12 3 12 8 3 7 10 3 14 7 4 8[3] 8 9 8 9 10 5 10 9 9 8
8:	2 10 7 3[3] 7 8 5 4 8 7 7 12 9 9 8
9:	2 3 5 6 7 4 8 8 10 12
Ideal 2	
10: 7 10 14 12	2 5 7 14 4
11:	2 12 7 4 5 2 5 5 7 13 14 12 4
12: 16	2 7 4 4 2 7 14 14 12
13:	2 4 2 3 8 7 14 14 4 2 4
14: 6	2 3 5 3 7 13 4
15: 14[4] 10	2 2 3 5 2 2 7 5 2 2 4 2 5 5 5 2
Ideal 3	
16:	10 6 5 7 8 14
17: 1	10 6 5 2 7 7 8 10 10 1 12 11 11 12 18 14[4] 10 14
18: 14	6 2 7 1 5 8 10 6 2 14 4 14 2[3] 14 9 11 8 5 7
19: 3 7	7 8 14 14 10
20:	10 14 4 6 2 3 9 14 8 8 14[5] 9 9 12 6 13
21: 1	10 4 6 7 7 8 8 10 10 14 8 8 3 13 14 10 10 13
22:	10 2 3 14[3] 8 5 2 3 1 14[4] 9 14
23:	10 3 6 14 2 5 6 7 3 6 7 8 14 1 11 2 8 8 14 12[3]
Ideal 4	
24:	2 3 1 4 5 6 7 8 13 9
25:	3 4 4 2 3 5 2 2 3 7 8 8 4 9 8[3] 13 9
26: 7 4	2 1 7 8 9 13 8 4 2 2 3 6 4 6 7 9 8 6 8 9 6 13 10 5 9 10 6 10 9

244

27:	2	3	1		5 2		7 2 3 4	8 8 6 8 6	13 8 7 5	9 1 4 8	10 14
28:	2		7 4				7 3 9	8 4 8 4		9 8 8 9	10 12 14
29: 2	8 1		1	4 6 1 1 2 3	4 1 4		1 4 4	8 4 3 12 14 13	13 8 8 10 10 8 14	9 10 8 12 8 11	10 14 14
30: 2 14	3	1		4 4 8 1 11 2	14 14 13 4 2 4	6	7 2 3 4	8 12 9 9	13	9 6 13	
31: 14				4 1 4 5	5 12 21 14 11 41 11 12 1		7 1 4 8	8 14 8 14 14 14		9 12 8 13 13	14 [3] 14 14 37
32: 4		14 1 4		4 1		6	7 1 4 8	8 8	13		14 14 8
33: 10 4 2	3	1 5		4 6 12 21 23	5 2[3] 3 3 8 14 2 11 4 8[4] 14 4	6 11 5 2 11 3	5 5 2	8 8	9 10 11	10[5]	10 14
Ideal 5	5	2		1	6	10	2	7	8		
34: 1	5	2 7 3 4[3]			6 6			8 6	9	10	14
35: 10		2 7		1 1 4 4			7 7	8 8	6 6	11	14 14
36: 14 14		2 14 14					7 4 4	8 8	6 8		
37: 14 6 10 6		2 3		1 1 4 5	6		7 4 4	8 8	9 1		14 [3]
38: 2 2 13	5	2 7 6 7 2 2 3 7		1 1 8 5	2 2		7 4	9 8 8 4 8	6 8	10 14 8 10	14 14 37
39:					10 2 4 4 6		23 8 23	9		10 8 3 14 14 14 18	14 14 8
40:				6	10		7 5 14	8 8	11	10 8 8 6 4 8	
41: 6 2 2 16	5	2 7 2 7 3	1[3] 4	6	4 8 10		7 2 3	8 8	11 8 6	10 13	
42: 10 10		2		6	2 3 2		7 7 4	8 9 10	11 12	10 11	
Ideal 6	2	3	1	4	6		10	8	9		
43: 3 1	2 5 4 6 1 2	3	1	4 13 13 8	6 6 2		10 10	8 10 10	9	12 13 5 14	10
44:		3		4 9 9 8[3] 12 1	6			8	9		
45: 5 7 6 3	2 7 14			4 4 6 10 2 7 1	6 7 2	10 2 2 6 2 4 9		8	9	12 3	8 8
46: 4	2			4[3] 5 12 9	6 1 2 6			8	9		10 14 12
47: 10		1 6 3 3 7		4 4	6 4 12 4 4 8 8 9 1 11	10 8 8 10 2 3		8 8 10 7 10	9	12 11	10 14 12
48: 4	2 2	3		4 4	6 8 4 7 3 4 8 11 2			8 12 11 2 10	9	12 4 12 2	
49:	2 7		1 3 1 7	4 10 8	6	10 1 5 6		8 14	9[3] 10 10 14	14	10 8 6 10
50: 5 5 1	2 1 2	3 4 3		4 1 4 4 2 3	6 6 4 4 3 7 3			8	9[5] 8 6 8 10	8 10 5	
51: 4		3 14	1	4		10	8 14	9 10 14	8 8 7 6	10 3
52:								9			
53: 7 6	2		1[3]	4[5] 1 1		8 2	9 9 6 10 8 8		12 14 13	14	

NOTE: Following cluster analysis, the sequences were renumbered in the order of clusters. The sequences within each cluster are given following the cluster's ideal sequence. Event sequences 5, 14, 23, 27, 37, and 48 are used in the text to illustrate the clusters. The event types represented by the numbers in the sequences are given in Table 9.2. Three or more consecutive repetitions of an event type are indicated by the event number followed by square brackets containing the number of repetitions; for example, in sequence 53, 1[3] indicates that event type 1 repeated 3 times in succession. We thank Andrew Abbott for suggesting this format for presenting the event sequences.

245

TABLE 9.5 The Frequencies of Event Types for Each Cluster

Event Types	Clusters						Total
	Cluster 1	Cluster 2	Cluster 3	Cluster 4	Cluster 5	Cluster 6	
1. Assignment of personnel to the IS project	2 (6.8)	1 (4.2)	9 (9.2)	16 (16.6)	15 (12.5)	21 (15.6)	64
2. Submission of proposal	9 (11.8)	18 (7.3)	11 (14.3)	27 (28.9)	23 (21.6)	23 (27.0)	111
3. Approval or authorization	17 (8.2)	4 (5.1)	7 (9.9)	18 (20.0)	12 (15.0)	19 (18.8)	77
4. Project definition	5 (10.3)	8 (6.4)	3 (12.5)	28 (25.2)	18 (18.9)	35 (23.6)	97
5. Seeking technical knowledge/ equipment	8 (5.3)	11 (3.3)	6 (6.4)	11 (13.0)	6 (9.7)	8 (12.2)	50
6. Assessment of performance	2 (7.9)	2 (4.9)	9 (9.5)	17 (19.2)	22 (14.4)	22 (18.0)	74
7. Selection of a specific vendor	12 (7.3)	7 (4.5)	10 (8.8)	10 (17.7)	17 (13.3)	12 (16.6)	68
8. Physical system construction	21 (15.9)	1 (9.9)	18 (19.2)	41 (38.8)	34 (29.0)	34 (36.3)	149
9. Training	10 (6.4)	0 (4.0)	5 (7.7)	18 (15.6)	6 (11.7)	21 (14.6)	60
10. Performance problems	7 (9.0)	2 (5.6)	15 (10.8)	19 (21.8)	15 (16.4)	26 (20.5)	84
11. Successful performance	0 (1.9)	0 (1.2)	2 (2.3)	7 (4.7)	5 (3.5)	4 (4.4)	18
12. Resistance	11 (4.7)	4 (2.9)	6 (5.7)	10 (11.4)	1 (8.6)	12 (10.7)	44
13. Acceptance/ cooperation	4 (3.0)	2 (1.9)	3 (3.6)	14 (7.3)	1 (5.5)	4 (6.8)	28
14. Reassignment of organizational roles	4 (10.7)	8 (6.6)	31 (12.9)	28 (26.0)	18 (19.5)	11 (24.4)	100
15. Others	4 (6.8)	4 (4.2)	5 (8.2)	19 (16.6)	19 (12.5)	13 (15.6)	64
Total	116	72	140	283	212	265	1088

NOTE: This table provides the actual frequency distributions and the expected distributions (given in parentheses). Of 90 cells, 17 had expected frequency below 5. The chi-square value was 204, significant at the 0.001 level with 70 degrees of freedom.

statistic is 204 ($p < 0.0001$), indicating that the clusters also differ in terms of the frequencies of occurrence of various event types. These frequencies, along with the sequences approximating cluster centroids and visual examination of the members of each cluster, were used to develop the "ideal types" for the six clusters. The comparison of the distance of each sequence from the ideal type for its cluster with the average distance from the ideal types for the other clusters produced a t statistic of 5.20 ($p < 0.001$), showing that the ideal types do indeed represent the clusters.

Table 9.6 summarizes the resulting taxonomy of IS implementation processes. It provides written versions of the ideal event sequences and the key features for each cluster. These key features are primarily based on the event types that occur frequently or rarely for each cluster. Table 9.6 also provides the names given to each cluster. References to other process models that bear resemblance to each cluster are also indicated in Table 9.6.

Interpretations of the Clusters: The Empirical Taxonomy

The clusters derived from our analysis appear to form six distinct types of implementation processes. As indicated by the "ideal" sequences of events, each type conveys a certain approach to developing an information system. The types are named logical minimalist, traditional off-the-shelf, problem-driven minimalist, textbook life cycle, outsourced cooperative, and in-house trial and error. We describe each type in more detail below, using the results from the cluster analysis. We also provide a summary of a typical case for each type.

Type 1: Logical Minimalist

The logical minimalist approach to implementation is typified by a logical sequence of events that meets the minimum requirements for system development. As Table 9.6 suggests, projects falling into type 1 typically begin with the submission of a proposal, followed by approval, vendor selection, physical system construction (including installation), training, and additional construction. Many of the systems implemented with this approach were actually delivered by external vendors or consultants, and the coordination of activities follows a logical sequence. This type of implementation process is similar to textbook life cycle (type 4), but it involves fewer types of events. Another difference is the relative infrequency of project definition in type 1 projects. Moreover, personnel are rarely assigned to the project, there is little performance assessment, and organizational roles are rarely reassigned.

An illustration of the logical minimalist type of implementation is the case of a public school system's adult education center, which had been serving the needs of older citizens in an urban setting for 30 years (case 5 in Table 9.4). The center provided classes in vocational training, English language, reading, and computers. The chairperson of the Computer Facilities Department

TABLE 9.6 The Taxonomy of Implementation Process

Cluster and Ideal Event Sequence	Frequency	Key Features	Relevant Models
1. Logical minimalist: submission of proposal; approval or authorization; selection of a specific vendor; physical system construction; training; physical system construction	9	Physical system construction, often using external vendors Infrequent project definition Little performance assessment Personnel rarely assigned Rarely affects organizational roles	Historical model process (Nutt 1984)
2. Traditional off-the-shelf: submission of proposal; project definition; seeking technical knowledge/equipment; submission of proposal; selection of a specific vendor; reassignment of organizational roles; project definition	6	System purchased off-the-shelf No physical system construction Personnel rarely assigned No training	Basic search process (Mintzberg et al. 1976) Off-the-shelf process (Nutt 1984) Industrial supplier choice process (Vyas and Woodside 1984)
3. Problem-driven minimalist: performance problems; assessment of performance; seeking technical knowledge/equipment; selection of a specific vendor; physical system construction; reassignment of organizational roles	8	Usually initiated by problems Infrequent project definition Frequently leads to reassignment of organizational roles	Model of innovation emergence (Usher 1954) Reactors (Miles and Snow 1978)

4.	Textbook life cycle: submission of proposal; approval or authorization; assignment of personnel to the project; project definition; seeking technical knowledge/equipment; assessment of performance; selection of a specific vendor; physical system construction; acceptance/cooperation; training; performance problems; reassignment of organizational roles	10	Considerable use of all the system development activities Frequent successful performance and acceptance	Conventional design approach (Lucas 1978) System development life cycle (Davis and Olson 1984)
5.	Outsourced cooperative: seeking technical knowledge/equipment; submission of proposal; assignment of personnel to the project; assessment of performance; performance problems; submission of proposal; selection of a specific vendor; physical system construction; training; assessment of performance; successful performance; performance problems; reassignment of organizational roles	9	System constructed jointly by assigned personnel and external vendors Frequent performance assessment Other (external) events influence the process	Outside consultant nova process (Nutt 1984)
6.	In-house trial and error: submission of proposal; approval or authorization; assignment of personnel to the project; project definition; assessment of performance; performance problems; physical system construction; training; resistance; physical system construction; performance problems	11	System frequently modified Frequent performance problems Technical knowledge/equipment rarely sought Extensive training Rarely affects organizational roles	Disjointed incrementalism (Braybrooke and Lindblom 1963) Dynamic design process (Mintzberg et al. 1976) Evolutionary design approach (Lucas 1978)

proposed the addition of a second IBM PC lab to complement the existing IBM PC lab already in the school. She believed that IBM computers would best serve the interests of the center's clients. The school system's Computer Advisory Committee first suggested that Apple computers would be more useful for educational purposes, but after several meetings the committee approved the chairperson's preference for IBM. However, the committee suggested using lower-priced machines in place of the 50Z models the chairperson had proposed. Again, the committee was persuaded that the more advanced equipment would better accommodate future conversion to the OS/2 operating system. After almost a year of review and discussion, an order was placed. The vendor's representatives installed the new computers and trained the instructors in their use. Necessary software was also developed by the vendor, and the instructors quickly began to use the new computers.

This case illustrates the sequence of proposal, approval, physical system construction (including installation), training, and use that characterizes the logical minimalist approach to implementation. The process allows for negotiation over an original proposal, but any modifications to the proposal are agreed upon before installation. Although the negotiations may take some time, the sequencing of events eliminates the taking of actions that may have to be reversed later. This is in direct contrast to the frequent modifications encountered in type 6, in-house trial and error.

The logical minimalist approach is similar to Nutt's (1984) historical model process in that there is little performance assessment. Nutt describes the historical model process as using concepts "drawn from the practices of others to guide solution development. The sponsor visits an organization or recalls an experience that offers a way to deal with the problem or further specify an opportunity" (p. 420). In our illustrative case the decision to buy IBM PCs was based on the personal experience of the chairperson rather than on a cost-benefit analysis or feasibility assessment. Because the first IBM PC lab had worked satisfactorily, it was assumed that the second lab should also utilize IBM PCs. Several scholars have observed that individuals commonly prefer known sources for their ideas and pursue alternatives that keep them on familiar terrain (Cyert and March 1963, Newell and Simon 1972). Moreover, by following familiar paths, they minimize organizational change, which is reflected in type 1 by the infrequent reassignment of organizational roles.

Type 2: Traditional Off-the-Shelf

The second type of process, traditional off-the-shelf, is marked by dependence on system applications provided by external vendors or consultants. Table 9.6 suggests that a project of this type usually begins with submission of a proposal and project definition. Technical knowledge and equipment are then sought, usually by sending out requests for proposals, followed by vendors' proposals and presentations. A specific vendor is selected, and some organizational roles are redefined. Unlike type 1, logical minimalist, the process starts with a clear project definition. A traditional off-the-shelf implementation process also allows for flexibility in reacting to new product announcements, and the ultimate definition of the project may not be complete until the project is nearly completed. This type also differs from logical minimalist in that considerable performance assessment is done and there is no system construction. The traditional off-the-shelf process also differs from type 4, outsourced cooperative, although both processes depend largely on external vendors or consultants. In the outsourced cooperative process, internal personnel and vendors' representatives are assigned and jointly construct the system. In the traditional off-the-shelf process there is little system construction because the system is simply being purchased. Hence there is also no assignment of personnel to the project. Interestingly, training is also completely absent from the cases that fall into type 2.

Traditional off-the-shelf process can be illustrated by the replacement of microfiche with optical storage for keeping student records in the registration department of a large public university (case 14 in Table 9.4). Maintaining these records was made difficult by the university's rapid growth and the need to keep records for all active and former students. This led the associate vice president of enrollment services to conduct a detailed evaluation of microfiche technology. He found that this technology constrained the ability to update the stored information and risked deterioration over time. Therefore, he proposed to the vice president of student affairs that the microfiche technology be replaced with an electronic database. After the VP of student affairs approved the proposal, the associate VP of enrollment services consulted with the purchasing department about the new technology. The purchasing department, in turn, contacted the vendors of this technology. Bids were received from several vendors. The VP of student affairs and associate VP of enrollment services decided to purchase an optical disk storage system, and selected hardware and software vendors. Once the system was in place, the users adapted to it within one week The optical disk storage overcame the problems associated with microfiche, improved the print quality, and drastically reduced the storage space required.

In this illustration, the implementation of a system was accomplished primarily by one person. Authorized to develop a tool to improve document storage, the associate VP of enrollment services used purchasing to seek external technical information and selected one alternative from vendor proposals. No other personnel were assigned to the project. Thus the process represents traditional off-the-shelf implementation, with the system being used without modifications or enhancements. Moreover, no training was provided to the users.

The traditional off-the-shelf process resembles a search process (Mintzberg, Raisinghani, and Théorêt 1976) wherein clear guidelines are established at the outset and the best available ready-made solution is then found. Nutt (1984) describes a similar type of process in his research. The traditional off-the-shelf process is comparable to the industrial supplier choice process (involving bid invitation, evaluation, and selection) that has been examined by several researchers in marketing (e.g., Sheth 1977, Vyas and Woodside 1984).

Type 3: Problem-Driven Minimalist

The third type of implementation, problem-driven minimalist, is reactionary in character. As shown in Table 9.6, the typical sequence is triggered by performance problems and proceeds through the seeking of technical knowledge, vendor selection, and system construction. It resembles the logical minimalist process (type 1), which also tries to solve problems as quickly and simply as possible, but it avoids the proposal and approval steps and rarely involves training. Moreover, whereas type 1 projects rarely affect organizational roles, problem-driven minimalist programs are very likely to end with the reassignment of organizational roles along with the implementation of technical changes.

The type 3 process can be illustrated using the case of an accounting firm that implemented a LAN system to integrate its office operations (case 23 in Table 9.4). The firm consisted of 11 partners and 50 professionals providing accounting services (preparation of tax returns and financial statements, audits, database management, and so on) to more than 2,000 clients. Problems first arose with the lack of internal memory and storage capacity on the firm's minicomputer, an IBM System 36. Accountants using personal computers to conduct clients' work found that their PCs placed too much demand on the System 36, which provided inadequate memory for running the software. With the approval of the managing partner in charge of administration, one of the accounting professionals in the firm took it upon himself to evaluate alternative solutions. He received suggestions from other professionals to develop a solution that would integrate the administrative staff with the functional departments in the organization. He then took a year to educate himself on the technologies available, after which he proposed that top management purchase a Novell LAN system. An outside consulting company was hired to purchase and install the network, which involved cabling 76 offices and connecting 32 terminals over a two-week period. The firm hired a network manager (with no previous accounting experience) to oversee network functions and established a network committee to develop file-naming procedures, menu systems, an operations manual, and so on. The committee excluded any administrative staff members.

Several conflicts resulted in the firing of the network manager at the end of one year. He had, among other things, acquired and installed an accounting software package that he mistakenly believed would be useful to the accountants in the firm. The network manager also could not resolve conflicts with a technical specialist who worked for him. Newly hired professionals were not offered any orientation to the system. Many users underutilized the system—for example, by using only its electronic mail features. Others were careless in file maintenance procedures, filling valuable storage space with unused files and personal software.

This case illustrates the problem-driven minimalist approach because events were responses to problems, with no person or group laying out a larger plan for implementation. The accounting firm implemented a new system in response to complaints, but the new system was selected and implemented haphazardly by an unqualified person. Implementation was done by a third party not involved in the specification of user needs, and administration of the system was assigned to someone else with poor interpersonal relationships with others in the firm. The project lacked definition, and implementation details were handled by people who misunderstood the needs of accounting professionals. Problem-driven minimalist implementation does not always lead to such trouble; responses to the problems posed along the way can be either effective or ineffective.

The lack of project definition and the focus on problems suggest some similarity between the problem-driven minimalist approach and the "reactor" organizations described by Miles and Snow (1978). The top managers in reactor organizations usually do not have a clear strategy, and they respond to problems rather than anticipate them. The problem-driven minimalist approach is also comparable to Usher's (1954) normative model of innovation, in which the perception of problems is followed by the collection of the elements needed for the solution. After the solution is found, critical revisions are made as new relations become understood and worked into context. This final step relates to the reassignment of organizational roles, which also frequently concludes the problem-driven minimalist approach.

Type 4: Textbook Life Cycle

The fourth type, textbook life cycle, most closely resembles the prescriptions for IS development found in traditional texts. As shown in Table 9.6, the event sequences included in this type reveal an elaborate, rational approach that carefully follows a logical sequence of defining needs, fully specifying system characteristics, modular construction and testing, installation, training, and so on. Compared with the logical minimalist approach (type 1), type 4 is more complete and elaborate, including the assignment of personnel to project teams, assessment of performance, and reassignment of organizational roles. Textbook life-cycle projects are often developed primarily by internal staff, but they may also be supported by vendors or consultants. Unlike the first three types of implementation, this type involves assessment of performance before too many resources are invested in the development effort.

The textbook life-cycle approach is illustrated by the case of a building materials distributor with four warehouse locations (case 27 in Table 9.4). The project involved the extension of the existing computer-based accounting system in one warehouse to include all four warehouses. This allowed each warehouse to be operated as a profit center capable of creating its own shipping tickets, invoices, and payments. The system was developed with the cooperation of an external consulting firm.

The project was initiated by the regional manager, who assigned his finance manager the responsibility to produce more timely reports on warehouse performance. The finance manager proposed to automate and decentralize accounting in all four locations and received approval from her supervisor, who delegated her to lead the project. The finance manager held a meeting with the warehouse managers, who ultimately supported the proposal after expressing initial disagreement about its merits. The finance manager then solicited bids and received two, including one from the company that had installed the original system in the one warehouse. This bid was selected, with the approval of the regional manager. The consulting firm assembled a design team, installed direct telephone lines for the warehouse employees to use for troubleshooting, and designed the complete system in three months. The consultants requested company data to use in testing the system and set up a prototype for approval. The finance manager was given a "structured walk-through" of the new system at the consulting firm, and she accepted it as an accurate representation of the operating environment of the warehouses. She ordered the piecemeal installation of the system on site and leased the necessary equipment from the consulting firm. The consultants trained the users on successive modules of the system as they were implemented. Except for some data-entry problems, the new systems were used effectively in each warehouse.

This case illustrates the extended logical sequence of events that typifies the textbook system development life cycle (Davis and Olson 1984, Lucas 1978). Early events in the textbook life-cycle approach include a proposal, its approval, discussion with users to gain support, solicitation of bids, and the awarding of a bid. Subsequent events involve design, testing, prototype construction, structured walk-through, and implementation by modules. Little is left to chance in this approach, which is probably why it is so widely advocated in traditional data-processing texts.

Type 5: Outsourced Cooperative

The outsourced cooperative process, our fifth type, requires the organization to cooperate extensively with one or more external parties to complete a project. As Table 9.6 reveals, the initial events in this type of project involve the seeking of technical knowledge and assessment of performance, followed by submission of a proposal and assignment of project personnel. Performance is then assessed, and new proposals (usually from vendors) are entertained. Vendor selection, system construction, and training follow, after which performance is again assessed. The entire sequence is an elaborate one, but it does not follow the logic of the textbook life-cycle process (type 4). The outsourced cooperative process seeks close coordination among internal and external parties over the entire course of the project. Consequently, the process is considerably affected by external events over which the organization may have little control. Frequent assessments help to monitor the performance of external parties.

The outsourced cooperative approach is illustrated by the case of a system developed to support the operation of a newly created hospital outpatient center (case 37 in Table 9.4). The system provided reports (referral summaries, collection productivity, bad debts, and so on) to aid in the management of the outpatient center. The project began with an evaluation of the hospital's other ISs, which determined that it would be more cost-effective to develop a new system for the new outpatient center than to add the new functions to an existing system. It was determined that the new system would have to be developed by an external party because the hospital's IS staff was not qualified to undertake the project.

A steering committee was appointed to oversee all phases of development, and a development task force was appointed to develop specific objectives. The steering committee solicited bids from vendors, evaluated vendor proposals, and selected a local vendor to build the system. A team of analysts from the consulting firm worked with the outpatient center's task force to study the system's data and hardware requirements. The consultants then developed prototypes, which the development team modified to their needs. Implementation proceeded smoothly, and consultants trained the users. The software was tested and the necessary revisions made.

The hospital's management then revised its estimates of the volume of demand for outpatient services by about 40%, a level that the system being implemented could not support efficiently. One member of the steering committee resigned after management expressed displeasure with the outpatient system, but implementation efforts continued. The consultants completed their work, but they did not provide user documentation or manuals because these were not specified in their original proposal. Users found the system unable to cope with the high volume of transactions and encountered delays in processing patients' accounts. Several users left the outpatient center, complaining of a heavier workload. Two years after implementation, the outpatient center upgraded its hardware and entered into contract renegotiations with the consulting firm to get the rest of what the center needed.

The outsourced cooperative approach utilizes external vendors and consultants to custom build the system to the organization's needs, thus resembling what Nutt (1984) calls the outside consultant nova approach. However, Nutt divides the nova process into two categories based on whether external consultants or inside staff build the solution, whereas our outsourced cooperative approach involves them working together. The coordination requirements are difficult to satisfy, as the case related here illustrates. The failure of the hospital to estimate properly the level of demand expected at the outpatient center placed additional requirements on the system and upon the coordination mechanisms between the two parties. The outsourced cooperative process attempts to address all the requirements of system development while depending heavily on an external provider. The chance of overlooking some important aspects, such as user manuals, is one of the pitfalls of this approach.

Type 6: In-House Trial and Error

The sixth and final type of implementation process, in-house trial and error, begins much like the textbook life-cycle approach, with the submission and approval of a proposal, assignment of personnel, and project definition. However, in-house trial and error is typified by performance problems and internal resistance throughout the project's life. This creates a situation in which systems are constructed, projects are redefined midstream, and then systems are reconstructed in response to problems encountered at different stages, as shown in Table 9.6. External vendors are not heavily involved in this type, as most of the work is performed in-house. The sequence of events appears to be a response to problems rather than a carefully executed plan, as is the case with type 3, problem-driven minimalist. However, the two processes are quite different. In-house trial and error begins with submission and approval of a proposal, whereas type 3 starts with performance problems. The project is clearly defined at the beginning of the in-house trial-and-error process, whereas there is little project definition in type 3. Moreover, the system is rarely modified in type 3. Finally, unlike the frequent reassignment of organizational roles caused by type 3, the in-house trial-and-error process rarely affects organizational roles.

In-house trial and error can be illustrated by a system developed by a manufacturer of innovative products for the construction industry (case 48 in Table 9.4). The corporation had been in business for 30 years, specializing in products such as connector plates and truss fabricating equipment. The "Customer Information System" was designed to centralize customer data from five subsidiary companies to enable better control and more standardized operations.

Corporate management began by establishing a methodology for the planning and development of all new information systems. Following the prescribed methodology, corporate management submitted a system request form and assigned a system analyst as project manager. The project manager examined the needs and requirements of each subsidiary company and evaluated its existing systems. Before considering specific design requirements, top management and the project manager determined what computer system they would use. They chose Hewlett-Packard's 3000 because the subsidiaries had more experience with HP than with the only alternative considered, Digital's VAX computer. At this time, the users were consulted about their information needs. The IS department took five days to design the system.

The system's design was presented separately to the users in each subsidiary, who suggested that more customer information be included. The project manager then formulated a budget for everything but the hardware and finished the system work well under budget. The system was then programmed by the project manager, following corporate policies, and hardware projections were increased to accommodate more users. The project manager conducted all the training for the new system's users, who were given manuals prepared by the IS personnel. Employees initially resisted the new system, but they eventually adjusted to the change and used the system productively. Further modifications were then made to the system.

This case illustrates the trials and errors of the implementation process. The policy for system development was created after the need for the system was realized, and equipment choices were made prior to the specification of user needs. The project budget was established well into the project, but it changed as the number of projected users increased. Planning seemed to serve decisions already made at this company, and the implementation process moved through a decidedly "nontextbook" sequence. There were not many errors committed by the company described, but a number of decisions were made without the support of prior analyses.

The in-house trial-and-error approach reflects disjointed incrementalism (Braybrooke and Lindblom 1963, Lindblom 1979), which is characterized by "a greater analytical preoccupation with ills to be remedied than positive goals to be sought" (Lindblom 1979, p. 517) and involves "a sequence of trials, errors, and revised trials" (p. 517). The in-house trial-and-error approach also resembles the dynamic design process (Mintzberg, Raisinghani, and Théorêt 1976), in which numerous interrupts complicate the flow of activities. Finally, the in-house trial-and-error approach is somewhat similar to Lucas's (1978) evolutionary design process, wherein an initial period of groping is followed by some mutual problem-solving dialogue between analysts and users. In evolutionary design, there is no final product as the system continues to evolve through reviews and modifications.

DISCUSSION

The availability of a widely accepted and usable taxonomy is a fundamental element in the development of a scientific body of knowledge (McKelvey 1975). Our analysis has produced a taxonomy of implementation processes based on the sequences of events that occurred in 53 IS projects. The events were classified into IS types, and the pairwise distances between event sequences were computed using optimal matching. Cluster analysis based on these intersequence distances was used to generate the empirical taxonomy of implementation processes.

The six archetypes literally represent the alternative courses of events that may be followed during the implementation process. We have labeled one of the process types (type 4) textbook life cycle because of its detailed, rational approach. The logical minimalist process (type 1) follows some of the basic steps of the textbook approach, but is characterized by little project definition and infrequent assignment of personnel. Whereas both textbook life-cycle and logical minimalist approaches use external vendors and consultants to some extent, the external dependence is much greater in the traditional off-the-shelf (type 2) and outsourced cooperative (type 5) processes. The latter two processes differ from each other. The traditional off-the-shelf process involves purchasing the system from an external vendor, with little system construction or assignment of personnel. The outsourced cooperative process consists of joint system development by internally assigned personnel and external vendors. The other two process types—problem-driven minimalist (type 3) and in-house trial and error (type 6)—are both considerably driven by performance problems. The problem-driven minimalist process begins with such problems and with little project definition, and results in a reassignment of organizational roles. The in-house trial-and-error process begins like the textbook life-cycle process, with clear project definition, but involves frequent system modifications to respond to performance problems encountered during the project.

Limitations

The research reported in this chapter relies upon innovative methodologies to generate a classification scheme for IS implementation. Although the results appear to be readily interpretable, it is necessary to understand their limitations. First, the taxonomy is based on actions rather than actors. Computationally, it is problematic to compare event sequences from different cases using more than one distance criterion. Our computations are based on action alone because our case descriptions were more specific on actions than on actors. In some cases joint action was specified, and in many others it was impossible to discern who was acting because of the use of pronouns and passive sentence construction. We dealt with this limitation by excluding actors from the analysis. Thus the resulting typology does not reflect who is acting, but only the actions taken.

Second, the use of student teams in research of this type has precedent, but its limitations must be acknowledged. Students have interests other than valid data collection, and the degree of training and control over their research activities is less than complete. Due to the several precautions discussed in our method section and in the appendices, we are confident that the descriptions given to us represent accurate events in the organizations studied. The descriptions are, to our pleasure, quite convincing and detailed, comparing favorably with professionally written cases. Where cases failed to provide adequate detail, they were excluded.

Third, our research may be limited by our excluding measures of the success of projects or the success of ISs that were implemented. Our data do not permit us to measure project success independently from the events described. Moreover, the success measures themselves may differ across clusters. Therefore, we resisted the temptation to conduct speculative analyses relating implementation types to success, however defined. Thus we are not sure that choosing an implementation type makes any difference to the success or failure of projects. We imagine, however, that choice of type does not "determine" the success or failure of a project, and that any type can be successful. This speculation is consistent with Nutt's (1986) findings that any implementation tactic can be successful and any can fail.

Fourth, the size of our sample does not permit us to explore within clusters to uncover variations of the six types of implementation. This approach would have yielded too many subclusters populated with too few members. A larger sample might have permitted the identification of meaningful subtypes.

Finally, as Table 9.1 indicates, the organizations in our study tend to be small organizations representing the economic demography of the geographic area in which students lived. This may have affected the generated taxonomy, for instance, by the inclusion of greater numbers of small business depending on outside consultants and vendors. Certainly, large organizations also subcontract IS development work and depend on hardware and software vendors to some degree, but very small organizations are unlikely to have much internal capacity for IS development at all. Perhaps this should not be treated as a limitation, however, because the development and implementation of smaller-scale systems is generally neglected in the literature on implementation. There are certainly many interesting implementation issues related to small organizations, and our typology may represent these issues better than studies using data drawn from larger organizations.

Implications

Despite the above limitations, our study has some potential implications for future research and practice. First, the results indicate the feasibility of generating a taxonomy based on events occurring during IS development projects. In other words, implementation projects can be classified in terms of the actions that constitute them. This differs from taxonomies based upon the conditions that surround projects (e.g., project size, technology, and degree of user involvement). The types are readily interpretable and meaningful, we believe, to both researchers and practitioners. Our results support the efforts of process researchers to analyze organizational phenomena that are dynamic in character.

Moreover, our findings provide researchers and practitioners with empirically grounded concepts that may find interesting future uses. Clearly, one important area to explore is the linkage between implementation types and project success. Future research could examine, for each cluster, the definitions of success as seen by various stakeholders within and outside the organization. Each stakeholder group is likely to regard specific outcomes of the implementation process differently, and future research could focus upon their interpretations. Approaching implementation success in this manner differs from attempts to find objective criteria, such as user acceptance or economic benefits.

Future research could also link the taxonomy to contextual conditions and states. This may be done at two levels. Across clusters, future research can examine the conditions, such as the size of the organization, that might be associated with the use of different implementation processes. Within clusters, the conditions associated with success in each of the process types may be examined. Such efforts would contribute to more complete explication of the theory underlying IS implementation and help to solve the implementation puzzle (Swanson 1988). Molding event sequences to particular theoretical assumptions about process dynamics would permit subsequent research to test specific propositions about the antecedents and consequences of implementation processes (Van de Ven 1992).

While it is difficult and time-consuming to conduct the type of analysis reported in this chapter, we believe that our taxonomy must be validated with additional samples and alternative methodologies. One approach would be to test the taxonomy with technological implementations different from information systems. It is also possible to improve upon the data collection and to control the generation of event sequences more closely.

Finally, it would be beneficial to include actors as well as actions in a more elaborate taxonomy. This would provide more indication of which stakeholders, inside and outside of the organization, are responsible for various actions. This part of the agenda for future work would almost certainly prove to be of practical value to those concerned with implementation.

Appendix A:
Some Relevant Portions of the Course Syllabus

A very important part of the paper is the description of the development history of the system. This history should include discussion of (a) how the organization decided to develop the system, (b) the design and development processes, (c) the implementation of the system, and (d) the way in which the system has been used, including the impacts it has had on the organization and on the various groups involved. The system's history should address such questions as: Who proposed the system? Who (if anyone) opposed the decision? How was this opposition conveyed? What were the objectives of those proposing the system? Why were the specific design features chosen? What happened during the various stages? How did those favoring the system behave during the various stages? and How did those opposing it behave during these stages? The better projects make explicit reference to the individuals involved in various stages of the process. Be sure that you present the various events that occurred during the development history in this manner. *AVOID SAYING simply, "The company decided to . . . ," wherever possible.*

The typical project might be organized as follows:

1. Summary
   an executive overview
2. Description of the Organization
   general background
   specific parts affected by the system
3. Functional Description of the System
4. The System Development History
   the decision-making process
   the design and development process

the implementation process

the use of the system

5. Recommendations

6. Appendices, which should definitely include:

   a. a list of all the individuals interviewed, including their titles and the approximate duration of each interview.

   b. an organization chart (or at least the relevant part of it) showing the various individuals involved in the process.

   c. indicators of the organization's size: annual sales, number of employees, etc.

   d. a list of all the articles you referred to in your paper. Can alternatively give these as footnotes.

Appendix B:
The Monitoring of the Student Projects

In an attempt to ensure that the student projects would be useful for the research study, the course instructor closely monitored the progress of these projects. Following the detailed description of the project in the first class, several formal and informal checkpoints were used, as briefly described below.

At the start of the case projects, the instructor encouraged personal discussions with the students about the organization and the system they wished to study. A large proportion of the groups did so. Moreover, all the groups submitted written proposals on their case projects. In these proposals they identified the organization, described the system, and indicated the executives they felt they would be able to interview (in most cases, a number of additional interviews were conducted as found necessary based on the initial interviews). The instructor provided detailed comments on these proposals, and in most cases asked the groups to modify the proposals to incorporate these comments. Through this involvement in the early stages of the project, the instructor tried to ensure that the groups understood what they needed to do and also to eliminate (a) projects where the interviewees might have been biased due to their close contact with one or more of the group members, (b) projects dealing with systems that were either so small as to be considered personal rather than organizational or so large and complex as to make it impossible to study adequately the associated implementation process in a one-semester course, (c) projects concerning systems that were so old as to raise questions about the ability of the interviewees to remember the implementation clearly (in most cases the system use had begun less than six months prior to the start of the case project), and (d) projects where the group of students seemed to be unable to get sufficient diversity of interviewee perspectives.

During the middle of the case projects, when the field research teams (student groups) were collecting the case data, the project requirements were discussed at least two more times. On both of these occasions, as well as at other times throughout the course, the students were encouraged to ask questions regarding the project. These discussions helped to keep the students on track in doing their case projects.

Finally, *toward the end of the case projects,* all groups were encouraged to submit initial drafts of their cases for comments. More than half of the groups took advantage of this opportunity. Also, all the groups presented their projects in class. Each presentation was about 15 minutes long, with another 10-15 minutes for questions. Two-thirds of the groups were able to utilize the comments made during their presentations to improve their final reports. Together, these two steps helped improve the quality of the case reports. In some cases, additional interviews were conducted based on the comments on the initial draft or the presentation.

Acknowledgments

The optimal matching programs in the Beldings Program Series were developed by David Bradley of the California State University at Long Beach and graciously provided to us by Andrew Abbott from the University of Chicago. We gratefully acknowledge the many helpful suggestions made by Andrew Abbott, Andrew Van de Ven, and the anonymous reviewers. We also thank Nicole Wishart for her valuable contributions to the data analysis and the students who conducted the case studies upon which this chapter is based.

Notes

1. Examples of events are included as part of Table 9.2.

2. We acknowledge that the results are potentially affected by the number of event types chosen. While this typology with IS types satisfies the criterion for interrater reliability, its superiority over others is not demonstrated. Conceptual overlaps between categories could be minimized with a greater number of categories, but this would reduce measurement reliability.

3. Forrest and Abbott (1990) have found that the calculated distances are not substantially influenced by even fairly strong perturbations in substitution costs.

4. Abbott and Hrycak (1990) note that the intersequence distances may be ill behaved, and t tests and F tests may be inappropriate. We conducted a goodness-of-fit test, dividing the 1,378 pairwise distances among the 53 sequences into 10 categories and comparing the actual frequencies with those based on a normal distribution. This test produced a chi-square value of 10%, which is not significant even at the 0.10 level, thus showing that the actual distribution of the distances does not differ from the normal distribution. Therefore, either the t test or the F test may be applied.

5. This is equivalent to setting insertion cost = 1.0 and deletion cost = 0.0.

6. For any given cell, the frequency predicted by chance is given by the product of the corresponding row and column totals, divided by the total frequency for the matrix. For example, for the top left corner cell (event type 1, logical minimalist process) in Table 9.4, the expected frequency is given by 64(116/1,088) or 6.8.

References

Abbott, A. (1990), "A Primer on Sequence Methods," *Organization Science,* 1, 375-392.

Abbott, A., and A. Hrycak (1990), "Measuring Resemblance in Sequential Data: An Optimal Matching Analysis of Musicians' Careers," *American Journal of Sociology*, 96, 144-185.

Alter, S. (1978), "Development Patterns for Decision Support Systems," *MIS Quarterly*, 2, 33-42.

Bakeman, R., and J. M. Gottman (1986), *Observing Interaction: An Introduction to Sequential Analysis*, New York: Cambridge University Press.

Bourgeois, L. J., and D. R. Brodwin (1984), "Strategic Implementation: Five Approaches to an Elusive Phenomenon." *Strategic Management Journal*, 5, 241-264.

Braybrooke, D., and C. E. Lindblom (1963), *A Strategy of Decision: Policy Evaluation as a Social Process*, New York: Free Press.

Bryman, A. (1988), *Quantity and Quality in Social Research*, London: Unwin Hyman.

Child, J. (1987), "Information Technology, Organization, and Response to Strategic Challenges," *California Management Review*, 30, 33-50.

Churchman, C., and A. Schainblatt (1965), "The Researcher and the Manager: A Dialectic of Implementation." *Management Science*, 11, B69-B87.

Cohen, J. (1960), "A Coefficient of Agreement of Nominal Scales," *Educational and Psychological Measurement*, 20, 37-46.

Cyert, R. M., and J. G. March (1963), *A Behavioral Theory of the Firm*, Englewood Cliffs, NJ: Prentice Hall.

Davis, G. B., and M. H. Olson (1984), *Management Information Systems: Conceptual Foundations, Structure, and Development*, New York: McGraw-Hill.

Doll, W. J. (1985). "Avenues for Top Management Involvement in Successful MIS Development," *MIS Quarterly*, 9, 17-35.

Ein-Dor, P., and E. Segev (1982), "Organizational Context and MIS Structure: Some Empirical Evidence," *MIS Quarterly*, 6, 55-68.

Eisenhardt, K. M. (1989), "Building Theories From Case Study Research," *Academy of Management Review*, 14, 532-550.

Forrest, J., and A. Abbott (1990), "The Optimal Matching Method for Studying Anthropological Sequence Data: An Introduction and Reliability Analysis," *Journal of Quantitative Anthropology*, 2, 151-170.

Harrigan, K. R. (1985), "An Application of Clustering for Strategic Group Analysis," *Strategic Management Journal*, 6, 55-73.

Harris, S. E., and J. L. Katz (1991), "Organizational Performance and Information Technological Investment Intensity in the Insurance Industry," *Organizational Science*, 2, 263-295.

Hartigan, J. A. (1975), *Clustering Algorithms*, New York: Wiley.

Henderson, J. C. (1990), "Plugging Into Strategic Partnerships: The Critical IS Connection," *Sloan Management Review*, 32, 7-18.

Hirschheim, R., H. K. Klein, and M. Newman (1991), "Information Systems Development as Social Action: Theoretical Perspective and Practice," *Omega*, 19, 587-608.

Hirschheim, R., and M. Newman (1991) "Symbolism and Information Systems Development: Myth, Metaphor and Magic," *Information Systems Research*, 2, 29-62.

Huber, G. P. (1984), "The Nature and Design of Post-Industrial Organizations," *Management Science*, 30, 928-951.

Huff, S. L., and Munro, M. (1985), "Information Technology Assessment and Adoption: A Field Study," *MIS Quarterly*, 9, 327-340.

Iivari, J. (1986), "An Innovation Research Perspective on Information System Implementation," *International Journal of Information Management*, 6, 123-144.

Isabella, L. A. (1990), "Evolving Interpretations as a Change Unfolds: How Managers Construe Key Organizational Events," *Academy of Management Journal*, 33, 7-41.

Ives, B., and M. Olson (1984), "User Involvement and MIS Success: A Review of Research," *Management Science*, 30, 586-603.

Jarvenpaa, S. L., and B. Ives (1991), "Executive Involvement and Participation in the Management of Information Technology," *MIS Quarterly,* 15, 205-227.

Leonard-Barton, D. (1988), "Implementation Characteristics of Organizational Innovations," *Communication Research,* 15, 603-631.

Lewin, A., and J. Minton (1986), "Determining Organizational Effectiveness: Another Look, and an Agenda for Research," *Management Science,* 32, 514-538.

Lindblom, C. E. (1979), "Still Muddling, Not Yet Through," *Public Administration Review,* 39, 517-526.

Lorr, M. (1983), *Cluster Analysis for Social Scientists,* San Francisco: Jossey-Bass.

Lucas, H. C. (1978), "The Evolution of an Information System: From Key-Man to Every Person," *Sloan Management Review,* 20, 39-52.

Lucas, H. C. (1981), *Implementation, the Key to Successful Information Systems,* New York: Columbia University Press.

Lucas, H. C., M. J. Ginzberg, and R. L. Schultz (1990), *Information Systems Implementation,* Norwood, NJ: Ablex.

Markus, M. L., and D. Robey (1988), "Information Technology and Organizational Change: Causal Structure in Theory and Research," *Management Science,* 34, 583-598.

McKelvey, B. (1975), "Guidelines for Empirical Classification of Organizations," *Administrative Science Quarterly,* 20, 509-525.

Miles, M. B. (1979), "Qualitative Data as an Attractive Nuisance: The Problem of Analysis," *Administrative Science Quarterly,* 24, 590-601.

Miles, R. E., and C. C. Snow (1978), *Organizational Strategy, Structure, and Process,* New York: McGraw-Hill.

Mintzberg, H. (1973), *The Nature of Managerial Work,* New York: Harper & Row.

Mintzberg, H., D. Raisinghani, and A. Théorêt (1976), "The Structure of 'Unstructured' Decision Processes," *Administrative Science Quarterly,* 21, 246-275.

Mohr, L. B. (1982), *Explaining Organizational Behavior,* San Francisco: Jossey-Bass.

Newell, A., and H. A. Simon (1972), *Human Problem Solving,* Englewood Cliffs, NJ: Prentice Hall.

Newman, M., and F. Noble (1990), "User Involvement as an Interaction Process: A Case Study," *Information Systems Research,* 1, 89-113.

Newman, M., and D. Robey (1992), "A Social Process Model of User-Analyst Relationships," *MIS Quarterly,* 16, 249-266.

Nutt, P. C. (1984), "Types of Organizational Decision Processes," *Administrative Science Quarterly,* 29, 414-450.

Nutt, P. C. (1986), "Tactics of Implementation," *Academy of Management Journal,* 29, 230-261.

Pelz, D. C., and F. C. Munson (1982), "Originality Level and the Innovating Process in Organizations," *Human Systems Management,* 3, 173-187.

Punj, G., and D. W. Stewart (1983), "Cluster Analysis in Marketing Research: Review and Suggestions for Application," *Journal of Marketing Research,* 20, 134-148.

Robbins, S. R., and R. B. Duncan (1988), "The Role of the CEO and Top Management in the Creation and Implementation of Strategic Vision," in D. C. Hambrick (Ed.), *The Executive Effect: Concepts and Methods for Studying Top Managers* (pp. 205-233), Greenwich, CT: JAI.

Robey, D., and M. L. Markus (1984), "Rituals in Information System Design," *MIS Quarterly,* 8, 5-15.

Sanders, G. L., and J. F. Courtney (1985), "A Field Study of Organizational Factors Influencing DSS Success," *MIS Quarterly,* 9, 77-93.

Sankoff, D., and J. B. Kruskal (Eds.) (1983), *Time Warps, String Edits, and Macromolecules,* Reading, MA: Addison-Wesley.

Schroeder, R. G., A. H. Van de Ven, G. D. Scudder, and D. Polley (1989), "The Development of Innovation Ideas," in A. H. Van de Ven, H. L. Angle, and M. S. Poole (Eds.), *Research on the Management of Innovation: The Minnesota Studies,* New York: Ballinger/Harper & Row.

Schultz, R. L. (1984), "The Implementation of Forecasting Models," *Journal of Forecasting,* 3, 43-55.

Sheth, J. N. (1977), "Recent Developments in Organizational Buying Behavior," in A. G. Woodside, J. N. Sheth, and P. D. Bennett (Eds.), *Consumer and Industrial Buying Behavior,* New York: Elsevier North Holland.

Smith, A. G., and A. E. Robbins (1982), "Structured Ethnography: The Study of Parental Involvement," *American Behavioral Scientist,* 26, 45-61.

Sutton, R., and A. Callahan (1987), "The Stigma of Bankruptcy: Spoiled Organizational Image and Its Management," *Academy of Management Journal,* 30, 405-436.

Swanson, E. B. (1988), *Information System Implementation: Bridging the Gap Between Design and Utilization,* Homewood, IL: Irwin.

Ulrich, D., and B. McKelvey (1990), "General Organizational Classification: An Empirical Test Using the United States and Japanese Electronic Industry," *Organization Science,* 1, 99-118.

Usher, A. P. (1954), *A History of Mechanical Invention,* Cambridge, MA: Harvard University Press.

Van de Ven, A. H. (1992), "Suggestions for Studying Strategy Process," *Strategic Management Journal,* 13, 169-188.

Van de Ven, A. H., and G. P. Huber (1990), "Longitudinal Field Research Models for Studying Processes of Organizational Change," *Organization Science,* 1, 213-219.

Van de Ven, A. H., and M. S. Poole (1990), "Methods for Studying Innovation Development in the Minnesota Innovation Research Program," *Organization Science,* 1, 313-335.

Van de Ven, A. H., H. L. Angle, and M. S. Poole (Eds.) (1989), *Research on the Management of Innovation: The Minnesota Studies,* New York: Ballinger/Harper & Row.

Venkatraman, N., and A. Zaheer (1990), "Electronic Integration and Strategic Advantage: A Quasi-Experimental Study in the Insurance Industry," *Information Systems Research,* 1, 377-393.

Vyas, N., and A. G. Woodside (1984), "An Inductive Model of Industrial Supplier Choice Processes," *Journal of Marketing,* 48, 30-45.

Ward, J. H., Jr. (1963), "Hierarchical Grouping to Optimize an Objective Function," *Journal of the American Statistical Association,* 58, 236-244.

Zmud, R. W. (1984), "An Examination of 'Push-Pull' Theory Applied to Process Innovation in Knowledge Work," *Management Science,* 30, 727-738.

10

Theoretical and Analytical Issues in Studying Organizational Processes

PETER R. MONGE

Formulation of dynamic theories and process hypotheses is a crucial component in longitudinal research. This chapter describes a framework for developing dynamic theory and hypotheses. The procedure requires the theorist to address six dimensions of process in each variable: continuity, magnitude of change, rate of change, trend, periodicity, and duration. Further, theorists are encouraged to explore the dynamic relations between sets of variables, including rate of change, magnitude of change, lag, and permanence. Consideration is given to the problem of feedback loops. A typology of analytical alternatives for studying dynamic processes and longitudinal research data is provided.

In a number of articles in the 1960s and 1970s, the eminent sociologist and methodologist H. M. Blalock argued that regression coefficients are the laws of social science (see, for example, Blalock 1972, p. 146). Blalock's assertion represented the vanguard of quantitative research methodology throughout much of the social sciences (economics and psychometrics excluded) at the beginning of the 1970s. Regression analysis was a well-understood statistical technique that was rapidly diffusing throughout sociology and the

This chapter originally appeared in *Organization Science,* vol. 1, no. 4, November 1990, pp. 406-430.

organizational sciences. It was the basis for the general linear model, which provided a comprehensive analytic framework for most univariate and multivariate techniques and which subsumed the classic ANOVA techniques as a special case. Further, regression was the basis for path analysis and structural equation modeling, which were developing rapidly at this time (see Blalock 1972, Duncan 1966, Land 1969). Stemming largely from the early work of Simon (1957) and Blalock (1964), these developments were motivated by the desire to develop techniques that would generate valid causal inferences from correlational data acquired in cross-sectional designs. It had taken nearly two decades of work to develop the logic and analytic techniques of causal inference from correlational data. To many social scientists at the beginning of the 1970s, Blalock's assertion must have appeared to represent a stunning achievement, if it were true.

The past two decades have witnessed even further rapid development of structural equation techniques for causal inference from static data. Yet during this time an alternative perspective has slowly emerged that changes the emphasis on causal inferences to a focus on dynamic processes (Box and Jenkins 1976, Mohr 1982, Monge et al. 1984). Further, coincident with the emergent focus on process has been an increasing emphasis on longitudinal rather than cross-sectional research. As a consequence of these two developments, a variation of Blalock's assertion is now much more appropriate: various dynamic representations, such as time-series coefficients, are slowly replacing static regression coefficients as the laws of social science.[1] This growing emphasis on dynamic processes is important because it has the potential to significantly alter and improve our fundamental knowledge about organizations.

Organizational science has long been concerned with developing and empirically testing theories about organizations (Parsons, Shils, and Bales 1949). Most theorists state that they are interested in developing dynamic or process theories (see, e.g., Hannan and Freeman 1977, Markus and Robey 1988, Mohr 1982, Tushman and Romanelli 1985). Yet despite this widely held ideal, few theories have been developed that meet the requirements of dynamic or process theories. Similarly, much exhortation abounds urging researchers to conduct longitudinal research (Kimberly 1976). Yet the percentage of published research articles that report data collected at more than one point in time is minuscule.

There are two reasons for this state of affairs. The first is that the organizational and social sciences generally lack the conceptual tools with which to develop dynamic theories. As Weick (1987) argues, for the most part, theory in the organizational sciences is based upon verbal and linguistic analysis. Blalock (1989) puts it even more strongly with regard to sociology:

> We seem to have the notion that "theory" involves the study of what dead sociologists (primarily European ones at that) have had to say about major historical processes, rather than, say, what a theoretical physicist such as an Einstein or a Hawking actually does, namely thinking in terms of mathematical equations. In this respect we are much closer to historians than to economists. (p. 448)

Weick's and Blalock's comments are not critical of verbal formulations. Process theories can and should be developed at the verbal level. However, as McPhee and Poole (1982) demonstrate, mathematical models provide an additional set of tools for thinking about process characteristics. Mathematics contains a reservoir of concepts and a framework for analysis that can increase the precision and rigor of conceptual and empirical work. These tools permit the scholar to examine the implications of different dynamic formulations and thereby explore the process ramifications of the theory in ways that are more difficult at the verbal level. As Blalock (1969) argues, moving from verbal to mathematical formulations provides considerable intellectual power for studying process characteristics.

The second reason for the paucity of process knowledge is that most of the empirical research has been conducted in single point in time, correlational designs. While it is possible to acquire parameters of processes from cross-sectional, correlational data, the required assumptions are so severe that they can rarely be met in social science data.

In one sense, the discipline suffers from a form of methodological determinism, a state of affairs where the methodological tools that are available determine the ways in which scholars think and develop their theories and research questions (Monge et al. 1984; see also Kaplan's 1964 discussion of the "law of the hammer"). Without a history and tradition of thinking in terms of processes, and without expertise in designing and executing longitudinal research, it is difficult to make progress in this domain (see Daft and Lewin's 1990 arguments about the normal science mind-set in organization science).

Despite the limitations that methodological tools often place on theorizing, methodological developments can provide a framework for theoretical advancement. Polanyi (1958) points out that Einstein studied non-Euclidean geometry developed by Reimann at the turn of the century. Polanyi argues that it was Einstein's familiarity with a geometry of infinite dimensions that enabled him to theorize about the world as a four-dimensional rather than three-dimensional system (see Hawking 1988, pp. 155-169, for a similar example in contemporary physics). Thus innovations in methodology can often provide the impetus for developments in theory, just as theoretical advancements often require the development of new methodologies.

An interesting organizational example of this phenomenon is provided in a recent article by Williams and Podsakoff (1989). They document the change in knowledge that occurred in the field of leadership as a function of changes in methodological strategies. Beginning with the early correlational strategies of the 1950s, they identify errors in inference that occurred as a result of the simple correlational techniques then in use. As researchers began to conduct panel studies, the earlier knowledge was replaced with a more accurate picture of leadership processes. However, because cross-lagged correlational analysis of panel data contains inherent flaws, this knowledge base has again been revised as researchers began to use structural equation modeling techniques such as LISREL.

The purpose of this chapter is to present a framework for the development of dynamic theories of organizational processes. Additionally, the framework and issues raised should lead to improvements in the conduct of longitudinal research. The first section of the chapter addresses several issues in theorizing about dynamic processes. The second section provides the framework for representing dynamic processes. This section is divided into three parts. The first part examines the dimensions of process characteristics that individual variables may display over time. These dimensions include continuity, magnitude, rate of change, trend, and periodicity. The next part provides a typology for examining dynamic effects in process theories by exploring the possible relations between two or more variables over time. This typology focuses on the history of the variables, the time lag, the rate of change, the magnitude of change, and the permanence of change. The final part discusses the issues of feedback and stability in process theories. The third section of the chapter presents a typology of alternatives for analyzing process data. The chapter concludes with a discussion of important unresolved issues in process research.

THEORIZING ABOUT DYNAMIC PROCESSES

The choice to conduct longitudinal research should be governed by theoretical issues. If theory specifies that several variables constitute a process that unfolds over time, then there is good reason to design longitudinal research to study the process. If theory specifies that two or more phenomena covary within a population at any point in time, then it makes little sense to conduct longitudinal research; a static, cross-sectional research design is preferable. For example, a theory that specifies that organizations evolve through periods of convergence and reorientation (Tushman and Romanelli 1985) requires a longitudinal design of sufficient duration to cover the theorized punctuated equilibria. A static, cross-sectional design would not generate the data required to test the theory.

The easiest way to design longitudinal research is on the basis of a dynamic theory and process hypothesis. A good process theory describes, at least in broad outline, plausible time parameters associated with change within and between the phenomena of interest. Given general theoretical specification of changes over time, it is relatively easy to develop a research design to correspond to the theoretical specifications (see Monge 1982). Ideally, scholars should address the issue of time specification in the theoretical phase of their work, before they address it in the research phase. Realistically, the current state of knowledge in organizational science rarely permits precise time specification. Nonetheless, even general time notions such as lag, sequence, and duration of change are important theoretical specifications. Vague and inexact specifications of process characteristics are preferable to no specifications at all.

Understanding the nature of process characteristics will sensitize both deductive and inductive scholars to focus on those characteristics in their research. The characteristics can be used to develop and test process theories, whether theorized in advance or discovered in the observational record. Each theoretical strategy has much to gain by focusing on process characteristics.

It is useful to ask the question, What form would knowledge eventually take if organizational scholars were able to create valid scientific theories of dynamic processes in human organizations? Irrespective of whether the theories were developed deductively or inductively, scholars would work toward the formulation of theories that correctly articulated the fundamental relations among variables over time. As with traditional theoretical work, attention would be given to the development of essential concepts. Similarly, the theories would stipulate the relations between the concepts, that is, the hypotheses. However, in contrast to traditional theories, process hypotheses would describe the expected or observed behavior of each variable over time as well as the interrelations among the variables over time. These specifications would pay particularly close attention to the time lags of causal influence among variables and to the feedback loops specified or emerging in the theory, if any.

These theoretical specifications would be summarized in formal representations of the systems. One useful formalization is a set of dynamic equations. Data would be collected in longitudinal designs that fulfilled the requirements of the theory. Specifically, the theory would indicate the number of times data would be collected, the length of the interval between data collections, and consequently, the overall duration of the research. The set of relations contained in the longitudinal data would be tested against the system of equations that formally represents the theory, thereby determining the truth or falsity of the theory. If the data supported the theory, the system of equations could be used with the longitudinal data to forecast the behavior of the dynamic processes under investigation. In such systems, the dynamic coefficients represent knowledge about the interrelated processes among pairs of variables,[2] in the same way that traditional regression coefficients represent knowledge about pairs of static relations in samples or populations at single points in time.

A FRAMEWORK FOR REPRESENTING DYNAMIC PROCESSES

Dynamic Processes in Individual Variables

Designing and executing a scenario like the above may seem a formidable task, but it can be simplified by subdividing it into more manageable subtasks. One strategy is to think about the dynamic nature of each variable arrayed in time before attempting to deal with the interrelations among variables. This is important because the field of organizational science has almost no information about how variables behave over time. Further, knowledge about how variables behave independently over time provides a basis for better understanding how they relate to each other over time. In short, in most forms of dynamic analysis it is essential to know how variables depend upon their own past histories, including trends and cycles (or previous developmental and evolutionary stages), as a basis for discovering how they relate to each other. This section provides a framework for representing dynamic processes in single variables. While extensive, it should be kept in mind that the current state of the framework is not yet exhaustive or comprehensive.

When theorizing about a dynamic variable in isolation—that is, unrelated to any other variables—it is important for the theoretician to consider six dimensions of dynamic behavior. These are continuity, magnitude, rate of change, trend, periodicity, and, if the variable is discontinuous, duration.

Continuity, the first dimension, refers to whether the variable has a consistent nonzero value through time, where zero typically represents the nonexistence of the variable. A continuous-time variable, such as organizational climate, is typically viewed as one that always exists at some value (Joyce and Slocum 1984). A discontinuous-time variable, such as the payment of the monthly bonus in the Scanlon management process, is one that occurs, then does not have a value until it occurs again at the next month (Monge and Cozzens 1986).

The second dimension, magnitude, refers to the amount of the variable at each point in time. Across time, magnitude may remain constant at any level or it can change considerably. The upper and lower bounds of magnitude are determined by the scale on which the variable is measured. Magnitude may be negative if the variable is measured on a scale with negative numbers.

Rate of change is the third dimension; it specifies how fast the magnitude increases or decreases per unit of time. Magnitudes, whether large or small, can change rapidly, even instantaneously, or they can increase or decrease slowly. For example, changes in organization climate are generally viewed as occurring quite slowly except in the case of organizational crisis. On the other hand, changes in the value of a firm's stock often occur quite rapidly, especially when new products are announced and hostile takeovers are attempted.

Trend, the fourth dimension, refers to the long-term increase or long-term decrease in the magnitude of a variable. Since trend can either increase or decrease it can have a positive or negative value. Further, the trend can be large or small, indicating a large or small long-term change in the magnitude. For example, salaries typically have a positive trend as a result of annual increases. Inflation that exceeds salary increases can give real income a negative trend. And executives tend to have large salary trends, while clerks have small trends. Variables that increase and decrease randomly fit the definition of trendless, as do variables that are constant.

The fifth dimension is periodicity. This is the amount of time that transpires between the regular repeating of the values of a variable, controlling for trend. If a variable does not repeat on a regular basis, it has no period. The length of the period can vary from very short to very long. For example, the number of employees in a large firm changes daily with retirements, firings, layoffs, and hirings. Other business cycles occur on a quarterly or annual basis. And Kondratieff cycles are long-term business cycles that are believed to have a period of approximately 50 years. Periods are usually measured from peaks to peaks (highest magnitude) or from valleys to valleys (lowest magnitude) in continuous-time variables, though any fixed-interval referent works as well. For a discontinuous-time variable, periods are usually measured from the onset of the variable or from the point at which it reaches maximum magnitude.

The final dimension is duration, which relates primarily to discontinuous-time variables. Duration refers to the length of time that a variable exists at some nonzero value. For example, the major network evening television newscasts occur once per day (their periodicity) and last for 30 minutes. Some variables have long durations, while others have short durations. Further, the length of the duration may change over time. For example, the length of time that an organization requires to manufacture a given product tends to decrease over time.

To explore these issues it is sometimes helpful to develop a time plot of the variable. Figure 10.1 presents an illustration of the six dimensions for representing the possible behavior of a single variable over time. The top half of Figure 10.1 is for discontinuous-time variables, the bottom half for continuous-time variables.[3] In the discontinuous-time case, the rate of change is instantaneous, the magnitude for the first occurrence is eight units, the

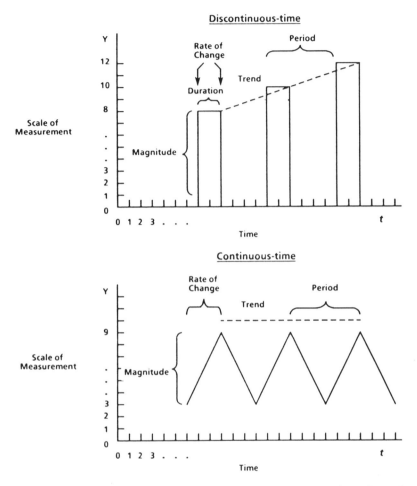

Figure 10.1. Five Dimensions of Dynamic Analysis: Continuity, Magnitude, Rate of Change, Trend, and Periodicity (additionally, it is useful to specify the duration of discontinuous variables)

variable has a duration of two time units, following which the magnitude drops instantaneously back to zero. Also, there is an upward trend of two units each time the variable recurs, and it recurs every six time units (onset to onset or termination to termination), indicating a periodicity of six.

The continuous-time variable illustration ranges in magnitude from a low of three units to a high of nine units. The rate of change is two units per time period. There is no trend, since the magnitudes of the peaks and valleys are

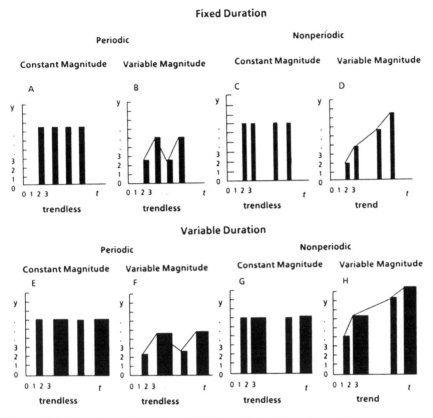

Figure 10.2. Examples of Eight Dynamic Patterns That a Discontinuous-Time Variable May Display

relatively constant. Finally, the periodicity of the variable is six units ·between peaks, valleys, or any other point on the graph.

It is informative to explore possible dynamic patterns that can occur in single variables as a function of different combinations of the six dimensions. Figure 10.2 presents eight possible scenarios for discontinuous-time variables, and Figure 10.3 presents another eight for continuous-time variables.

The top four examples in Figure 10.2 show patterns for variables that occur for fixed durations; the bottom four show patterns of variable duration. The examples were further created by distinguishing between periodic and nonperiodic variables and between those that were of constant versus those that were of variable magnitude. It is important to recognize that in the case of discontinuous-time variables the focus is on variable versus constant

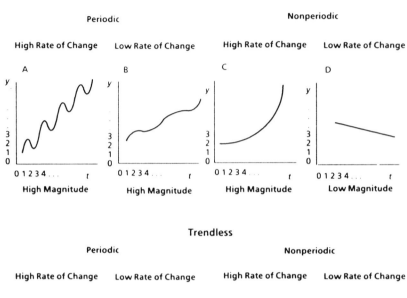

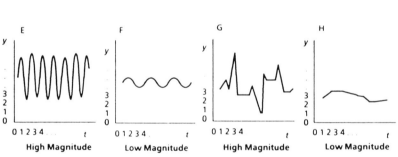

Figure 10.3. Examples of Eight Dynamic Patterns That a Continuous-Time Variable May Display

magnitude rather than on rate of change. Finally, the distinction is made between those situations that display trends and those that are trendless. For example, Cell A shows a discontinuous-time variable of fixed duration that occurs at a regular period at a constant or fixed magnitude without trend. Cell H presents a discontinuous-time pattern of variable duration that is nonperiodic and of varying magnitudes with a trend. For comparison, Cell A shows a highly predictable pattern, while Cell H shows a pattern that would be more difficult to predict.

Figure 10.3 provides eight possible examples for continuous-time variables. Duration is not an issue in continuous-time variables, so the dimensions illustrated in Figure 10.3 are trend, periodicity, rate of change, and magnitude. Cell A shows a continuous-time variable that has a positive trend, is periodic, and has a high rate of change and a high magnitude of change. Cell H illustrates a trendless continuous-time variable that is nonperiodic, with a low rate of change and relatively low magnitude of change.

DYNAMIC PROCESSES AND EFFECTS: A TYPOLOGY

Dynamic theorizing requires an important change in the way hypotheses are stated. The traditional form, "An increase in X is related to an increase in Y," is appropriate for static, cross-sectional research, but it does not capture the dynamic aspects of process. Rather, it is essential to formulate hypotheses in such a way that they include the relevant aspects of time. This can be done by specifying one or more of the six dimensions of process analysis described in the previous section. One possibility is something like the following: "A change in the magnitude of X during the time interval between a and b leads to a change in the magnitude of Y during the time interval between c and d." Another hypothesis specifically addressing the lag dimension might take the following form: "Changes in variable A will precede changes in variable B by two to four weeks." Yet another possibility that focuses on trend and period could be: "There will be a positive trend of one to two units per month together with a quarterly cycle in the magnitude covering six to eight units." None of these hypothetical hypotheses is terribly precise, but each specifically addresses one or more of the six essential process characteristics. It may not be possible to capture all of the relevant aspects of the process in a single verbal hypothesis. Rather, multiple hypotheses may be required.

Formulating process hypotheses such as these requires an understanding of various possible cause-effect relations. The analysis in the previous section produced six dimensions for theoretically specifying the time-dependent behavior of individual variables. This knowledge is crucial for theorizing about the dynamic relations among two or more variables, specifically dynamic causes and effects. The present section describes a typology of dynamic effects to assist in theorizing about organizational phenomena. The typology consists of five components: the history of the variables, the lag (immediacy), rate of change, the magnitude of change, and the permanence of change. Some of these components are identical to the six dimensions of dynamic analysis presented in the previous section (e.g., rate of change); others are different (e.g., lag). Despite the overlap between the two schemes, all five components are useful in identifying cause-effect relations.

Consider the five components of the typology in the simplest case where there are two variables. First, each variable has an empirical history that approximates one of the behavioral patterns in Figures 10.2 and 10.3, at least theoretically. This history may be known or it may be hypothesized as part of the theory. As is well known, in order to determine a cause and effect, it is necessary to observe change in one variable that precedes change in the other, and, of course, to rule out spurious causes. Thus it is necessary to theoretically array the two variables such that changes in the cause precede changes in the outcome variable. The second component of the typology, lag, indicates the amount of time between the onset of change in the causal variable and the onset of change in the outcome variable. In other words, lag specifies the immediacy with which a change in one variable begins to affect the other variable.

The third component of the typology is rate of change, which refers to the rapidity of change in the causal variable and the rapidity with which the effect occurs, once it begins to take place. Rate of change can vary from very slow to virtually instantaneous.

The fourth component of the typology, magnitude, refers to the amount of change in each variable. Independent variables can change anywhere from a small amount of their possible variation over time to all of their possible variation. The same is true of dependent variables.

Permanence, the final component, refers to the degree to which a cause or effect continues throughout time. If an effect is permanent, then once the effect has occurred, the value of the variable remains unchanged until some other event causes it to change. If it is temporary, then the effect will terminate at some later point in time, if no intermediate events occur to sustain it.

Figure 10.4 shows the components of this typology of effects. Two vertical axes are provided in order to include a causal, independent variable, X, and an effects-dependent variable, Y, that are measured on different scales (a 5-point scale for X, a 10-point scale for Y). The horizontal axis represents time. The graph is divided into two parts. The history of the variables on the left side provides the context for interpreting the causal process. The right side is the causal process that displays how the cause and effect are theorized to occur. All of the components of the typology—history, lag, rate of change, magnitude of change, and permanence—are indicated on the graph. The example in this graph is a constant value for both variables throughout their relevant history. The rate of change in the independent variable (X) is theorized to be instantaneous; thus it changes from a value of 1 to 2 at a specific point in time. The cause is viewed as lasting for one period of time and then returning to its prior value. Thus the permanence of the independent variable is one. Its magnitude of change is one unit or one fifth of its potential variation on a 5-point scale.

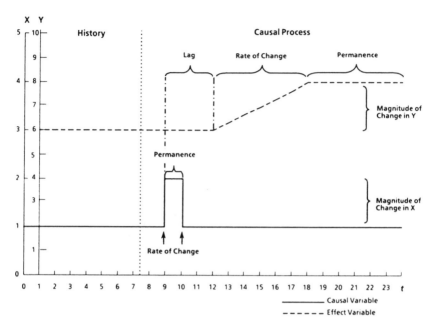

Figure 10.4. Components of a Causal Process: History, Rate of Change, Magnitude of Change, Lag, and Permanence

The dependent variable, *Y*, is also theorized to have a constant history. There is a lag of three time periods before it begins to change relative to the onset of change in *X*. Rate of change is hypothesized to be two units of change in *Y* over an interval of six time units, or a rate of change of 1/3 (i.e., 1/3 unit change in *Y* per unit change in time). The graph shows that it requires six units of elapsed time before the effect is complete. The magnitude of change in *Y* is 2 units over a 10-unit scale of variation, yielding a magnitude of 1/5. This change is theorized to be permanent, at least until another change occurs in *X* to produce further changes in *Y*.

Figure 10.4 can be summarized as a set of dynamic hypotheses something like the following: An increase in variable *X* of at least one unit of magnitude for a period of one unit of time will cause a change in *Y*. The change in *Y* will begin three time periods after the onset of *X* and will require six periods of time to increase a maximum of two units. Thereafter, it will remain unchanged until another change occurs in *X* (or another variable to which *Y* is related). The focus of these hypotheses is on the change in the levels of the variables over time. Dynamic hypotheses can also be developed about the relations between levels and rates of changes and between just rates of change (see Tuma and Hannan 1984).

Imagine a scholar focusing attention on the components of cause-effect processes in a case study being conducted as a part of a larger effort to inductively develop organizational theory. Let us further imagine that what the scholar observes roughly corresponds to the general features shown in Figure 10.4. From knowledge of the variables, the researcher establishes a six-month observation plan in which measurements are made on the two variables on a weekly basis. What would the researcher observe? For eight weeks the variables would remain constant at their respective X and Y values of 1 and 6. At the beginning of the ninth week the X variable would increase rapidly from a value of 1 to a value of 2. The researcher may have expected this change in X beforehand, though this is not necessary. Also, the researcher may or may not have participated in making X change. The X variable would remain at the value of 2 for one week and then return or be returned to its original value of 1. During this time the researcher would continue to measure Y, but Y would continue to remain constant at a value of 6 until three weeks after the beginning of change in X. Then, Y would change slowly for six weeks at the rate of 1/3 of a scale unit per week. During this time, X would remain constant at its prechange value of 1. At week 18, Y would stop changing, and throughout the remainder of the research, Y would remain at a value of 8.

With this observational record in hand, the scholar could identify and plot the history, rate of change, lag, magnitude, and permanence of the process. The history of the variables was a constant until X changed. The rate of change in X was virtually instantaneous; in Y, 1/3. The lag was three weeks before change in X produced any observable change in Y. The magnitude of change in Y was 2 units on its 10-point scale, while for X it was 1 unit of change on its 5-point scale. And the change in Y was permanent even though X returned to its original value of 1 within a week after it changed to 2.

The distinctions made in the typology of causal effects provide a rich basis on which to explore possible causal patterns. For example, Figure 10.5 presents four causal scenarios that occur by different combinations of the two components of rate of change and permanence, specifically, contrasts between rapid and slow causes and between permanent and temporary causes. (For simplicity, the effects variable is not shown.) A fifth scenario shows a discontinuous, repetitive cause. Many other scenarios are possible.

It is also important to consider different plausible patterns of effects. Eight examples are provided in Figure 10.6. These effects scenarios assume that the history of each variable is constant prior to the onset of the causal process. For simplicity, they also assume that the causal variable occurs instantaneously and is temporary, returning quickly to its prechange value. This

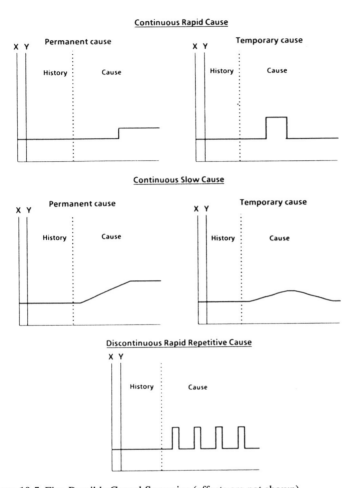

Figure 10.5. Five Possible Causal Scenarios (effects are not shown)

research design, where an event at an single point in time (or over a specific period of time) is viewed as causing a change in an ongoing process, is called intervention analysis (see Cook and Campbell 1979, Cook, Dintzer, and Mark 1980, and McCleary and Hay 1980). In this type of design, sorting out cause and effect is relatively straightforward. Since X does not vary over the history of the relation, then occurs briefly at a specific point in time and then not again, it is possible to determine its influence on Y.

The examples in Figure 10.6 show contrasts between immediate and delayed effects, rapid and slow effects, and permanent and temporary effects

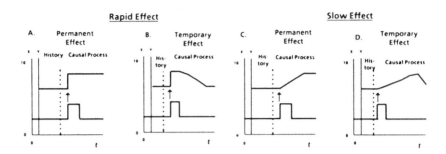

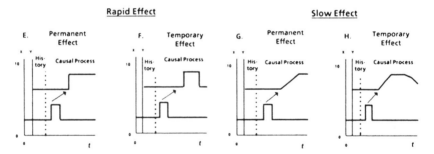

Figure 10.6. Examples of Cause-Effect Scenarios (derived from the three components of lag, rate of change, and permanence; the causal variable, X, is a simple intervention that occurs rapidly at one point in time with minimal duration)

for a simple intervention by a causal variable. For example, Cell A shows an immediate effect (no lag) that is rapid and permanent. By contrast, Cell H shows a delayed effect that occurs slowly and is temporary.

It is worth exploring the implications of more complex causal relations. Figure 10.7 provides several. The first example (A) shows an X that causes an instantaneous change in the level of Y but does not affect the cyclicity of Y. Example B represents a discontinuous repeating cause that occurs twice at different magnitudes. It affects the level of Y twice, once for each occurrence of X, but it does not affect the cyclicity of Y. Further, there is a five-unit time lag before the effect takes place. Determining causality in these situations is analytically more complex, but the theorizing is relatively straightforward.

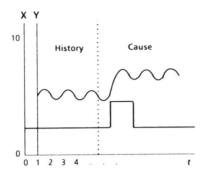

A. X causes a change in the level but not the cyclicality of Y.

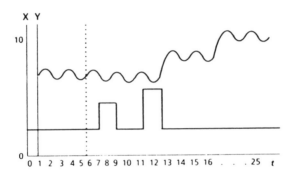

B. X is a discontinuous cause that occurs twice at different magnitudes.
It affects the level but not the cyclicality of Y. The effect is delayed by
5 time units.

Figure 10.7. More Complex Causal Relations

Dynamic theorizing frequently focuses on the relations between two or
more variables that vary continuously over time. This case is known as
concomitant variation. Three examples are provided in Figure 10.8. Example
A shows two time series where X is historically the cause of Y in an inverse
relation, so that when X increases, Y decreases. During the causal effect
period of interest, when X stops increasing, Y stops decreasing one unit in
time later. A common example of this occurs in the housing market, where
increases in the cost of funds lead to decreases in mortgage applications until

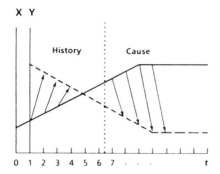

A. Historically, X & Y are inversely related When X stops increasing, Y stops decreasing one time period later.

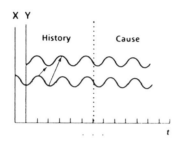

B. X is a countercyclical cause of Y at a lag of one time unit. A peak (or valley) in X causes a valley (or peak) in Y one time unit later.

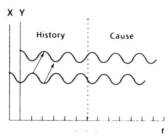

C. Cyclical X causes cyclical Y A peak (or valley) in X causes a peak (or valley) in Y one time unit later.

Figure 10.8. Concomitant Causes

the increases in cost of funds level off, leading to a stabilizing of mortgage applications at or near their obtained level.

Example B shows *X* as a countercyclical cause of *Y*. Peaks of *X* lead to valleys of *Y*, one time unit later. Similarly, valleys of *X* cause peaks of *Y* one unit later. An example of this kind of relation (though not the specific time lag) occurs in geographic regions that experience dry and wet seasons. In many western states, an increase in rain during the winter months leads to a decrease in forest and brush fires; a decrease in rain during the summer months leads to an increase in fires. Example C represents two processes whose cycles are aligned, with X leading Y by one time period. A peak in X leads to a peak in Y, and X valleys cause Y valleys.

The issue of cause and effect is more complicated in the case of concomitant variation than in the case of intervention analysis. Whether changes in one variable lead to changes in the second or the second leads to the first is a matter of perspective. Since both variables vary together through time, it is difficult to determine which causes which. One solution to this problem has been proposed by Granger (1969, 1980) and has become known as Granger causality. Granger was the first to point out the necessity of controlling for the past history of a variable in order to determine causal effects on variables. Granger's definition of causality is that one variable can be taken as a cause of another only after the influence of the past history of the second variable on itself has been controlled (Van de Ven and Poole 1990). The section prior to this one describes several techniques for theorizing about the behavior of individual variables across time, including their histories; those techniques are directly relevant to the determination of Granger causality.

The identification of causes and effects is a fundamental aspect of organizational science. The notion of Granger causality described in this section identifies procedures that can be used to determine causality in dynamic systems. Sometimes, however, the research goal is less to determine causal relations than it is to specify the overall dynamic process. Feedback loops are an important aspect of dynamic processes. The next section describes the role of feedback loops in dynamic theories and their place in the central issue of stability analysis.

Dynamic Processes in Systems With Feedback Loops

Many theories in the organizational sciences postulate one or more links that create feedback loops (see, e.g., Bagozzi 1980). A link is a relationship between two variables (or between the same variable at two points in time). Feedback loops are one or more links that eventually relate a variable to itself at a later point in time. By definition, feedback loops represent processes that occur over time. Analysis of the nature of the links and loops can provide important insights into the dynamics of the theory. This section provides an explication of the central features of feedback loops, primarily, stability analysis. It also relates the analysis of feedback loops to the forms of dynamic theorizing described above.

Feedback links represent positive (direct) or negative (inverse) relations (the sign of the link) that are typically viewed as causal (Kenny 1979). Further, feedback links are characterized by the magnitude of the relation,

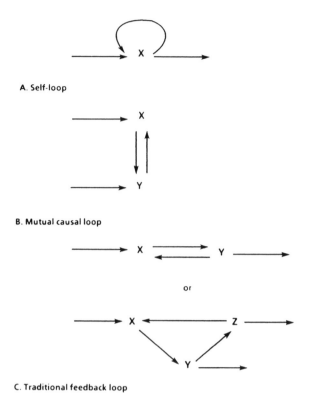

Figure 10.9. Three Types of Feedback Loops: (a) Self-Loop, (b) Mutual Causal Loop, and (c) Regular Loop

most often in the form of verbal descriptions or, quantitatively, in the form of standardized or unstandardized regression coefficients.

Feedback loops also have a positive or negative sign and are characterized as stable or unstable. The sign of the loop is determined as the algebraic product of the signs of each of the links in the loop (Kenny 1979). Stability is determined as the product of the magnitude of the coefficients of each of the links in the loop.

There are three well-known forms of feedback (Blalock 1969, Kenny 1979); they are presented in Figure 10.9. A self-loop represents the influence of a variable on itself, that is, the influence of its own history. A mutual causal loop represents the (nearly) simultaneous influence of two variables on each other. Finally, a standard loop represents the effect a variable has on itself through its influence on a chain of other variables.

Theorists who postulate the existence of feedback loops should be explicit about the time-dependent nature of the feedback links and loops. Correct specification of a self-loop is equivalent to explication of the historical behavior of a variable as illustrated in the previous sections. Theorists should specify whether the variable increases or decreases over each cycle of the loop and by what magnitude. (Most self-loops are nonlinear, implying exponentially increasing or decreasing self-influence over time.) Also, it is important to specify the frequency at which each cycle occurs. Similarly, theorists need to be specific about the signs, magnitudes, and time dimensions of mutually causal and traditional feedback loops. Drawing time graphs of concomitant variation like those in Figure 10.8 can provide useful precision.

Stability analysis is an important aspect of dynamic systems. Maruyama (1968) introduced to the social sciences the notions of deviation amplification and deviation counteraction to represent the influence that a feedback loop has on the initial variable. Deviation counteraction is a negative feedback loop where a magnitude of change in one direction in the initial variable leads in time through the feedback loop to an eventual change in the initial variable in the opposite direction. Thus an increase in the magnitude of X will lead eventually to a decrease in X through the subsequent influence of the other variables in the loop. Since X has changed a second time, it causes the process to repeat. However, since X decreased this time but the loop is still negative, this decrease in X leads eventually to an increase in X. Obviously, this is oscillatory behavior over time as X switches back and forth from increasing to decreasing with each cycle of the feedback loop. The same oscillatory pattern holds if X initially decreases rather than increases.

Deviation amplification represents a positive loop in which an initial change in a variable leads eventually to further changes in the variable in the same direction. Thus an increase in the initial variable leads eventually to a further increase in the variable. Likewise, an initial decrease leads to a further decrease.

Obviously, variables cannot continue to increase or decrease indefinitely. At some point they will reach the limits of their capacity for change. Consequently, when theorists specify feedback loops, it is crucial that they identify whether the system is stable or unstable. As Blalock (1969) indicates, stability is determined by the sign and magnitude of the product of the coefficients along the loop. Two general rules specify the type and stability of feedback. First, if the product of the coefficients is above zero, the feedback is positive; if below zero, the feedback is negative. Second, if the absolute value of the product is below one, the feedback is stable; if above one, the feedback is unstable. Figure 10.10 presents examples of the four possibilities: stable and unstable deviation-amplifying (positive) and deviation-counteracting (negative) feedback loops. The figure also shows the two product rules governing each case.[4]

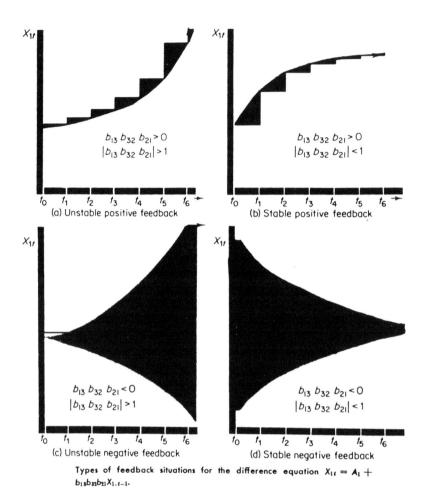

Figure for panels (a) Unstable positive feedback, (b) Stable positive feedback, (c) Unstable negative feedback, (d) Stable negative feedback.

Types of feedback situations for the difference equation $X_{1t} = A_1 + b_{13}b_{32}b_{21}X_{1,t-1}$.

Figure 10.10. Stable and Unstable Feedback Loops
SOURCE: From Hubert M. Blalock, Jr., *Theory Construction: From Verbal to Mathematical Formulations,* © 1969, p. 82. Reprinted by permission of Prentice Hall, Inc., Englewood Cliffs, New Jersey.

Theorists who develop one or more feedback loops as a part of their theories should also specify the expected sign of the coefficient for each link and estimate the magnitude of the relation between each pair of variables. The rules above then make it possible to theorize whether the feedback is positive or negative and whether the model is stable or unstable.

A Typology of Analytical Alternatives

Theorizing about dynamic processes is essential for meaningful longitudinal research. Nonetheless, an important part of the research design is the selection of an appropriate statistical technique for analyzing the longitudinal data. The discipline's collective experience in this domain is modest at best.

Table 10.1 presents a typology of statistical techniques for analyzing longitudinal designs. One axis of the typology represents the "research design" in terms of the number of points in time at which data are gathered. This varies from static to dynamic or, equivalently, from cross-sectional to longitudinal. This axis of the table is divided into three sections: single point in time, two or a few points in time, and many points in time.

The second dimension of the table pertains to the "type of model" being analyzed. Of course, this model should correspond to the theory. There are four types of models. Independence models examine single variables or single-variable processes. Dependence models look at relations between two or more variables. Interdependence models focus on relations within a set of variables rather than relations between variables. Finally, hybrid models constitute a residual category for techniques that seem to fit into more than one category.

These four models are subdivided further by number of variables and levels of measurement, where applicable. The number of variables is divided into single variables and into multiple independent and multiple dependent variables. The levels of measurement are split into categorical, which typically represents nominal or weak ordinal level of measurement, and continuous, which represents ratio, interval, and strong ordinal measurement.

The cells of the typology represent statistical techniques that are appropriate for the type of model and the research design chosen by the researcher. For example, Glick et al. (1990) asked top executives to recall retrospectively the occurrence of major organizational changes. Though each event is different, at a higher level of abstraction each is an instance of the categorical variable "organizational change." Though the data were gathered at six-month intervals over a two-year period, the dates of change provided by these informants permitted the approximate location in chronological time for each change, thus producing a distribution of a single categorical variable across time. Table 10.1 shows that an independence model with a longitudinal design can properly be analyzed with Markov models in general and the sociological variant known as event histories (Tuma and Hannan 1984, pp. 91-115). The latter was the method they chose for this part of their analysis.

An article by Monge, Cozzens, and Contractor (1992) provides another example. These researchers theorized that increases over time in two communication factors and three motivational factors would lead over time to

TABLE 10.1 A Typology of Analytical Alternatives for Longitudinal to Static Research Designs

| | Research Design | | |
| | Longitudinal | | Static |
Type of Model	Many Points in Time	Two or a Few Points in Time	Single Point in Time
Independence Models			
Single continuous variable	Time series	t test	t test
	Lagged regression	Structural equations[a]	
Single categorical variable	Markov models	χ^2	χ^2
	Event history analysis		
Dependence Models			
Single continuous dependent variable			
Continuous independent variable			
single	Transfer function time series	t test	Simple regression
	Lagged regression	Structural equations[b]	
multiple	Multivariate time series	Multiple regression	
Categorical independent variable			
single	Intervention time series	Repeated measures	ANOVA
		ANOVA	Dummy regression
multiple		Repeated measures	ANOVA
		ANOVA	Dummy regression
Multiple continuous dependent variable			
Continuous independent variable			
single	State-space analysis	Structural equations	
multiple	State-space analysis	Panel analysis	Canonical correlation
	Dynamic modeling	Structural equations	Structural equations[b]
			Multivariate multiple regression
Categorical independent variable			Hotelling's T^2
single		Repeated measures	
		MANOVA	
multiple	State-space analysis	Repeated measures	Structural equations[b]

(continued)

TABLE 10.1 Continued

| | Research Design | | |
| | Longitudinal | | Static |
Type of Model	Many Points in Time	Two or a Few Points in Time	Single Point in Time
Single categorical dependent variable			
Continuous independent variable			
single	Event-history analysis		Discriminant analysis
multiple	Event-history analysis		Multiple discriminant analysis
Categorical independent variable			
single			Cross-break analysis Log-linear analysis
multiple			Cross-break analysis Log-linear analysis
Multiple categorical dependent variable			
Continuous independent variable			
single	Log-linear analysis		
multiple	Log-linear analysis		
Categorical independent variable			
single			
multiple			
Interdependence Models			
Multiple continuous variables	Confirmatory factor analysis	Metric multidimensional scaling Confirmatory factor analysis	Principal components analysis Confirmatory factor analysis Metric multidimensional scaling
Multiple categorical variables		Nonmetric multidimensional scaling	Smallest space analysis Nonmetric multidimensional scaling
Hybrid Models			ANACOVA

a. Also known as reliability and stability analysis.
b. Also known as path analysis.
c. Logit and probit analysis.

increases in the number of innovations generated in a sample of firms. This dynamic theoretical framework implies the "longitudinal" category of the research design dimension of Table 10.1. The specification of predictor variables and outcome variables implies a dependence model in the type of model dimension of the table. There was one dependent variable measured at the ratio level (number of innovations generated per week per firm), so the first appropriate subdivision is single continuous dependent variable. There were five predictor variables measured at the strong ordinal and interval levels. Consequently, the appropriate subcategories are "continuous independent variable(s)" followed by "multiple." The cell representing this combination of research design and type of model contains the entry "multivariate time series." Since the researchers had collected weekly data on all six variables for 52 weeks, multivariate time series was the analytic method of choice.

CONCLUSION

The central thesis of this chapter has been that the design and conduct of longitudinal research should be a theoretical enterprise. This means that researchers must specify the over-time behavior of each variable in the design and should theorize about the dynamic interrelations among the set of variables. The chapter has provided a framework to assist organizational researchers in this process.

Yet there are numerous issues that a primer such as this cannot address within the confines of a chapter-length piece. In this final section several of these will be briefly mentioned as an agenda for future investigations of dynamic process. Some of these issues are intellectual, others empirical. All provide rich areas in which to work.

Two broad classes of process theories exist in organization science: (1) those that conceptualize phenomena as recurring patterns of a cycle, and (2) those that conceptualize the processes as a sequence of events or stages. When viewing a process from this latter perspective, important considerations include the identification of the stages in the sequence and the specification of the conditions of movement from one stage to the next. Several stage theories exist in the organizational literature. For example, organizational life-cycle theories (Kimberly and Miles 1980) propose that organizations proceed regularly through the stages of emergence, growth, maturity, decline, and death. Tushman and Romanelli's (1985) metamorphosis model argues that organizations go through successive stages of convergence and reorientation. Van de Ven and Poole's (1990) theory of innovation processes describes a sequence of stages as innovations emerge, develop, grow, or terminate over time. These researchers have developed a set of techniques to determine empirically the stages and transitions between stages of innovating. The current chapter has focused primarily on the cyclical form of theory. A similar explication of how to develop process stage theories, hypotheses, and research would enrich the organizational literature (see Abbott 1990, Mohr 1982, Tuma and Hannan 1984, Van de Ven and Poole 1989).

At the center of all dynamic analyses is the assessment of change over time (Kelly and McGrath 1988). There are several models of change that have been used in organizational and other social science theories. For example, Meyer, Brooks, and Goes (1989) present a typology of change models based on the distinction between continuous and discontinuous change and between firm and industry levels of analysis. The intersection between these two dimensions leads to four classes of change models: adaptation, metamorphosis, evolution, and revolution. Further examination of the nature of various change models, the development of appropriate forms of hypotheses for each type of model, and the specification of relevant longitudinal research designs would substantially increase our understanding of dynamic processes.

Closely related to this issue is the one of linear and nonlinear systems, or of order and chaos. Linear systems are generally viewed as orderly, steady-state, equilibrium-maintaining systems. Nonlinear systems may be orderly or they may be chaotic. *Chaos* generally refers to the fact that a small change in the initial parameters of a system can lead to radically large changes in the behavior of the system (Gleick, 1987). The framework described in this chapter assumes that change occurs in a rather orderly fashion. Other frameworks need to be developed that focus on chaotic change (see Glass and Mackey 1988). For example, Fombrun (1986) argues that structural dynamics within and between organizations is a dialectic between convergence (equilibrium) and divergence (chaos), either of which may be dominant at any point in time (see also Child and Kieser's 1981 discussion of the nature of change in organizational development).

Whatever the content, studying the dynamics of human systems places time at the center of all theory and research. Although time has been included in the analytic frameworks described above, nothing has been said about the nature of time. Jaques (1982) argues that the way we view time fundamentally affects the way in which we view phenomena. Much of the preceding analysis has been based on the notion of "clock time" or "real time." Yet Clark (1985) asserts that clock time should be viewed as only one of the several alternatives for determining time. He argues that organizational theorists should employ a plurality of time-reckoning systems. One example of analyzing an alternative to clock time comes from Gersick's (1989) recent research on group time reckoning during decision tasks with fixed deadlines.

Her results show that most groups utilize the first half of their allotted time in relatively nonproductive activities, but at the halfway point they shift to highly focused, productive work. A thorough examination is needed of the differences between the nature of time in organizational theories and the role of time in hypotheses and research designs (see, for example, Kelly and McGrath's 1988 discussion of real time versus experimental time).

There are a number of practical issues that must be addressed in the conduct of longitudinal research. One of these is the question of how often to gather data. In the case of cyclical processes, Arundale (1980) presents a theorem demonstrating that in order to reproduce the cycle, data must be gathered at least as often as one-half the periodicity of the phenomenon. Thus, for periodic phenomena, the issue of how often to gather data is directly related to the theoretical and/or empirical issue of how long it takes the phenomena in the theory to complete one cycle of change. Similar criteria would be helpful in stage theories and in chaotic phenomena.

Another practical issue related to sampling is that of who or what to observe. Almost by definition, process research requires multiple observations on the same entity. Yet when the phenomena of interest are human processes, a host of problems arise pertaining to the effects this has on the people involved (see Cook and Campbell 1979). A number of solutions have been proposed, such as institutionalizing the data collection process as an inherent part of work (Monge et al. 1984) and taking unobtrusive measures— for example, in studying electronic mail (Fulk, Schmitz, and Steinfield 1990). Another solution has been to draw random samples from organizations without replacement until everyone in the firm is sampled and then repeat the sampling frame as often as necessary. This strategy reduces the reactivity problem but produces a quasi-panel rather than a true panel design. Further research on this issue should help researchers make important choices in the conduct of longitudinal research.

Another practical issue is how to analyze process phenomena in multiple cases. For example, most time-series analyses focus on a few variables of a single entity measured at many points in time (e.g., several measures of the economy at quarterly intervals over several years). In essence, most time-series analyses are case studies, or what Kratochwill (1978) calls "single subject research." Process techniques such as time-series analyses have not yet been developed for analyzing many variables on many cases at many points in time. The work by Monge, Cozzens, and Contractor (1992) described above contained weekly measures on six variables over 52 weeks for five firms. Their analysis provided separate time-series models for each firm, the results of which differed somewhat across companies. The researchers then conducted a meta-analysis of the results from the five models. This strategy provided an estimate of the dynamic relations across all the firms in the study as well as an estimate of the stability of the coefficients across the firms. This is an indirect way to achieve what someday should be available for all process researchers: methods for directly analyzing dynamic processes across multiple cases.

Forecasting is an important but little-known aspect of process research. It provides a unique way to test the adequacy of the process models, yet almost no organizational studies exist that utilize forecasting techniques. Forecasting is the dynamic equivalent of prediction in static research. By developing forecasting models on a part of the data, researchers can test their theories and models on later parts of the same data set. For example, Monge, Cozzens, and Contractor (1992) developed their models on the basis of 42 weeks of data. They used these models to forecast the accuracy of their hypotheses over the remaining 10 weeks of data. In four out of the five models, the forecasting accuracy for all six variables ranged from 72% to 85%. The forecasts for the fifth model were less successful leading to an exploration of anomalies in this firm to explain the results.

There is little doubt that major contributions in empirical work in organizations will be made on the basis of longitudinal research (though see Blalock's 1989 recent despair about methodological advances in sociology). As researchers acquire more experience in designing and conducting longitudinal research, they should also develop experience in thinking and theorizing dynamically. Eventually, new theories will be developed that are inherently dynamic. While that expertise is being developed, valuable progress can be made by translating existing static theories into dynamic form (see Contractor and Monge's 1990 dynamic reformulation of equity theory).

Organization science is moving slowly in the direction of studying dynamic process. Someday, through a combination of inductive and deductive efforts, organization theories will be dynamic rather than static. Research will be based on longitudinal designs rather than single point in time designs. And data will be analyzed with inherently dynamic techniques such as time-series and Markov models rather than with static correlational methods. This chapter provides a framework designed to assist in the development of that vision of organization science. Yet, as this final section has amply demonstrated, much more needs to be known about the process of studying process.

Acknowledgments

This chapter was prepared in part with support from the National Science Foundation, Grant No. ISI-8412761, Peter R. Monge and Richard V. Farace, co-principal investigators. I would like to acknowledge the assistance of several individuals who commented on earlier drafts of this manuscript: Noshir Contractor, Janet Fulk, Bill

Glick, George Huber, Arie Lewin, Bob McPhee, Scott Poole, Tom Reed, Andy Van de Ven, and an anonymous reviewer for *Organization Science*. I would also like to acknowledge the contributions of the students in my research methods classes at the Annenberg School, who over the years have pressed me hard to clarify my ideas about process. Finally, I would like to thank Linnea Berg for her usual outstanding job of preparing the manuscript and graphics (with the assistance of Judy Chan).

Notes

1. Regression techniques can be used to analyze longitudinal data. Hibbs (1974) describes these well, but they are rarely employed in organizational research. Further, there are clear advantages to using nonlinear techniques such as those developed by Box and Jenkins (1976) if the longitudinal data contain cyclicity.

2. Each dynamic coefficient represents the relation between the changes in the dependent variable over time and changes in one independent variable over time, controlling for the over-time influence of all other independent variables.

3. This distinction is different from discrete and continuous measurement. Variables may be measured either discretely (categorically) or continuously (i.e., on a scale). This measurement is independent of whether the variables are viewed in a process as continuous-time (occurring at all points in time with nonzero values) or discontinuous-time (occurring with nonzero values at some points in time and having zero values at other points).

4. These criteria are for difference equations with lagged variables. Blalock also provides the criteria for linear differential equations, as do Tuma and Hannan (1984), who also provide the criteria for nonlinear equations.

References

Abbott, A. (1990), "A Primer on Sequence Methods," *Organization Science,* 1, 375-392.

Arundale, R. B. (1980), "Studying Change Over Time: Criteria for Sampling From Continuous Variables," *Communication Research,* 7, 227-263.

Baggozi, R. P. (1980), *Causal Models in Marketing* New York: Wiley.

Blalock, H. M., Jr. (1964), *Causal Inferences in Non-Experimental Research,* Chapel Hill: University of North Carolina Press.

Blalock, H. M., Jr. (1969), *Theory Construction,* Englewood Cliffs, NJ: Prentice Hall.

Blalock, H. M., Jr. (Ed.) (1972), *Causal Models in the Social Sciences,* New York: Aldine.

Blalock, H. M., Jr. (1989), "The Real and Unrealized Contributions of Quantitative Sociology," *American Sociological Review,* 54, 447-460.

Box, G. E. P., and G. M. Jenkins (1976), *Time Series Analysis: Forecasting and Control,* San Francisco: Holden-Day.

Child, J., and A. Kieser (1981), "Development of Organizations Over Time," in P. C. Nystrom and W. H. Starbuck (Eds.), *Handbook of Organizational Design* (Vol. 1, pp. 28-64), Oxford: Oxford University Press.

Clark, P. (1985), "A Review of the Theories of Time and Structure for Organizational Sociology," in S. B. Bacharach (Ed.), *Research in the Sociology of Organizations* (Vol. 4, pp. 35-79), Greenwich, CT: JAI.

Contractor, N., and P. R. Monge (1990), *A Dynamic Reformulation and Empirical Test of Equity Theory.*

Cook, T. D., and D. T. Campbell (1979), *Quasi-experimentation: Design and Analysis Issues for Field Settings,* Chicago: Rand McNally.

Cook, T. D., L. Dintzer, and M. M. Mark (1980), "The Causal Analysis of Concomitant Time Series," in L. Bickman (Ed.), *Applied Social Psychology Annual* (Vol. 1, pp. 93-135), Beverly Hills, CA: Sage.

Daft, R. L., and A. Y. Lewin (1990), "Can Organization Studies Begin to Break Out of the Normal Science Straitjacket? An Editorial Essay," *Organization Science,* 1, 1-9.

Duncan, O. D. (1966), "Methodological Issues in the Analysis of Social Mobility," in N. Smelser and S. M. Lipset (Eds.), *Social Structure and Social Mobility in Economic Development* (pp. 51-97), Chicago: Aldine.

Fombrun, C. J. (1986), "Structural Dynamics Within and Between Organizations," *Administrative Science Quarterly,* 31, 403-421.

Fulk, J., J. A. Schmitz, and C. W. Steinfield (1990), "The Social Influence Model of Technology Use," in J. Fulk and C. W. Steinfield (Eds.), *Organizations and Communication Technology* (pp. 117-141), Newbury Park, CA: Sage.

Gersick, C. J. G. (1989), "Marking Time: Predictable Transitions in Task Groups," *Academy of Management Journal,* 32, 274-309.

Glass, L., and M. C. Mackey (1988), *From Clocks to Chaos: The Rhythms of Life,* Princeton, NJ: Princeton University Press.

Gleick, J. (1987), *Chaos: Making a New Science,* New York: Penguin.

Glick, W. H., G. P. Huber, C. C. Miller, D. H. Doty, and K. M. Sutcliffe (1990), "Studying Changes in Organizational Design and Effectiveness: Retrospective Event Histories and Periodic Assessments," *Organization Science,* 1, 293-312.

Granger, C. W. J. (1969), "Investigating Causal Relations by Econometric Models and Cross-Spectral Methods," *Econometrica* 37, 424-438.

Granger, C. W. J. (1980), "Testing for Causality: A Personal Viewpoint," *Journal of Economics, Dynamics and Control,* 2, 329-352.

Hannan, M. T., and J. H. Freeman (1977), "The Population Ecology of Organizations," *American Journal of Sociology* 82, 929-964.

Hawking, S. W. (1988), *A Brief History of Time,* New York: Bantam.

Hibbs, D. A., Jr. (1974), "Problems of Statistical Estimation and Causal Inference in Time Series Regression Models," in H. L. Costner (Ed.), *Sociological Methodology 1973-1974* (pp. 252-308), San Francisco: Jossey-Bass.

Jaques, E. (1982), *The Form of Time,* New York: Crane Russak.

Joyce, W., and J. Slocum (1984), "Collective Climates: Agreement as a Basis for Defining Aggregate Climates in Organizations," *Academy of Management Journal,* 27, 721-742.

Kaplan, A. (1964), *The Conduct of Inquiry: Methodology for Behavioral Science,* New York: Chandler.

Kelly, J. R., and J. E. McGrath (1988), *On Time and Method,* Newbury Park, CA: Sage.

Kenny, D. A. (1979), *Correlation and Causality,* New York: Wiley.

Kimberly, J. R. (1976), "Issues in the Design of Longitudinal Organizational Research," *Sociological Methods and Research* 4, 321-347.

Kimberly, J. R., and R. H. Miles (1980), *The Organizational Life Cycle,* San Francisco: Jossey-Bass.

Kratochwill, T. R. (1978), *Single Subject Research: Strategies for Evaluating Change,* New York: Academic Press.

Land, K. C. (1969), "Principles of Path Analysis," in E. F. Borgatta and G. W. Bohrnstedt (Eds.), *Sociological Methodology 1969* (pp. 23-37), San Francisco: Jossey-Bass.

Marcus, M. L., and D. Robey (1988), "Information Technology and Organizational Change: Causal Structure in Theory and Research," *Management Science, 34,* 583-598.

Maruyama, M. (1968), "The Second Cybernetics: Deviation-Amplifying Mutual Causal Processes," in W. Buckley (Ed.), *Modern Systems Research for the Behavioral Scientist* (pp. 304-313), Chicago: Aldine.

McCleary, R., and R. A. Hay, Jr. (1980), *Applied Time Series Analysis for the Social Sciences,* Beverly Hills, CA: Sage.

McPhee, R. D., and M. S. Poole (1982), "Mathematical Modeling in Communication Research: An Overview," in M. Burgoon (Ed.), *Communication Yearbook 5* (pp. 159-191), Beverly Hills, CA: Sage.

Meyer, A. D., G. R. Brooks, and J. B. Goes (1989), "Environmental Jolts and Industry Revolutions: Organizational Responses to Discontinuous Change," Working paper, Graduate School of Management, University of Oregon.

Mohr, L. B. (1982), *Explaining Organizational Behavior,* San Francisco: Jossey-Bass.

Monge, P. R. (1982), "Systems Theory and Research in the Study of Organizational Communication: The Correspondence Problem," *Human Communication Research, 8,* 245-261.

Monge, P. R., and M. D. Cozzens (1986), "Innovation Through Participatory Management: The Case for the Scanlon Process," in D. Gray, T. Solomon, and W. H. Hetzner (Eds.), *Strategies and Practices for Technological Innovation* (pp. 319-329), Amsterdam: Elsevier.

Monge, P. R., M. D. Cozzens, and N. S. Contractor (1992), "Communication and Motivational Predictors of the Dynamics of Organization Innovation," *Organization Science, 3,* 250-274.

Monge, P. R., R. V. Farace, E. M. Eisenberg, L. White, and K. I. Miller (1984), "The Process of Studying Process in Organizational Communication," *Journal of Communication, 34,* 22-43.

Parsons, T., E. A. Shils, and R. C. F. Bales (1949), *Working Papers in the Theory of Action,* New York: Free Press.

Polanyi, M. (1958), *Reliable Knowledge,* New York: Harper & Row.

Simon, H. (1957), *Models of Man,* New York: Wiley.

Tuma, N. B., and M. T. Hannan (1984), *Social Dynamics: Models and Methods,* New York: Academic Press.

Tushman, M. L., and E. Romanelli (1985), "Organizational Evolution: A Metamorphosis Model of Convergence and Reorientation," in L. L. Cummings and B. M. Staw (Eds.), *Research in Organizational Behavior* (Vol. 7, pp. 171-222), Greenwich, CT: JAI.

Van de Ven, A. H., and M. S. Poole (1989), "Methods for Studying Innovation Processes," in A. H. Van de Ven, H. L. Angle, and M. S. Poole (Eds.), *Research on the Management of Innovation: The Minnesota Studies* (pp. 31-54), New York: Ballinger/Harper & Row.

Van de Ven, A. H., and M. S. Poole (1990), "Methods for Studying Innovation Development in the Minnesota Innovation Research Program," *Organization Science, 1,* 313-335.

Weick, K. (1987), "Theorizing About Organizational Communication," in F. M. Jablin, L. L. Putnam, K. H. Roberts, and L. W. Porter (Eds.), *Handbook of Organizational Communication* (pp. 97-122), Newbury Park, CA: Sage.

Williams, L. J., and P. M. Podsakoff (1989), "Longitudinal Field Methods for Studying Reciprocal Relationships in Organizational Behavior Research: Toward Improved Causal Analysis," in L. L. Cummings and B. M. Staw (Eds.), *Research in Organizational Behavior* (Vol. 11, pp. 247-292), Greenwich, CT: JAI.

11

Organizations Reacting to Hyperturbulence

ALAN D. MEYER

JAMES B. GOES

GEOFFREY R. BROOKS

EDITORS' SUMMARY:[1] In this chapter, Meyer, Goes, and Brooks
provide two new and extraordinarily important insights. The first has
to do with the nature of change in a hyperturbulent environment.
Few researchers have encountered hyperturbulent environments;
fewer still have recognized hyperturbulence when they saw it; and
no one else has made as much sense out of the nature of organizational change in hyperturbulent environments as have these authors.
Hyperturbulent situations are unusual. These researchers were lucky.
But "luck" is preparation meeting opportunity. It is hard to imagine
how any researchers could have exploited their opportunity more
fully than did Meyer and associates.

The second extraordinarily important insight is that certain prescribed ways of thinking and acting (ways that are so much a part of
the organizational science culture that deviations from them are akin
to heresy) must be discarded when studying organizational change
under hyperturbulent conditions. This insight, well argued and supported with unsettling examples, will cause considerable consterna-
tion in the research community. The authors state that "as our study
progressed, one research design parameter after another slipped the

shackles of experimental control and started behaving like a variable." For example, they had to change "the operationalization of the [dependent] variable 'organizational performance' as industry restructuring altered the meaning of high performance." Executive-level managers, although not necessarily interested in the nature or process of organizational science, will recognize in this chapter that the problems that hyperturbulent environments pose for researchers are also problems that managers face when attempting to understand, to plan for, or to control organizational change under hyperturbulent conditions.

The industry studied was the hospital industry during the 1980s. Fortunately, Meyer and associates recognized that what they learned about managing change in hyperturbulent conditions is not limited to this industry—indeed, the authors' conclusions do not and need not mention any particular industry. Of course, this simply highlights the fact that one of the important contributions of this chapter will be to stimulate research on hyperturbulent environments and research on radical change in other industries. Examples of observations that merit investigation in other contexts are the following: (1) "While discontinuous changes were overturning the existing industry order, there was no equilibrium to be sought"; (2) strategic reorientations were most frequently associated with major environmental changes; (3) "hospitals were more likely to reorient their strategies in response to low performance relative to their competitors . . . reorientations were less likely to follow decline over time in their own performance"; and (4) hyperturbulence led to changes at three levels of analysis—the organization, the industry, and the interorganizational network.

Managing in changing conditions is qualitatively different from managing under steady-state conditions. Two important messages for managers in this chapter are that (1) hyperturbulence, which is likely to occur with increasing frequency, demands that organizations adopt radically new strategies in order to survive and that (2) hyperturbulence *is* survivable and presents unique opportunities for top managers who are prepared to reinvent their organizations.

Order is heav'n's first law.

Alexander Pope

Toto, something tells me we're not in Kansas anymore.

Dorothy in *The Wizard of Oz,* by L. Frank Baum

Organizations change continuously and discontinuously, and so do their environments. Demographic, economic, and social trends prompt routine organizational adjustment (March 1981). Geopolitical revolutions, technological breakthroughs, and stock market crashes jolt organizations into periodic reactions (Meyer 1982). Quantum changes occasionally sweep through industries, altering competitive structures, redefining viable niches, relocating industry boundaries, and triggering metamorphic changes in organizational form (Meyer, Brooks, and Goes 1990).

Based on a longitudinal field study in the health care industry, this chapter builds a general framework classifying these varieties of change within organizations and industries. It investigates causal processes operating over time and across levels of analysis. It describes environmental conditions ranging from steady state to hyperturbulence, the situation in which "environmental demands finally exceed the collective adaptive capacities of members sharing an environment" (McCann and Selsky 1984, p. 460). Such conditions are not unique to the health care industry. Telecommunications, computers, airlines, electric utilities, and financial services are other industries in the throes of revolutionary change. Events that alter the trajectories of entire industries can overwhelm the adaptive capacities of resilient organizations and surpass the understanding of seasoned managers. However, our observations also suggest that hyperturbulence is survivable and may offer unique opportunities for collective action.

This chapter challenges some prescribed ways of thinking and acting when researching organizational change under hyperturbulent conditions. It chronicles an attempt to rigorously research organizational change that was confounded by the very changes the researchers were trying to understand. Selecting "change" as a research problem and adopting a longitudinal data-collection strategy forced us to reconceptualize the study on the fly, led us into methodological mine fields, and produced results that continue to surprise us.

Thus discontinuous change is the central theme of the chapter. We offer concepts, data, and interpretations germane to the causes of discontinuous change, to its effect on industries and on organizations, and to its impact on the social scientists who research it. The chapter's first section provides a retrospective overview of the study. The second section presents a chronological report of the research project, which unfolded in four phases. The third section takes stock of the processes and products of the research and suggests some conceptual, methodological, and practical implications.

PROLOGUE: A RETROSPECTIVE OVERVIEW

Social science research is usually partitioned into five sequential stages: conceptualizing, designing, observing, analyzing, and reporting. We began this study by moving through these stages in the prescribed sequence. But when we reached the "observing" stage, discontinuous change occurred in the research setting that threatened to invalidate our conceptual model and research design. As the study proceeded, we were obliged to cycle back, rethink our concepts, change our research methods, and update our findings. As the change processes we were studying grew more chaotic, the focus of the research expanded to include industry-level as well as organization-level change, discontinuous as well as incremental change, and historical as well as contemporary change. Figure 11.1 reconstructs the research process. Over the four-year course of the longitudinal study, the research team's focus oscillated among conceptualizing, designing, and observing.[2]

PHASE 1: ORGANIZATIONS ADAPTING TOWARD EQUILIBRIUM

Model 1: Organizational Adaptation

In January 1987, we set out to learn about the processes that keep organizations in sync with their environments. We decided to limit the study to a single industry. One reason was theoretical: Since organizations' environments consist largely of other organizations, changes often reverberate through a group of competitors, and only a single-industry study could assess the extent to which changes observed in a given organization had been induced by prior changes in its competitors. A second reason was methodological: A single-industry study would let us compare organizations' responses with a uniform set of exogenous changes and estimate effects on performance. These considerations, coupled with experience gained in prior research in hospitals, led us to select as our study population the 55 medical-surgical hospitals located in four counties contiguous to the San Francisco Bay. Background interviews and journalistic reports indicated that environmental turbulence was increasing in the hospital industry. Costs were rising, new technologies were diffusing, and significant regulatory changes were afoot. So this seemed an appropriate setting for studying environmentally induced changes in organizational design and effectiveness.

We adopted a model developed in our prior research in this setting. This study (Meyer 1982) conceived of organizations as adaptive systems and reported on hospitals' responses to environmental jolts. The adaptation model theorized that when jolts emanate from environments, organizations observe and interpret events according to theories of action encoded in their strategies and ideologies. After interpretation, events elicit organizational

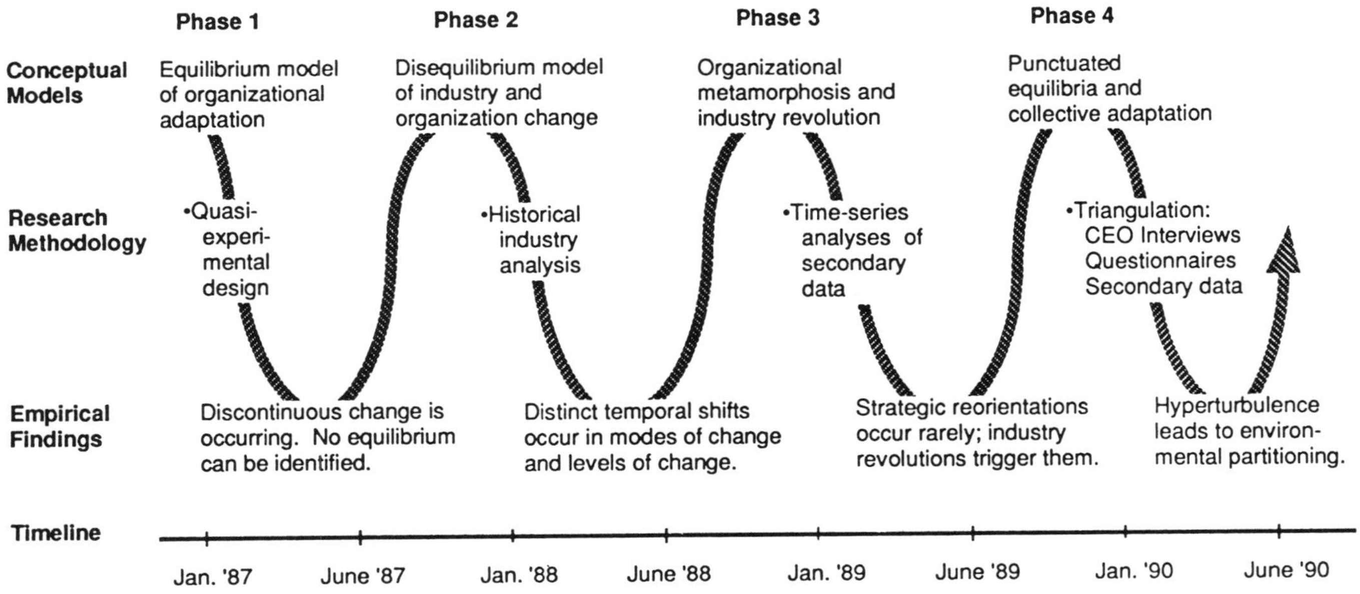

Figure 11.1. Phases in the Hospital Study

responses that exploit stockpiles of slack resources, as constrained by behavioral repertoires crystallized in the organizations' structures.

Our intention in January 1987 was to extend this model of organizational adaptation by applying it to a broader spectrum of environmental changes. We expected, for instance, to observe responses to secular trends and step-function shifts as well as adaptations to transitory environmental jolts. We developed hypotheses linking adaptive responses to organizations' subsequent performances.

Methodology 1: A Quasi-Experiment

The study was designed as a quasi-experiment that would exploit naturally occurring environmental changes (see Figure 11A.1 in the appendix to this chapter). Our plan was to observe hospitals' antecedent states, wait for the environment to change, watch hospitals adapt, and then evaluate the effects of various antecedent-adaptation combinations on subsequent levels of performance and on the hospitals' final configurations of strategy, structure, ideology, and slack. During July 1987, two members of the research team spent three weeks in the San Francisco area conducting the first of four scheduled waves of interviews with CEOs in a 30-hospital sample and gathering baseline questionnaire data on organizational variables. (The appendix to this chapter describes data-collection procedures.)

This method was designed to capitalize opportunistically on environmental change. Although we hoped for change, we failed to anticipate the type or the intensity of environmental change that we would encounter. Signs of trouble first surfaced during the six weeks immediately before our first wave of interviews, when two of the 30 hospitals in the sample merged, three hospitals were acquired, and six CEO successions occurred. As we hastily rescheduled interviews and recruited new informants, it became clear that we had taken to the field during a period of quantum change in the hospital industry. As Oscar Wilde once remarked, "When the gods wish to punish us, they answer our prayers."

Findings 1: Discontinuity and Disequilibrium

Discontinuous Change

Organizations' environments occasionally undergo cataclysmic upheavals—changes so sudden and extensive that they overwhelm organizations' adaptive capacities and transcend top managers' understanding. In 1987, changes of this magnitude were sweeping through the California hospital industry. Our CEO informants agreed that the character of competition was undergoing rapid change, but they attributed changes to different causes and foresaw different outcomes. Most CEOs recognized that the industry's boundaries were shifting, but they expected future boundaries to stabilize in different locations. A number of hospitals, physicians, and insurers were experimenting with new organizational forms that intruded into each other's traditional domains, and many CEOs were forging linkages with competing hospitals and with firms in related industries.

In sum, data collected in our first wave of interviews indicated that organizational change was rampant, but the data displayed no systematic pattern. Some changes produced increases in interorganizational cooperation, while others produced increases in competition. Some hospitals were expanding their domains of activity, while others were consolidating. The exact causes of changes were unclear. CEOs found all this confusing and disorienting, as did the researchers.

Conceptual Disorientation

The assumption that social systems exist in a state of equilibrium—or at least gravitate toward quasi-stationary equilibria—permeates both theories of organizations and the research methods routinely used to test the theories. Building on this implicit assumption, our Phase 1 conceptual framework treated adaptations as equilibrium-seeking responses by organizations. But it became apparent early in the first wave of CEO interviews that this adaptation framework could neither encompass the discontinuous environmental changes in progress nor account for the disparate organizational responses we were observing. The study's quasi-experimental research design, which also implicitly assumed equilibrium seeking, was invalidated as well. Simply stated, while discontinuous changes were overturning the existing industry order, there was no equilibrium to be sought.

PHASE 2: INDUSTRIES IN DISEQUILIBRIUM[3]

Model 2: Modes and Levels of Change

Both of the above "findings" suggested that the most pressing need was to develop a broader framework for thinking about organizational change. In the study's second phase, a review of the literature suggested classifying theories of change according to the *mode* of change (continuous or discontinuous) and the *level* at which it occurs (organization or industry).

The physical, biological, and social sciences portray the world changing in two fundamentally different modes. Continuous, or first-order, change occurs within a stable system that itself remains unchanged (Watzlawick, Weakland, and Fisch 1974). Indeed, system stability often *requires* ongoing first-order change, such as the myriad small compensatory steering movements that permit a bicyclist to maintain his or her equilibrium. Discontinuous, or second-order, change transforms fundamental properties or states of the system.

The level at which change occurs provides a second dimension for classifying theories about organizational change (Astley and Van de Ven 1983). Traditionally, theorists have taken the organization as the relevant unit of analysis and have focused on actions designed to alter organizational attributes to match environmental conditions. Recently, theories fashioned at the level of industries, populations, or groups of competing organizations have been imported from biology (Hannan and Freeman 1977), human ecology (Hawley 1950), and sociology (Scott 1987), helping focus organizational researchers' attention on industry-level change processes.[4]

Figure 11.2 combines these two dimensions to classify theories about how organizations create and maintain alignments with their environments. It organizes the literature according to implicit and explicit assumptions about the nature and level of change. Four types of change are distinguished; of these, the one called revolution in the figure has been neglected by organization theory and research.

Adaptation

The figure's top left quadrant corresponds to theories of first-order change constructed at the organization level of analysis. These are termed *adaptation* theories, and they maintain that organizations track their environments more or less continuously and adjust to them purposively. Two mechanisms of adjustment have been proposed. Theorists espousing a "strategic choice" approach maintain that managers experiment with new products, structures, and processes. Successful variations are retained in organizations' structural designs and product-market domains. An alternate mechanism of organizational adaptation is proposed by the "resource dependence" perspective, in which managers are relegated to a lesser role since organizational changes are viewed as responses dictated by external dependencies. Nevertheless, the organization remains the principal unit within which change is seen as occurring, and first-order change is the principal mode emphasized in resource dependence theory. But whichever of these approaches is taken, the domain of theoretical explanation is limited to incremental changes within firms. Other events are exogenous to adaptation models. Adaptation models posit organization-level processes that construct idiosyncratic product-market domains, and thus increase interorganizational diversity over time.

	First-Order Change	Second-Order Change
	Adaptation	**Metamorphosis**
Firm Level	Focus: Incremental change within organizations Mechanisms: •Strategic choice •Resource dependence Authors: Child (1972) Lindblom (1959) Miles & Snow (1978) Pfeffer & Salancik (1978) Weick (1979)	Focus: Frame-breaking change within organizations Mechanisms: •Life cycles •Strategic reorientations Authors: Greenwood & Hinings (1988) Kimberly & Miles (1980) Miller & Friesen (1984) Tushman & Romanelli (1985) Greiner (1972)
	Evolution	**Revolution**
Industry Level	Focus: Incremental change within established industries Mechanisms: •Natural selection •Institutional isomorphism Authors: Hannan & Freeman (1977) McKelvey & Aldrich (1983) Meyer & Rowan (1977) Scott (1987) Zucker (1987)	Focus: Emergence, transformation, and decline of industries Mechanisms: •Quantum speciation •Environmental partitioning Authors: Astley (1985) Barney (1986) Gould & Eldredge (1977) McCann & Selsky (1984) Schumpeter (1950)

Figure 11.2. Models of Change Within Organizations and Industries
SOURCE: Adapted from "Environmental Jolts and Industry Revolutions: Organizational Responses to Discontinuous Change," by Alan D. Meyer, Geoffrey R. Brooks, and James B. Goes. *Strategic Management Journal,* 11 (Summer): 93-110. Copyright © 1990 John Wiley & Sons, Ltd. Reprinted by permission.

Evolution

In the figure's lower left quadrant are models addressing how industries, or populations of competing organizations, undergo first-order change. We refer to these as *evolution* models because they maintain that although individual organizations are relatively inert, various forces propel populations of organizations toward alignment with prevailing external conditions. Two streams of evolutionary theory are differentiated by the dominant change mechanisms they posit. Population ecologists (e.g., Hannan and Freeman 1977, 1984, McKelvey and Aldrich 1983) emphasize blind variation, selection, and retention. They maintain that differential rates in the entry and exit of organizations cause populations to evolve gradually to fit the technical and economic constraints of environmental niches. Alternatively, institutional theorists (e.g., Meyer and Rowan 1977, Scott 1987) argue that organizations experience pressure to conform to the normative expectations of their institutional environments. Achieving "isomorphism" with such expectations allows organizations to gain legitimacy, garner resources, and increase their chances of surviving. Whereas population ecology theory assumes that competition for resources shapes populations by affecting entry and exit rates, institutional theory emphasizes competition for legitimacy and entertains the possibility of change within existing organizations. But although they emphasize different causal mechanisms, both the ecological and institutional approaches to evolution postulate population-level processes that increase the homogeneity of organizations over time.

Metamorphosis

The top right quadrant of Figure 11.2 contains organization-level theories focusing on second-order changes. These are termed *metamorphosis* theories, because they maintain that organizations adopt stable configurations and possess inertia, but periodically undergo rapid, organizationwide transformations. Theorists have proposed various causal mechanism that might drive metamorphic changes. These include progression through life-cycle stages (Kimberly and Miles 1980), shifts between strategic types (Miles and Snow 1978), changes in structural gestalts (Miller and Friesen 1984), and technological breakthroughs (Tushman and Romanelli 1985). In any case, metamorphosis theories focus on frame-breaking changes confined within the boundaries of single organizations.

Revolution

The figure's lower right quadrant is reserved for theories focusing on second-order change in industries. Following Schumpeter (1950), we label these *revolution* models, because they propose that industries are restructured and reconstituted during brief periods of quantum change that punctuate long periods of stability. "Quantum speciation," a biological notion, has been proposed as a mechanism through which new organizational forms might emerge during such periods (Astley 1985), and "environmental partitioning" has been suggested as a likely collective response of organizations already present in the industry (McCann and Selsky 1984).

Organization theorists have rarely ventured into this quadrant. Metamorphosis theorists argue that progression between developmental stages (Kimberly and Miles 1980) or radical innovations in technology (Anderson and Tushman 1990) lead to second-order changes *within* organizations—but they have not addressed the issue of why or how second-order changes in the structure of an industry *itself* unfold. Van de Ven and Garud (1987) explain the emergence of new industries, but their framework is less germane to second-order changes that restructure existing industries. Barney (1986) discusses industrywide Schumpeterian shocks, but he does not delineate their dynamics. Population ecologists describe how sets of competing organizations evolve, yet, as noted by Astley (1985) and Carroll (1984), they have little to say about how exogenous second-order changes redefine viable niches or trigger the emergence of new organizational forms.[5] Institutional theorists argue that coercive, mimetic, and normative forces bring organizations into alignment with each other and with the institutions upon which they depend (DiMaggio and Powell 1983), but, as Barley and Tolbert (1988) note, processes through which institutions form and re-form have not been considered.

Methodology 2: Historical Industry Analysis

At this point in the study, the most pressing questions concerned the antecedents and dynamics of the surprising barrage of changes observed during the first wave of interviews. We believed that the model shown in Figure 11.2 could help isolate and interpret the cross-level processes connecting changes in industry structures with changes in organizations. A historical approach seemed necessary to delineate the industry's longitudinal cycle of contextual change, organizational response, and new context formation. Consequently, we shifted the unit of analysis from the organization to the industry and changed the time frame from real-time observation to retrospective data collection.

The analysis presented below draws on a data set assembled using a variety of methods: structured interviews with industry experts and hospital CEOs, naturalist observations, responses to mailed surveys, inspection of organizational documents, and analysis of secondary data. Details are provided in the appendix to this chapter. In the discussion that follows, key conclusions of the analysis are presented as propositions.

Findings 2: Three Decades in the California Hospital Industry

During Phase 1 fieldwork, we developed a generic "environmental map" to help each CEO chart his or her hospital's position within the evolving industry (as described in the appendix). Depicted in the map were three distinct but interdependent sectors of health care: (1) the provider sector in which hospitals actually deliver acute care, (2) the insurance sector that insures and pays for such care, and (3) the pre/post acute-care sector that funnels patients into hospitals and provides care after their discharge. Our Phase 2 analysis of the industry's history focused on these sectors and examined their changing relationships over time. Figure 11.3 depicts the

310

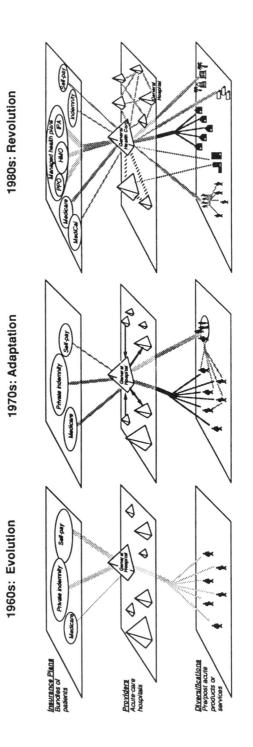

Figure 11.3. Industry Change Across Three Decades

SOURCE: Adapted from Figures 2-4 in "Environmental Jolts and Industry Revolutions: Organizational Responses to Discontinuous Change," by Alan D. Meyer, Geoffrey R. Brooks, and James B. Goes. *Strategic Management Journal, 11* (Summer): 93-110. Copyright © 1990 John Wiley & Sons, Ltd. Reprinted by permission.

position of "General Hospital," a typical provider in the industry,[6] during each of three decades.

The 1960s: Evolution Through Isomorphism

For hospitals in the San Francisco area, the 1960s was a period when institutional forces produced a high level of interorganizational homogeneity. Perrow (1965) argues that medical professionals dominated hospital power structures during this period, imposing what institutional theorists term "normative isomorphism" (DiMaggio and Powell 1983). In addition, governmental largesse funded by the Hill-Burton Act imposed pressures for "coercive isomorphism."

Many hospital administrators of this era equated strategic planning with writing a mission statement and commissioning an architect to draw up blueprints for expansion. Serious attempts by hospitals to differentiate their services or segment their markets were virtually nonexistent. The absence of strong competition for resources rendered such efforts unnecessary, and intense institutional pressures for conformity rendered them ill-advised. Any gains in market share won through adaptive change were likely to be offset by losses in legitimacy. Accordingly, hospitals' goals, structures, and missions closely resembled those of their competitors. CEOs perceived their environments as relatively tranquil and munificent. Metamorphic changes were rare, as hospitals grew incrementally by adding services in a well-established sequence. Conditions were predictable and competition was orderly. As Figure 11.3 suggests, interorganizational linkages to other hospitals were largely unnecessary. Links up to the insurance sector and down to the pre/post acute-care sector were straightforward.

Proposition 1: Over time, an industry's evolutionary changes tend to increase the homogeneity of organizations within the industry.

In economists' terminology, during the 1960s, hospitals resembled regulated, homogeneous oligopolists. Industry boundaries were distinct, entry barriers were high, and competition was negligible. In terms of the conceptual model in Figure 11.2, this was an era of evolution: Industry-level first-order change was the primary change process operating, the most potent mechanisms of change were institutional ones, and the result was homogenization of the industry.

The 1970s: Organizational Adaptation

In the decade that followed, adaptation replaced evolution as the dominant form of change, strategic and structural differentiation occurred, and diversity within the industry increased. As new technologies such as CT scanners, kidney dialysis, and intensive care units came on line, hospital costs rose, resource scarcities emerged, and regulatory actions were triggered. Competition for patients increased, and newly imposed regulatory reviews or facility expansions and equipment purchases fomented political skirmishing. Hospitals grew to appreciate the concept of competitive strategy, and some hired consultants to help them develop one. By the mid-1970s, industry experts could readily classify many San Francisco area hospitals according to Miles and Snow's (1978) generic strategy types, as prospectors, defenders, analyzers, or reactors. Emerging competition, however, turned on nonprice factors, since roughly 80% of all reimbursements were made on a cost-plus basis. The pre/post acute-care sector at the bottom of Figure 11.3 shows that fee-for-service medicine was fragmenting as specialties multiplied and group practices proliferated. Thus both normative and coercive forces for isomorphism among providers were dwindling.

Proposition 2: Over time, adaptive changes undertaken by individual organizations increase the collective diversity of organizations within the industry.

In fact, adaptive changes undertaken by individual organizations very likely had the collective effect of constraining industry-level change. Strategic differentiation partitioned patients into diagnostic subgroups, channeling certain subgroups to particular hospitals. This began to produce domain consensus (Thompson 1967), which reduced uncertainty and limited rivalry. Hospitals' service differentiation and physicians' specialty referral networks developed in tandem, setting up predictable resource flows that both complicated and solidified the industry's collective structure. As Aldrich and Whetten (1981) have argued, dependence relations can stabilize interorganizational networks and hold environmental selection pressures in check.

Proposition 3: Over time, adaptive changes undertaken by individual organizations inhibit evolutionary changes within their industry.

In the language of our framework, the 1970s was primarily a decade of adaptation. First-order change at the organization level became the predominant mode of change, driven both by resource dependence and by purposive incremental change. Executives luxuriated in a sense of professional progress and mastery of the environment. Hospital management was emerging as a bona fide profession with established educational institutions and recognized credentialing mechanisms. The industry environment was changing, but in ways that seemed comprehensible. Interorganizational diversity

was increasing as many hospitals settled into distinctive strategic configurations. However, unseen stresses were accumulating, and the industry was
drifting toward a period of rapid restructuring.

The 1980s: Industry Revolution

Second-order changes swept through the hospital industry during the
1980s (Shortell, Morrison, and Friedman 1990). An early by-product of this
industry revolution was a burst of metamorphic change within organizations.
During the first half of the decade, most freestanding hospitals in the Bay
Area underwent corporate reorganization. The chief impetus for their metamorphoses was resource scarcity, and the chief objective was to expedite
diversification strategies. For instance, as shown in Figure 11.3, General
Hospital metamorphosed into General Health Corporation, a regional holding company that owned one hospital outright and was formally affiliated
with four others. Then, General diversified into a number of pre and post
acute-care products and services. Some, including a string of five urgent-care
centers and several upscale residential nursing homes, probably qualify as
vertical diversifications. Other projects are best viewed as related diversifications, such as a joint venture with another hospital to acquire a wheelchair
manufacturer. Still other diversifications—such as the purchase of a local
trucking business—are clearly unrelated.

Although the aforementioned changes were substantial, other changes occurring in the insurance sector overshadowed them. As shown in Figure 11.3, the
health insurance market fragmented, largely due to explosive growth in "managed health plans." Initially, hospitals were so reluctant to turn away business
that some contracted simultaneously with as many as 90 different plans, often
at discounts exceeding 30%. These contract negotiations took place without
sound actuarial data about the incidence of different diagnoses within the
populations served, and without reliable internal data on the cost to the hospital
of providing services. As the contract share of volume increased, hospitals
rapidly found themselves holding considerable risk.

The 1980s was a decade of revolution in health care. Discontinuous
changes restructured the industry. Long-established barriers partitioning
health care into the medical-surgical sector, the insurance sector, and the
pre/post acute-care sector were breached. Hospitals were thrust into the
insurance business as insurance carriers built and bought medical clinics. In
their offices, doctors began competing directly with the hospitals with which
they were affiliated to perform outpatient procedures, to control diagnostic
imaging, and to provide other lucrative ancillary services. Revolution in the
industry cascaded down to the organization level, inducing organizational
metamorphoses and spurring CEOs' efforts to adapt.

Proposition 4: Revolutionary changes within an industry are
associated with metamorphic changes within organizations.

In sum, changes occurring within the hospital industry during these three decades are characterized as evolution of a population of firms, giving way to adaptation within individual firms, followed by industrywide revolution. Our historical analysis shows that the changes confronting organizations vary dramatically over time, as shifts occur in the predominant mode of change and the level at which it unfolds. However, the analysis also suggests that adaptation, metamorphosis, evolution, and revolution are not independent and mutually exclusive forms of change. That is, change processes associated with all four quadrants in Figure 11.2 may occur simultaneously, and the incidence or intensity of change in one quadrant may influence the incidence or intensity of change in another. A group of competing hospitals, each seeking to adapt within the same domain by cultivating distinctive competencies (first-order organization-level change), may simultaneously experience institutional pressure to display identical structural features (first-order industry-level change). The interplay of adaptive and evolutionary change will, over time, determine whether this particular set of organizations becomes more heterogeneous or more homogeneous.

After repacking our theoretical bags to include these new ideas, adding new questions to the interview schedules to address industrywide issues, and recruiting new informants who occupied industry-level vantage points, we returned to the field for the second wave of data collection. This time CEO interviews were easier to conduct, because we had achieved some rapport during the first wave. The observations during Wave 2 strengthened and clarified our conviction that discontinuous changes at the industry level were under way and that these changes were linked to metamorphoses at the organization level.

PHASE 3: METAMORPHOSIS THROUGH
STRATEGIC REORIENTATION

The historical industry analysis discussed in the last section generated four propositions about the relationships between industry and organizational change. Using Proposition 4 as a starting point, we next conducted a more systematic and quantitative investigation of the role metamorphic organizational change plays in aligning organizations and environments. Our goal was to test hypotheses on the relationships among revolutionary environmental changes, metamorphic organizational changes, and performance outcomes over time in a large sample of organizations. We developed and evaluated two models: (1) an organization-level model positing a reciprocal

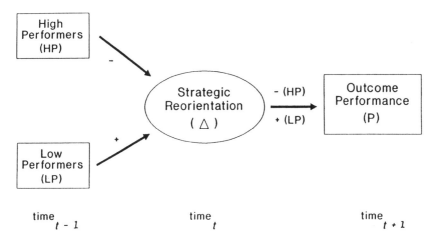

Figure 11.4. An Organization-Level Model of Strategic Reorientation Processes

relationship between organizational performance and metamorphic changes in organizations and (2) a cross-level model predicting that metamorphic changes in organizations are influenced by revolutionary changes in organizations' industry environments.

Our focus was on metamorphic changes in organizational configurations of strategy and structure, termed "strategic reorientations" (Tushman and Romanelli 1985). For our purposes, strategic reorientations were conceptualized as discretionary moves by top managers to improve competitive position. Unlike incremental or "fine-tuning" changes in strategy or structure, reorientations are radical shifts in strategic position and management perspective (Ginsberg 1988). Reorientations "take organizations outside their familiar domains and alter bases of power" (Starbuck 1983, p. 99); they involve simultaneous changes in a host of variables; and they shift organizations from one strategic type, configuration, or generic strategy to another (Greenwood and Hinings 1988).

Model 3: Reorientations and Revolutions

Our organization-level model of strategic reorientation is shown in Figure 11.4. The model posits that strategic reorientations within organizations are related to their prior performances, and that reorientations can have positive or negative effects on subsequent performances, depending on performance levels prior to the reorientations. These relationships are formalized in the first three hypotheses below.

Pressures for strategic reorientation can originate within or outside organizations (Ginsberg 1988). Even when no environmental imperative for change exists, top management may feel a need to develop a fundamentally new competitive posture. Such changes are often undertaken to improve organizational performance or competitive position. Indeed, unexpected environmental events such as exogenous technological breakthroughs or regulatory changes can act to trigger or enable strategic reorientations that have long been contemplated by management (Meyer 1982). In general, therefore, reorientations may occur within both low-performing and high-performing organizations.

However, discontinuous changes are risky and costly, since they propel organizations into new domains and impose new demands on their structures and members (Miller and Friesen 1984). These may include developing new competencies, products, or markets that require expenditures of time, money, and human capital. The potential gains from a reorientation must be sufficient to offset the risks and costs incurred in the attempt. Since low-performing organizations have less to lose and more to gain if a reorientation succeeds, we expect low-performing organizations to undertake strategic reorientations more often than high-performing organizations.

Hypothesis 1: Organizations with low performance in one period (t − 1) are more likely to undergo strategic reorientations in a subsequent period (t) than are organizations with high performance.

As rational decision makers, strategic managers are believed to recognize the threats implicit in chronic low performance and to react by formulating appropriate strategic changes. Assuming that the reasons for low performance were correctly diagnosed, and that a new strategy is successfully implemented, achievement of strategic reorientation should have a positive impact on subsequent performance.

Hypothesis 2: Among organizations with low performance in prior periods (LP_{t-1}), those that undergo strategic reorientations (Δ_t) will achieve higher performance in later periods (P_{t+1}) than will those that display strategic persistence.

For organizations that are performing poorly, an imperative for strategic change seems obvious. However, strategic reorientations are sometimes seen as a means for already successful organizations to maintain or improve their competitive positions. Strategic managers are said to recognize opportunities for change, to accept the risks implicit in change, and to manage the process to achieve reorientation successfully (Chandler 1990). However, as we

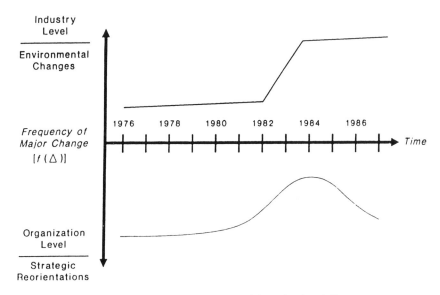

Figure 11.5. A Cross-Level Model of Industry and Organizational Change

noted, reorientation is time-consuming, expensive, and risky, leading Peters and Waterman (1982) to advise managers that "if it ain't broke, don't fix it." Therefore, we propose that when successful organizations reorient their strategies, they place their record of superior performance in jeopardy.

Hypothesis 3: Among organizations with high performance in prior periods (HP_{t-1}), those that undergo strategic reorientations (Δ_t) will have lower performance in later periods (P_{t+1}) than will those that display strategic persistence.

Figure 11.5 shows our cross-level model, which depicts the relationship between revolutionary environmental change and metamorphic organizational change. As Meyer and Starbuck (1993) have noted, strategic reorientations almost always encounter resistance. They entail discontinuous changes that would redefine organizations' domains in fundamental respects. People lack experience outside their domains, so proposed reorientations evoke confusion and uncertainty. Reorientations invariably alter existing power distributions, and they often impugn current top managers' wisdom. Thus managers may oppose reorientations to avoid uncertainty, maintain power, and protect their reputations. As a result, we propose that strategic reorientations will be infrequent events.

Hypothesis 4: Over a number of time periods ($t_1 \ldots n$), the number of organizations in a population that exhibit strategic reorientations ($\Sigma\Delta_t$) will be less than the number of organizations that do not exhibit strategic reorientations ($\Sigma\Delta_t$).

Since individual organizations generally resist change due to strategic or structural inertia (Hannan and Freeman 1984), they can collectively act as a "brake" that slows down industry change processes.[7] Large organizations in particular can resist change by expending slack resources, co-opting environmental constituencies, or driving out marginal competitors. Meyer (1982) found that San Francisco hospitals reacted to a short-term environmental jolt (a doctor's strike) by absorbing slack and making temporary adjustments in their strategies and structures. When the strike ended, most hospitals returned to their prior forms and strategies. The jolt was insufficient in magnitude and duration to compel the hospitals to reorient their strategies fundamentally.

The enduring changes wrought by an industry revolution, however, demand more than temporary changes in organizations. Bedeian and Zammuto (1991) argue that major environmental changes produce discontinuities in the size or shape of environmental niches and thereby spur strategic changes in organizations. In fact, since organizations are usually so resistant to change, industry revolutions may sometimes be *necessary* to trigger reorientations. Both our historical analysis and our field interviews suggested that revolutions in the health care industry were likely to trigger reorientations in hospitals. Thus, as illustrated in Figure 11.5, we formulated the following hypothesis:

Hypothesis 5: Strategic reorientations will be more prevalent during periods of industry revolution than during periods of industry evolution [$f(\Delta_t|revolution) > f(\Delta_t|evolution)$].

Methodology 3: Multivariate Time-Series Analyses

Strategic reorientations and organizational performance were tracked in approximately 450 California acute-care hospitals over a period of 11 years. Hospital strategies were measured along three dimensions; product/market domain, competitive methods, and organizational resources. Performance was conceptualized in two ways: cross-sectionally relative to competitors and longitudinally within the organization over time. Three elements of performance (profitability, efficiency, and growth) were assessed. Strategy and performance measures were constructed from a time series of secondary data collected annually by the state. Factor and cluster analyses were used to generate a taxonomy of strategic configurations and track changes between configurations (i.e., reorientations). Hypotheses were tested using discriminant analyses and ANOVA. (Further details can be found in the appendix to this chapter.)

Findings 3: Organization-Level and Cross-Level Effects

We proposed that organizations undertake strategic reorientations in order to increase their performance and improve their competitive position (Figure 11.4). Three longitudinal relationships between performance and strategic reorientations were hypothesized at the organization level. Considerable support was found for Hypothesis 1, that low prior performance is associated with strategic reorientations (Goes 1989). The strength of the relationship, however, varied depending on the conceptualization of performance used. Low performance measured relative to competing organizations proved a much better predictor of strategic reorientations than did measures of decline in performance within the focal organization. In other words, hospitals were more likely to reorient their strategies based on weaknesses in relative competitive position. Reorientations in a particular hospital were less affected by the hospital's own track record of performance over time.

Mixed and limited support was found for Hypothesis 2, which predicted that low-performing organizations that reoriented strategies would subsequently outperform those that did not. Again, the strength of the relationship varied considerably by performance measure. Reorientations had stronger effects on profitability and growth than on efficiency. Reorientations also seemed more likely to lead to higher future performance measured within the focal organization over time than to higher future performance measured relative to competitors. Reorientations by low performers rarely resulted in improved competitive position.

Finally, strong support was found for Hypothesis 3, which predicted that reorientations in high-performing organizations would have negative effects on performance. Strategic reorientations in high performers were generally found to be followed by substantial declines in profitability, efficiency, and growth. This finding implies that reorientations carry serious performance risks for organizations that are already succeeding with current strategies.

Overall, these results square with the image of organizations aligning and periodically realigning with their environments by undergoing strategic reorientations. Although the importance of particular performance measures as predictors or outcomes of reorientation varied, the hypotheses were generally supported. Prior performance emerges as a key variable in driving metamorphic changes in organizational strategy. In addition, future performance outcomes were influenced by strategic reorientations. Metamorphic change seems to play an important role in realigning organizations with changing environments.

TABLE 11.1 Cross-Tabulation of Strategic Reorientations Over Time

Year	Total Number of Hospitals	Total Number of Reorientation Opportunities[a]	Strategic Reorientations			No Strategic Reorientations	
			Number of Hospitals	% of Hospitals	% of Total Reorientations (1979-1986)	Number of Hospitals	% of Hospitals
1979	453	453	13	2.9	6.4	440	97.1
1980	449	436	39	8.9	19.2	397	91.1
1981	451	412	14	3.4	6.9	398	96.6
1982	457	443	40	9.0	19.7	403	91.0
1983	451	411	42	10.2	20.7	369	89.8
1984	459	417	17	4.1	8.4	400	95.9
1985	448	431	18	4.2	8.9	413	95.8
1986	443	425	20	4.7	9.9	405	95.3
Total	—	3,428	203	5.9	100.0	3,225	94.1

a. Given our coding scheme, strategic reorientations could occur only in years 1979-1986, and only hospitals that had *not* reoriented in the previous year could undergo a strategic reorientation.

However, as stated in Hypothesis 4, we expected strategic reorientations to be relatively rare events given the cost, time, and effort necessary to achieve them. This expectation was largely supported by the data. Table 11.1 presents the distribution of strategic reorientations observed in our sample over time. No more than about 10% of the hospitals made a reorientation in any given year. Across all years of the study, about 6% of the opportunities for reorientations resulted in actual changes between configurations. Indeed, only 142 hospitals in the sample (31%) underwent a strategic reorientation at any time during the eight years. Only 61 hospitals (14%) experienced more than one reorientation during this time span. In other words, almost 70% of the sample hospitals never made a strategic reorientation. This is an important finding, since it is at odds with another study finding that change in hospitals' "generic strategies" is common (Zajac and Shortell 1989). While this contradiction may result from the different methodologies used in measuring strategic change, our findings nonetheless imply that formidable inertial forces within organizations resist reorientations.

However, significant variation in the pattern of strategic reorientations over time was also evident. The results in Table 11.1 indicate that strategic reorientations were positively associated with revolutionary changes in the structure of the industry, as we predicted in Hypothesis 5.

It has been argued that quantum changes in the California hospital industry peaked between the years 1981 and 1983 (Meyer, Brooks, and Goes 1990; Shortell, Morrison, and Friedman 1990). Our secondary data analyses suggest that this discontinuous industry-level change may have triggered discontinuous organization-level changes: more than 40% of all metamorphoses we observed over an eight-year period (1979-1986) occurred during the latter two years (1982-1983) of the industry revolution. Indeed, the number of strategic reorientations was significantly greater during this two-year period than during other periods of the study.

Additional support for this cross-level relationship comes from an examination of time-dependent changes in the emphasis hospitals placed on several strategic dimensions that we elicited with factor analysis. Figure 11.6 plots over time the average factor scores observed for two of these strategic dimensions: "low margin defense" and "service differentiation."[8] Major discontinuities in both curves coincided with the industry revolution (1981-1983), and the curves' individual trajectories appear congruent with the particular character of the health care revolution.

In other words, the preferred mix of strategy variables changed considerably as the structure of the industry underwent major changes. Consistent with increased regulatory emphasis on cost containment, the factor we label low margin defense received sharply higher emphasis throughout the industry. Key variables in the low margin defense strategy were innovation in service delivery and an emphasis on efficiency. Regulatory disincentives for inpatient hospitalization were invoked in 1982, followed almost immediately by incentives for increased delivery of outpatient services. Consistent with these regulatory changes, the factor we label service differentiation fell sharply and then rebounded. Hospitals rapidly abandoned marginal inpatient services, yet moved just as quickly into a variety of new outpatient delivery programs.

In sum, our findings suggest that organization-level strategic reorientations in the California acute-care hospital industry were strongly associated with performance, were relatively uncommon over time, and seemed to correspond to major structural changes under way in the industry. Proposition 4, which contended that revolutionary changes within industries trigger metamorphic changes within organizations, was generally supported in our longitudinal, quantitative analyses of secondary hospital data.

PHASE 4: COLLECTIVE RESPONSES
TO INDUSTRY REVOLUTION

Methodology 4: Building Grounded Theory

Based on the Phase 2 historical analyses and Phase 3 time-series analyses, we reinterpreted Phase 1 reports of widespread CEO successions, restructuring, and strategic reorientations as organization-level responses to discontinuous

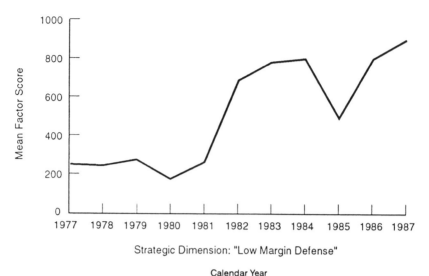

Strategic Dimension: "Low Margin Defense"

Calendar Year

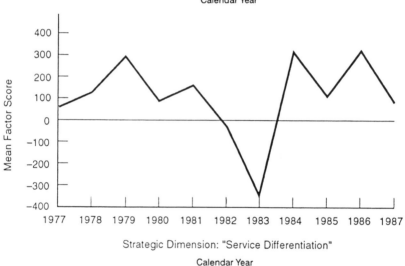

Strategic Dimension: "Service Differentiation"

Calendar Year

Figure 11.6. Time-Dependent Changes in Strategic Emphasis

industry-level change. However, as the fieldwork progressed, the growing significance of *inter*organizational responses became apparent. Hospitals were entering into operating agreements, asset-sharing arrangements, long-term contracts, and joint ventures with insurers, groups of doctors, employers, and other hospitals.

These collective responses to discontinuous change became the focus of the fourth phase of the study. Our goal at this point was to build theory by triangulating among data from observations, interviews, questionnaires, and archives. The process was largely inductive, and, as Eisenhardt (1989) recommends, it involved continuous comparison of data and theory. The methods are described in the appendix to this chapter, and the key findings are stated as propositions.

Findings 4: Responses to Hyperturbulence

Table 11.2 summarizes in tabular form the trends ascertained through content analyses of data gathered at six-month intervals. In hospital executive suites, we noticed profound shifts over time in CEOs' activities, in their emotional states, and in the issues commanding their attention. The collective mood swung from optimism, through despair, to resignation; foci of attention shifted from primarily external to primarily internal; and pivotal activities moved from strategy formulation, to implementation, to retrenchment.

In the insurance sector, traditional indemnity insurance almost disappeared during this period, while executives' attitudes toward managed care ricocheted from optimism, to disenchantment, to determination to build equity positions in managed care plans. The financial naïveté and "promiscuous contracting" that characterized the beginning of the period were replaced by tougher negotiation and a clearer understanding of hospital cost structures.

Early 1980s diversification into pre/post acute-care products and services gave way first to divestment and then to disaggregation. Nearly all hospitals that invested in primary-care clinics or acquired unrelated businesses absorbed losses. Fierce competition for diagnostic imaging, laboratory, and other profitable ancillary services arose from physicians and external entrepreneurs. Frequently, to avoid ceding services outright to unaffiliated investors, hospitals spun them off in joint ventures with physicians from their own medical staffs. The result, in either case, was a hollowing out of the hospital.

The most intriguing change we observed over the two-year period was a pronounced shift away from competition between freestanding hospitals toward affiliation into overlapping regional networks. Network formation was in its early stages when we began our fieldwork, and it continued throughout the study. The processes generating networks, however, did not operate in a stable or consistent fashion over time. As shown in the collective action row of Table 11.2, we observed systematic longitudinal differences in (1) CEOs' self-reported motives for affiliating with networks, (2) the nature of linkages connecting networked organizations, and (3) the function, or role, that networks played in the industry. In the process of reconceptualizing

TABLE 11.2 Time-Dependent Changes in Hospitals' Responses to Discontinuous Industry Change

	Wave 1, July 1987	*Wave 2, January 1988*	*Wave 3, July 1988*	*Wave 4, January 1989*
Medical-Surgical Acute-Care Sector	Great emphasis placed on formulating competitive strategies; less on implementation. Little change in organization structure. Performance: financial indicators and volume generally good. Mood is decidedly upbeat.	Strategy implementation now under way. Many structural reorganizations are in progress. Performance: generally high occupancy, but dwindling medicare reimbursement is troubling. Mood grows increasingly somber.	Many CEO successions, downsizing top management teams, adopting internal focus. Skim and differentiation strategies abandoned. Performance: mounting financial losses. Mood is to cut losses and weather storm. Gloom and doom abound.	Retrenching to core businesses. Downsizing continues at top and middle management levels. Performance: losses in competitive markets, profits in protected markets. Mood of realization that industry changes are irreversible, permanent.
Risk/Reimbursement Sector	General optimism about managed care, coupled with fear of turning away business. Tempered by concerns about magnitude of discounting and ignorance about costs of providing services.	Disenchantment with managed care and renegotiation of contracts. More awareness of costs of providing services and overhead costs of low-volume contracts. Curtailment of "promiscuous contracting."	HMOs experience heavy losses, levy sizable premium increases. Indemnity insurance vanishing. Hospitals are growing more experienced and selective in negotiating with managed care contractors.	Competition increasingly revolves around managed care. New products being developed and marketed. Many hospital CEOs seek to supplement arms-length contracting with equity in HMOs to retain control.

Pre/Post Acute-Care Sector	Diversification into pre- and post-acute care continues, but a retreat from primary care clinics is apparent. Concerted efforts are under way to foster a bottom-line orientation among M.D.s via education and indoctrination.	Back-to-basics sentiment surfaces. Divestiture of unrelated and many related businesses is now well under way. Hospital executives are devoting more attention to romancing and recruiting physicians to boost patient occupancy.	Divestment continues. Conviction grows that diversification does not make sense for hospitals. More vigorous physician recruitment by offering equity in joint ventures and subsidized medical office space as inducements.	Divestment gives way to disaggregation as core technologies are siphoned off or spun off. Joint ventures lead to hollowing out of the hospital. Joint ventures now essential for physician retention as well as recruitment.
Collective Action	Strong enthusiasm for affiliation: 70% of unaffiliated hospitals are actively courting network partners. Main benefit anticipated in areawide contracting for managed care.	Marked decline in enthusiasm for affiliation. Many CEOs opt for either full merger or freestanding posture; avoid intermediate positions. Main benefit perceived now is better access to financing.	An unprecedented number of acquisitions, affiliations, and mergers have just been completed or are under way. Most link hospitals to HMOs or other "managed care" plans. Key motive now is survival.	No major new affiliations since July, but many deals hang in abeyance. Air of expectation; extensive and durable groupings may jell at any time. Sitting in limbo.

SOURCE: Adapted from "Environmental Jolts and Industry Revolutions: Organizational Responses to Discontinuous Change," by Alan D. Meyer, Geoffrey R. Brooks, and James B. Goes. *Strategic Management Journal*, 11 (Summer): 93-110. Copyright © 1990 John Wiley & Sons, Ltd. Reprinted by permission.

networks, a set of concepts from the organizational literature was pressed into service.

Punctuated Equilibrium

Gersick (1991) describes recent shifts in theorizing about the development of human individuals, groups, and organizations, linking them to concurrent theoretical developments in evolutionary biology, physical science, and the philosophy of science. At issue in all these fields is the best way to conceptualize change. The older, better established *gradualist* position maintains that change unfolds in a piecemeal fashion through the incremental accumulation of many infinitesimal changes. The newer *punctuated equilibrium* view maintains that short bursts of quantum change are interspersed between long periods of stability. Gould and Eldredge (1977) characterize punctuated equilibria as changes that occur in large leaps. These changes follow a gradual accumulation of stress, which a system resists until it reaches its breaking point, or until a triggering event precipitates discontinuous change. Van de Ven (1993) reports that organizational innovation involves similar dynamics.

The notion of punctuated equilibria corresponded closely to events affecting our sample. As hospitals entered the 1980s, three stresses had been accumulating for some time. The first resulted from spectacular growth in "managed care," a term referring to health maintenance organizations (HMOs), preferred provider organizations (PPOs), and other new vehicles for financing and delivering health services. Second, a hospital building boom fueled by federal largesse during the 1960s and 1970s had saddled the industry with substantial excess capacity. Third, entry and mobility barriers had been weakened by competence-destroying innovations in medical technologies and services.[9] Characteristically, industry participants resisted change, and the stresses continued to build.

However, during 1982 and 1983, state and federal governments launched a fusillade of regulatory actions in an attempt to contain health costs by increasing competition. The most important actions were (1) initiating sealed-bid contracting for state-subsidized low-income patients, thereby creating incentives for operating efficiently and requiring hospitals to assume risk; (2) sunsetting the Certificate of Need review process, thereby removing a regulatory barrier to entry and mobility within the industry; and (3) basing the medicare payment system on diagnostic-related groups (DRGs), thereby reimbursing services according to predetermined rates. In comparison with the demographic, technological, and epidemiological changes then buffeting hospitals, these regulatory actions appeared relatively innocuous. But small causes can have large effects—the outcome was discontinuous change that surged through the California hospital industry.

Proposition 5: Weak forces can trigger revolutionary change by releasing the accumulated pressure of prior technological, social, and political changes.

Quantum Speciation and Dynamic Networks

In the biological process termed quantum speciation, new species arise when a small segment of an ancestral population is isolated at the periphery of its ecological domain. Here, because peripheries mark the edge of ecological tolerance for the form, conditions are harsh and selection pressures are intense. In these settings, favorable mutations spread quickly. If unsaturated ecological space exists, mutations proliferate. They occasionally displace the ancestral form and thus punctuate the evolutionary equilibrium.

Quantum speciation was a promising notion for conceptualizing the rapid formation of regional hospital networks. The networks themselves had properties akin to the organizational form that Miles and Snow (1986) term the "dynamic network"; they say this form is appearing "especially in service and high technology industries, as both a cause and a result of today's competitive environment" (p. 62). Dynamic networks connect selected components of formerly independent organizations. They are assembled for finite time periods to produce specific products or achieve specific objectives.

The 55 hospitals clustered around the shores of San Francisco Bay inhabit an ecological niche that is isolated from other hospital organizations in geographic, demographic, and regulatory terms. As competition and resource scarcities intensified in the early 1980s, several regional networks (like the one depicted in Figure 11.3 for General Hospital) appeared in this organizational population. These new interorganizational structures did not evolve in any gradual fashion. They did not, for instance, arise from the formalization of emergent social networks, the accretion of historical exchange patterns, or the crystallization of dependency relationships. Rather, our interviews indicated that these networks were analogous to biological mutations. They were brokered purposively by entrepreneurs to create new competitive vehicles for financing and delivering health care. They linked hospitals by superimposing governance structures ranging from markets to hierarchies. These linkages formed multiple layers of informal alliances, year-to-year contracts, joint ventures, and interlocking equity holdings. Hospitals connected by collaborative linkages for specified undertakings often competed vigorously in other areas. This cooperative overlay seems to fit Emery and Trist's (1965) assertion that, in turbulent environments, individual organizations, however large, cannot cope successfully in isolation but must establish cooperative relationships.

Proposition 6: Revolutionary change within an industry stimulates the formation of transorganizational networks.

During the study's second interviewing wave, we expanded the research design to obtain additional data from network brokers and affiliated executives. Brokers, we found, usually took the lead in connecting organizations. In some cases they linked participants by establishing an entirely new hierarchical entity. In others they acted as intermediaries who negotiated and contracted with participants individually. In still other cases, brokers merely established and maintained various formal relationships, leaving the affiliated organizations as equal partners in an evolving network. As industry boundaries became permeable, many brokers formed linkages that spanned industries—acting at once as respondents to and as agents of industry revolution.

Brokers maintained that they added value by reconfiguring components of hospitals and connecting them to insurance providers and physician organizations. When asked to spell out how value was added, brokers gave responses that fell into three categories: efficiency, power, and synergy. The efficiency argument emphasized economies of scale and scope. Pointing to the network's ability to deliver health services at geographically dispersed locations under a single contractual relationship, brokers said they provided access to superior executive talent, contracting expertise, and management information systems. The power argument maintained that coalescing amassed bargaining power vis-à-vis large public and private customers, and that it facilitated lobbying and other collective strategies. The synergy argument turned on linking separate components with unique competencies, each pursing its core mission single-mindedly after diversionary activities had been stripped away and superfluous enterprises had been spun off. But whatever rationales brokers offered for affiliation, the networks they assembled forged brand-new linkages among hospitals, physicians, and insurers.

Proposition 7: Revolutionary change within an industry precipitates affiliations spanning industry boundaries.

A less optimistic appraisal, however, came from our later interviews with hospital executives, the principal actors whom the brokers were trying to connect. The enthusiasm voiced by executives for networks during Wave 1 had dwindled sharply by Wave 2, when several remarked that the benefits ascribed to networks had been exaggerated and were not obtainable without legally merging the affiliated institutions. As indicated by entries in the bottom row of Table 11.2, the rate at which network affiliations were being consummated and the benefits ascribed to affiliation proved highly unstable over the period of our study. One trend, however, was unmistakable: As time passed, CEOs' anticipation of benefits from synergy, efficiency, or power gave way to an overpowering desire to mitigate the uncertainties and scarcities arising from revolutionary change in the industry.

Partitioning the Environment

McCann and Selsky (1984) propose that when the collective adaptive capacity of a population of organizations is exceeded by environmental demands, a condition that they call *hyperturbulence* ensues. This, they contend, can lead to a partitioning of the environment. Organizations that are relatively resource rich come together to form *social enclaves* within which resources are sequestered and turbulence is reduced. Selective membership criteria restrict admission to social enclaves. Prospective organizational members must demonstrate their control of slack resources available for contribution to the enclave, and they must hold values and goals compatible with those of existing members. In a process of *social triage,* resource-poor organizations are left to fend for themselves in hyperturbulent *social vortices,* wherein "attempts at collaboration either will be highly fragile, episodic, and prone to setbacks or will be impossible" (McCann and Selsky 1984, p. 466).

Events observed during and subsequent to Wave 4 suggested that environmental partitioning was under way in California's hospital industry. Faced with declining financial performance, disaggregation, downsizing, and the realization that their industry had undergone a quantum change, many executives were actively preparing their organizations for affiliation. The involution of embryonic dynamic networks and social enclaves over the two-year period of our field interviews was evident in the increasing disparity in size and wealth of affiliated and unaffiliated hospitals and in the failure and abandonment of one network formed to link less-affluent hospitals. Other evidence for the shift from dynamic networks to social enclaves comes from the case of a provisional alliance of several prominent hospitals. Legal affiliation was held in abeyance for more than a year because one potential member was losing money. In interviews with the alliance broker and CEOs of the hospitals involved, it was stated that the flow of red ink would have to be stanched before the arrangement could become permanent. When the beleaguered alliance member failed to return to profitability, the other hospitals severed their tentative links with it and formed a smaller enclave among themselves.

Proposition 8: Revolutionary change in conjunction with resource scarcity fosters partitioning of industry environments and formation of social enclaves.

According to McCann and Selsky's (1984) view of partitioning, when certain organizations amalgamate to form relatively affluent enclaves, others that are isolated tend to be drawn into social vortices in which uncertainty is higher and resources arc scarcer. The collaboration of some organizations actively worsens the conditions that confront others. These processes became increasingly evident in our sample. County-owned hospitals in particular seemed to be spiraling into vortices of extreme resource scarcity. They were obliged to treat medicaid patients and were expected to treat indigents. As the AIDS and crack cocaine epidemics advanced, private hospitals erected barricades to divert these patients to public hospitals. Because emergency rooms create portals affording entry to unwanted classes of patients, some private hospitals were led to cut emergency staffing levels or to discontinue emergency services altogether. (The proportion of all emergency services delivered by networked—as opposed to freestanding—hospitals in the San Francisco metropolitan area declined from about 35% to 20% just during the two years of our study.) Allegations were made of "patient dumping," where uninsured patients were transferred, or dumped, from private emergency rooms into public emergency facilities before they had been medically stabilized.

By 1990, emergency services had contracted to the point that periodic episodes of excess demand were occurring. Occasionally the entire region's emergency-care system crashed. Such an episode would typically begin when an overloaded county hospital placed its emergency room on "diversion" because no vacant critical-care beds were available. The result was to divert or reroute ambulances to other emergency facilities, inundating them with patients, absorbing their critical-care capacity, and leading them to go on diversion as well. These events then touched off a chain reaction that could throw an entire city into critical-care diversion, leaving emergency patients literally circling the city in ambulances. These events graphically illustrate how organizations coalescing into social enclaves can inadvertently isolate other organizations, plunging them into the vortex of hyperturbulence. In this grim example, social triage among organizations has cascaded down to produce medical triage among patients.

Proposition 9: The amalgamation of certain organizations into social enclaves fuels social vortices that threaten the survival of unaffiliated organizations.

In Phase 4 of our study, qualitative analyses probed the origins, functions, and transformations of regional health care provider networks. These collective structures appeared to represent a new organizational form emerging at a level between the organization and the industry. Our analyses suggest that, initially, the key functions of networks were pooling information and pursuing opportunities. However, as resource scarcities mounted, threats displaced opportunities and the networks began to function as enclaves. Indeed, some of our CEO informants expected these new collective forms to drive their organizational ancestors into extinction. One predicted that by the year 2000 no freestanding hospitals will be left in the Bay Area. Other executives, determined to preserve their hospitals' autonomy, resolved to continue adapting existing strategies and structures incrementally. The relative effectiveness of changes unfolding at these two levels of analysis may well determine the structure of the industry during the 1990s.

EPILOGUE: TAKING STOCK OF
RESEARCH PROCESSES AND PRODUCTS

This chapter has chronicled our study of organizations in a hyperturbulent industry. Our selection of "change" as a research problem and adoption of a longitudinal data-collection strategy led to unforeseen conceptual and methodological difficulties. Like the study, our account here has been more complex and fragmented than we intended initially. Therefore, in summing up we will try to synthesize our findings and speculations around three themes. First, we consider the nature of change in and around organizations. Second, we extract from our experiences some lessons about designing and conducting social science research. Third, we suggest some implications of our work for executive-level managers.

Implications for Theory:
The Nature of Organizational Change

While tracking a homogeneous set of organizations over a brief span of time, we observed a broad spectrum of changes. These changes varied both cross-sectionally and longitudinally in terms of rates, modes, and levels of analysis. Back in the library, however, it was a different story. Here, we were struck by how little attention organization theorists had devoted to differentiating change processes and specifying when, how, and why organizations in context undergo different types of change. Of particular note was the field's affinity for first-order change—adaptation models outnumbered metamorphosis models at the organization level; evolution models overshadowed revolution models at the population level. Perhaps this favoritism arises from

TABLE 11.3 First- and Second-Order Change Paradigms

Assumptions	First-Order Paradigm	Second-Order Paradigm
Equilibrium	Quasi-stationary equilibrium	Punctuated equilibrium
Primary mode of change	Incremental change	Quantum change
Temporal distribution of change	Continuous progression	Episodic bursts
Rates of change across levels	Slower at high levels of analysis	Faster at level of punctuation
Social system cohesion and constraint	Amalgam of weakly constrained components	Configuration of strongly constrained components
Origin of new organizational forms	Adaptation and/or selection	Speciation

tacit theories of change subsumed in paradigmatic constellations of assumptions, values, and taken-for-granted understandings.

Paradigms of Change

The first-order change paradigm summarized in Table 11.3 underpins most organization theory and research. Researchers usually assume quasi-stationary equilibrium conditions and focus primarily on incremental changes within organizations. Changes at all levels of analysis are seen as generally slow, steady, gradual, and continuous. Environments, however, are thought to change more slowly than organizations, organizations are thought to change more slowly than individual members, and the whole system is expected to change more slowly than an organization researcher's capacity for comprehending it. Organizations typically are viewed as loosely coupled aggregates whose separate components may be fine-tuned incrementally once weak constraints have been overcome. New forms of organizations are thought to evolve incrementally in response to new environmental conditions. Environmental discontinuities, according to some disciples of the first-order paradigm, are mere figments of observers' imaginations. Lenz and Engledow (1986), for instance, argue that environments actually change continuously, but observers' cognitive limits lead them to *experience* the changes as discontinuities. They speculate that "what executives reference as new competitive realities are probably new meanings assigned to continuous adjustments" (p. 343).

These first-order notions reinforce each other in subtle but powerful ways, and they fit Beyer's (1981) definition of an ideology—"relatively coherent sets of beliefs that bind some people together and explain their worlds to them in terms of cause and effect relations" (p. 166). Granted, organizational researchers do acknowledge cases where first-order change assumptions are violated. But researchers typically discount such cases, portraying them as unrepresentative settings, outlying organizations, or noisy data containing unexplained variance. The ideological status of the first-order paradigm may explain the ease with which exceptions to first-order change have been brushed aside.

The second-order paradigm in the right-hand column of Table 11.1 represents a different set of assumptions, ones that have entered the organization literature more recently. Those who embrace it expect alternation between disequilibrium and equilibrium, with quantum change punctuating periods of stability. Change is seen as highly episodic, largely because organizations are viewed as configurations of tightly coupled components. These linkages are pliable up to a point, but if stretched beyond that point, they actively prevent change. Adherents to the second-order paradigm expect substantially more organizational change to occur through rapid transformations between comparatively stable states than through incremental transition within those states. One result is that major transformations in organizational structure are expected to occur rapidly without a smooth series of intermediate stages. Another is that new organizational forms will emerge in rapid, episodic speciation events. The second-order paradigm ascribes no stable hierarchical ordering to rates of change. Since quantum changes can occur at multiple levels in social systems (Gersick 1991), changes unfolding within a particular individual, department, organization, or industry may temporarily outstrip rates of change at all other levels. As we discovered in our study, quantum changes in industry structure can outrun organization researchers' efforts to understand them.

Within the second-order paradigm, organizational metamorphoses and industry, revolutions are not regarded as mental events, outliers, or aberrations. Rather, they become natural by-products of routine processes. Stresses accumulate covertly during stable periods of first-order change, and they overturn the existing order when punctuated by second-order change. Extended periods of disequilibrium are likely to follow, sharply limiting the value of static analysis.

Multilevel Change

Our research underscores the multilevel nature of change processes. The study's initial design took the organization as its principal unit of analysis, but discontinuous changes led us to add two more inclusive units—the industry and the interorganizational network. At each of these levels, we observed discrete structures changing according to their own dynamics. At the organization level, top management teams formulated strategies intended to align hospitals with industry conditions. At the industry level, boundaries shifted and were breached as rivalry intensified. At the interorganizational level, "competitors" were drawn into networks of symbiotic relations that overlaid competitive relationships with collaborative and collusive ones. Although change processes at these different levels were distinct, our historical analysis (Phase 2), our time-series analysis (Phase 3), and our qualitative analyses (Phase 4) all suggest that events on one level strongly influenced events on other levels.

An implication is that industries' structures cannot be adequately described by aggregating attributes of individual organizations, and that organizations' actions cannot be inferred or understood solely through analyses of industry-level data. However, the temporally lagged and idiosyncratic character of these cross-level relationships makes them hard to discern unless longitudinal research designs are adopted. Our experience highlights the limitations of studying environmental change and organizational adaptation using survey methods in multi-industry samples. However, studying change at multiple levels over time may require a second-order change in organizational research methods, which Pettigrew (1987) describes as "ahistorical, aprocessual, and acontextual in character" (p. 655).

Most theories of change assume implicitly that organizational boundaries are distinct and remain intact throughout change processes. In times of revolutionary change, however, boundaries between organizations and their environments may become porous. In Kaufman's (1975) terms, organizational surfaces etherealize, permitting fluid exchange between organizations' interiors and their environments. In the aftermath of revolution, boundaries congeal, reducing exchange and increasing organizations' insularity. Moving up one level of analysis, our observations suggest that boundaries separating industries or populations of organizations also become permeable and mobile during periods of revolutionary change.

Our analyses indicate that organizations do not respond to their environments as independent, isolated actors. The hospitals we studied took collective action, and in so doing they shaped their future environments. Their collective interpretations and actions in a confusing milieu created the conditions they subsequently encountered. Intraindustry linkages superimposed cooperative relationships on competitive relationships and ushered in entirely new strategic options. Interindustry linkages joined diverse organizations in symbiotic relationships that helped lower and relocate industry boundaries. As resources grew scarcer, networks turned into social enclaves, and the collective action of members depleted resources available for nonmembers. Organizations are entangled in an ecology in which one competitor's actions help construct another competitor's environment. But since organizations are able to influence the context that influences them, they can play an active role in their own development.

Time-Dependent Change

Our research directs attention to the temporal ebb and flow of change processes across levels of analysis. The competitive and institutional pressures that environments impose vary over time, defining and altering niches for organizational populations. Our findings suggest that these pressures do not impinge on organizations continuously or shape them gradually. Tushman and Romanelli (1985) have argued that leaders have their most profound effects on organizations during major reorientations. Our study extends this line of argument to other potential influences on organizations at other levels of analysis. Technological and social change, for instance, appeared to affect hospitals' functioning most intensely during periods of discontinuous change, but these changes affected organizations indirectly, having their greatest influence at the industry level rather than at the organization level. If this observation generalizes, it may explain the inability of past research to demonstrate strong effects of technology, societal culture, and other exogenous conditions on organizational structure. We may have been searching for effects at the wrong level of analysis.

Implications for Research:
Turning Parameters Into Variables

As mentioned in the chapter's prologue, the research enterprise is traditionally partitioned into sequential stages: conceptualizing, designing, observing, analyzing, and reporting. During the conceptual and design stages, investigators are enjoined to make choices that remain in effect throughout the inquiry. They are directed, for instance, to spell out assumptions, identify theoretical models, select appropriate units and levels of analysis, specify independent and dependent variables, choose sampling frames, and so forth. During the subsequent stages of observation, analysis, and reporting, these choices become parameters. To change them on the fly could contaminate data or even be interpreted as scientific fraud. Stigmas attached to "post hoc theorizing," "data mining," and "dust-bowl empiricism" are handed down across generations of researchers. In short, researchers are indoctrinated to think first, then act.

But as our study progressed, one research design parameter after another slipped the shackles of experimental control and started behaving like a variable. Efforts to keep the sample of organizations intact, for example, were beleaguered by mergers, acquisitions, exits, and CEO turnovers. Sample attrition would have resulted not only in lost data, but also in nonresponse bias if organizations or informants who dropped out differed in analytically important ways. Consequently, we worked hard at maintaining friendly relations with CEOs; and, when successions occurred, we worked doubly hard to "reenter" by building rapport with the new CEO (who had no stake in the research and suspected, no doubt, that our study might be part of the mess he or she had been hired to clean up). Despite considerable effort, the study's organizations and informants varied over time in ways that introduced unknown biases. The lesson is that samples in longitudinal research always present a moving target. One implication is that researchers should treat organizations' beginnings, endings, alliances, amalgamations, and boundaries as variables rather than as parameters.

Other research principles were violated in our study as well. Using different theories to explain the same phenomenon occurring at different times was one transgression. In a sense, theoretical models took on the role of dependent variables in our study: "Are the relationships observed between Variable X and Variable Y during Wave 1 best explained by Theory A, Theory B, or Theory C? Which theory offers the best explanation during Waves 2, 3, and 4?" Another infraction arose from our practice of occasionally changing the operationalization of the variable "organizational performance" as industry restructuring altered the meaning of high performance. In effect, the question "What's your dependent variable?" became an *empirical* question, not a theoretical one. Moreover, we conceptualized the same fundamental processes at different levels of analysis over the course of the study. The principal locus of strategy formation, for instance, shifted between Wave 1 and Wave 4 from individual organizations, to expanding interorganizational networks, and finally up to the industry level, as discontinuous change made organization-level strategic planning pointless.

Much like our CEO informants, we found that the burst of changes punctuating the industry equilibrium created paradoxes and violated assumptions of the schemata we used to frame and interpret our worlds as social scientists. Like our informants, we were forced to act first and think later as we tried to discover the implications of our actions and the meaning of the data they had elicited. Researchers typically justify code-of-conduct violations such as these by labeling the enterprise as "exploratory" and attempting to "build grounded theory." Yet even this avenue was closed to us, since, as Karl Weick remarked in his role as consultant to this research project, "you can't build grounded theory while the ground is moving."

In sum, in the setting we studied, conventional research design parameters turned out to be among the most important empirical variables. It is a truism that you can only get answers to the questions you are asking. Perhaps questions about social systems in disequilibrium are not being asked simply because they violate current conceptions about rigorous methodology. Industries in flux make unappealing research settings. Like earthquake victims, researchers are inclined to run for cover, wait for the dust to settle, and then return cautiously to sift through the debris. But analyses of data collected at a single point in time can lead only to an account of stable structures.

It is conceivable that conventional research designs have camouflaged the fact that the most significant variation in organizations occurs over time rather than across organizations, and it stems from discontinuous changes that simultaneously affect entire populations or industries. If this conjecture is correct, and if the recent upsurge in discontinuous industry-level change persists, then organizational research could become increasingly irrelevant to organizational practice.

Implications for Managerial Practice: Change Isn't What It Used to Be

What are the practical implications of viewing change as a discontinuous, multilevel, time-dependent process? In certain respects, our study leads to clear managerial prescriptions.

Inculcate Shared Values

Shared values are intangible aspects of organizations that often escape notice. Members take them for granted, and outsiders seldom observe them. Yet members of the high-performing hospitals we studied share sets of explicit values about what their organizations are doing and why. Because shared values inspire commitment and elicit cooperation, they can take the place of elaborate organizational structures and formal control systems. During periods of first-order change, shared values function as internal gyroscopes to ensure self-control by members. During periods of second-order change, they supply reservoirs of goodwill that countenance unorthodox maneuvers. Our research on hospitals' responses to a disruptive doctors' strike (Meyer 1982) showed that those faring best had value systems that endorsed dispersed influence in decision making, frequent strategic changes, and responsiveness to environmental events. Such hospitals both anticipated the strike and used it as a stimulus for long-run improvement. But although values favoring responsiveness may help organizations adapt to transitory environmental jolts, adjusting to major discontinuities is likely to demand more vigorous action.

The Best Defense Is a Strong Offense

Performing effectively during tranquil periods of first-order change probably remains the best preparation for discontinuous periods of second-order change. Most industries will concurrently support different competitive strategies, so top managers have considerable latitude in conceiving a strategic configuration for their organization. Among the hospitals we studied, those having unique strategies mated with internally consistent organizational structures appeared not only to perform best while their environments were changing gradually but also to adjust to discontinuities with somewhat more aplomb. This advantage accrued both to consistently aligned defenders pursuing low-cost strategies and to consistently aligned prospectors pursuing differentiation strategies. It arose not from executing ingrained action programs, but from tapping accumulated stockpiles of slack resources. The lesson is that top managers should articulate clear strategies for their organizations, develop structures that support those strategies, inculcate harmonious values, and invest slack resources wisely.

But Don't Rest on Your Laurels

When industrywide revolutions come, shared values, slack resources, and lucid strategies merely buy time for organizations. These characteristics produced past successes, but in the face of changed environments they promote rigidity and complacency. Hard-won gains create resistance to change, and coherent values make abandoning ingrained responses difficult. Indeed, these are sensible organizational responses in normal circumstances, for as our time-series analyses of strategic reorientations suggest, high-performing organizations undertake such changes at considerable risk. However, discontinuities are abnormal circumstances, and managers encountering them must invent ways to slip the bonds of tradition, precedence, and past practice. This is not to say that executives experiencing industry revolutions should always initiate strategic reorientations. The considerable costs and risks attendant to organizational metamorphoses are magnified by industry revolutions. Executives should first consider updating existing strategies to fit new demands of postrevolutionary environments. In some cases this may be accomplished through unilateral organizational adaptation, but, as suggested below, it more often will involve multilateral collective action.

Prepare for Paradoxical Pressures

The discontinuous industry-level change we studied placed paradoxical demands on organizations. When the dust settled, the restructured health care industry contained much stronger incentives for cost-effective delivery of health services. This aspect of the change clearly favored habitually efficient, cost-conscious defender hospitals. Unfortunately, many defenders lacked the prowess in environmental scanning and interpretation needed to envision a new strategy for cutting costs in the radically changed industry, as well as the capacity for restructuring swiftly to implement an up-to-date defender strategy. As a result, defenders' responses often were too little, too late. Ironically, many defenders languished, locked into obsolete approaches in pursuit of an increasingly valued objective.

On the other hand, the velocity and extent of the discontinuity called for rapid and bold responses. This aspect of the industry revolution clearly favored habitually innovative prospector hospitals. But although prospectors' extensive environmental surveillance mechanisms forewarned them, and their entrepreneurial values encouraged bold responses, prospectors' lack of experience in efficient operations left them ill equipped to implement cost-control policies. As a result, prospectors' responses often were well conceived and comprehensive, but, lacking experience, skills, or values promoting cost-effectiveness, their responses were unsuccessful. Prospectors rarely store slack in financial form, preferring to invest it in human resources and state-of-the-art technologies (Meyer 1982). Consequently, although some prospectors progressed rapidly down the efficiency learning curve, their financial reserves were consumed faster.

Due to paradoxical demands of this sort, we believe that the most promising responses to discontinuous changes are those that combine disaggregation and collective action.

Disaggregate and Affiliate

Fixed costs reduce organizational flexibility. As resource scarcities mounted in the hospital industry, many executives in our sample retrenched to their core businesses by stripping away nonessential activities and divesting unrelated ventures. Although these actions were motivated by financial exigencies, in many cases they yielded unexpected gains in flexibility and human resources. The flexibility came from cutting fixed costs and contracting or venturing for services previously offered in-house. The human resources became available when divestment released what often turned out to be a hospital's highest-caliber managers from their preoccupation with unrelated ventures.

However, realizing the full potential of divestiture and disaggregation seemed to require coupling these activities with collective action. As we have noted, this involved a variety of cooperative linkages with suppliers, insurers, entrepreneurs, and competitors. The most appropriate pattern of collective action seemed to depend on a hospital's prior competitive strategy. Prospector hospitals, for example, often took the lead in brokering regional networks. Their networks were usually built around the concept of a "continuum of care," defined as a system linking primary, acute, and post-acute health services with some financing mechanism. Defender hospitals, on the other hand, were more likely to serve as low-cost producer nodes in a network, with executive talent, contracting expertise, information systems, and other services supplied from elsewhere in the system.

Industries undergoing revolutionary change pose dilemmas for managers. Revolutions create entrepreneurial opportunities by redefining potential niches and opening ecological space for new strategies and structural forms. Nevertheless, discontinuous change is enigmatic and paradoxical for managers. How can one prepare for conditions that are by definition unforeseeable? The events triggering discontinuous changes can appear so inconsequential, and the onset can be so sudden, that managers are forced to act before they understand the consequences of acting. But even in the throes of revolutionary change, astute managers can recognize and seize the opportunity to revitalize their organizations and reshape their environments. In the final analysis, we cannot predict the future—we can only invent it.

Appendix: Data-Collection and Analysis Methods

Retrospective Overview: Using Historical Methods

A data-based approach was used to reconstruct the research chronology and reduce self-serving biases. First, all available artifacts produced by the research were assembled. These included proposals, progress reports to the funding agency, pages from research notebooks, agendas of research team meetings, memos and letters exchanged by team members, electronic mail messages, methodological notes, raw data from interviews, handwritten field notes, hundreds of newspaper articles provided by a clipping service, working papers, and journal submissions. These documents were sorted into three categories: conceptual frameworks, research methods, and empirical findings. Documents were arranged in chronological order. Content analyses of these data were used in constructing the timeline in Figure 11.1 and in writing up the study's four phases.

Phase 1: Adapting Toward Equilibrium

Quasi-Experimental Research Design

Of the 55 medical-surgical hospitals in the four counties contiguous to San Francisco Bay, 40 were selected randomly and their CEOs' participation was solicited; 30 agreed to participate. Health care experts were impaneled to identify important environmental changes as these occurred over the course of the study.

Data were collected using multiple methods, with observations scheduled as shown in Figure 11A.1. During Wave 1, data on organizational antecedents (strategies, structure, ideology, and slack) were collected, as were measures of past performance and control variables. In Wave 2, hospitals' responses to subsequent environmental changes

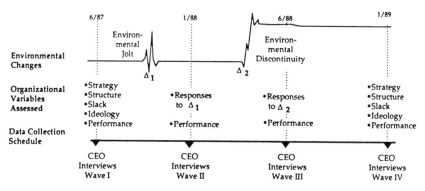

Figure 11A.1. A Quasi-Experimental Research Design

(the experimental treatments identified by the expert panel) were to be measured and performance was to be assessed. In Waves 3 and 4, responses and performances would again be measured. Organizational strategy, structure, ideology, and slack were to be measured in Wave 4. However, when discontinuous industrywide change invalidated this research design, it was abandoned.

Field Interview Methods

Interview procedures were as follows. During each three-week data-collection wave, structured interviews were conducted with CEOs about changes in organization design, strategy, environment, and performance. Most interviews were face-to-face in the CEOs' offices (55%); others were conducted via telephone conference calls (45%). Two researchers were present at each interview. Interviews were transcribed as near verbatim as possible, and transcripts were cross-checked. More than 1,500 pages of transcripts were produced.

Mapping Evolving Environments

Techniques for collecting "visual data" were developed to tap CEOs' capacities for making sense of discontinuous changes. This technique is useful when informants possess more complex cognitive maps than they can verbalize (Meyer 1991). A generic diagram of the industry environment was constructed to show both the traditional domain of medical-surgical hospitals and adjacent domains offering new sources of competitive threats and opportunities. Three sectors were represented: (1) *providers,* the set of hospitals competing to supply acute care in the local market; (2) *insurance plans,* the set of patient groups amalgamated by some form of insurance plan; and (3) *diversifications,* the set of pre/post acute-care products and services into which hospitals potentially could diversify. Figure 11A.2 shows the visual instrument used to allow CEOs to map their hospitals' positions in the industry. The three sectors were depicted as planes floating in three-dimensional space, with different

342

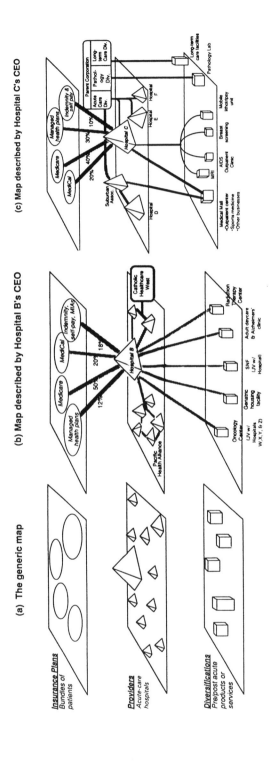

Figure 11A.2. Computer-Generated Maps of Industry Environments

SOURCE: From "Visual Data in Organizational Research," by Alan D. Meyer. *Organization Science*, 2 (May 1991). Copyright © 1991 The Institute of Management Sciences, 290 Westminster Street, Providence, RI 02903.

icons representing elements within each sector. Part a of the figure shows the generic map as presented to all CEOs; parts b and c show how this generic map was revised to show the unique positions described by two CEOs during Wave 1 interviews. Shifts in each hospital's position in the industry over time were charted by asking CEOs to update their latest map during Waves 2, 3, and 4.

Phase 2: Industries in Disequilibrium

Our historical analysis of the California hospital industry in the 1960s, 1970s, and 1980s drew on three types of data: (1) archival data from published sources, such as journalistic reports, newsletters of industry trade associations, and reports compiled by state and local governments; (2) time-series data obtained from the California Office of Statewide Health Planning and Development, the American Hospital Association, and the Northern California Hospital Council; and (3) two primary data sets containing transcripts of structured interviews with industry experts and hospital CEOs, questionnaires, and naturalistic observations (Meyer 1982, Meyer, Brooks, and Goes 1990).

Phase 3: Metamorphosis
Through Strategic Reorientation

We obtained highly detailed time-series data on medical-surgical hospitals collected by the state of California. Covering a period of 11 years (calendar years 1976-1987), these data were uniquely suited to our Phase 3 objectives.

Sample

The sample consisted of all acute-care general surgical hospitals in the state of California, excluding those administered by the Kaiser Foundation. Kaiser hospitals were omitted due to incomplete data at the organization level. The sample size ranged from 443 to 457 hospitals over the study period.

Variables

Table 11A.1 lists variables used to tap three dimensions of organizational strategy: product/market domain, competitive methods, and organizational resources. Variables were selected based on widespread use in the industry and prior research, and for their demonstrated ability to discriminate among strategic configurations. Performance was conceptualized in two ways. The first reflected a hospital's performance relative to peer organizations (cross-sectionally), and the second reflected change in performance within the focal organization over time (longitudinally). Based on prior research (Dess and Davis 1984, Venkatraman and Ramanujam 1986, Smith and Grimm 1987), we used three operationalizations: profitability, efficiency, and growth. Table 11A.1 lists the different performance indicators used: relative profitability, relative efficiency, and relative growth, along with change in profitability,

TABLE 11A.1 Strategy and Performance Variables

Dimension	Variable	Operational Definition
Product/market domain	Service diversity (SERVDIFF)	Scope of medical services provided
	Service concentration (SERVCON)	Average depth of medical services
	Service volume (VOLUME)	Gross patient revenues/bed
	Market demographics (MCARINT/MCALINT)	Ratio of medicare/mediCal patient revenues to gross patient revenues
Competitive methods	Advertising/promotion (ADSALES)	Advertising/gross patient revenues
	Marketing innovation (OUTPMIX)	Outpatient revenues/gross patient revenues
	Efficiency focus (EFFIC)	General services expenditures/gross patient revenues
	Research/development (RESEARCH)	Research expenditures/gross patient revenues
	Service innovation (NEWSERV)	Annual development of new services
Organizational resources	Size (LOGBEDS)	Log of acute care beds
	Staff diversity (STAFFDIV)	Number of different medical specialties
	Education/training (EDUCATE)	Education expenditures/gross patient revenues
	Administrative ratio (ADMRATIO)	Administrative payroll/total payroll
Performance	Profitability	Operating margin
		Profit margin
		Return on assets
	Efficiency	Average daily occupancy
		Fixed assets per patient day
		Average length of stay
	Growth	Annual growth in licensed beds
		Annual growth in patient days
		Annual growth in net revenues

change in efficiency, and change in growth. Three lags were computed for each performance indicator.

Measuring Strategic Reorientations

We used a two-step method for identifying strategic configurations and tracking changes between them. First, strategy measures were factor analyzed following Gal-

TABLE 11A.2 Count of Variables Loading on Four Strategy Dimensions Over Time

Factor			
No.	Title	Variables Loading at ≥ .4	Years[a]
1	Integrated defense	Service concentration	11
		Service volume	11
		Size	11
		Staff diversity	11
		Education/training	11
		Administrative ratio	(–)11
		Research and development	7
		Service differentiation	3
		Marketing innovation	(–)2
2	Low margin defense	Market demographics	(–)11
		Marketing innovation	11
		Education/training	10
		Efficiency focus	5
		Service differentiation	1
3	Service promotion	Advertising/promotion	11
		Efficiency focus	7
		Research and development	5
		Service concentration	(–)1
		Staff diversity	1
		Administrative ratio	1
4	Service differentiation	Service innovation	10
		Service differentiation	9
		Service concentration	(–)2
		Research and development	2
		Efficiency focus	1
		Staff diversity	1
		Education/training	1

a. Number of years in which the variable exhibited a substantial loading (≥.4) on the factor. Minus signs (–) signify negative loadings.

braith and Schendel (1983) and Dess and Davis (1984). Eleven common factor analyses (one for each data year) were conducted, and a four-factor solution was determined to be superior across all 11 years. This yielded a set of four strategic dimensions (factors) that explained the greatest variance among hospitals in the sample. Factor selection and identification were based on prior theoretical expectations, overall interpretability, and various diagnostic statistics (see Table 11A.2 for a count of strategy variables loading on factors over time).

The second step used cluster analysis to generate strategic configurations. Organizations were clustered into groups on the basis of their relative emphasis on the four strategic dimensions, as indicated by factor scores. A series of k-means iterative cluster analyses (Hartigan 1975) were conducted over the 11-year period, and a five-cluster solution was selected based on prior theoretical expectations, interpretability,

and diagnostic statistics. Each organization was thereby classified into a single configuration (cluster) for each year. Miles and Snow's and Porter's strategy typologies
were used as general templates for identifying and labeling strategic configurations.
For a complete discussion of factor and cluster characteristics, interpretations, and
procedures, see Goes (1989).

By definition, a move from one cluster to another over time represented a strategic
reorientation. However, underlying strategies are unlikely to change on an annual
basis (Miller and Friesen 1984, Greenwood and Hinings 1988). Consequently, a
conservative approach was adopted: If a hospital was classified into one cluster for
two or more years, and subsequently classified into a different cluster for two or
more years, a strategic reorientation was coded for the year of transition between
clusters. This mitigated the problem of an organization's falling near the boundary
separating two clusters and cycling back and forth. As a result of this coding scheme,
no strategic changes could occur in data years 1, 2, or 11.

The unit of analysis was a strategic reorientation or, more precisely, an "opportunity"
for a strategic reorientation. In any given data year each hospital had an opportunity to
change or not change its strategic configuration. Over the entire study, therefore, the sum
of potential strategic reorientations (i.e., the sum of opportunities) equaled the sum of
opportunities in each year pooled across eight years of potential change.

Hypothesis Testing

Hypothesis 1 was tested using discriminant analyses to assess the extent to which
prior performance (lagged 0, 1, 2, and 3 years) predicted hospitals' membership in
reorientation and nonreorientation groups. Hypotheses 2 and 3 were tested using
single-factor ANOVA to assess performance differences (lagged 0-4 years out) between low and high performers that did or did not reorient their strategies. Hypotheses 4 and 5 were tested using frequency analyses, cross-tabulation analyses, and
ANOVA.

Phase 4: Responding Collectively to Industry Revolution

Assessing Collective Action

In Wave 2, we expanded the research design to obtain data from regional network
brokers and CEOs of affiliated hospitals. Open-ended interviews were conducted
with representatives of seven networks during Waves 2-4. Questions about collective
actions and their consequences were added to interviews with hospital CEOs. Data
from questionnaires, archives, and documents were also obtained.

Identifying Temporal Changes

Upon leaving the field after each wave, we reviewed our notes, identified changes
in CEOs' environmental "maps," met to discuss key issues and concerns voiced by
informants, and created tabular displays showing common themes characterizing the

sample at that time. Each display suggested an interpretation of the industry that differed from previous interpretations. To elaborate and verify these temporal differences, we content analyzed interview transcripts according to the four analytic categories shown in Table 11.2.

Acknowledgments

The CEOs of 30 hospitals each participated in our field interviews and completed three lengthy questionnaires for this study. We thank them for their cordiality, patience, and invaluable assistance. We also are indebted to Raymond Miles for his advice in research design; to Arie Lewin, Peter Monge, John Slocum, Andrew Van de Ven, and Karl Weick for consultation throughout the project; and to William Glick, George Huber, Reuben McDaniel, Steve Shortell, and Ray Zammuto for their constructive comments on earlier drafts.

Notes

1. The authors of this summary are George P. Huber and William H. Glick, editors of the volume in which this chapter first appeared, *Organizational Change and Redesign: Ideas and Insights for Improving Performance.*

2. As with any retrospective reconstruction, there is a risk that logic, order, and rationality will be attributed post hoc to haphazard events. To guard against such biasing, we used the data-based approach described in the appendix to this chapter to identify and verify the phases and activities shown in Figure 11.1.

3. This section draws on Alan D. Meyer, Geoffrey R. Brooks, and James B. Goes, "Environmental Jolts and Industry Revolutions: Organizational Responses to Discontinuous Change," *Strategic Management Journal,* 11 (Summer): 93-110. © 1990 by John Wiley & Sons, Ltd.

4. McKelvey (1982) notes that the locus of an organizational population's boundaries depends on both conceptual and empirical issues (e.g., the specific research question being addressed and the particular organizations under investigation). For the purposes of our general discussion, the terms *population* and *industry* are used interchangeably to refer to a relevant set of competing organizations.

5. Although the population-level analyses conducted by Hannan and Freeman have attracted the largest share of attention, it should be noted that the population is one of several possible levels in the ecological analysis of organizations. Carroll (1984) terms this larger domain *organizational ecology* and argues that it includes analyses conducted at a lower level focusing on developmental changes within individual organizations (*organizational demography*), as well as analyses conducted at a higher level focusing on interactions between multiple populations (*community ecology*).

6. "General Hospital" is a fictitious name given to one of the hospitals in our research sample. Certain characteristics have been disguised to protect informants' anonymity.

7. We thank Reuben McDaniel for suggesting this notion.

8. The characteristics of these two dimensions are briefly summarized in the appendix to this chapter. For a complete discussion of the characteristics and interpretations of the four strategic dimensions, see Goes (1989).

9. For example, advances in outpatient surgery lower barriers separating acute care, primary care, and group medical practice; ultraexpensive diagnostic and treatment technologies, such as magnetic resonance imaging and mobile lithotripsy, encourage nonmedical entrepreneurs to enter medical services markets.

References

Aldrich, H., and D. A. Whetten (1981), "Organization-Sets, Action-Sets, and Networks: Making the Most of Simplicity," in P. Nystrom and W. H. Starbuck (Eds.), *Handbook of Organizational Design* (pp. 385-408), New York: Oxford University Press.

Anderson, P., and M. L. Tushman (1990), "Technological Discontinuities and Dominant Designs: A Cyclical Model of Technological Change, *Administrative Science Quarterly,* 35, 604-633.

Astley, W. G. (1985), "The Two Ecologies: Population and Community Perspectives on Organization Evolution," *Administrative Science Quarterly,* 30, 224-241.

Astley, W. G., and A. H. Van de Ven (1983), "Central Perspectives and Debates in Organization Theory," *Administrative Science Quarterly,* 28, 245-273.

Barley, S. R., and P. S. Tolbert (1988), "Institutionalization as Structuration: Methods and Analytic Strategies for Studying Links Between Action and Structure," paper presented at the National Science Foundation Conference on Longitudinal Field Research Methods for Studying Organizational Processes, Austin, TX, September.

Barney, J. B. (1986), "Types of Competition and the Theory of Strategy: Toward an Integrative Framework," *Academy of Management Review,* 11, 791-800.

Bedeian, A. G., and R. F. Zammuto (1991), *Organizations: Theory and Design,* Chicago: Dryden.

Beyer, J. M. (1981), "Ideologies, Values and Decision Making in Organizations," in P. C. Nystrom and W. H. Starbuck (Eds), *Handbook of Organizational Design* (pp. 166-202), New York: Oxford University Press.

Carroll, G. R. (1984), "Organizational ecology," *American Review of Sociology,* 10, 71-93.

Chandler, A. D. (1990), *Scale and Scope: The Dynamics of Industrial Capitalism,* Cambridge, MA: Belknap.

Child, J. (1972), "Organizational Structure, Environment, and Performance: The Role of Strategic Choice," *Sociology,* 6, 2-22.

Dess, G., and P. Davis (1984), "Porter's (1980) Generic Strategies as Determinants of Strategic Group Membership and Organizational Performance," *Academy of Management Journal,* 27, 467-488.

DiMaggio, P. J., and W. W. Powell (1983), "The Iron Case Revisited: Institutional Isomorphism and Collective Rationality in Organizational Fields," *American Sociological Review,* 48, 147-160.

Eisenhardt, K. M. (1989), "Building Theories From Case Study Research," *Academy of Management Review,* 14, 532-550.

Emery, F. E., and E. L. Trist (1965), "The Causal Texture of Organizational Environments," *Human Relations,* 18, 21-32.

Galbraith, C., and D. Schendel (1983), "An Empirical Analysis of Strategy Types," *Strategic Management Journal,* 4, 153-173.

Gersick, C. (1991), "Revolutionary Change Theories: A Multilevel Exploration of the Punctuated Equilibrium Paradigm," *Academy of Management Review,* 16, 10-36.

Ginsberg, A. (1988), "Measuring and Modeling Changes in Strategy: Theoretical Foundations and Empirical Directions," *Strategic Management Journal,* 9, 559-575.

Goes, J. B. (1989), "Strategic Change and Organizational Performance: A Longitudinal Study of California Hospitals," doctoral dissertation, University of Oregon.

Gould, S. J., and N. Eldredge (1977), "Punctuated Equilibria: The Tempo and Mode of Evolution Reconsidered," *Paleobiology,* 3, 115-151.

Greenwood, R., and C. R. Hinings (1988), "Organizational Design Types, Tracks, and the Dynamics of Strategic Change," *Organization Studies,* 9, 293-316.

Greiner, L. E. (1972), "Evolution and Revolution as Organizations Grow," *Harvard Business Review,* 50, 4, 37-46.

Hannan, M. T., and J. Freeman (1977), "The Population Ecology of Organizations," *American Journal of Sociology,* 83, 929-964.

Hannan, M. T., and J. Freeman (1984), "Structural Inertia and Organizational Change," *American Sociological Review,* 49, 149-164.

Hartigan, J. A. (1975), *Clustering Algorithms,* New York: Wiley.

Hawley, A. (1950), *Human Ecology: A Theory of Community Structure,* New York: Ronald.

Kaufman, H. (1975), "The Natural History of Organizations," *Administration and Society,* 7, 131-149.

Kimberly, J. R., and R. H. Miles (1980), *The Organization Life Cycle,* San Francisco: Jossey-Bass.

Lenz, R. T., and J. L. Engledow (1986), "Environmental Analysis: The Applicability of Current Theory," *Strategic Management Journal,* 7, 329-346.

Lindblom, C. E. (1959), "The 'Science' of Muddling Through," *Public Administration Review,* 19, 79-88.

March, J. G. (1981), "Footnotes to Organizational Change," *Administrative Science Quarterly,* 26, 563-577.

McCann, J. E., and J. Selsky (1984), "Hyperturbulence and the Emergence of Type 5 Environments," *Academy of Management Review,* 9, 460-470.

McKelvey, W. (1982), *Organizational Systematics: Taxonomy, Evolution and Classification,* Berkeley: University of California Press.

McKelvey, W., and H. Aldrich (1983), "Populations, Natural Selection and Applied Organizational Science," *Administrative Science Quarterly,* 28, 101-128.

Meyer, A. D. (1982), "Adapting to Environmental Jolts," *Administrative Science Quarterly,* 27, 515-537.

Meyer, A. D. (1991), "Visual Data in Organizational Research," *Organization Science,* 2, 218-236.

Meyer, A. D., G. R. Brooks, and J. B. Goes (1990), "Environmental Jolts and Industry Revolutions: Organizational Responses to Discontinuous Change," *Strategic Management Journal,* 11 (Summer), 93-110.

Meyer, A. D., and W. H. Starbuck (1993), "Interactions Between Politics and Ideology in Strategy Formation," in K. Roberts (Ed.), *New Challenges to Understanding Organizations: High Reliability Organizations* (pp. 99-116), Beverly Hills, CA: McMillan.

Meyer, J. W., and B. Rowan (1977), "Institutionalized Organizations: Formal Structure as Myth and Ceremony," *American Journal of Sociology,* 83, 340-363.

Miles, R. E., and C. C. Snow (1978), *Organizational Strategy, Structure, and Process,* New York: McGraw-Hill.

Miles, R. E., and C. C. Snow (1986), "Organizations: New Concepts for New Forms," *California Management Review,* 28, 3, 62-73.

Miller, D., and P. H. Friesen (1984), *Organizations: A Quantum View,* Englewood Cliffs, NJ: Prentice Hall.

Perrow, C. (1965), "Hospitals: Technology, Goals and Structure," in J. March (Ed.), *Handbook of Organizations* (pp. 910-971), Chicago: Rand McNally.

Peters, T. J., and R. H. Waterman (1982), *In Search of Excellence: Lessons From America's Best-Run Companies,* New York: Harper & Row.

Pettigrew, A. M. (1987), "Context and Action in the Transformation of the Firm," *Journal of Management Studies,* 24, 649-670.

Pfeffer, J., and G. R. Salancik (1978), *The External Control of Organizations,* New York: Harper & Row.

Schumpeter, J. A. (1950), *Capitalism, Socialism and Democracy,* New York: Harper & Row.

Scott, W. R. (1987), *Organizations: Rational, Natural and Open Systems* (2nd ed.), Englewood Cliffs, NJ: Prentice Hall.

Shortell, S. M., E. M. Morrison, and B. Friedman (1990), *Strategic Choices for America's Hospitals,* San Francisco: Jossey-Bass.

Smith, K. G., and C. M. Grimm (1987), "Environmental Variation, Strategic Change and Firm Performance," *Strategic Management Journal,* 8, 363-376.

Starbuck, W. H. (1983), "Organizations as Action Generators," *American Sociological Review,* 48, 91-102.

Thompson, J. D. (1967), *Organizations in Action: Social Science Bases of Administrative Theory,* New York: McGraw-Hill.

Tushman, M. L., and E. Romanelli (1985), "Organizational Evolution: A Metamorphosis Model of Convergence and Reorientation," in L. L. Cummings and B. M. Staw (Eds.), *Research in Organizational Behavior* (Vol. 7, pp. 171-222), Greenwich, CT: JAI.

Van de Ven, A. H. (1993), "Managing the Process of Organizational Innovation," in G. P. Huber and W. H. Glick (Eds.), *Organizational Change and Redesign: Ideas and Insights for Improving Performance* (pp. 269-294). New York: Oxford University Press.

Van de Ven, A. H., and R. Garud (1987), "A Framework for Understanding the Emergence of New Industries," in R. Rosenbloom and R. Burgelman (Eds.), *Research on Technological Innovation, Management and Policy* (Vol. 4, pp. 195-225), Greenwich, CT: JAI.

Venkatraman, N., and V. Ramanujam (1986), "Measurement of Business Performance in Strategy Research: A Comparison of Approaches," *Academy of Management Review,* 11, 801-814.

Watzlawick, P., J. H. Weakland, and R. Fisch (1974), *Change: Principles of Problem Formation and Problem Resolution,* New York: Norton.

Weick, K. E. (1979), *The Social Psychology of Organizing,* Reading, MA: Addison-Wesley.

Zajac, E. J., and S. M. Shortell (1989), "Changing Generic Strategies: Likelihood, Direction, and Performance Implications," *Strategic Management Journal,* 10, 413-430.

Zucker, L. G. (1987), "Institutional Theories of Organizations," *Annual Review of Sociology,* 13, 443-464.

Index

351

About the Editors

George P. Huber is the Charles and Elizabeth Prothro Regents Chair in Business Administration and Associate Dean for Research of the Graduate School of Business at the University of Texas at Austin. He received his B.S.M.E. and M.S.I.E. degrees from the University of Missouri and his Ph.D. from Purdue University. He has previously held full-time positions with the Emerson Electric Manufacturing Company, the Procter & Gamble Manufacturing Company, the U.S. Department of Labor, Execucom Systems Corporation, and the Universities of California and Wisconsin. He has also served as a consultant to many corporations and public agencies. His current research focuses on organizational change, organizational design, and organizational decision making. He has also conducted research in the areas of information technology and individual and group decision making. His pioneering article "The Nature and Design of Post-Industrial Organizations" was awarded First Prize in the International Prize Competition sponsored by the Institute of Management Sciences in 1983. His coauthored article "Fit, Equifinality, and Organizational Effectiveness: A Test of Two Configurational Theories" was selected as the Best Article of the Year in the *Academy of Management Journal* for 1993. He is coeditor, with William H. Glick, of *Organizational Change and Redesign: Ideas and Insights for Improving Performance.* He is a Fellow of the Academy of Management and of the Decision Sciences Institute.

Andrew H. Van de Ven is Vernon H. Heath Professor of Organizational Innovation and Change in the Carlson School of Management of the University of Minnesota. He received his Ph.D. from the University of Wisconsin at Madison in 1972, and taught at Kent State University (1972-1975) and the Wharton School of the University of Pennsylvania (1975-1981) before his present appointment. He teaches courses in the Carlson School on theory building and research design, macroorganizational behavior, and organizational innovation and change. He also directs the Minnesota Innovation Research Program in the Strategic Management Research Center. Since 1983, this program has been conducting longitudinal studies of how a wide variety of innovations develop from concept to implementation in organizations. The research has been supported with $1.7 million through 16 grants and contracts from the Office of Naval Research, the National Science Foundation, and other organizations. In addition to his publications dealing with organizational innovation and change, his books and journal articles over the years have dealt with the nominal group technique, the program planning model, the Organization Assessment Framework and Instruments, interorganizational relationships, and methods for building theories and designing research studies. He is senior editor of *Organization Science* (since 1989), has served on the editorial boards of various journals, such as the *Academy of Management Journal* and *Review,* and is a section editor for the Sage Publications book series Foundations for Organizational Science. An active member of the Academy of Management for more than 20 years, he has been elected an officer of the Organization and Management Theory Division (1979-1982), a representative on the Board of Governors (1982-1984), and a Fellow of the Academy of Management (1988).

About the Contributors

Andrew Abbott is Professor of Sociology at the University of Chicago. His work addresses the theoretical and methodological issues of analyzing temporality in social processes. He has conducted empirical analyses of careers, stories, policies, and other "narratively structured" social data. He has adapted a variety of sequence-analytic methods from biology and computer science for social science applications. Substantively, his work focuses on occupations and professions.

Stephen R. Barley is Associate Professor of Industrial Engineering and Engineering Management at Stanford University's School of Engineering. Previously, he served for 10 years on the faculty of Cornell University's School of Industrial and Labor Relations. He holds a Ph.D. in organization studies from the Massachusetts Institute of Technology. He is the editor of *Administrative Science Quarterly,* and he has written extensively on the ramifications of new technologies on work, the social organization of the technical labor force, and organizational culture. He is currently writing a book on the role of technicians in modern organizations titled *The New Crafts,* and has just finished an edited volume of original essays on technical work titled *Between Technology and Society: Technical Work in the Emerging Economy.*

Geoffrey R. Brooks is Assistant Professor of Management at the Wharton School of the University of Pennsylvania. His current research focuses on how organizations interact with and shape their environments. His recent work has dealt with the definition of markets and industries and the relationships between market conditions and the occurrence and consequences of hospital mergers.

D. Harold Doty is Assistant Professor in the Department of Management at the University of Arkansas, Fayetteville. He received his Ph.D. in management from the University of Texas at Austin. His research has appeared in such journals as *Organization Science, Academy of Management Journal,* and the *Academy of Management Review.* His current research interests focus on configurational theories of organizations; business unit structure, strategy, and effectiveness; and the use of human resource systems to further organizational, strategic, and performance goals.

Kathleen M. Eisenhardt (Ph.D., Stanford University) is Associate Professor of Strategy and Organizations at Stanford University. Her research interests center on the management of firms in fast-paced markets and include strategic decision making, entrepreneurship, and evolutionary processes, using inductive, theory-building, and hypothesis-testing methods. She is currently studying strategic alliance formation in the semiconductor industry, product innovation in the computer industry, and the evolutionary dynamics of global firms. Her work has appeared in numerous managerial and academic journals, and she has received the Pacific Telesis Foundation Award for her work on fast decision making. Her recent research on the dynamics of multinational firms (with D. Charles Galunic) received the Whittemore Prize for Outstanding Research on Hypercompetition. She currently serves as co-principal investigator for the Stanford Computer Industry Project.

William H. Glick is Associate Professor of Management of the University of Texas at Austin. He received his Ph.D. from the University of California at Berkeley (1981). His main research has been in the areas of job and organization design and business process redesign. His most recent work on organization design includes an edited book with George Huber, *Organizational Change and Redesign: Ideas and Insights for Improving Performance* (1993) and the article "Fit, Equifinality, and Organizational Effectiveness: A Test of Two Configurational Theories," with D. Harold Doty and George Huber, which won the award for the Best Article in the 1993 *Academy of Management Journal* from the Academy of Management.

James B. Goes is Associate Professor of Management in the School of Business and Public Administration at the University of Alaska Southeast. He previously served on the faculties of the University of Minnesota and Montana State University. He holds a Ph.D. in strategic management from the University of Oregon. His research focuses on major change processes and innovation in organizations, and has been published in the *Academy of Management Journal, Strategic Management Journal,* and *Health Services Research.* He is currently working on an evaluation of Alaska's product preference program and an advanced program for business professors from the Russian Far East.

Dorothy Leonard-Barton is William J. Abernathy Professor of Business Administration at the Harvard Business School, where she has taught in M.B.A. and executive education programs since 1983. She received her Ph.D. from Stanford University. Previously, she was on the faculty of the MIT Sloan School. She conducts research on and consults about new technology commercialization, new product development, and the transfer of knowledge across geographic, cultural, and cognitive boundaries. She has published more than two dozen articles based on field research in academic journals such as *Organization Science.* Her most recent publication, *Wellsprings of Knowledge,* describes and illustrates the managerial activities that sustain innovation and enhance strategic technological capabilities.

Robert D. McPhee is Associate Professor of Communication at the University of Wisconsin—Milwaukee. His focal interests include organizational communication and communication/social theory. He has recently served as Chair of the Organizational Communication Division of the Speech Communication Association, and as associate editor (overseeing organizational communication manuscripts) of *Human Communication Research.* Two of his recent publications, which appeared in *Communication Monographs,* concern the evolution of climate themes in a governmental organization and the determinants of a communication network in a local church.

Alan D. Meyer is the Edwin E. and June Woldt Cone Professor of Management at the University of Oregon. He received his doctorate in organizational behavior and industrial relations from the University of California, Berkeley. He likes using multiple research methods and collecting data by talking with informants on their own turf. He is interested in organizational behavior away from equilibrium, and is currently studying the impacts of quantum changes in the structure and boundaries of the health care, electric utility, and savings and loan industries. He is senior editor of organization theory and design for *Organization Science* and a former consulting editor for the *Academy of Management Journal.* Before entering academia, he worked as an industrial engineer, a market researcher, and a ski instructor.

C. Chet Miller is on the faculty of the Hankamer School of Business, Baylor University. He received his doctoral degree at the University of Texas at

Austin. His current research interests center on organizational design, strategic decision processes, and diversity within upper-echelon executive groups. His previous publications on these topics have appeared in the *Academy of Management Journal, Organization Science,* and as book chapters. In 1992, he was awarded the Outstanding Young Researcher Award by the Hankamer School of Business.

Peter R. Monge is Professor of Communication at the Annenberg School for Communication, University of Southern California. He is former editor of *Communication Research* and the Academic Press Series on Human Communication. His research interests lie in the areas of collaborative communication technologies and communication networks, with particular focus on dynamic systems and longitudinal research.

Andrew M. Pettigrew is Professor of Organisational Behaviour and Director of the Centre for Corporate Strategy and Change, Warwick Business School, University of Warwick. His published research includes studies of organizational politics and decision making, organizational culture, strategic change processes in organizations, and the study of managerial elites. He is the author or coauthor of 10 books and many scholarly articles.

Marshall Scott Poole (Ph.D., University of Wisconsin, 1980) is Professor of Speech-Communication at Texas A&M University. His research interests include group and organizational communication, information technology, conflict management, organizational innovation, and process research methods. He has published more than 70 articles and chapters, and his coauthored or edited books include *Communication and Group Decision-Making, Working Through Conflict,* and *Research on the Management of Innovation.* He is one of the principal developers of the computerized meeting support system Software Aided Meeting Management (SAMM) and is currently working on a Windows-based group support environment. He has consulted for 20 years on organizational communication, teamwork, conflict management, innovation, and computerized communication technologies.

Daniel Robey is Professor of Information Systems at Florida International University. He earned his doctorate in 1973 from Kent State University, and he has served on the faculties of the University of Pittsburgh, Marquette University, Gannon University, and the Copenhagen School of Economics and Business Administration. He is currently an associate editor for *Management Science* and serves on the editorial boards of *Information Systems Research, Organization Science,* and *Accounting, Management and Information Technologies.* He is the author of three books and has published numerous articles in such journals as *Management Science, Organization Science, Human Relations, Academy of Management Review,* and the *Academy of Management Journal.* His current research deals with the consequences of information systems in organizations and the processes of system development and implementation. This research includes empirical examinations of information systems development work and of the effects of a wide range of technologies on organizational structure and patterns of work. It also includes the development of theoretical approaches to explaining the development and consequences of information technology in organizations.

Rajiv Sabherwal is Associate Professor in the Department of Decision Sciences and Information Systems at Florida International University. He earned a Ph.D. from the University of Pittsburgh in 1989 and a postgraduate diploma in management from Indian Institute of Management, Calcutta, in 1983. He has authored numerous articles, which have appeared in such journals as *Organization Science, Decision Sciences, European Journal of Information Systems, Information and Management, Journal of Information Systems,* and *Journal of Management Information Systems.* His research interests include strategic utilization of information technology, organizational decision making, information systems planning, behavioral aspects of information systems development, and global information systems.

Kathleen M. Sutcliffe is Assistant Professor of Organizational Behavior and Human Resource Management at the University of Michigan, School of Business Administration. She received her Ph.D. degree from the University of Texas at Austin. Her primary research interests include top management team perception, interpretation, and sense-making processes; organizational responsiveness to environmental change; and understanding the link between perceptual accuracy and performance.